*Shakespeare in Production*

Late nineteenth-century depiction
of Agincourt by W. Paget.

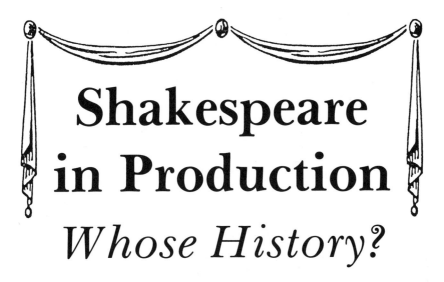

# Shakespeare
# in Production
## *Whose History?*

BY

## H. R. COURSEN

**Ohio University Press**
Athens

Ohio University Press, Athens, Ohio 45701

01 00 99 98 97 96   5 4 3 2 1

Ohio University Press books are
printed on acid-free paper ∞

Library of Congress Cataloging-in-Publication Data

Coursen, Herbert R.
    Shakespeare in production : whose history? / by H. R. Coursen.
        p.    cm.
    Includes bibliographical references (p.    ) and index.
    ISBN 0-8214-1140-3 (alk. paper)
    1. Shakespeare, William, 1564-1616—Dramatic production.
    2. Shakespeare, William, 1564-1616—Film and video adaptations.
    3. Shakespeare, William, 1564-1616—Stage history.   4. Theater—
    History.   I. Title
    PR3091.C675   1996
    792.9′5—dc20                                                            95-43091
                                                                                 CIP

Design by Laury A. Egan

*This book is for Ken Rothwell*

# Contents

# Acknowledgements

Some of this material appeared in review form in *The Marlowe Society Newsletter, Shakespeare Bulletin,* and *Shakespeare Quarterly.* I am grateful to editors Bruce Brandt, Alan Dessen, James Lusardi, Barbara Mowat and June Schlueter. I also thank Robert F. Willson, Jr. who edited *Shakespeare: Entering the Maze* (Peter Lang, 1995), in which a version of my chapter on *Hamlet* on film appears. As always, Theatre in England and Homer and Laura Swander were a huge help in getting me to the theater and in providing lively classes in which to discuss and debate the issues of production and interpretation. People who also provided formats for evaluating performance materials include James Andreas of Clemson, James Bulman of Allegheny, Michael Bristol of McGill, Walter Cannon of Central College, Samuel Crowl of Ohio, William Godshalk of Cincinnati, James Lake of Louisiana (Shreveport), Joan Langley of the Oregon Shakespeare Festival, Susan Lewis of Motlow, Stuart Omans of the Orlando Shakespeare Festival, Hassel Shedd and David Skeele of Slippery Rock, Gary Sloan of Tudor Hall, Ed Taft of Marshall, and John Van Meter of The McDonogh School. Thanks also for a variety of assists to David Bevington of Chicago, Sharon Beehler of Montana State, Richard Bornstein of Samuel Goldwyn, Amy Cuddy of the Oregon Shakespeare Festival, Peter Donaldson of M.I.T., Dale Duffy of Theatre in England, Bernice W. Kliman of Nassau Community College, Barry Kraft of the Oregon Shakespeare Festival, Eva McManus of Ohio Northern, Pamela Mount, Marion Pringle and the accommodating staff at the Shakespeare Centre, Stratford on Avon, Pat Quigley of the Stratford Ontario Shakespeare Festival, William C. Watterson of Bowdoin, and Stanley Wells and the helpful staff of the Shakespeare Institute, Stratford-on-Avon.

# Introduction

The need to "historicize" has become obvious, even to those of us who grew up and lived (and, some would say, died) with the New Criticism for most of our professional lives. The "New Historicism" insists that we contextualize, as opposed to extracting well-wrought urns from their museum cases and holding them up to the light of "irony" and "ambiguity" as articulated by the tweedy, leather-patched, pipe-smoking old boys of academe. But if the New Historicists are right, it follows that we do not merely scratch around in the 1590s for the anecdote or tattered document that will help us discern "early modern construction of this or that" and thus, possibly, to say something original about a play by Shakespeare by recuperating "meaning." The historical imperative means that we place productions in context, as best we can. Productions sometimes say something original about Shakespeare's plays. The "originality," when it does occur, occurs in a context that at once defines originality and helps us recognize it. The medium itself—film, which spans the immediately premodern, modern, and postmodern epochs; television, which is "modernist"; and stage, which goes back, obviously, much further than the "early modern" period—demands to be recognized as a motive force underlying any manifestation of a Shakespeare play in that medium. The historical moment of production, insofar as it can be recognized from the 1990s, also conditions what any production can show us and tells us what it cannot show us. There the thesis of historicity is right. Whether Shakespeare could "transcend his time" or not, a Hollywood film of 1936 had to contend with the Hays Office and a censorship that had not affected the films of the less inhibited 1920s. Had Clark Gable not said *"give* a damn," Will Hays would have censored the line (Safire 1994, 18).

A specific production's contact with time—with history—comes not in its mere addition to and minute alteration of what has already been done, as in the mode of "Tradition and the Individual Talent," but in its challenge to what has already been done. A good production confronts past productions and changes them, forces them to justify themselves, and must show them to be products of their zeitgeist, daring and innovative perhaps, but of a time even as *they* challenged the historical

xii     Shakespeare in Production

moment into which they emerged. Such productions include Orson Welles's *Chimes at Midnight,* Peter Brook's *King Lear*s and *A Midsummer Night's Dream,* Trevor Nunn's *Antony and Cleopatra* for television (from which BBC stubbornly refused to learn as it launched its series a few years later), Terry Hands's *Henry V,* Jane Howell's *Henry VI* sequence for BBC-TV (once they had relaxed their "rules"), and Deborah Warner's *King John* and *Titus Andronicus.* As I suggest in the last chapter, little innovation is occurring these days in the big theaters in Great Britain. If the Royal Shakespeare Company insists on trying to please tourists, it will end up pleasing nobody, and even the "experimental" spaces that "traditional" productions claim to support will go dark.

The essays that follow are not merely a single response—though they include one, without apology—but incorporate the moment of production, through reviews and responses contemporary to a given production, and through critical and scholarly responses that disagree with mine. The idea here is not to get people to agree with what I have to say about productions that are available on cassette or that a reader may have seen on this stage or that, but to get them to disagree and thus add to the discourse that is developing within the relatively new and increasingly exciting area of performance criticism.

The first chapter deals with "script" and its components. Basically, they are two, as defined by Robert Weimann (1991): *locus,* or what is present in the script, and *platea,* who is producing the script. The former is always conservative and indeed falls inexorably back into time. The latter can be radical and can reshape *locus* into something powerfully contemporary. I will argue, however, that the production that loses contact with one aspect of *locus*—its moment of origin, which can be ascertained, for example, through the meanings of words that have specialized or generalized since, say, 1601—loses contact with an *essential* element that can still be communicated in modern and postmodern productions. Franco Zeffirelli's film of *Romeo and Juliet,* for example, incorporated a *platea*-dimension that emphasized the generational conflict that attitudes about Vietnam so exacerbated in the late 1960s. In doing so, Zeffirelli energized an element that most would agree is in the *locus.* Certainly, Juliet's youth is in the *locus,* a fact strongly noted when Norma Shearer, old enough to be Lady Capulet, essayed the role in 1936. Suffice it that the overdetermination of *platea* can harm a production. One that is merely contemporary becomes almost immediately irrelevant. The same can be said of a production that allows itself to be completely absorbed by the time selected for its setting, as I have argued about the Joseph Papp/A.J. Antoon *Much Ado About Nothing* (1992).

It is probably a better idea to let good actors have at the *locus,* as in a spirited production of the 1603 Quarto of *Hamlet* by the Medieval Players on a bare platform in the yard of the George Inn in August 1992.

I make an effort here to "contextualize" productions. The way in which *Hamlet* opens on film shows us something about the problems of translating that script to film—that is an issue "in history"—and also shows us something about the historical moment at which the effort was made. I think that the 1936 Hollywood *Romeo and Juliet* is better than most of today's film critics believe it to be, but my judgment is based to some extent on trying to see the film as a film of 1936. Seeing the film as artifact hardly brings it forward in time but does place it in its own time. Since the film has just been released on cassette, placement of it in its own time should help bring it into *our* historical moment. I ask why *The Comedy of Errors* does not translate well to television—or seems not to have done so so far—and suggest that a medium trapped in its modernist premises lacks the flexibility to accommodate a script whose origins are in ancient drama. Comedy itself, as genre, encounters difficulties when it attempts to move from the premises of stage to film. This is particularly true of a play like *As You Like It,* with its pastoral conventions and its insistence that we suspend our disbelief and accept the multiple fictions that Rosalind introduces to Arden. A script less rooted in literary and stage conventions, and less embedded in blank verse, like *Much Ado About Nothing,* has an easier voyage to the light-sensitive medium. I ask, however, whether Kenneth Branagh's version does any challenging of received beliefs and traditions.

It is the history play, of course, that is interrogated most obviously for its commentary on our times, even if Dennis Kennedy finds that Shakespeare productions are becoming "trans-historical or anti-historical . . . creating, through irony, a disjunction between the pastness of Shakespeare's plays and the ways we now receive them" (1993, 267). I agree that the script probably works best within a setting that does not pin it to a specific time, though there was much to be said for the exciting late-1930s *Richard III* that Richard Eyre presented in 1992, which contrasted with the intense minimalism of Sam Mendes's almost simultaneous version—about which, also, much was to be said, as I have suggested (1995). I think, however, that it is impossible for a contemporary audience not to perceive the parallels that the history plays draw with our own moment in time, simply because they depict men and women struggling for power. When John Barton's famous *Richard II* hit Brooklyn in 1972, it picked up a lot of energy from an audience experiencing Watergate. This coincidence provided the production a lot of praise for its "relevance" (see Coursen 1992).

Zeitgeist is inevitably a part of *platea*. The more minimally recognized *in* production the more powerful a response *to* production it is likely to generate. Several versions of *Hamlet* suggested in 1994 that the matter of Ophelia is now much more central to the script than it seemed to be before feminist criticism demanded that attention be paid to her. I find, however, that "larger" dimensions of the *locus*—the issues of dynasty and of the supernatural—tend to be neglected in this tighter focus on character and relationship. If so, that does not mean a diminution of the script's power but it does mean that the play is developing a centripetal, implosive energy in our time. Its ability to become "as the time is" remains remarkable, regardless of the case being made for *King Lear* by R. A. Foakes (1993a).

Finally, I look at the 1994 season in Great Britain and issue another indictment of what the big theaters are doing these days. In that the tourists seem to be pleased, no one is listening. But—things are about to change. The Globe, Sam Wanamaker's dream, is about to open in Southwark. It will bring many productions from many companies to its stage. There, the plays will be heard in a context resembling the original conditions of performance. That *platea* will insist that we learn—as we must keep relearning—how these plays work and how we discover what we mean as people and as *a* people in their workings.

*Shakespeare in Production*

# I

# Whose History?

Obviously, "historical" factors influence, condition, and sometimes control the production of any Shakespeare script. The script itself has a history, which directors must take into account and about which critics must be knowledgeable. If a director merely borrows from other productions—as Michael Kahn did for his 1993 *Hamlet* in D.C.—the theft may go undetected. In D.C. that is a good bet. If the borrowings are not fused with an imaginative recreation of the script, however, they serve only to confuse our response. Why, in Kahn's production, did Hamlet wash his hands in a bucket after killing Polonius, when Polonius had shed no jot of blood?—so Hamlet could call Guildenstern a sponge, of course, but basically because Mark Rylance had washed his hands after a very bloody dispatch of Polonius in Ron Daniels's Royal Shakespeare Company (RSC) production, and Kahn apparently liked that piece of business.

It may be that the "intertextualities" of a production are other productions of the same play, and, indeed, the history of that play in performance. If the play is *not* well known, the actor has an advantage, as did Brian Cox, Titus in Deborah Warner's splendid production at the Swan in Stratford-on-Avon in 1987: "Playing Titus was a unique experience in that the part was relatively uncharted. Actors over the years have put their stamp on many Shakespearean roles, which for each succeeding generation of players then present a new challenge" (Jackson and Smallwood 1993, 176). Mimi Kramer goes further: "The problem with star-centered Shakespeare as the British serve it up is that it leaves the actors thinking they have nothing to do—which is to say, nothing to act. The star ends up playing the history of the role rather than the role itself—anything, just to be different—and the secondary characters mostly play to some antiquated notion of theatricality" (1992, 85). That can happen, of course, as in the 1994 *Hamlet* at Regent's Park, featuring a young Damian Lewis in the title role and a Claudius (Paul Freeman) and Polonius (David Collings) playing in a tradition that Hamlet himself would scorn ("Do not saw the air too much with your hand, thus"). But Kramer overstates the case, as we realize when we see the very different Hamlets of Mark Rylance, Kenneth Branagh, and Damian Lewis, or the Lears of Brian Cox, John Wood, and Richard Briers, or the very different Richard IIIs of Anthony Sher, Ian McKellen, and Simon Russell Beale.

Whatever the *director* may be thinking, the auditor may well have seen other performances of the same script that play subtextually through his or her experience of a given production. Furthermore, the zeitgeist is an inevitable subtext in any production, whether the production represents a conscious "modernization," is set in a specific historical period, or is rendered in an eclectic zone, with automatic weapons and medieval armor simultaneously visible. Obviously, different modes of production react differently with the historical awareness and perception of zeitgeist that a spectator brings to the theater and applies, consciously and unconsciously, to the experience of the play.

The effort to establish the conceptual premises of early modern England can help the modern practitioner of drama to shape a production so that it can *re*-create meanings for a modern—or postmodern audience—that approximate those that might have arrived clearly to an Elizabethan ear. (A lot of audience members do not realize that they inhabit a "post" modern world). Older meanings can be recuperated even as the language changes and those meanings recede into the past. It helps, for example, to know that "desert" to the Elizabethan meant any wild and uninhabited place, and not Sahara or Mojave. Such an historical grasp might have avoided a sandbox *Midsummer Night's Dream* in Portland, Maine, in September 1994, a production also influenced by Robert Lepage's abysmal version, in that plastic was placed over the knees of those in the front row so that people would not have sand kicked in their faces as in the old "Hero of the Beach" ads. The allusion to Lepage did not enhance my anticipation or enjoyment of what followed. Suffice it that I take "historicism" a step further—a big step further—than the new historicists and say that any production must be "historicized," regardless of its moment of inception. It must be probed for its affinities to the moments surrounding its creation and its presentation. The process may not reveal a given production's quality—that judgment is a product of "final cause," the communal response of an audience as a play ends *and* an experience based on individual psychology of perception—but it will suggest the circumference within which the specific interpretation of a given script is to be organized.

The script is not "free of time," and is therefore not a totalizing text that gathers "universal truth" unto itself, but is an energy source, a site of interrogation, a collection of words that make sense only when deconstructed by actors for an audience that is a participant in the process and not a detached and uninvolved observer. The spectator's "interactivity" with Shakespeare onstage may not be physical, but if it has not been psychologically and imaginatively intense, then the entire enterprise has failed.

The transaction on which Shakespeare insists—its reciprocal quality and the nature of the response it elicits—cannot be overemphasized. If a production is "deconstructing" the script by exploring its marginalizations and the anxieties that power produces in its deployment of power, the audience does more than observe this activity. The audience becomes, as Kent Cartwright says, *"the* audience [that] the playwright sets out to construct with each play" (1991, 29. My emphasis). The play, as Norman Rabkin, says is "a dynamic interaction between artist and audience. [We must] learn to talk about the process of our involvement rather than our considered view after the aesthetic event" (1977, 27). "The eddying signals communicated by a play arouse a total and complex involvement of our intellect, our moral sensibility, our need to complete incomplete patterns and answer questions, our longing to judge, and that involvement is so incessantly in motion that to pin it down to a 'meaning' is to negate its very essence" (22–23).

That assumption of "essence" needs to be qualified. I would say, "to negate a *process*." "We have been betrayed by a bias toward what can be set out in rational argument," says Rabkin (1977, 19)—indeed, betrayed by a misunderstanding of the *event* of drama—which is not an appeal to rationality. I would qualify Rabkin further by saying that we must use the rational faculty to work toward what our experience has been— to order it, to articulate it, and not to *mistake* it for the further process of exploring and explaining it in language that we and others can understand. I, at least, often do not know how I *am responding* to a given production until I begin to write about it.

Historicism cannot recapture "the moment," although we can suggest some of the swirl of zeitgeist surrounding a production, particularly if we look at the *immediate* critical response to productions, response that may say something about the production but invariably says something about the moment of a script's emergence *into* history. Historicism tends to misinterpret the event of drama, making it part of an intellectual context. It is that, but it is much more than that. It is also more than a product of a literary context. It is an event. "A play is not an artifact but a process," says Philip McGuire, "unique with each performance, of making physically present (of *realizing*) possibilities of perception and feeling that lie attenuated and frozen in the script" (1979, xx. McGuire's emphasis). As necessary as it is to "contextualize" a moment in history, the danger is that, if that moment is a performance, its artifactualization destroys what is intrinsic to it. We cannot reestablish what was intrinsic at that moment, but we can suggest some of the ways in which zeitgeist and script interacted to create that third component of the process—the production.

Stephen Orgel, in discussing the Peacham sketch of *Titus Andronicus*, which shows a mixed mode of costuming—Elizabethan and Roman —and a coal-black Aaron, emphasizes the importance of the auditor of Shakespeare's drama in integrating the experience: The plays exhibit a "basic fluidity or disjunctiveness [that] depends for its truth upon its audience . . . [the Peacham sketch] persuades the viewer of the significance, position, status of its figures. It does not mime a consistent world but expresses an action. Its elements fit together only insofar as a viewer interprets and understands them . . . [T]he real play is the performance, not the text . . . [T]o fix the text, transform it into a book, is to defeat it" (1983, 43–44).

One of the signs of transition from New Criticism to current historicist modes is that a stage production or a film is no longer seen only as a separate production, or only in relation to other films made by its director, or only in contrast to other versions of Shakespeare's scripts. The film is viewed as part of an economic, political, and cultural process. The film, as Leslie F. Sharman suggests, is seen as "taking sides," or as *un*committed because playing it safe (1993). Branagh's Hamlet for Adrian Noble was so criticized, particularly by Frank Rich, as merely a Muzak version serving to roll the red carpet out in front of the steady tread of Branagh's career. It would seem that few productions of Shakespeare will be able, any longer, to receive any unanimity of praise. If the production involves a subversive undercutting of received opinion about the script or about how "Shakespeare should be done," the productions will be blasted by the right, with the weight of authority that the right brings to all the wrong reasons. If delivered in the received standard mode, the cultural materialists will indict productions for merely confirming the established hegemony, or, as Alan Sinfield would say, for silencing the subcultures (1995). This schism is a "given" from which this study emerges and with which it deals in its discussions of specific productions. There "is no such thing as an apolitical or unpolitical Shakespearean film," says Sidney Gottlieb (1992, 245), or, I would add, *production*.

Another issue that these essays confront is that of postmodernism. Shakespearean productions have long gone beyond the Brechtian device of calling attention to the seams in the garment even as the fiction continues to generate its fictions. In the American Repertory Theatre (ART) *Henry IV* plays, for example, King Henry and Falstaff inhabited worlds that could not exist together in time. The king lived in a late-medieval era, full of the kinds of icons we see exhibited at The Cloisters, Falstaff in the Jersey City of the 1970s, when Ballantine's Three Rings dominated the tavern windows. Glendower was a Native American of the Little Bighorn era. This was postmodernism, of course, defended on the premise that the plays are anachronistic. The problem with Hotspur in the script would seem to be that he clings to creeds outworn. He would have been a superb soldier of the king had the king been Edward III. In the world of Henry IV, however, he is the cartoon character who has already taken several steps over the cliff before gravity asserts itself. A production, however, that creates different zones of time for us is not the same thing as characters, in an admittedly confused historical moment—when concepts of time and of history's intersection with time are themselves in conflict—who attempt to define the time. Hotspur is a critique of medieval concepts of honor precisely because the times have changed.

But how do we reconcile ourselves to the narrative—suspend our disbelief—when characters in the same time up there on stage step in and out of different times, unless that is one of the explicit premises of the fiction? Another way of framing the question would be—if we assume that Shakespeare's plays have a "thematic unity," must the production? We can disagree about what the themes are, of course, but is the production itself permitted to be incoherent because critics disagree about its unifying principle or about the possibility of there being one? (see Berger 1991). It is probably true that Falstaff is an *Elizabethan* rapscallion loose in the early fifteenth century, and therefore an anachronism in a late sixteenth century play, but the world that Shakespeare creates for the Second Tetralogy is assuredly Tudor, as many critics have argued.

Is coherence a value in production? "If," says Philip McGuire, "we are to understand the multiplicity generated by the freedom inherent in Shakespeare's plays, we must put aside assumptions and methods shaped by the themata of simplicity, completeness, and causality" (1985, 135)—that is, we must discard the concept of "text" in favor of "script": a set of signs to be completed by actors and an audience. A given production can still mean different things to different people without itself reflecting confusion—or simplicity, completeness, and causality—to the audience. The play, if by Shakespeare, cannot *mean* "confusion." It can depict confusion, as after the assassination of Caesar or after the Battle of Shrewsbury, or even confusion among the characters as to what world they are in. It can even include a kind of parallel time scheme, in which two different worlds compete against each other. Baroque Shakespeare draws these contrasts—Edmund invokes "Nature," the outlaw moment of his own conception, but at the end, against his own "nature" tries to do "some good," recognizing, it can be argued, another order of things, an order represented in this play by Cordelia. Yet she dies anyway, a fact that may suggest that the question of who is in charge now is irrelevant. But that irrelevance does not add up to confusion, rather reveals the face of something stern and inscrutable that sees beyond human intention.

In *Antony and Cleopatra*, two worlds are poised against each other, and the one that can move its armies with celerity wins against the epic values of individual heroism, which Antony claims for himself and seems to validate on the second day of Actium. Caesar, obviously, is "modern" and is the future, however diminished from the "mystic oxymoron" that Antony and Cleopatra frame for themselves. But we would probably object were the point made by equipping Antony and his troops with bronze helmets, while Octavius's army deployed automatic weapons and napalm ("the shirt of Nessus"). Egypt and Rome are different, but they exist at the same moment in history, even if the characters, as in Shakespeare's history plays, have different *visions* of history (see Coursen 1984, 1988b). The play can be brought forward in time, as in an opulent but empty production at Stratford, Ontario, in 1993, where Octavius was a fascist and Antony had "gone native," but both worlds must emerge into the same historical epoch so that they retain the symmetry that does make sense in the script. That is, unless one argues that the play depicts something like spear-carrying Ethiopians charging Mussolini's infantry, or a troop of Polish uhlans attacking a panzer unit in September 1939. That historical anachronisms do occur does not mean that they can be introduced into Shakespeare's scripts without causing confusion—as opposed to transmitting different possible interpretations to an audience.

The same production *can* produce diametrically different responses in an audience, as witness Branagh's *Henry V*, which some critics find "antiwar" and others do not. A history play like *Julius Caesar*, with its generic insistence on shifting from one dominant character to another, *should* promote disagreement among its auditors. The emphasis of the spectator, in admiring Brutus and despising Antony—*or* vice versa—is part of the occasion of production, an occasion that crucially involves an audience. "Final cause" can also can also be primarily a response to the most superficial aspects of the production. Peter Hall's *Coriolanus* at the National Theatre some years ago depicted the evolution of weaponry—showing Coriolanus (Ian McKellen) fighting early on with a sword but assassinated by weapons that could have been on the grassy knoll at Dallas in November 1963. This "concept" was merely a gimmick, of course, but permitted signs outside the auditorium to deliver all the politically correct warnings to people with hearing aids, pacemakers, and electronically activated elbows. Too many directors these days are indulging their idiosyncrasies under the all-licensing banner of postmodernism. Some, of course, as I will suggest later, are parading to the permissive beat of "popular culture."

Assuming that "final cause"—the effect of a work of art on its auditor—will always be a matter of debate, the question becomes, Must art link up to something called "formal cause"? Visual art itself, of course, has gone beyond anything that we might call formal cause. Its history since the last decades of the nineteenth century depicts a war *against* form. The same could be said for music. Shakespeare's plays, however, emerge from generic principles and agreed-upon conventions of language and are based on what Robert Weimann calls *locus*—the thing represented, which is always, for example, the fall of Richard II, no matter how the action is depicted and no matter who is doing the representation. The *locus* never permits us to learn that Zeus created a Bolingbroke figure and sent it to England, while the real Bolingbroke relaxed in the Loire Valley. It is in the area of the other "authority," *platea*—the specifics of production (the company, space, audience, editing decisions, moment in history) that the variables occur. *Platea* can create friction between itself and *locus*, making the script a site for contestation, problematizing it, possibly radicalizing what is, according to Weimann, invariably a conservative "given." The "Elizabethan theatre," says Weimann, "was not, by any stretch of the imagination, a subversive institution, hostile to the Tudor balance of socioeconomic forces old and new . . . the *locus*-centered authority of what was represented tended to be defined spatially, socially and linguistically in terms of a certain verisimilitude, decorum, aloofness from the audience, and representational closure. For instance, in Shakespeare's drama, we have the throne as a *locus* of privileged royalty" (1991, 409–10).

Even *presentational* closure could, of course, uphold this conservative *locus*, as in the Chorus at the end of *II Henry IV*. But against *locus* could be poised the "*platea*-directed mimesis . . . the actor (the real person who is representing) behind the role (the fictional person who is represented): moving between these two different types of identity (and authority)" (410). The "other authority"—the creator of the immediate fiction that we are hearing and in which we are participating in a theater—must be, whether consciously or not, a product of the moment of production and the many contexts of that moment. It is to *platea* that Stephen Greenblatt addresses himself when he says that Shakespeare's plays "offer no single timeless affirmation or denial of legitimate authority. [His] language and themes are caught up, like the medium itself, in unsettling repetitions, committed to the shifting voices and audiences, with their shifting aesthetic assumptions and historical imperatives, that govern a living theater" (1980, 254).

*Platea*, broadly construed, becomes a mode of interrogation—or, if *platea* is considered by a director to be "popular culture," it becomes an excuse for *not* challenging *locus*. The effort here will be to attempt to describe a given *platea*—the assumptions and the mode of a given production and the space in which production occurred—in relationship to the prior authority of *locus*, an authority that, as Greenblatt suggests, moves through time to encounter the *platea*s that time must impose on *locus*. The method, of course, is subject, as response to Shakespearean production must be, to the subjective viewpoint of the third authority—the auditor. That third area, part of an extended *platea* cannot be controlled by those who create the production. Samuel Crowl describes the contrast between the intentions of Houseman and Mankiewicz as they made the 1953 film of *Julius Caesar* and its impact on its audience: "Houseman believed that the Forum would inevitably 'evoke memories of the Fuhrer at Nuremberg and of Mussolini ranting from his high balcony overlooking the wildly cheering crowd.'" The film, however, seems to allude to "both the extension of America's international influence and internal hysteria about supposed subversives" (1994, 149). Fortunately, the film is set in a 'neutral' zone—that of ancient Rome—and so its audience was free, and, in a sense, is free to respond to *new* historical circumstances that its *locus* continues to identify.

Even if Shakespeare keeps challenging generic principles as most of his scripts do, it helps us to know what they are—what a revenge play tends to be, for example, in light of *Hamlet*. That is, as Helen Gardner pointed out in a forgotten essay (1963), that revenge plays incorporate clever traps into which their designers themselves tumble, something that happens twice in *Hamlet,* once at the "Mousetrap" and again in the final scene. Genre is, however, debatable, part of the *locus* component that Weimann describes. Genre can be challenged internally by the script itself, as Bolingbroke says when he labels the playlet in which he is a character "The Beggar and the King." Genre can be a question that *platea* must answer, as in the instance of a "problem play" like *Measure for Measure* or in the case of a play that can be played as farce or as romantic comedy—*The Taming of the Shrew*, for example. What happens when *The Comedy of Errors* is treated as "problem play" is a question I will ask later, in Chapter 4.

The interplay between *locus* and *platea* is nicely expressed by Alan Sinfield: "*Henry V* can be read to reveal not only the ruler's strategies of power, but also the anxieties informing both them and their ideological representation. In the Elizabethan theater, to foreground and even to promote such representations was not to foreclose on their interrogation" (127). The force of the interrogation varies, of course. Branagh's *Henry V*, for example, was not as clearly antiwar as was Michael Kahn's version of the late 1960s. I will argue, though, that Branagh's *platea* for *Henry V* is more subversive than for his *Much Ado About Nothing*, in which Benedick, particularly, accepts the notion of romantic love as *Branagh* seems to. It is the latter, the director Branagh, who provides a sentimentalizing musical score for the former skeptics, Beatrice and Benedick. Again, Barbara Hodgdon deals with the *locus* and the possibilities for *platea* that are inherent in the script and awaiting the emphasis of a production: "the history play inscribes the *idealized* dominance of the institution of kingship [and] interrogates that ideal by representing alternative values, meanings, and practices capable of contesting its hegemony" (1991, 12. Hodgdon's emphasis). Because the distinction is crucial to any analysis of production, I will reiterate the relationship between *locus* and *platea* in specific terms as I look at specific productions on the pages that follow.

Given the pressures of recent criticism, its antitheatrical bent, its postmodernist bias, and particularly its unwillingness to explore the discrepancy between *locus* and *platea*, one might ask whether Shakespeare's plays can work as anything other than fragmented fragments. Has the pressure for intertextuality made each script merely a datum in a web of other meanings, a site for valorization of, or contestation *with*, those meanings? Has the postmodern stage *not* learned how to incorporate Shakespeare, as the modern stage did learn (in that, as it was discovered, Shakespeare incorporated "The Theater of the Absurd" already)? Some postmodernist interpretations—Lepage's *A Midsummer Night's Dream*, which occurred in a huge mud puddle, and Peter Greenaway's *Prospero's Books*—would seem to have obliterated whatever "Shakespeare" may be for the sake of making some statement that is ultimately banal, where the mud or the nakedness becomes the "play" and the statement becomes (a) "Comedy is a cleansing medium" (the mud is finally washed from the bodies of the hapless young lovers by a benevolent shower) or (b) "Prospero is a fine fellow after all," as we should have known from his imperviousness to all those nude young persons of both genders scampering around the premises. Here post-modernism serves no "meaning" but the ego of the director who basks as critics praise his genius or, in the case of Lepage, chuckles as his revenge for French Canada detonates on the banks of the River Thames.

But Lepage and Greenaway do not signal the end of Shakespeare, merely their ability to fund their aberrations, and to discover critics who, in turn, cry out delightedly as they discern the emperor's clothes. Lepage and Greenaway usefully define the limits beyond which whatever "Shakespeare" may continue to mean no longer generates meaning in a culture, as do some of the projects that the National Endowment for the Arts insist on funding, claiming that they support the avant-garde while really underwriting the lunatic fringe *and* some crushingly conventional projects, and sometimes worthy enterprises as well. The basic point about postmodernism and Shakespeare is well put by Michael Mullin, who says that "disparate, ambiguous cultural icons . . . are often expressed as abstract symbols drawn from art and architecture, that challenge the audience to formulate individual responses to the plays and the cultural issues they raise. Instead of saying, in performance terms, 'This is what we the director, designers, and actors think the play means,' postmodern Shakespeare is open-ended, at times deliberately suggesting opposed interpretive stances" (1994, 5). I would suggest that directors, designers, and actors *can* say, "Here is what we think the play means"—indeed, I think that they have to *interpret* the script. I think it is also possible for their interpretation to evoke the final cause that Mullin posits—namely, that different meanings can be drawn from the experience by different spectators. To some extent, then, I am arguing for coherence *in* production.

But whose history is it? Response is dictated by the individual psychology of perception of a single spectator. *This* spectator puts himself in the stance of Emerson's "American Scholar" or Camus's existentialist and says, here is what I find there. What I inscribe as "responses" are, of course, *my* meanings, though they attempt to account for what directors and designers have done and for the historical moment into which a specific production intruded. The quality of what is found depends largely on the quality of the response. In the case of drama, criticism becomes *part* of the performed work of art and not some activity conducted separately from the experience. A work of art is an appeal to the imagination and, secondarily, to the intellect. I reassert the old claim that the production is revitalized, even re-created by the critic, *after* the performance is over, true, but as part of the continuum of energy that the performance built between it and that spectator. Study, research, and personal history are part of that process, as is, if possible, a return to the performance, something not often feasible for the live performances I discuss in this book. There is something to be gained by seeing well *the first time*—and "instant replay" usually proves that the official call, made with the *naked* eye and open ear, *was* right. Those activities and that experience do not substitute for the performance itself, but can enhance it and may help to articulate its imaginative and emotional appeal to others who were there and to others who were not. This is to argue an extension of Weimann's *platea* that includes *response* at the outer edge of its parenthetical closure.

In his introduction to *Screen Shakespeare*, Michael Skovmand says, "We are no longer caught between the virtuality of the playscript and the ephemerality of the performance. Indeed, we are faced with texts with a social life of their own, films which relate in a much more direct way than previous Shakespeare performances to the international marketplace of culture and communications" (1994, 7). Additionally, we are charged by recent critical imperatives to examine the ideology underlying filmed translations of the scripts (see Holderness 1993) and to ascertain the historical circumstances from which a film emerges. It may be "based" on Shakespeare but it is equally a product of its zeitgeist.

The issue of "interpretation" is further complicated by a conflation of media. We understand film better than we once did. Indeed, Shakespeare-on-film has shown us in many ways what film is, and is not. At the same time, however, film and television, light-sensitive and magnetic media, have become, at times, almost the same thing—almost, because neither a television production nor a film-on-cassette can approximate the field of depth that a film in a cinema can achieve. The need to make distinctions becomes more imperative as the distinctions blur in the media's all-out effort to *sell* something to us. That we become confused about which medium we are in at any given moment— as in Greenaway's *Prospero's Books*—helps in the selling. The long "Home Shopping" sequence in Greenaway on high-definition television superimposed on the film, in which many naked people line up to show products to Ferdinand and Miranda, is an example. History itself, as it is intersected by the process of politics, becomes a history of sales and selling and, sometimes, the chronicle of an effort to unload products after their "sell by" date has long expired. Shakespearean productions are themselves not only conditioned by their times, but are also "time's subjects." That is one reason why it is important that the recorded production be contextualized—placed at its level in the archaeological scheme.

It may be that the return to an emphasis on Shakespeare as basically and even exclusively a site for performance is premised on the making of films and on our study of those films. If we look at a good silent-film version of a play we may discern an inheritance that goes back *to* Shakespeare. Later on these pages, I quote Max Herzberg on the similarities between Shakespeare's scenic fluidity and the techniques of the filmmaker. In the Nielsen-Gade *Hamlet* (1920), from the title card that tells us that the actors are setting up for their play right on into the prayer scene, the flow is almost uninterrupted. Hamlet mimes her objections to the Player's style, "Gonzago" occurs, Hamlet borrows Horatio's sword and rushes up the castle steps after Claudius, and the prayer scene follows in a wonderful flow of long shots, tracking shots (as Hamlet crawls from Ophelia to Claudius), and reaction shots—a montage virtually uninterrupted by title cards. "Gonzago" has been clearly set up for us so that this sequence can *flow,* with what Peter Holland calls "cinematic theatricality" (1993b, 141). The line of inheritance would be, as James Andreas has pointed out to me, back through Dickens's novelistic techniques, so loved of the early filmmakers, to Dickens's model, Shakespeare. For the exception, if it is one, we would look at Emil Jannings's 1922 version of *Othello,* in which poor Desdemona would have plenty of time to escape during the many interruptions that the title cards interpose at the end of the film, cards timed to the ability of the slowest reader in the audience. Shakespeare's language could interfere with a silent film, as it certainly interfered with talkies.

Although few would argue that a filmed or televised version of a play is a substitute for a stage production, the filmed or taped performance does treat the "text" as *script*—that is a system of signals designed to be variously interpreted by actors and audiences within the ongoing energy known as history. The concept and actualization of "script" should be the basis of our debates and discussions. The continuity that we celebrate is that the plays *are* plays, even if adapted to media undreamed of in Shakespeare's dramaturgy. Historicism, an effort to reconstruct the ideational framework of Elizabethan-Jacobean England, can help us understand postmodern productions because it provides a trace memory of an early-modern zeitgeist and thus permits us to measure—without much precision, it is true—how a production recaptures or deviates from the contexts of the culture out of which the plays emerged. That measurement creates a zone wherein we can evaluate our response to productions in our own times. This is particularly important when we respond to postmodernist productions which might try to refute the premise of any "history of ideas." (Some would say that "history of ideas" is a fiction invented by a dominant ideology designed quite simply to keep certain controlling concepts in force and thus keep the elite in power. "The American Dream" would be an example of a construct that dampens revolutionary impulses.) It remains true, however, that as Michael Pursell says of Branagh's *Henry V*, the "discourse . . . of any historical fiction . . . is much more heavily franked with the cultural conditions of its point of production than its point of reference" (1992, 273). And it remains true that the point of production *of* production is often more accessible to us than is the point of production of the script and of its initial manifestation as production.

New Historicists help directors to construct an equivalent to what may have been an Elizabethan/Jacobean understanding. That is not to suggest that the director must necessarily ignore immediately contemporary analogues. If insisted upon in *platea*, however, those allusions can confuse the issues of the plays by making them merely contemporary, thus removing any resonance with a moment other than our own. The director should attempt to illuminate the early-modern context so that a modern, or postmodern, audience can respond effectively to *locus:* what "is there." That involves not just a visual equivalent for the language—as in Olivier's film, where dirt falls from the skull of Yorick ("his fine pate filled with fine dirt") or in Zeffirelli's, where Gertrude is "like Niobe, all tears"—but a visual, vocal, and emotional equivalent for concepts that meant something in 1600 and can still mean something like what they meant then in performance today. The director is a maker of metaphors that connect two unlike worlds and that allow the former to communicate with the latter. If contemporary analogies do exist, they can be recognized only through an understanding of the "early modern" meanings that lie on one shore that the metaphor bridges. Those early modern meanings will usually arc their metaphors to *us,* and therefore do not need to be made explicitly "postmodern" in the production. If the production itself is overly contemporized, we are robbed of our response to anything other than "today." We are robbed of history, or, to put it more accurately, of an interpretation of history. The script is a medium for exploration of what is past, and passing, and to come, a source of meanings in the future that performance of the scripts *will* reveal in time.

Dr. Pinch in *Errors* need not be wildly overdone, as he tends to be in modern productions. Antipholus of Syracuse is not mad—angry, yes, but not clinically mad—and is therefore not in need of an exorcist. The play shows that exorcism is unnecessary, and when we look back, we learn that exorcism was officially frowned upon. The exorcist claimed control of the supernatural, a claim that the new Church and the authority under which it functioned were unwilling to sanction (see Neely 1994). To overdo the scene may be to sacrifice a serious point that performance can still make without losing the laughs that will still be there, even if the scene is played at a pitch below that of frantic farce. The late sixteenth-century context provides clues about playing the scene in the late twentieth century. *Locus,* properly weighed, does undercut exorcism, a fact that *platea,* as in, for example, the RSC production of *Errors* of the late 1970s, can obliterate.

When Michael Skovmand says that "there are no *organizing* metaphors in Zeffirelli's *Hamlet*" (1994, 126. Skovmand's emphasis), he is applying a modernist critique, whether we agree with his judgment or not. It may be that directors still seek those old-fashioned elements known as "thematic unity" and "narrative continuity." Perhaps they still believe that the plays are "about" something. Perhaps Zeffirelli did not believe as much when he made his *Hamlet,* but he certainly did when he made his *Romeo and Juliet.* It is possible, of course, that *we* as a culture were keenly aware of the generational conflict in the late 1960s in this country, partly a result of the Vietnam War, but it is difficult to believe that the same conflict is not "in" the script as it is certainly in Zeffirelli's interpretation of it. Perhaps he has become a postmodernist in the twenty years between.

One basic question, then, is the issue of evaluating our response to a production recorded in the past that we will see in the future. An issue in the *continuity* of evaluating productions is: Can productions escape the necessity of artistic coherence? A corollary question is: Are some conceptual spaces more conducive to postmodernism than others? Stage more than TV? Film more than TV? Stage more than film? The stage, given a *non*proscenium format, is more amenable to postmodernist critical theory than is film, and film is a more flexible medium than television, the latter a development that occurred in the modern era and that is, perhaps, trapped in that zeitgeist. If film is not trapped within modernist premises, is it now necessary to look at recent films—Van Sant's *My Own Private Idaho,* for example—in comparison and in contrast to the artistic premises underlying "modernist" films—Welles's *Chimes at Midnight,* for example?[1]

My own sense of the history plays is that they contain within themselves the "conflicts" (to use an ancient term) that render them less than monolithic or "totalizing." The plays are, if not better than, certainly different from their sources or "intertextuality." They contain plenty of "irony," "ambiguity," and "paradox" (or "multiple signification"), and are effectively "problematized." Does anyone argue anymore that "the voice of the dominant culture is not the only one that speaks through the text" (Freeman 1990, 112)? Is it not a commonplace that "Shakespeare's plays can be seen as effecting their own political management of reality in the consolidation of Tudor power and, at the same time, in the questioning of that power" (110)? Such a New Historicist stance avoids easy "universalizing" and avoids making Shakespeare a Tudor apologist. And again, the argument that the plays are "sites where many voices of culture and many systems of intelligibility interact," as opposed to "monologic, organically unified wholes" (Jean E. Howard 1986, 20), helps us as teachers. We need not be apologists for a point of view, whether political or critical, and can open the play up to the variables of student response, and show them not only that no "right" answers exist but that politicians and some teachers are likely to try to sell them on a wrong answer.

Still, without reviving Tillyardism, I find it useful to recall what Moody Prior said over twenty years ago:

> Even the most original and powerful minds are subject to the limitations of their times. When we attempt to reconstruct the age by means of scholarship, what emerges for the most part is the common denominator, a synthesis deeply colored by the contributions of those less creative minds, the official ideologists, the popularizers, the shapers of common opinion, the propagandists. To make notions of the age the primary measure by which the plays are to be understood is not only to make the lesser the measure of the greater; it is to reverse the process of creation and to return to the plays the limited vision . . . from which the complexity of Shakespeare's forms, the richness of his art, the breadth and humanity of his understanding, and the transcendent quality of his creative power have freed them. (1973, 24)

The transcendence of which Prior speaks is, of course, a fallacy within the concept of "historicity," but it is an equal fallacy to see Shakespeare only as a function of the constructs that were being put together in early-modern England. Shakespeare's critique of those constructs in drama created that extra dimension—whatever it is—that has kept the scripts alive as critiques of cultures other than his own. Part of the extra dimension is the fact of the script—that is, that these words are meant to be performed within a space that includes an audience. The script is a generator of meanings that are not in the script in its latent form of words on a page.

An example of this mode of generating meaning is nicely described by Michael Shurgot. He sees *Henry IV* as a contest "between history and holiday, between Burbage and Kempe, the one trying to enact a history play in which fat, unruly knights are serious threats to order, the other committed only to his own comic existence and contemptuous of authority and the very idea of history" (forthcoming, 227). Each invents a different time, a process available since Richard II has permitted time to become a variable of power or of imagination, as opposed to a rhythm independent of human agency (see Coursen, 1984 and 1988). Falstaff provides a constant challenge from *platea* to a conservative *locus* which has become problematized as a result of the competition between Richard and Bolingbroke that the latter "wins" even as most of the valuable attributes of kingship go with Richard to the grave. Falstaff challenges "presumptions that history is a verifiable construct about whose content and meaning people can agree." He challenges "the structures of authority that history requires" (Shurgot, 228). Characters in the history plays (and in history) are always reciting history and theories of history to back their diverse claims. Part of the *platea* here, Shurgot argues, must be that the audience is "complicit in [Falstaff's] consummate theatrical 'revising of history'" (260).

It may be that the plays can be read "atemporally" without imposing a conservative or fascist bias on the reading—but atemporality, if possible, is not a useful approach, as Gary Waller suggests: the "Shakespearean script [is] a mode of producing, not merely *reproducing* meanings . . . as it is loosed into the world as production, within changing signifying systems and historical formulations. [It is not a set of] fixed textual meanings waiting to be read atemporally . . . by the attentive critic armed with the appropriate terminology" (1992, 103). The text seems undisturbed by time in that it tends to be a collection of fragments, variants, and emendations that print can disguise as something "whole" and "complete." The script is invariably disturbed by time and represents a disturbance *in* time and an inevitable deconstruction of "text." The text's intrusion into history and history's simultaneous intrusion into the version of text known as production are perhaps the most significant manifestations of "intertextuality." It is important to recall, however, that the original script intruded into the audience, insisting on its interactivity: "Shakespeare's theatrical language—every element of it, from word to gesture to costume—was native to and developed in a place in which the actors were surrounded by and within touching distance. No playwright of genius could fail to include in his plays, in a most basic way, the theatre space and the actor-audience relationship that he knew was a given for him" (Swander 1984, 8). Spaces that do not incorporate that dynamic—like the Shakespeare Theatre in D.C.—must, I believe, overcome some basic conflicts between the play as scripted and the play as performed. That victory is possible, as I will suggest later, but one wonders why the challenge must be met in the first place.

Niels Herold asks, *"Will historicists shake [Coursen's] strategic hand of containment?"* (1995, 48. Herold's emphasis), suggesting that my effort to accommodate historicism to performance criticism is really an attempt at the cooption of historicism. Herold cites the antitheatrical tradition as represented by Harry Berger and quotes Richard Poirier, who talks of "those inflections of language which most teachers of literature . . . often cannot hear or which they ignore in the interest of a variously motivated eloquence" (48)—"variously motivated," Herold says, meaning "political." Herold goes on to say that "For those who can hear them, Shakespeare's plays somehow exist prior to and beyond any theatrical performances of them, performances which can never be definitive or ideal but are always embedded in the 'variously motivated' facts of their particular moment" (48). And that is true: performances are never "definitive," as I replied in response to Berger (Coursen 1992). Even a listener who tried to hear the *un*variously motivated inflections would be hearing his or her own interpretation, modified by his or her experience and his or her *history*. The individual, like the production, is embedded in those facts. It cannot be otherwise. To reach the point where one can understand Shakespeare's language, one can no longer be *a*historical.

Louis Montrose says that "The metaphorical identification of the world and the stage is not an incidental commonplace; it is one of the reflexive dramatic and theatrical strategies by which Shakespeare asserts a reciprocal relationship between his work and his world" (1979-80, 51-2). As time has gone on, the work, although edited by textual scholars and debated by critics, has remained a constant, although "translations" like those of Cibber, Tate, and modern filmmakers have been made. But with the sheer movement of history, *locus* has encountered *platea*—the zeitgeist, the challenge launched *to* the script by an era to make the work intelligible or to re-create the "reciprocal relationship" between work and world. In *Julius Caesar, locus* (Rome) could become fascist Italy in the late 1930s (= *platea*). Welles's was an extreme example of what any good production does—it pulls the script forward in time, and it limits the number of possible meanings latent in the script. In this instance the anachronistic setting was a clear and intended analogy that probably blurred or oversimplified the tangle of right and unright that the *locus* provides. But no production can escape *platea*. If it tries, *platea* becomes something repressed—a "shadow" that the production will still communicate. It is probably true, as well, that our response to fascism today cannot be as urgent as was the response of a New York audience to Welles's production in the late 1930s.

I remember many years ago when a student sneered at *The Tempest*.

"Not very convincing," she said. I did not try to convince her. I merely said, "Antonio agrees." Shakespeare often builds the disapproving or alienated position into his comic closure in characters like Malvolio, Jaques, Shylock, and possibly Egeus, depending upon what a director decides to do with Egeus after Theseus overrules him. But this insight is merely an extension of the New Critical "irony" *into* a dramatic text, which can discharge "multiple signification" through different attitudes in the characters. Thus the text becomes a *script,* which can be, as Fox says, "an instrument of analysis rather than a definitive statement" (1983, 51) and which, as Hapgood says will "not only allow the performers to make certain interpretive emphases but also allow for individual differences among the spectators" (1986, 218). A script, designed to be performed, is inevitably an instrument of analysis within which, as Hodgdon says, "critics [and] performers fill in an elliptical text [therefore rewriting] the play's intentionally puzzling narrative rhythms" (1985, 63).

In the BBC *Richard II,* for example, Northumberland's revelation of Bolingbroke's return with an army occurs at Gaunt's funeral. That is a normalizing *platea* decision. In the script, however, Northumberland's knowledge is imparted during the same scene in which Richard has seized the Lancastrian estates. A production could show that Bolingbroke executes his return *as* Richard provides the justification for that return. The implication would be that Bolingbroke is counting on Richard's playing into his hands, as Richard seems to do so often in the play. The puzzle is intentional, designed to be put together by the actors, and never producing the same aesthetic shape as that created by another group of actors working with the same puzzle—the script.

It is a lie, promulgated by many of the newer critics, that New Criticism involved merely the application of a set of terms to a monolithic text. *Reading* with the New Critical vocabulary—though not the primary activity that Shakespeare encourages—does not necessarily result in "univocal statements about texts" that cannot "reflect fully the tensions and ideological conflicts which such texts embody" (Freeman 1990, 111). That the New Critical approach *can* produce sealed interpretations is true, but so can the New Historicism. When, for example, a psychological approach to the plays is dismissed because it is "not historical," such sealing has occurred.

The basic premise of "historicity" is that no one can know what is beyond the knowledge of a given culture, as even Prior, whom I quote approvingly above, tends to suggest. We must be "intertextual." This is nonsense, of course, because the inevitable corollary is that nothing new can be thought, or can occur. (In the middle of the nineteenth century, the director of the U.S. Patent Office resigned because everything that could be invented had been invented.) The "explanation," of course, is that there is nothing really "new," but what seems to be new is a development from what has been there already, even if the new element seems sudden, even revolutionary. It is the accretion of weight that produces the avalanche. The early nineteenth century, for example, created much of the intellectual context which Darwin would pursue in the specifics of *The Origin of Species by Means of Natural Selection*. If my own view includes some Carlyle with the inevitable Engels—that is, that whoever the existential Shakespeare may have been, he was more than merely a product of a lot of contexts—then that becomes "my" history. I believe that there is a mystery here—a miracle perhaps—that cannot be explained, or explained away, by intertextuality or even by a remarkably protean collision of zeitgeists.

That is not to deny what Louis Montrose says: The "writing and reading of texts [are] historically determined and determining modes of cultural work," and that "apparently autonomous aesthetic and academic issues are being reunderstood as inextricably though complexly linked to other discourses and practices" (1989, 15). Miracles inevitably represent a qualification. If the New Historicists demonstrate "the embeddedness of cultural objects in the contingencies of history" (Greenblatt 1990, 164), one must not *bury* the cultural object in that history. The dirt is part of the history, but the archaeologist clears it away from the object and links the object with others on the same plane to create *a* history, or context that is made up of what else belonged in that room. The room stands for a context within which a particularly "theme" and its objects are to be discovered—whether it was a kitchen or a dungeon. That definition begins to become primary, of course, and begins to rule out other possibilities, but limitation is necessary within contextualization. Pressure is part of history, but it is the fossil that communicates to us and the stone only more generally. Other *fossils* at the same level, though, create a context.

Whatever we find "history" to be, or not to be, a script moves forward in time. It shows us something *new* as it moves, partly because time is the infinitely renewable medium within which the fragile entity known as history and that fragment known as script, which carries its history with it, also move. I would amend Ann Thompson's statement that "In some sense all future readings could be said to be already 'there' in the text, but we have to wait for the historical circumstances which will make them visible" (1988, 81). My amendment would be that what makes the text visible is its production as play. Atemporality does not permit the script to uncover what we believe is new in our own culture. The "New Critical" approach searches for confirmation of its own method, for the presence in literature of its own terms. Nor, however, does New Historicism, strictly defined, permit the uncovering that Thompson suggests. The New Historicism can only discover what is old—intertextual—in the texts. The possibilities of the *script*, however, range forward in time, or can do so within the coordinates described by Philip McGuire: "*The play text . . . is not its enduring essence abstracted from the particularities that inhere in all performances. It is a verbal (rather than mathematical) construct that describes the ensemble of possibilities.* It establishes a range, a distribution of possible events during a performance, including acts of speaking . . . Its statements do specify what *cannot* happen, and in doing so, they permit whatever possibilities are not prohibited" (1985, 138–39. McGuire's emphasis).

Historicizing may avoid fallacy—attributing, for example, a consciousness/unconscious dichotomy to characters who do not have that conception in their cultures. "Unconscious" is a word not available to Shakespeare in his culture—nor did he invent it. "Conscience" meant both "consciousness" *and* "moral voice," but the tradition of the latter as an "inner" activity emerges long before Montaigne. Oedipus is already in the culture, even if Sophocles is not available to Shakespeare. Much of Jung was in the culture, from Augustine ("archetype") and mythology. The concept of the split personality and the compensatory psyche emerges from St. Bernard into, for example, Richard III's debate between conscious intention and the repressed guilt represented by the "Fool," or truth sayer, that some part of Richard sets up in opposition to his conscious agenda.

One could also argue, if necessary, that if the examples of the "construction of interiority" available from, for example, Christ, St. Jerome, St. Bernard, St. Augustine—were somehow *not* available to Shakespeare, he could have thought of the concept himself. He had his sonnet experience, the débat tradition of medieval literature, his exploration of dramatic characters, and Marlowe's example of putting the Good and Evil Angels within Faustus, as his inner voices, making them *psychological,* as opposed to theological or theatrical stereotypes. It is possible, however, that "history" ignores the imagination that might precede the historical fact: "Once in an interview . . . the essayist George Steiner made the provocative suggestion to me that the nightmare world of the death camps might not have been realizable had not Kafka's imagination first embodied their possibility in his fiction" (Rosenbaum 1994, 30). Oscar Wilde once said that life imitates art as often as art imitates life. Rupert Sheldrake has proposed a theory of "formative causation" that challenges the materialist premises of modern science (1981, 1995. See Coursen, 1988a).

Historicizing brings a work into time and into zeitgeist, and that is useful in contrast to the "well-wrought urn" tradition. But historicizing does not necessarily show us all that is there. It is useful to see Olivier's *Hamlet* as a film of its decade—Eileen Herlie's hairdo as Gertrude is Vivien Leigh's as Scarlett in *Gone with the Wind*. The conventions and limitations of film in the 1940s pertain, but that is not the whole story. The "text" may be atemporal but "the script" is inevitably trapped in the time of its production and by all the signifiers that show that the production itself unconsciously reflects its time. Photographs of productions of the turn of the century, for example, done in "the dress of Shakespeare's time" demonstrate that the productions were done in what was *thought* to be the dress of Shakespeare's time. To us they are dated, and historical only in that they reflect what was thought to be known in 1900. Enough time has passed since Jan Kott's infamous reduction of Shakespeare to the range and scope of modern dramatists so that a book can emerge entitled *Is Shakespeare Still Our Contemporary?* The answer, of course, is yes, as long as we agree that Shakespeare is also his own contemporary, as it were. And that is useful, since we avoid saying silly things like "Others abide our question. Thou art free," or "Not of an age, but for all time." Those are half truths. Shakespeare is of an age and must abide some of the questions that his zeitgeist imposes on him.

Still, however, he does continue into time, freely enough in one sense but absorbing the prejudices and biases of new times and different cultures, even as we recover ways in which the plays manifest his own times. Shakespeare was hardly "free" after the Restoration but was cabined within a set of critical assumptions that insisted on radical revision of his scripts—as film does today when it essays Shakespeare. And some highly developed cultures—those emerging from and employing the Romance languages, for example—are not at all enthralled by Shakespeare. The Muslim world must see Shakespeare as a Satan. Other cultures—India, for example—discover in Shakespeare a set of moral allegories that modern American and British critics scorn as passé.

R. W. Desai, for example, offers a cultural corrective to Gary Taylor's *Reinventing Shakespeare*. "Do we really believe," Taylor asks, "in the overwhelming moral importance of premarital female virginity? . . . Do we believe in the influence of the planets? Do we worry ourselves about the divine right of kings? Do we actively believe, all of us, in the fundamental premises of Christianity?" (quoted by Desai 1991,

112). Desai says that, in India, "for the vast population that lies between [the two extremes of erstwhile maharajahs and nawabs and
bottom-of-the-rung manual workers], a population highly conservative, traditional, orthodox, the answers to the questions would be an
emphatic 'yes'" (113). "Today's India is truly Shakespeare's contemporary" (113)—that is, assuming that all of Shakespeare's England believed all that is implied in Taylor's questions. Western culture tends
to turn the question of a woman's virginity into a matter of her domination by a phallocentric orientation and the issue of kings into an exploration of power. Some of Gary Taylor's questions, when translated
into another allegory, do require a "yes." (See Rooks 1990, 116–29.)

At times, and perhaps in spirit, this book represents a piece of "old
historicism," in which the work of art is still granted some primacy.
That is not to say that something called "the text" is the "authority." I
am suggesting that performance is authoritative, but not in the way
that Anthony Dawson attributes to Harry Berger: "Berger seems to assume that performance is single and unchanging, incapable of irony,
its meanings univocal" (1988, 340 n. 41). That is to place Berger in a
position more rigid than he occupies, as Berger has placed me in a position more comfortable than I occupy, as "an academic interpreter . . .
an armchair reader [as opposed to a] theater-centered interpreter" (1991,
226). My own stance toward performance is that (a) it is heavily conditioned by the historical moment into which it intrudes and (b) it is just
as important, perhaps more important, than its intertextuality. I will
suggest, for example, that the 1936 film version of *Romeo and Juliet* is
a more significant emblemization of its zeitgeist than, say, Tony Martin's record of the Walter Bullock-Richard Whiting song, "When Did
You Leave Heaven?," recorded with Victor Young and his Orchestra
on 18 July 1936, if only because the latter lasts for two minutes and
fifty-two seconds, which was all the time an eight-inch 78-rpm record
offered in 1936, space being very much a determinant of what could occur within it. For those who prefer the song to the film, I am willing to
grant their obvious intertextuality, but am unwilling to grant that each
is an equal thread in the cultural fabric of 1936 as we re-weave it from
the loom of our current vantage point.

"Intertextuality" itself, I would suggest, is sometimes best employed
to help us understand "Shakespearean meanings" and how they might
resonate to his audience and thus help an actor understand them for us.
As has often been noted, Hamlet's soliloquies are usually "closed" or
ineffectual—"sit still my soul," "My tables, meet it is I set it down,"
"and lose the name of action," "I will speak daggers to her, but use
none," "Up sword, and know thou a more horrid hent," "My thoughts

be bloody, or be nothing worth." One ends with action—"the play's the thing." It moves from self-laceration to activity. This soliloquy is easy to "historicize." Hamlet's reference to "guilty creatures sitting at a play" is very probably to the famous Townswoman of Lynn, who confessed to her husband's murder during a performance of *Fair Francis* (see Hardison 1969). If that episode was not available to W.S. he could have invented it—and he would not have had to "transcend" his time to do so, since confession was a well-known activity and was, in his Church, a *"general"* confession, as opposed to one privately rendered to an anonymous priest. *Hamlet* is a script suffused with references to Christian ritual and to the failure of any and all God-contacting activity within the world of Elsinore.

But that a contemporary example did exist in no way informs the way the script works today. In fact, most New Historical approaches can render only very conventional and usually unoriginal readings of the plays themselves. That is only partly because the concepts of "historicity" and "imagination" are so at odds with each other. More basically, the reason is that New Historicism stops short at the very moment when it might transcend itself. It is in performance that the plays confront their history and the historical circumstances of their point of production. In Adrian Noble's *Hamlet* of 1992, with Kenneth Branagh, people made efforts or moves to embrace each other, but failed or stopped short. Their inability to contact each other physically reflected their world's inability to give and receive the larger positive energies of the universe in a kingdom as exiled from health as is Oedipus's Thebes. Noble gave us a "modern" reading of a concept that emerges from deep history into Shakespeare's play and thus suggested the continuity that is one positive consequence of the New Historicist orientation, broadly construed.

It may be that the trend for Shakespeare productions to move *away* from television and to film (see Davies 1994a, xi) reflects the movement from modernism to postmodernism and film's ability to make the transition. Although television was developed before World War II, it is a postwar phenomenon. Its programming, its spread from very regional to national and satellite formats, and the development of color are all products of the years from 1948 to 1960. Its segmented format, to incorporate commercial breaks, is inherited from radio, which is also a *modern* medium. Is television trapped in "modernist" criteria—thematic unity, coherence, structure, and the expectation of a homogeneous audience? Possibly—meaning that the medium is *intrinsically* limited.[2] Certainly it has no field of depth technically and, it follows, must be a close-up and shallow medium with very conventional camera techniques. Even with the advent of larger screens, it has developed no field of depth intellectually or emotionally. To some extent it is a victim of what has been put on the screen and therefore of our expectations—CBS once believed that it could bring culture through its networks but brought the NFL instead—and it never stood for more than entertainment. Its one transcendent moment was the Kennedy funeral. It is not accidental that the wars reported on television are small wars, regional and guerrilla, or that sound bites and rapid montage reporting are its modes of transmitting "information." It was "radio with a picture," but the picture took away, absorbed the imaginative completing of radio that we provided, whether listening to Don Dunphy broadcast the fights of Joe Louis, or Mr. North waking up after a midshow commercial break to ask Mrs. North where he was, or Hop Harrigan coming in for a landing.

Film, which began, with the photograph, in a premodern era, which incorporated radical changes, like the addition of sound (a radical transition that transformed the industry), which enjoys a deep field that makes it far more flexible than television, and which is light sensitive, as opposed to magnetic—making it more like *our* way of seeing things than TV is—is not trapped in specific modernist categories. The automobile, which can be improved in all kinds of ways, is a good example of a *modern* agent. The addition of air bags (almost over Lee Iacocca's dead body, who then, still living, trumpeted his championship of them) merely points at the intrinsic *limitations* of the automobile.

It may be that television will remain trapped in its own banality, for the reasons that Peter Brook gives—that it emerged at a moment of stasis at which it is frozen:

> The cinema degenerated because, like many a great empire, it stood still: it repeated its rituals identically again and again—but time passed and the meaning went out of them. Then television arrived at the very instant when the dramatic cliches of the cinema were being dished up for the nine millionth time. It began showing old movies—and rotten movie-like plays—and enabled audiences to judge them in a completely new way. In the cinema the darkness, the vast screen, the loud music, the soft carpets added unquestionably to the hypnosis. On television the cliches were naked: the viewer is independent, he is walking around his room, he hasn't paid (which makes it easier to switch off), he can voice his disapproval out loud without being sssshed. Furthermore, he is forced to judge, and to judge fast. He switches on the set and immediately judges from the face that he sees (a) whether it's an actor

or someone "real"; (b) whether he's nice or not, good or bad, what his class or background, etc., are; (c) when it's a fictional scene, he draws on his experience of dramatic cliches to guess at the part of the story he has missed (because, of course, he can't sit round the program twice, as he used to do at the movies). The smallest gesture identifies the villain, the adulteress, and so on. The essential fact is that he has learned—from necessity—to observe, to judge for himself. (1987, 26)

But this unknown citizen makes only the judgments dictated by the conventions with which he has been inundated. The insidiousness of television is that it is not merely itself, which is more than enough, but that the shallow psychology of perception that it has engendered has become the expectation of most spectators at any "live" event, sporting or dramatic. Too often the practitioners of drama have surrendered to these expectations. Perhaps the most valuable contribution of the New Historicism will turn out to be that it forces us "to judge for ourselves" by insisting that as individuals we discern the flow of history as it moves *us*—not as it may move others, or cultures, or countries. It may be, then, that as we return to things old—the scripts of Shakespeare and some of their manifestations, like the 1936 film of *Romeo and Juliet*— the dead do not speak to us. Rather, we speak to them, and, through the act of our speaking, they rise.

### NOTES

1. On post-modernism and its implications for performance, see Samuel Crowl's excellent summary (1992, 51–53).
2. On television's "modernism," see Raymond Williams, 1974, particularly his analysis on pp. 86–118.

# II

# *Romeo and Juliet:* A Beautiful Film for Beautiful People?

One might have supposed that with the advent of talkies in 1927, filmed Shakespeare would have become more popular than during the days of silents. That was not the case, however.

Between *The Jazz Singer*, with Al Jolson's "Wait a minute, wait a minute, you ain't heard nothin' yet" (1927), and Olivier's *Henry V* (1944), the "first Shakespeare film to be both a popular and an artistic success" (Hapgood 1986, 274), only *four* major films based on a Shakespearean script were produced: *The Taming of the Shrew* (Pickford and Fairbanks in 1929), the Dieterle-Reinhardt *Midsummer Night's Dream* (1935), the Czinner *As You Like It* (1936), and the Thalberg-Cukor *Romeo and Juliet* (1936). By way of contrast, Robert Hamilton Ball (1968, 385–91) indicates that in the three years immediately preceding the advent of sound (1924–26), twelve Shakespeare films were produced (not all of them in English, not all of them feature length, and some of them "off-shoots"). The evidence suggests that it was easier to make silents of Shakespeare, using visual equivalents for the language and plenty of title cards. Why, once the words and sound were synchronized with the celluloid and adequately amplified for huge movie palaces, did so few Shakespeare films appear in the 1930s?

A basic reason, of course, is that, as Ball says, "film was essentially a business" (1968, 300). As the famous *Variety* headline announced, "Sticks Nix Hicks' Pix." Hollywood had to turn out films that would attract the nickles and dimes of Depression-ridden moviegoers. At the same time, however, "the silent film created an enormous audience, potentially a large audience for Shakespeare" (Ball, 302). That audience came to the films in the 1930s, perhaps seeking escapist fare, Ginger Rogers and Fred Astaire, but not to see Shakespeare. The only "success" among the '30s Shakespeare films was the *Dream*, with its well-known stars and its use of gauzy special effects appropriate to the script and choreographed to the tune of Korngold's arrangement of Mendelssohn. As America's romance with the stockmarket was breaking up in 1929, its sweethearts, Pickford and Fairbanks, were nearing the end of their relationship—a fact that might have served as subtext for their *Shrew*—but Pickford was far too coy as Kate. She claimed that it was director Taylor's fault. He, she accused, said, "We don't want any of this heavy stage drama. We want the old Pickford tricks." So "instead of being a forceful tiger-cat [she became] a spitting little kitten" (Pickford, 1956, 311–12). She was permitted to eavesdrop on Fairbanks's soliloquy ("to kill a wife with kindness"), which he delivered to his hound, Troilus. Pickford eclipsed her "submission" speech with a wink to Bianca. Elisabeth Bergner's Rosalind in the Czinner *As You Like It* was also intolerably arch. Her antics kept blocking Olivier's effort to play Orlando.

The *Romeo and Juliet* remains perhaps the least evaluated sound film of them all. Of the '30s films "only [*Dream*] has much interest today," says Hapgood (1986, 274). Roger Manvell devotes several pages to the *Romeo and Juliet* (1971, 27–35), about which he is unenthusiastic. Jack Jorgens condemns the film's "static, ornate prettiness" and finds that Howard and Shearer are not "credible and likeable lovers" (1977, 91). Bernice W. Kliman calls the film a "clunker" (1994, 26). The only contemporary critic to say a kind word is Kenneth Rothwell: "I believe the film should be cherished as a masterwork from antiquity: a bit archaic, a little rigid, slightly overdone, but, yes, still withal warm and good" (Rothwell and Melzer 1990, 249).[1]

The mythology, of course, is that both Norma Shearer at thirty-five and Leslie Howard at forty-two were too old for their roles. As Manvell says, "Norma Shearer, a fully mature actress . . . appeared utterly out of character, a middle-aged woman masquerading as a virgin," while Howard "did his best to bring a youthful ardour and sincerity to the poetry, but his evident age made his task impossible" (1971, 30). Age was a factor, along with the puritanical attitude of the censors—the Hays Office—because the film, like the expurgated texts that tenth graders read even today, did not/ could not "portray . . . violent and sex-driven youth confronting their repressive, counter-violent, and counter-sexual elders, not just idealistic and fate-haunted lovers lost in bookish poetry" (Frey 1992). The script had to wait for Franco Zeffirelli and the 1960s to "free" it from age and an era.

Since the film has recently been made commercially available, it deserves an examination it has never received. If we historicize the moment of its production, we discover that one of the basic issues the film confronts is that of the inherited text itself and the corollary question of how "high poetry" is to be spoken in a realistic medium that requires little or no projection from the actors. These issues inhibited the Shakespeare films of the 1930s, helping make all but one of them both artistic and financial failures, although Robert Osborne of Turner Broadcasting claimed, in introducing *Romeo and Juliet* on 20 April 1994, that it was "amazingly popular with audiences."[2] Rothwell and Melzer, however, say that "the film did poorly . . . at the box office" (1990, 249). Since talkies were far more expensive to make than silent films, they had to succeed at the box office. This film, says *The Literary Digest*, left 138,000 feet of film on the cutting-room floor, before arriving at the *12,000* feet of the "shrewdly compressed" final version ("Boy Meets Girl" 1936, 20). It could be argued that *Romeo and Juliet did* do well at the box office, making $1.1 million. But it cost $2 million, "double its original budget" (Flamini 1994, 251). The deficit obviously inhibited the making of any Shakespeare films from 1936 to 1944 (along with the continuing cultural and economic disaster of the Great Depression and World War II, of course).[3]

In a report from Hollywood, *The New York Times* summarized the issue as of 19 April 1936:

> Hollywood is awaiting the preview [of *Romeo and Juliet*] with considerable interest. The town, frankly, didn't care much for "Dream," but Metro promises that this will be different. If the money and thought and care that have gone into "Romeo" result in box-office success, then other of Shakespeare's works will be filmed. But if this fails, the town's strivings toward culture must find another outlet. The Bard will be regarded as one of Hollywood's major flops. ("Report," 1936)

Richard Watts said of the 1935 *Midsummer Night's Dream* that

> There is something almost wistful about [the motion-picture producers's] anxiety to prove to us that they are missionaries of culture and pioneers of a new aesthetic form . . . they can hardly forget that they are also supposed to be businessmen [and] can only succeed when their pictures appeal to widespread audiences and show a neat profit . . . these warring emotions in the magnate's soul . . . almost invariably result . . . in the deadening spirit of compromise. It would certainly be much better for the aesthetic quality of the films if the motives could be divided and two definite types of photoplay could be made: the one that frankly

was intended as a piece of trade goods and the other that made a thoughtful and complete effort to be dramatically distinguished, even though forced to appeal to a comparatively limited group. (1935, 311)

It may be, though I do not intend to explore the thesis here, that it was easier for silent films to be both "popular" and "artistic," particularly since silent films were not burdened with the weight of "Shakespeare's language." If so, the "division" occurred as soon as the sacrosanct words of a given play became available to a medium that had relied upon the visual image. As Granville-Barker said of the Reinhardt and Cukor films, cinema could use Shakespeare's narratives "to suit its pictorial purpose, without respect to him . . . Shakespeare in the cinema will do—with Shakespeare left out" (1936, 425).[4]

While a film like Zeffirelli's *Romeo and Juliet* has been very successful, directors and producers have hardly stampeded to create filmic versions of the canon. Commercial considerations may no longer be a major barrier these days, given the success of Kenneth Branagh's two films, but the difficulties of the playtext when translated to film and of the speaking of the verse have hardly been solved since 1936. It is questionable, for example, whether most films based on a Shakespeare script have transcended the problems that Max Reinhardt outlined during the silent era:

There is no creative film literature; only more or less arbitrary adaptations of dramas, novels, sentimental or detective stories. . . . [T]he film cannot dispense with the excessive use of the word, although freedom from the word is one of its chief potential characteristics. . . . The film . . . must live on its own soil, without borrowing everywhere else. It must stand on its own foundations, so that it can dispense entirely with the photographed word. (1926, 62–64)

If Michael Skovmand is right, some recent cinematic versions of the scripts are as derivative as were the films that Reinhardt scorned: Branagh's "approach is that of finding the right cinematic *equivalent* of a primarily *theatrical* concept, in which the dynamics of character and verbal delivery are essential ingredients" (1994, 9. Skovmand's emphasis).

The 1936 *Romeo and Juliet* summoned an intense debate about how Shakespeare's language should or could be translated to film. Zeffirelli's late 1960s production solved the problem by cutting the script drastically and creating a luxurious high Renaissance suffused with light,

brocade and velvet, lutes and recorders, and fuzzy-cheeked teenage sexuality. It was a film we could stroke. Branagh solved the problem of
high poetry by working with the script of *Much Ado About Nothing*, a
play written mostly in prose. For the 1936 *Romeo and Juliet*, "Talbot
Jennings, who wrote the script . . . resolved all the poetry into the
form of prose so that there would be no inclination to read it other than
in a natural fashion" ("Report from Hollywood," 1936).

John Marks wondered in 1936 "why they have to film Shakespeare"
—as if live versions were easily accessible. Marks concedes that Shakespeare "was the first man to write scenarios . . . cuts, continuity, comp.
shots and all." Marks claims that the *Romeo and Juliet* is Shakespeare's
"first successful translation into active cinematic terms" because of "a
certain dawning realisation that it's the dialogue that counts, however
difficult verse may be to film." The difficulty, Marks argues, is that the
verse is "rich in metaphor and so is the screen, because its pictures
dance, allude and illustrate" (1936, 38). The point, of course, is that
Shakespeare's language is high in sensory data, as McLuhan would
say, demanding our participation in the images, whereas film itself is a
"hot" medium which does most of the sensory work *for* us, particularly
if the film is in Technicolor (which the 1936 *Romeo and Juliet* is not).
Still, as Marks suggests, "the camera is not always obliged to skip as
quick as thought; so that not invariably when the poet mentions say, a
bear, need we have one lumbering into view" (38). Marks alludes to the
moment in Reinhardt's *Dream* when Jean Muir's Helena complains of
being shunned by beasts. A huge bear emerges from behind a bush,
takes one look at her, and flees back into the forest. Reinhardt provided
a consciously simpleminded visual equivalent for the verse, looking
ahead to the obsessively literal interpretation that the artisans would
impose on "Pyramus and Thisbe." Reinhardt and Dieterle sometimes
made their film self-referential, as when the donkey that has pulled the
player's properties into the woods bolts at the sight of the transformed
Bottom. While Marks calls the *Romeo and Juliet* a success, he does
point at its internal tug-of-war between film and poetry:

> Shakespeare is appreciated as a librettist: the camera serves to
> clarify the incidents and outline of his plot. That is half the battle
> —the easier half. His words are poetry, an awkward fact which
> most of [the] actors did their best to overlook, shying as far as pos-
> sible into prose . . . [T]o film Shakespeare, with all the magnifi-
> cent resources of the screen at one's disposal, to use them well—
> though much too lavishly—and yet to miss, or dodge the verbal
> values of his poetry, is surely to fail, without excuse, in an enter-

prise which deserved to be undertaken with greater confidence. (1936, 38)

But would "confidence"—the launching into the verse *as* verse—have accomplished anything other than a "staginess" or "operatic effect" inappropriate to film?

The problem of speaking itself should have been solved by 1936. Robert Benchley's short talkie of 1925 had, of course, aroused great interest in films that spoke. Benchley's satiric thrust of 1928, "Enter the Talkies," suggests what was happening in Hollywood:

> Perceiving the advent of the Film Which Talks Like a Man, hundreds of movie stars who have attained their eminence because of a dimple in the chin or a bovine eye, but whose speaking voices could hardly be counted on to put across the sale of a pack of Fatimas in a night club, are now frantically trying to train their larynxes into some sort of gentility. Voice culture has become the order, even the command, of the day. (1928 [1994], 100)

The transition was satirized in the great musical of 1952, *Singin' in the Rain*, with Gene Kelly, Debbie Reynolds, Donald O'Connor, and the late Jean Hagen as a beautiful actress of the silent screen with a deplorable "Joisey" accent.

The verse, as opposed to the voice, had to be cut from filmed Shakespeare in favor of the image, or "naturalized" so that it sounded like prose. The exception, of course, would be a Mercutio, who is characterized as a flamboyant speaker. The problem is that Shakespeare's script creates the imagery, whereas it is the camera that does so for film—words and sound accounting for no more than a quarter of the total effect of film (see Styan, 1981). Thalberg, for example, called his film a "picturization" (*Motion Picture Edition*, 13). What Stephen Hearst says of a television script is even truer of a film script, since film relies more heavily on the visual image and, it follows, much less heavily on the spoken word than does television:

> A written text on the right-hand side of any script page which makes complete sense in itself is a bad text. What are the pictures there for? . . . The words, except in exceptional circumstances, need to follow the pictures. . . . Pictures have their own grammar, their own logic . . . and cannot easily be kept waiting. . . . To such a picture you could speak no more than about 25 words. . . . [L]anguage seems to play a secondary role in television. (1978, 4–5)

As Peter Hall suggests, in Shakespeare "what is meant is said. Even his stage action is verbalized before or after the event. This is bad screen writing. A good film script relies on constasting visual images. What is spoken is of secondary importance. And so potent is the camera in convincing us that we are peering at reality, that dialogue is best underwritten or eliptical" (1969).

Into the 1936 debate charged George Bernard Shaw, who defended Shakespeare, in spite of Shaw's long-standing reservations, against the potential tyranny of the camera. Although this was one playwright standing up for another, and though Shaw displayed a remarkable sense of how the microphone works, he tended to ignore the *inevitable* domination of the camera:

Q. Is it possible to do justice to Shakespeare's verse as verse through the medium of the screen?

G.B.S. . . . [Y]ou can do things with the microphone that you cannot do on the ordinary stage. . . . [O]n the screen you can employ nuances and delicacies of expression which would be no use spoken by an actor on the ordinary stage in the ordinary way. They might reach the first row of the stalls; they would not get any further. . . . The main thing that you require nowadays is to get people who understand what they are saying when they are speaking Shakespeare. . . . [I]f people do understand and feel what they are saying they get all sorts of inflexions without thinking about it. . . .

Q. With the use of the camera you are able to get the spirit of the aside, the soliloquy, much better than you are able to get it on stage . . . ?

G.B.S. . . . [O]ne of the difficulties now is to keep the camera in its place . . .

Q. Don't all these devices in themselves constitute an interruption of the verse, the rhythm, the sweep of the verse?

G.B.S. . . . It is extraordinary how much can be spoiled if you let the photographer, as photographer pure and simple, get the upper hand. There is the human voice; you have the verse and the lines . . . You have to remember for instance that you are speaking Shakespeare, not giving an exhibition of photography. . . .

(quoted in Manvell 1971, 33–34)

Clearly, Shaw came out in favor of the verse and the voice, the former inimical to a "naturalistic" medium, the latter almost superfluous. As Norma Desmond says in *Sunset Boulevard*, "Dialogue? We had faces!" The *Time* reviewer saw things very much as Norma Desmond did:

> In the avowed effort to make the production what Shakespeare would have wanted had he possessed the facilities of cinema, it apparently occurred to no one that, could he really have gone to Hollywood to work on the script, Shakespeare would simply have thrown away *Romeo and Juliet* and written a new play, as was his inflexible habit with the classics of his own day. Instead, [the adapters] scrupulously arranged a script without a line of dialogue not written by the Bard. (Review of *Romeo and Juliet*, 1936b)

In other words, while Shakespeare may not have been as inflexible as *Time* suggests (he could steal verbatim when he wanted to), he would have "adapted" the antique and unwieldy old play into a cinematic space. The suggestion has merit. Some of the great "Shakespeare" films, as has often been noted, are the ones the most removed from the specific language of the script. One thinks of Kurosawa's *Throne of Blood*, Kozintsev's *King Lear,* and Welles's *Chimes at Midnight.* Even films that translate Shakespeare into modern metaphors but stay close to the scripted story can be as technically and emotionally shallow, as tensionless, as mumbled and as banal as, for example, the recent *Men of Respect,* a hoodlum version of *Macbeth.* Kozintsev, speaking for the maker of films, grants the playwright only half of the collaborative credit: "half of the text of any play [is] a diffused remark that the author wrote in order to acquaint actors as thoroughly as possible with the heart of the action to be played" (1966, 215). In other words, a film "based" on Shakespeare must become a separate work, with its own inner logic and integrity. Peter Hall's advice is to "throw away the text altogether . . . and develop the fable with all its atmosphere. This is what happens in *Throne of Blood* and the Russian *Hamlet*" (1969).

Summarizing the debate about the Shakespeare films of the 1930s, Manvell says that none "displayed any realization that an imaginative adaptation of normal film technique would be necessary to allow Shakespeare's greatness as a dramatist to reach its proper fulfillment through the screen. The mid 1930s was possibly the wrong period for this to be understood or attempted; film-makers were still over-preoccupied with establishing the first principles of matching sight and sound, while at the same time rebuilding an impregnable star system after the silent era in order to sustain the very costly medium which sound films had become" (1971, 34–35). That may be unfair to the

*Dream,* which incorporates some long and stunning sequences backed only by Mendelssohn's pizzicato strings and mellow horns, but Manvell is correct to suggest that the filmmakers of the 1930s had yet to learn what to do with their newfound sound. They tended to overuse it—often in long, climactic speeches in locker rooms or before the Senate or in a courtroom. It was the speech that had to be put in its place, not the camera. Shaw's comment demonstrates that the lesson had not been learned in 1936. Its learning would be to the detriment of the inherited script. That issue—Shakespeare's language, however unascertainable within the intertextual flux of variants, versus the grammar of the camera—remains. The debate surrounding the 1936 *Romeo and Juliet* focuses the question clearly.

The "packaging" of the 1936 *Romeo and Juliet* was similar to what goes on today. Branagh's *Much Ado* arrives with a separate book containing commentary, photographs, and film script and, of course, enjoys the secondary market of video cassette (perhaps the *primary* market for some films, like *The Last Action Hero*). In 1936 Random House produced a book edited by Professor William Strunk that included the film script of *Romeo and Juliet.*

The trailer, presented around the country after the premieres in New York and later in Los Angeles, tried to sell many things and to create the aura of a successful history for the film. It is itself an opulent film, a fascinating artifact of the 1930s.

It creates an immediate link with popular print media by flashing "Extra—another sensational SCOOP for this theatre" on top of a conventional shield-and-crossed-swords motif. The words go on to tell of a "Special limited popular-priced engagement of one of the greatest triumphs in screen history! The sweethearts of 'Smilin' Through' . . . come smiling through again in William Shakespeare's great love story—." We wait to find out what that story might be as the words "starring the first lady of the screen, lovely Norma Shearer" appear below two soft-focus shots of Shearer, one, standing by one of the stanchions of Juliet's balcony, the second, feeding a fawn (which turns out to be our first view of her in the film itself). Howard also gets two shots, slightly less close-up, as "the passionate dreamer and romantic lover." Both Shearer and Howard are smiling. Finally, *Romeo and Juliet* appears over trumpets and a procession. The background shifts to big-city streets at night. More words appear on the screen: "A sensation at the Astor Theatre in New York . . . *eagerly applauded* by happy throngs who paid $2.20 to witness this supreme dramatic sequence." The stately music that has accompanied the trailer continues. Two dollars and twenty cents for a film was a high price, of course, at a time when dinner at the Central Park Casino cost that much and caused Commissioner Robert Moses to close the place down because it was beyond the means of the common man. The midnight showing of *The Road to Glory,* directed by Howard Hawks and starring Fredric March, was available four blocks from the Astor at the Rivoli, at Broadway and Forty-ninth, for a quarter. One could precede that excitement with filet mignon or broiled lobster at the Cafe Loyale on East Forty-third for $1.25., or enjoy dinner and a view of lower Central Park at the St. Moritz for a $1.75, or listen to Peg La Centra sing "Moonlight and Shadows" with Art Shaw and his Orchestra at the Lexington on Forty-eighth Street for $1.25 (no cover).

The scene shifts to a tower and a "Carthay Circle" [sic] neon sign under the text "Then across the continent where Los Angeles and the great of Hollywood pay tribute." We see "Romeo and Juliet" again, in the gleaming art deco print of '30s trailers. Then Clark Gable stands at a microphone to announce that *"Romeo and Juliet* makes me proud to be a member of the motion picture industry." He had turned down the part of Romeo however, as had one of the most popular actors of the '30s, Fredric March, and as had Olivier—the latter because "Shake-speare cannot be filmed" (Manvell 1971, 36), and as had Brian Aherne, who "decided he was too old to be convincing as Juliet's youthful lover" (Flamini 1994, 246). Tenor Nelson Eddy follows Gable to the mike to compare "the dialogue of *Romeo and Juliet* [to] a symphony or a glorious tone poem." Over a montage of scenes from the film showing Shearer and Howard, we read about "the thrilling drama of the star-crossed lovers who met on Monday, loved on Tuesday, were married on Wednesday, separated Thursday, and on Friday [by this time Juliet is pleading with C. Aubrey Smith's angry Capulet] the girl rose to heroic heights of sacrifice for her love." We are not told what happened the next weekend, but the narrative outline does suggest the impetuous haste built into the inherited script. We read of "The famous potion scene," and Shearer contemplates her marriage to Paris. "This shall forbid it," she says, looking down at a dagger. We see and hear marching and trumpets again and read that *"Magnificent* pageantry surrounded the warring houses of the girl and boy" (who appear in separate cutouts smiling). The camera cuts to a duel (Tybalt and Romeo, though they are not identified) and then to a balcony—"The most famous scene of stage or screen." The claim for screen is probably correct, since Ball lists some forty-one silent versions or variants on the play in his index, and such stars as Theda Bara, Francis X. Bushman, and Will Rogers had appeared in silent versions of the play, as had

Shearer herself, when, in "an early indiscretion . . . years ago in the silent era, she dared a short balcony scene to the late John Gilbert's [Romeo]" ("Boy Meets Girl," 1936, 20). "The never to be forgotten balcony scene," reads the trailer, in the hope that Shearer's previous adventure with that scene *has* been forgotten. In a brief snippet from the film itself, Shearer calls Romeo back, forgetting why, with Tchaikovsky's tone poem in the background. The trailer returns to images of print media, as newspapers flop from the presses. "Only a picture as great . . . as important as 'Romeo and Juliet' could win this praise." From Universal Services: "Whole town talking about Norma Shearer's Juliet." From the St. Louis *Post Dispatch*: "Stage never dreamed such a production!" A voice-over tells us that *"Romeo and Juliet* is the talk of the world, this, the world's finest picture, embodies every attribute of perfect entertainment." The screen is then divided into four frames showing the town square, the duel, horses, the city—the expanse, depth, action, and variety of the production. The stars, Shearer and Howard, are reintroduced, and Barrymore, Oliver, Rathbone, and Smith each get a quarter of the screen as their names are announced. "And thousands of others." The shields and crossed swords reappear beneath the urgent message, "Now you may see this *greatest* motion picture of our time / At popular prices. / The engagement of 'Romeo and Juliet' is limited. / We urge you to see it as soon as possible." The orchestra crescendos into its final chord.

In retrospect, this is a strange version of "Coming Attractions." No raves come from either the New York or the Los Angeles press, and certainly only an ambiguous notice from whatever "Universal Services" might have been—people may have been talking about Shearer's Juliet, but what were they *saying?* The trailer could have used some of the reviews cited above, or Euphemia V. R. Wyatt, who said, "Those who love [Shakespeare] need not fear to see *Romeo and Juliet.* This is Shakespeare" (1936, 85), an assertion that would have pleased anyone afraid that this was a lowbrow enterprise, including that breed known as "purists," who would be heard from years later when Zeffirelli chopped so much of the language from his film script. The 1936 version received a rave from Frank Nugent of the *New York Times* after its opening in August:

> Metro the Magnificent has loosed its technical magic upon Will Shakespeare and has fashioned for his "Romeo and Juliet" a jeweled setting in which the deep beauty of his romance glows and sparkles and gleams with breathless radiance. Never before, in all its centuries, has the play received so handsome a production as

that which was unveiled last night at the Astor Theatre. All that the camera's scope, superb photography and opulent costuming could give it has been given to it here. Ornate but not garish, extravagant but in perfect taste, expensive but never overwhelming, the picture reflects great credit upon its producers and upon the screen as a whole. . . . Metro has translated the play into sheerly cinematic terms. (1936b)

Surely Nugent said *something* here that could have been condensed into a preview bite. Or, if he did not, he provided further hyperbole on 30 August:

If there is to be a Shakespearean cycle in the cinema, it must be along the lines indicated by MGM's superb craftsmen. . . . [T]he magnificent motion picture . . . has been described as a handsome production, one that is truly cinematic, lavishly costumed, opulently framed, performed by a company which, considered en masse, is little short of brilliant. Adjectives come glibly to the tongue, and there are many synonyms for extraordinary. . . . The play has been liberated from the spatial boundaries of the stage. Verona and its citizens have come alive in all the vivid splendor of Renaissance Italy. The tempo of the tragedy has been accelerated, its action made more compact and more convincing. For the first time in its centuries, the play has received a setting which does justice to the magnificence of its lines. By the magic of the closeup and the microphone we may hear its singing stanzas as they were meant to be heard—softly, in the silver-sweet whispers of two lovers. (1936a)

It may be that the person charged with condensing all of this into a few, flashing phrases was simply overwhelmed.

When it came time to rate the films of 1936—just before the New York film writers made their selections in early January 1937, Nugent put *Romeo and Juliet* in sixth place: "the cinema restored the bard to his proper pedestal by according his tragedy the most opulent production it has ever received. The camera released his play from the limitations of the stage; the microphone caught and perfectly preserved the matchless loveliness of his language and a clever company . . . played the roles with rather surprising competence" (Nugent, 1937). Ahead of the film on Nugent's list were *Carnival in Flanders,* a French farce "which managed somehow to elude the Hays office" (Nugent, 1937), *Fury,* directed by Fritz Lang, with Spencer Tracy, *Dodsworth,* with Walter Huston, *Mr. Deeds Goes to Town,* with Gary Cooper and Jean

Arthur, directed by Frank Capra, which won the New York Writers Award, and *Winterset,* the Sherwood Anderson script based on the Sacco-Vanzetti case, starring Burgess Meredith and John Carradine. In the writers' poll, Luise Rainer's portrayal of Anna Held in *The Great Ziegfeld* beat out, in order, Ruth Chatterton, Shearer, Carole Lombard, Katharine Hepburn, and Rosalind Russell. *Ziegfeld* and Rainer won the Academy Awards, along with Paul Muni for his Louis Pasteur and Capra for *Deeds.* Douglas Shearer, Norma's brother, won for the sound recording of *San Francisco. Romeo and Juliet* was shut out.

The mythology of creaking middle age that sprang up around Shearer and Howard may have emanated from the trailer's insistence on "girl" and "boy." The film itself necessarily deletes references to Juliet's age and, as much as possible, to the youth of the lovers. Suffice it that it was hard to package these well-known stars as part of a "boy meets girl" film. Their pairing in *Smilin' Through* had occurred in 1932.[5] Judy Garland and the already-experienced Shakespearean Mickey Rooney would probably not have worked out either, except possibly as characters in a film featuring an amateur production of *Romeo and Juliet* in Andy Hardy's backyard. The trailer deceptively sells smiling, the inevitable antidote to the Depression. It trades on what would be Susan Snyder's 1979 thesis that the opening sequences of the play promise a comedy. Indeed, according to a *New York Times* article, "Until the climax there is no hint that it is a tragedy. Metro's 'Romeo' is a rollicking, gay affair" ("Report from Hollywood," 1936). The effort to keep the tone light may explain why, as the film begins, the prologue— which *does* warn us about what is to come—is delivered from a proscenium stage, here an emblem of tawdry make-believe. Some people, innocent of the ending, may have plunked down their quarter and received a letdown along with their free soup dish.

The film's marketing may have suffered from some vague perception on the part of the public, or some rumor that crept out after the opening that things end up gloomily and tombily to boot. That was hardly escapism, the *raison d'etre* for films of the 1930s and certainly what the trailer was trying to sell. As early as 1917, as the United States was entering World War I, *Photoplay* argued that "American art, to reach the hearts of Americans, must be happy art. This, then, is the mandate of America to the photoplay—to exercise its high privilege and opportunity of making an art of happiness and a happiness of art" ("Screening of America" 1994, 12). MGM films may have been, as L. B. Mayer was fond of saying, "Beautiful films for beautiful people," but except for those who worship golden statues, the last words of *Romeo and Juliet* are not happily ever after.

The trailer was deceptive on one count. It claimed that the audience for the Astor premiere paid $2.20. The price for evening performances ranged from $.50 to $2.00. (Professor Eugene Waith tells me that the 20 extra cents was the tax). The air-conditioned Astor, at Broadway and Forty-fifth Street, did promise that "This picture will not be shown in any other theatre in New York this year." Did that limitation on the market contribute to the film's losing money, or was it just that the "gamble [of] about two million dollars (in 1936 currency)," as Rothwell calls it (1977, 1) could not be made up by many more millions of 1936 nickels, dimes, and quarters? The film did appear as a "second run" at the Capitol in New York in March of 1937.[6]

The pamphlet designed to accompany the production was Volume 2, number 3 of *Photoplay Studies* which appeared in March 1936, some five months before the film opened. It is "A Preliminary Study Guide to the Screen Version of Shakespeare's *Romeo and Juliet*," prepared by Max J. Herzberg of Weequahic High School, Newark, New Jersey. Herzberg would prepare a similar pamphlet for Olivier's film of *Hamlet*. Other pamphlets in the series included, as of 1936, preliminary study guides to the 1935 *Dream*, and to *Mutiny on the Bounty, The Last Days of Pompeii, Les Miserables, Mary of Scotland, Fang and Claw*, and *Things to Come*.[7]

The pamphlet is useful, naive in its view of the film as a kind of "visual aid" to the study of the text and as a medium for general cultural uplift, but illuminating in many ways. The film of *Romeo and Juliet*, Herzberg says,

> is a momentous event . . . the first serious attempt to give, with all the scenic, histrionic, and artistic resources of Hollywood, a cinematic version of one of Shakespeare's great tragedies. If the public, by a cordial response to this endeavor, shows that it truly appreciates and admires Shakespeare in a worthy screen version, a great step forward will have been taken. It will then be more likely than ever that we shall have similar first-rate versions of other literary classics, and, in general, the standards of motion-picture production will have been raised. In this way, moreover, a new impetus will be given to the admirable movement now under way in our schools to teach photoplay appreciation and give photoplays the status of an art. (1936, 3)

Other classics did follow: *Wuthering Heights* in 1938 (with Olivier and Merle Oberon) and *Pride and Prejudice* in 1940 (with Olivier and Greer Garson). The hope that filmed Shakespeare would become a respectable, even central, component of an academic program may finally have been fulfilled these many years later. Herzberg could not know in March of 1936 that no more Shakespeare films would come until Olivier changed his mind about the possibilities of making films of the plays, and until Welles produced three brilliant, if uneven, filmed translations of Shakespeare.

"For the first time," Herzberg continues, "the *script* of the play is lifted into proper prominence" (1936, 3). His points of contrast, of course, are the 1929 *Shrew,* which is "silent" in its camera technique even if it contains a sound track and dialogue, and the 1935 *Dream,* which is most impressive in its nondialogic sequences. The *Romeo and Juliet* is probably also best in its visual mode, but the film does not suffer much disruption from the addition of an inherited script. "Of course," says technical assistant William Strunk, "it was not possible to keep all the 3050 lines of the play, but the dialogue of the script was all good Shakespeare" (Herzberg 1936, 12). (Even the 1994 Zenger Media catalogue making the film available again says, "Although condensed, the dialogue is entirely the bard's" [161]). Herzberg makes the often repeated claim that "It is, I think, unquestionable that if [Shakespeare] were alive today, he would in some way be concerned with the art of making photoplays," partly because, Herzberg asserts, a "screen version" allows for "clear crystallization of speech and motion" (3). The inference, of course, is that word and action can be fitted to each other on the screen, as obviously they can be coordinated on the stage.

Producer Irving Thalberg adds Norma Shearer (his wife) to the list of those who have "stepp[ed] into the historic role that served as the crowning achievement on the stage of such famous actresses as Mrs. Siddons, Fanny Kemble, Modjeska, Adelaide Neilson, Ellen Terry, Mary Anderson, Mrs. Patrick Campbell, Julia Marlowe; and, more recently, Jane Cowl, Eva Le Gallienne, and Katherine Cornell" (Herzberg, 1936, 13). Thalberg had always been enamored of the stage and leaned toward it for his films (*Private Lives, Strange Interlude,* and *The Barretts of Wimpole Street,* for example, all vehicles he acquired for Norma Shearer). Thalberg argues film's suitability for Shakespeare: "With its greater scope, the screen will present the classic with unlimited movement and authentic backgrounds, so as to secure fluidity in story unfoldment through the elimination of the episodical division of acts necessitated in the original works" (Herzberg 1936, 13). It might have been the proscenium stage and not the "original work" that caused the "division" of which Thalberg speaks. Like Herzberg, Thalberg presages a great future for Shakespeare on film: Shakespeare's "dramatic form is practically that of a scenario . . . [he wrote] not in acts but in scenes" (Strunk 1936, 14). There, Thalberg seems to suggest Shakespeare's own fluidity, the movement from scene to scene without pause. "If the popularity [of this film] should warrant other of the bard's plays being translated to the screen," Thalberg says, "there is no reason why a revival of world interest should not follow in its wake" (Herzberg 1936, 13).

That prospect would seem to be embodied in the trailer, but it was not to be. The film and Norma Shearer were nominated for Academy Awards, but Thalberg died on 14 September 1936, a month after the film opened. The frail Thalberg, born with a bad heart, succumbed to pneumonia, from which he had almost died in 1933. His obituary said that his *Romeo and Juliet* was "the most successful of Hollywood's attempts to translate Shakespeare for the cinema" and that the "acclaim for [the] production . . . was still dinning at the time of his death" ("Irving Thalberg," 1936). Thalberg, the inspiration for F. Scott Fitzgerald's *The Last Tycoon,* had been instrumental in promoting the careers of John Gilbert (the silent star who famously failed in talkies) Greta Garbo, Clark Gable, Joan Crawford (though she was often angry when Shearer got roles that Crawford coveted) Myrna Loy, and Jean Harlow. Director George Cukor had a further brush with Shakespeare in 1947, when he directed Ronald Colman in *A Double Life,* about an actor playing Othello who murders his Desdemona. Colman won the Academy Award for best actor that year. After directing forty-four films, Cukor got his Oscar in 1961 for *My Fair Lady.*

Herzberg's pamphlet reveals one flaw inherent in the film's creation —the compulsive need for authenticity. The script, as noted, is edited but is "all Shakespeare," a naive statement but no great problem given the uncomplicated textual situation of the play. While one would not wish for "additional dialogue," the script might have been pared even more, though not necessarily down to Zeffirelli's concession to his inexperienced actors. As Herzberg says, perceptively, "the photoplay director . . . tells his story somewhat differently from the stage dramatist, and he may find it necessary and desirable to cut down the amount of *spoken* drama. He relies for his effect on pictures, on sound, on rapid suggestion, on pantomime, where the Elizabethan dramatist appealed to the imagination of his audience by rich lines, weighed down with descriptive data, as a means of obliterating the bare boards of the stage" (1936, 17–18). The film, however, pulls free neither of the inherited script nor of the awe described by an English critic in 1936: "The cinema is not yet at ease with Shakespeare; it approaches him with an anxious sense of occasion, not venturing to make a friend of him but determined to do him proud" ("Films," 1936). Herzberg's pamphlet claims that Strunk "pays tribute to the care and reverence with which the production of the play . . . was handled" (1936, 12–13). Such reverential treatment, of course, kills invention, spontaneity, and any sense that the modern director and actor are *collaborators* with the playwright. That the film has little, if any, tension is not just a function of our knowing what happens, but of a script perhaps more "recorded" than performed. The film, then, suffers from the problem that Mark C. Miller describes when talking about the *Richard II–Henry V* plays in the BBC series: "Struggling to create the proper aura, the BBC has blown a wad on late medieval bric-a-brac: hogsheads, cross-bows, goblets, scrolls . . . These irrelevant items clutter irrelevant sets, all those dungeons and taverns and banquet halls which Shakespeare mentions . . . the BBC has meticulously reconstructed" (1980, 56).

MGM reconstructed on an even grander scale: "to provide a site on which to rebuild Verona . . . one hundred acres were set aside. The Herzberg study guide goes on to describe what was done within those hundred acres:

> Cedric Gibbons . . . designed fifty-four models, actual reproductions of historical Veronese buildings associated with the story of *Romeo and Juliet,* from which the mammoth settings . . . were constructed, so that there might be a faithful atmosphere of the fifteenth century capital of Northern Italy. Similarly, old masters of this same century unconsciously contributed their art to help this production . . . Gozzoli, Botticelli, Carpaccio, Fra Angelico, Bellini . . . furnished a wealth of details for the costumes and settings. . . . All told, 1250 costumes were designed [and] the largest number of costume sketches ever assembled for a single production were made for *Romeo and Juliet.* [Subjects researched included] bubonic plague, falcons, rapier and dagger fighting, costumes, Veronese churches, Renaissance furniture, burial ceremonies, and period musical instruments. (1936, 16)

It is startling to learn that fifty-four buildings are associated with the *Romeo and Juliet* story! The Capulet garden, said the *Literary Digest* was "as large as the air-port in Fort Worth, Texas. [The] Cathedral Square . . . covers eight acres. The ballroom is 250 by 400 feet . . . The balcony to which Romeo clambers on a rose-trellis is twenty-four feet above garden level . . . One cloak for Romeo used up nine yards of material. Leslie Howard wore it four times" ("Boy Meets Girl," 1936, 20). Remarking on the height of the balcony, Graham Greene wrote "that Juliet should really have conversed with Romeo in shouts like a sailor from the crow's nest sighting land" (Flamini 1994, 247).

All of this tends, of course, to pull a script and the issues it explores *into* "historical authenticity," making the latter the point of the film. "After all this preparation the only thing the film lacked was imagination," says Ian Johnson, who lists the film's positive features: "that the balcony was high enough to provide a genuine obstacle, the tomb sufficiently maze-like to make Romeo's search seem necessary, and a trumpet call announc[ed] the beginning of the film, as in Elizabethan days, [a framing device later] adopted by Olivier in his *Henry V*" (1972, 13). *Romeo and Juliet* is, as Flamini says, "burdened with its own significance" (1994, 245). As Rothwell suggests, the film is an "example of the kind of archaeological production that dominated the theatrical imagination of the nineteenth century" (1973, 347). Zeffirelli also uses the old masters, not as subjects for research or as guarantors of "authenticity," but as emblems of the opulence and grandeur of a world not necessarily built for the young lovers, in which some delicate ships have somewhere to get to and sail calmly on.

The *quality* of the sets for the 1936 production, however, makes the film more than a series of footnotes.[8] The settings often reflect, literally and figuratively, what is happening to the characters. Romeo, for example, battles Tybalt from a down-ramp position. Tybalt balances for a moment, his pride punctured, falls, and, in a reverse angle shot, lands in the dust below. It is fair to say, as the Herzberg pamphlet does, that the film's technique "may be contrasted with the free-and-easy imaginative methods of the Elizabethans" and that the film's "backgrounds . . . as compared with those of the stage play, are enormously enlarged, to include both full and detailed 'shots' of cities, great landscapes, a cathedral, tumultuous street scenes, crowds, revelry," and that "the photoplay director calls thousands into action. The result is, undoubtedly, greater variety and greater verisimilitude in action" (1936, 17). In other words, all the research and resultant "reality" serves an audience that refuses to suspend its disbelief when it watches a film.

Herzberg's pamphlet is filled with stills of the film, some of them magnificent, and contains some of Cedric Gibbons's splendid scenic designs, which convey an art-deco tonality that did not get into the film. It may be that all the reproduction of the fifteenth century canceled a 1930s style that Gibbons had discovered but could not introduce to the camera.

The film itself begins by presenting each major actor in costume within an ornate framing possibly influenced by the opening scene of the Reinhardt *Dream*. It is a version of playbill in motion, the introduction to a photo*play*. Then comes what Rothwell calls "the curious anachronism of John Barrymore acting as prologue at the center of a proscenium stage [and] the establishment shot of fair Verona . . . after the style of Hogenberg's *Civitates Orbis Terrarum*" (1977, 8). This staged approach to the prologue "distances" the words from the "reality" of the city and its activities, almost as if the inner narrative is claiming, "This can't happen to *me*."

The opening depicts the ceremonial approach of both the Capulet and Montague trains, on a collision course, toward the cathedral at the top of the vast city square. The aristocrats enter the portals, the families frowning at each other. The retainers remain outside, Andy Devine's Peter biting his thumb, a brawl commencing to disturb the Sunday calm. Basil Rathbone's Tybalt rushes out of the church to reignite the fight just as Reginald Denny's Benvolio has almost quenched it. The others flock from church and stand on the steps, sinners in the hands of an angry prince. The opening balances formal processions and the rituals of peace expected of a Sunday mass against the enmity that lies just below the facade and, here, breaks into a riot at the heart of the city.

Black-and-white photography, of course, can provide more depth than color, which erases depth, and Cukor often employs his camera superbly. When Romeo first climbs the Capulet walls and steps along a dark pool in the moonlight, the mood of mystery, danger, and lurking death is powerfully evoked. At that moment the theme of love and death so often linked in the poetry of the play, and in Marvell, Keats, and Rollo May later, is realized visually, the camera work becoming the poem. After the ball, as the Nurse and Juliet walk down a long hallway, a servant douses the torches behind them, a superb Tenebrae that is repeated by the Nurse on a much smaller scale later, as she puts out the candles in Juliet's room just before Juliet takes the potion. Juliet's funeral procession, down a steep hillside into the valley of the graves, and the Poe-like luminescence of the Capulet tomb are also vividly realized. These scenes alone make the film worth watching and they are, of course, virtually silent, certainly wordless. The duel scenes are quick—not exploiting Rathbone's superb swordplay—and lack the dusty, fear-soaked violence that Zeffirelli achieves.

The acting is often good. Devine, for example, carries off his scene with Romeo in the street very well. We get a sense of the why of the Shakespeare script. Romeo is full of witty responses; the illiterate Peter needs help. The latter begins to wander away before Romeo reads the list for him. For one of the few times, the film captures a small and seemingly inconsequential moment on which the hinge of fatality swings. Romeo's decision to go to the Capulet fete in spite of his foreboding is not as precisely timed or emphasized. Rathbone's Tybalt is, as Paul Dehn says, "played with a white-hot, whipping elegance that matches his sword play" (1954, 59). This Tybalt is, however, not "a fiery young man, but a calculating courtier" (Flamini 1994, 252). Barrymore's Mercutio rolls his eyes and trills his *r*s. Mercutio is all talk, of course, but here he tends to stop the action cold as he emotes. I was not sorry to see him dispatched. Dehn suggests that Barrymore is " 'old-style' Shakespeare . . . 'Ham' possibly—but how exquisitely cured!" (59). The question of "old-style" is complicated, of course, since Edwin Booth spoke the verse more and more naturally as his career evolved (as proved by the early Edison recordings of Booth's readings). Flamini says that Barrymore's "testy, middle-aged queen, though colorful, is overacted and at odds with the rest of the picture, an ornate Victorian couch in a roomful of contemporary furniture" (251). The idle Veronese ladies who constantly observe the city square from their balcony—the equivalent of teenagers prowling the malls of the latter twentieth century—are directed to appear sorry to see their primary entertainer depart at the touch of Tybalt's point.

The ensemble acting is often very strong. The film is particularly effective in mirroring the Nurse-Juliet sequences with the Friar-Romeo scenes, neatly depicting the age vs youth concerns of the script, and contrasting both sets of characters, particularly Henry Kolker's sober Friar with Edna Oliver's shallow gossip of a Nurse. That they are meant as a "pair" is suggested by her nunlike garb.

The two leads, Flamini says, are "surprisingly plaintive and moving." According to Graham Greene, they are "satisfying in the conventional and romantic and dreamy mode" (Flamini 1994, 251). Rothwell, however, calls them "a stylized matinee idol . . . and a simpering, somewhat plump young lady" (1973, 346).

Shearer's coy hand gestures suggest an effort to *play* the teenager. She "made a dumpy twelve-year old" (Johnson 1972, 13). She is kittenish in a way that can be very unseemly in any woman, particularly an "older" one, though this tendency drops away as the film develops—as if Juliet were maturing. As Nugent said, "barring a slight shallowness in her earlier scenes [she] is a tender, lovely, and gracious Juliet" (1936a.). The exceptions to a more convincing style are some silent-screen histrionics during her aria on the terrors of the tomb, when she places the back of her hand to her forehead, for example. Shearer is consistently an example of that soft-focus technique that Laura Mulvey attributes to the "male gaze" (1985). A "mystic white light suffused her while the other actors were in shadow" (Flamini 1994, 249). Shearer had by this time "somewhat dropped from her zenith" (Dehn 1954, 59). Herzberg's pamphlet notes that "Miss Shearer dances for the first time in a photoplay appearance" (1936, 29). She keeps deserting poor Paris in her fascination with Romeo, who smiles at her from the platform around the dance floor as he doffs his mask. Among the assignments the pamphlet suggests is "Give an account of the career of Norma Shearer. In what famous photoplays has she appeared? (If you have seen her in any of these, give your impression.) What are the traits of her personality and her acting that have made her so popular?" (1936, 29). No such questions are provided for Howard.[9]

Howard's Romeo is restrained and gentle, as was his wont as actor. He had the wisdom not to play the youth, not to surrender to the Peter Pan syndrome, but to be a mature man who happens to have fallen in love for the first time after the youthful infatuations for which Rosaline is a synecdoche. He was "old enough to understand Romeo, and the camera made him young enough to play him" (Dehn 1954, 59). Nugent found him, however, "indefinably disappointing . . . possibly because of his maturity or perhaps because he lacks the fiery spirit which tradition has attached to the young Montague" (1936a.), but there, Howard was blamed for a "tradition" that Nugent claimed had grown up around the role, as opposed to the givens of the role itself. Flamini agrees with Nugent: "Howard is a mature Romeo who should have known better" (1994, 252). Rothwell suggests that "Howard's super-sensitive archetypally poetic face, so plausible to audiences of the . . . romantic thirties comes through today as looking too etherial, too underfed, for anyone to believe that even a whiff of phylogeny breathed in his soul" (1973, 347). A contemporary critic said that "that sensitive horse's face of his, wrapped in disguises, leads to giggles" (Ferguson 1936, 104).

If anyone deserved an Academy Award nomination it was Leslie Howard. Later that year, on 10 November, Howard would open in Hamlet at the Imperial Theater in New York. Thalberg's selection of Howard for the film may "have been inspired by news stories that the handsome blonde actor was planning to play Hamlet on Broadway. Howard, meanwhile, though reluctant at first, began to see Romeo as "a baby Hamlet" and also as a means of earning money for the Broadway production, which he was financing himself (Flamini 1994, 246). Howard's *Hamlet* was compared unfavorably with that of John Gielgud, who had brought his 1934 New Theatre revival of his 1930 Old Vic production to the Empire on Monday, 12 October 1936. The latter had Judith Anderson, Lillian Gish, and Whitner Bissell. The former had Celeste Holm and Wesley Addy as extras. Joseph Wood Krutch appreciated Howard: "strong precisely where Mr. Gielgud is weak . . . he brings to vivid life exactly those aspects of Hamlet's character which, in his rival's performance, simply do not exist. He is above all else the intellectual and the ironist, the tender and ingenious thinker" (1936,

40). John Mason Brown, however, said "Compared to Mr. Howard . . . Mr. Gielgud is Hyperion to a Satyr" (1936), and Grenville Vernon claimed that "The bitterness, the passion, the tortured despair of the Prince is beyond Mr. Howard's compass" (1936).[10]

The competing Hamlets became part of a moment that was credited, along with the film, with "[r]escuing Shakespeare from the doldrums" (Nugent 1937). Howard would die in early June 1943, when the plane on which he was a passenger was shot down by the Nazis. Although Howard was English, his countrymen called him "that American actor," because of the amount of time he spent in the United States. He played Americans, of course, as in *Gone With the Wind,* in which he is the pallid Ashley Wilkes.

Herbert Stothart's score features the "Romeo and Juliet" tone-poem for the lovers—a more modern motif (however late nineteenth-century) than the "authentic" music by which the rest of Verona parades. The Tchaikovsky places the lovers in a world removed from the codified rivalries and expectations of Verona. Rothwell reports that "in Paris, Thalberg suddenly heard Tchaikovsky for the first time and cried out, 'Why did no one ever tell me of this?'" (1994). Stothart wrote "Cuban Love Song" and "Donkey Serenade." The Tchaikovsky would become "Our Love" in 1939, as translated by bandleader Larry Clinton. The hit songs of 1936 suggest the popular context with which the film merged: "Easy to Love," "The Glory of Love," "A Fine Romance," "Goodnight, My Love," "Moonlight and Shadows," "The Night is Young and You're So Beautiful," "The Touch of Your Lips," "The Way You Look Tonight" (which won the Academy Award for best song in 1936), and "When Did You Leave Heaven?" (David 1982, 32–33).

The only editing to which an alert auditor might object is that portion of Romeo's soliloquy in the tomb about death's "pale ensign," which argues his coming to a mature and self-generated poetics, *and* suggests his being aware just below the level of conscious statement that Juliet is alive. If he would only generalize on the basis of what his senses are telling him! How did Mercutio's line about "the bawdy hand of the dial" get past the Hays Office? The censors must have been looking for that fatted calf and not listening to what the ham was saying. According to *The Literary Digest,* Strunk "permitted no gross liberties, [but i]nsisted on inclusions of words and lines that would never have been allowed in a typical Hollywood program-picture. Shakespeare's magic condoned the audacities" ("Boy Meets Girl" 1936, 20). The Hays Office must have been pleased to see that, on the dawn of Romeo's departure from Juliet's chamber, the lovers are clothed as if about to make a dog-sled run for the South Pole. For audiences "nurtured on the nakedness of the Zeffirelli version," says Rothwell, they appear to be "two egregiously overdressed and rather stuffy people insincerely spouting poetry" (1973, 346).

Rothwell, in an unpublished essay that he has kindly sent me, provides an excellent method for understanding Cukor's technique. The camera, Rothwell suggests, contrasts order, depicted by long takes balanced against each other, with disorder, shown by rapid, montage juxtapositions. The camera techniques, then, visualize the conflicts in the script. The "symmetry in sequences of parallel shots"—for example, of the opening procession—"correlates with a Verona ruled by reason and responsive to authority; while the montage effects, and random cuts, become metaphors for the overthrow of reason by passion" (1977, 3). "For Talbot Jennings [the film's scenarist] repetitive allusions to impetuosity in words like 'sudden,' 'speed,' 'swift,' and 'haste' were of notable frequency," and, it follows, Rothwell argues, that the film "works symbiotically with Shakespeare's text by taking its cues for editing and camera angles from the thematic implications and rhythms of the play itself" (7). The opening sequences demonstrate a "pattern of parallel editing . . . supportive of the elements of conjunction and disjunction in the play's structure." The Capulets enter, then the Montagues—"Mirror opposites" (1977, 10). The "feelings [of] ordinary people [are] registered through intercut reaction shots [that] allow audience identification with the perceptions of [a] citizenry [that] conveys the anxiety of the city over two such powerful houses" at enmity with each other (9–11). The camera, then, can "record experience from multiple angles" (6), can capture aristocratic rivalry and its bawdy reflection in the serving men, public anxiety, ducal authority, and, crucially, the contrast between the rhythms of antagonism and reconciliation. The latter possibility, of course, is represented by Romeo and Juliet, who have their own theme song and their own secret garden, set apart from the tilting and brawling of the town square and the martial trumpets and drums of Veronese public music. Rothwell's concentration on the "tempo of the editing" (12) is extremely useful. Of the stately opening procession and its reduction to a brawl, he says "The orderly design of parallel and converging lines that has so far been the dominant image of the film now tumbles before an onslaught of antithetical and diverging images. Cinematically this involves a shift from parallel editing to montage, and thematically from array to disarray" (14).

This film deserves a reintroduction here in the 1990s—not just as a vivid contrast with the Zeffirelli version, which it certainly is—but as an early and valid effort to translate a Shakespeare script into a modern cinematic format.

NOTES

1. For a brief but lucid commentary on Shakespearean films in the 1930s, see Davies 1994b, 2-3. See also Rothwell's discussion of the three Shakespeare films of the 1930s (*The Taming of the Shrew, A Midsummer Night's Dream,* and *Romeo and Juliet*) in Rothwell and Melzer 1990, 4-5.

2. Indeed, many contemporary comments were positive: "beautiful . . . authentic . . . moving, and when all is said and done, it is still Shakespeare," wrote the *Scholastic* reviewer (Review of MGM *Romeo and Juliet* 1936a); a "great picture," commented Laura Elston (1936) in *Canadian Magazine;* "an engaging obeisance to the Bard," declared Howard Barnes (1936) in the *New York Herald-Tribune;* "sensitive, delicate and as human as any of the great classics to reach the screen," said *Commonweal*'s James P. Cunningham (1936); *Time*'s reviewer found it "certainly the best [*Romeo and Juliet*] since the Jane Cowl-Rollo Peters version and quite probably the best ever shown" (Review of MGM *Romeo and Juliet* 1936b); "Hollywood's best joust with Shakespeare to date" was the judgment of the *Literary Digest* ("Boy Meets Girl," 1936). *Literary Digest* was soon to lose its joust with posterity by predicting Alf Landon's victory in the 1936 presidential elections. Only a few of the reviews were lukewarm: "the framing of an old picture rather than the execution of a new one," astutely declared Otis Ferguson (1936, 104). This film "seems hardly more than a gorgeous valentine—overlarge to the point of boredom at that"; movies, Ferguson suggested, "having known higher pastures in their own right" (104); "falls short of being a great picture," said Elizabeth Creelman (1936); a "faithful and not too imaginative translation to the screen" read the review in *Variety* (Review of MGM *Romeo and Juliet* 1936c).

3. MGM's willingness to produce prestige films that lost money, however, may well have been responsible for *The Wizard of Oz,* which was not expected to be the spectacular success it turned out to be (Flamini 1994, 134-35).

4. See Alfred Hitchcock's reply to Barker (Hitchcock 1936).

5. *Smilin' Through* was a very popular film and had been reissued by MGM, so its mention in the trailer was not merely gratuitous. To call Shearer and Howard "the sweethearts of *Smilin' Through,*" however, was not really accurate. The effort to pair them may have stemmed from Mayer's conviction "that a successful team *more* than doubled the gross of a film" (Edwards 1974, 108; Edwards's emphasis). In *Smilin' Through,* Shearer and Howard played Moonyean and John in the flashback sequences, wherein a rejected suitor shoots Moonyean at her wedding. Her orphaned niece, Kathleen (also played by Shearer) comes to live with John many years later and falls in love with the son of the murderer, Ken, played by Fredric March, who also played Brian, the father. Ken and Kathleen are really the sweethearts of the film, which, for all its tear-jerking melodrama is an effective variation on the "double story." It has its *Romeo and Juliet* moments, when John forbids Kathleen to see Ken, by now ready to ship off to France and the Great War that rattles the windows in the film (*a la* Hardy's "Channel Firing"). But she and love prevail. Shearer is beautiful in gowns by Adrian and handles a wide emotional range with skill and conviction. March, who played with many of Hollywood's leading actresses, Claudette Colbert, Joan Crawford, Greta Garbo, Katharine Hepburn, Miriam Hopkins, Grace Kelly, Carole Lombard, Myrna Loy, Evelyn Venable, *et. al.* during his long career said in an interview that Shearer was the best of them (Osborne 1994b). Shearer and Howard also appeared together in the 1931 film, *A Free Spirit,* but that film is remembered as Clark Gable's first big hit. Gable plays Ace Willfong, a criminal. Howard plays Dwight Winthrop, a polo player whom Shearer's impetuous Jan Ashe jilts in favor of the exciting Willfong. Winthrop shoots Willfong. Lionel Barrymore, Jan's father, emerges from alcoholism to save Winthrop with a dramatic appeal in court, and we

assume that Jan and Dwight will get together at some future point. Barrymore won the Academy Award for 1931 for his portrayal of Stephen Ashe. MGM remade *Smilin' Through* in 1941, with Jeanette MacDonald and Brian Aherne.

6. One reason for the film's cost was that Oliver Messel's designs for sets and costumes were not accepted by MGM, in spite of his having been sent to Verona by Thalberg for on-site research (Flamini 1994, 245–47). Messel is given a consultant's credit in the film and a credit for costumes with Adrian.

7. The 1936 film version of H. G. Wells's *Things to Come* was a vivid contrast to *Romeo and Juliet*, and helps contextualize the Thalberg-Cukor effort towards historicity. In *Things to Come*, produced by Alexander Korda and directed by William C. Menzies, a war consumes the world from Christmas 1940 to 1966. The film's air raids on London foreshadow what would happen in 1940, although St. Paul's is more badly damaged in the film than it was by enemy bombing. Cabal (Raymond Massey), one of the "last trustees of civilization," arrives in feudal London to confront the warlord Rudolph (Ralph Richardson), who has been given a speech rationalizing his fiefdom's lack of books. Rudolph is defeated by the "Peace Gas," dropped by Cabal's air force. The film swings into the future—2036—by means of a long montage of machinery—hydraulics, robotics, mono-rails, turbines, and gyroscopes—with automaton human beings tending it. The future does not include rocketry or jet propulsion, advisor Nigel Tangy's concept of aeronautics being very much conditioned by the flying wing and pusher propeller concepts being developed in the 1930s. The Roman-like civilization that has ensued incorporates the smokeless air and architecture that was featured inside the Perisphere of the 1939-40 World's Fair in New York, where the observers, emerging into the smoky air of Flushing Meadows, were given a pin proclaiming "I have seen the future." A somewhat unmotivated, but understandable, revolt does occur against this sterile technology in the film. These scenes are indebted to Antony's oration in *Julius Caesar*, but the two young people who have volunteered for a moon shot out of a space gun are projected towards the stars before the mob can smash the equipment to pieces. The space gun presages the supergun developed by the late Gerry Bull, who recognized that nine-tenths of a space shot's weight goes into a first-stage booster. The film's Dr. Harding, who refuses to develop poison gas for Rudolph, says something that many victims of modern politician —that is, almost all of us—can agree with: "All my life has been interrupted, wasted, and spoiled by war." Recent eulogies to the likes of Richard Nixon and Dean Rusk might provoke a "let them rest, and the victims mourn a space." The film is an odd mixture of humanism and technology, and the blending of the two amounts to an unconvincing rationalization—perhaps more convincing in 1936, before World War II, than it is today.

8. The gigantic sets for D.W. Griffith's *Intolerance* (1916) were recently discovered in the California desert. Where is the Verona of the 1936 film? Was it, like the *King Kong* set, burned as Atlanta in *Gone With the Wind?* Apparently not. Flamini says that it was dismantled and replaced by Shanghai for *The Good Earth* (1994, 254). The one setting that would have been very familiar to any filmgoer was the dirt road on which Romeo and Balthazar galloped back to Verona from Padua. It had recorded the hooves of William S. Hart, Tom Mix, Ken Maynard, Tim Holt, Bill Boyd, et. al.

9. After almost a decade in silents, Shearer had made her talkie debut as a showgirl accused of murder in *The Trial of Mary Dugan* in 1929. One of her most famous roles was in *Private Lives* (1931). She won one of the first Academy Awards in 1929/30 for *The Divorcee* and was nominated five other times, including her nomination for Juliet. Her last film was *Her Cardboard Lover* for Cukor in 1942. She died on 12 June 1983. According to Douglas Gomery, "her acclaimed talent as an actress rested on little more than fan magazine publicity, [but] she was, undeniably, a major star . . . She had learned from

working in silent films . . . how best to utilize her limited talents to create the penultimate image of a glamorous woman. After Thalberg's death, she completed her studio contract and then retired to a life of wealth and leisure, only rarely appearing in public" (1986, 570). According to Lillian Hellman, Shearer had "a face unclouded by thought" (Devine 1984, 277). She is reported to have turned down the parts of Scarlett O'Hara, Mrs. Miniver (which won an Academy Award for Greer Garson), and Norma Desmond in *Sunset Boulevard* (278), a role splendidly delivered by Gloria Swanson.

10. Howard's place in film history was enhanced by his insistence that Humphrey Bogart play Duke Mantee in the film version of Robert Sherwood's "Petrified Forest." Bogart had originated the role opposite Howard on Broadway, but Paramount wanted Edward G. Robinson for the film. The film gave Bogart his first major break in Hollywood. Later, the grateful Bogie named his daughter Leslie.

# III

# "What's There?": Opening *Hamlet* on Film

With a seventy-year history on film, *Hamlet* provides a wonderful opportunity to chart and describe the ways in which locus has been challenged by *platea* in the twentieth century. Clearly this enigmatic script picks up and amplifies the enigmas that history has formulated and, invariably, the film versions are aware that the script is an exploration of depth psychology. This is more true in a black-and-white film like Olivier's, in which the camera itself does some wild whirling—bouncing in and out of focus as a giant beat shakes the parapets and swish-panning up and around staircases—than in Zeffirelli's opulent color film, which seldom pauses to contemplate its *locus*; but the film versions of the script, when unearthed a thousand years from now, will confirm that ours was, among other things, a century of the psyche.

Roger Manvell calls *Hamlet* "the least immediately filmable of the great poetic tragedies" (quoted in Davison 1983, 52). Robert Duffy talks of "the resistance of the source play to cinematic adaptation" (1976, 142). "Much discussed 'epic' qualities," Duffy says, "particularly the emphatic and rapid shifting of locale and time frame—so often cited as one of the most 'cinematic' of Shakespeare's techniques—simply do not operate to any great extent in the play" (141). Films of Shakespearean scripts, says Anthony Davies, "can be articulated to varying degrees through the relationship of men to things, of ideas to the concrete world and of motives to actions, without conscious distortion. But of all the plays of Shakespeare," Davies suggests, "*Hamlet* is least of all a play which readily enlists spatial detail and the world of objects for its major thematic developments" (1988, 40).

Some of the soliloquies in *Hamlet* are, as Peter Davison says, "bravura set-piece[s] for an actor, and . . . require . . . amplitude and a theatre audience to make the most of" them, like the "rogue and peasant slave speech," for which "there was no place," Davison says, "in Olivier's film" (1983, 51). We may recall him racing through a midnight palace shouting so loudly of "the conscience of the king" that even a wine-sodden Claudius might have started from his slumber. And, of course, if films erase Fortinbras, as Olivier and Zeffirelli do, they also eliminate the splendid, "How all occasions do inform against me!" soliloquy.

And, of course, the words themselves fight against the medium. Peter Hall indicts Shakespeare for "bad screen writing. A good film-script relies on contrasting visual images. What is spoken is of secondary importance. And so potent is the camera in convincing us that we are peering at reality, that dialogue is best under-written or elliptical." (1969). Kozintsev goes so far as to call the text "a diffused remark that the author wrote to acquaint actors as thoroughly as possible with the heart of the action to be played" (1966, 215). The sheer amount of language in *Hamlet* must stretch a director's imagination as he seeks visual equivalents for it. A film of *Hamlet* demands transitions that, in this play, often occur in the mind of Prince Hamlet and not in some exterior and potentially cinematic space. Yet for all of the problems, *Hamlet* is one of the most filmed of all the plays, and successfully filmed at that.

Of all the plays, *Hamlet* has, I believe, summoned the greatest artists in response to it, and that includes filmmakers. I want to deal here only *with* films and not with television productions, like the Franz Peter Wirth-Maximilian Schell (1960), the Christopher Plummer (1964), Ian McKellen (1971), Rodney Bennett-Derek Jacobi (1980), and Kevin Kline (1990), but including films that seem to have been designed for television and destined for cassette, like the Tony Richardson-Nicol Williamson (1969) and the Ragnar Lyth (1984). The "straight" films I will consider are the Sven Gade-Asta Nielsen (1920), Laurence Olivier (1948), Grigori Kozintsev (1964), and Franco Zeffirelli (1990). My question is, How does the director get us into the *Hamlet* story? That is another way of asking, what does the director believe the *Hamlet* story to be, or not to be? Since the films considered cover a seventy-year period, their examination constitutes a history of *Hamlet* on film and, of course, must treat the assumptions about Shakespeare and about film that conditioned the production of each film.

The Gade version succeeds perhaps because it tells a story other than what most believed the *Hamlet* story to be as of 1920. It is also much more than "extended pictorial allusion . . . to the source play," as Duffy calls most silent films up until the Gade (1976, 141). The "Gade version," he says, "makes evident the central reality of *Hamlet* adaptation: cinematic effectiveness demands the sacrifice of some traditional, even sacrosanct, Shakespearean values" (142). Robert Hamilton Ball says of the Gade-Nielsen film that "by adaptation and acting appropriate to pictures in motion, the least Shakespearean *Hamlet* becomes the best *Hamlet* film in the silent era" (1968, 278). It "succeeded," Ball claims, "because it started with, developed from and adhered to a conception of the *Hamlet* story, which, however unShakespearean, made cinematic sense" (279). The star, Asta Nielsen, was an actress of power and grace, with a remarkable ability to suggest nuances of emotion without the exaggeration we often associate with the silent screen. A contemporary review remarked her "mature art [in which] appearance, gesture, even the movement of an eyelid—show forth the soul of . . . Hamlet" (*Exceptional Photoplays*, quoted in Ball 1968, 277).[1]

The film opens with an ominous piano score, obviously added at some point, and, after her name appears, a picture of Nielsen. Edward P. Vining is given a credit for suggesting that the problem of *Hamlet* is that Hamlet is really "eine Frau"! (Sarah Bernhardt should also be credited with playing Hamlet, though she did not embrace the Vining thesis in her portrayal.) The opening of the film per se is a series of crosscuts, with title cards, depicting events on a battlefield and back in Elsinore. (The technique is, of course, pure D. W. Griffith.) The King of Denmark defeats Norway on a muddy hillside as battle ebbs and sways against a gray wash of sky. Denmark is himself wounded and carried off on a stretcher. At Elsinore, a crowd of *danische Volk* awaits a royal birth. *"Ein Prinz fur Danemark?"* asks the queen. *"Nein, meine Konigin,"* says the nurse. *"Es ist eine Prinzessin."* A messenger reports the severe wounding of the king. The queen and nurse devise a scheme. They will claim that it's a boy and so maintain the line of succession. The conspiracy is sealed with an iris close. From the steps of the palace the good news is delivered: *"Ein Prinz ist geboren!"* The king rises from his stretcher, however, returns and is let in on the secret by the queen. Another iris close links the scene with the one between queen and the nurse.

Hamlet grows—a winsome youth with luminous eyes framed in dark lashes. This Hamlet loves his father, dislikes his mother, and is suspicious of a really nasty looking *"Onkle."* We get a strong depiction of the "Electra Complex" in a film uncannily aware of the gender issues it raises by making Hamlet really a woman, as opposed to a Bernhardt or a Judith Anderson depicting a male Hamlet.

Jeff Hush suggests that "the precise way in which Hamlet's womanish heart (his delays and excuses), which Hamlet himself sees as being like a strumpet's heart . . . gained great prominence in the major strands of the late nineteenth-century acting tradition. Hamlet's becoming a woman is a pointed reversal of and commentary upon the slanders heaped on women in Shakespeare's *Hamlet*" (1991). I have argued elsewhere that Hamlet is a character out of touch with his "anima" (or "femaleness": 1986). The film makes that point poignantly by creating a Hamlet forced into a role that defies her "nature," at least as consciously constructed ("persona"). We have Viola's story without a Sebastian to permit her to reassume her desired gender role. Nielsen's Hamlet is in love with Horatio but has no genre to save her. It is a moving and deeply realized film, both in its grasp of the ramifications of the femininity of Hamlet—the taking literally of the insight that Vining offers literally—and in Nielsen's remarkable performance.

Laurence Olivier, of course, was a director looking for a starring role for himself and he may have perceived that the post-World War II world would accept a hero other than the dashing Henry V he had provided in 1944. The reasons for his taking on Hamlet, however, lie in the role. Olivier's films all feature characters who are also consummate "actors"—Henry V, Hamlet, and Richard III. Even his filmed version of his *Othello* shows him *playing* the stereotype, rather than *being* it, as some critics charge in light of recent racial sensitivity.

Olivier called his film an "essay on Hamlet" (1948, 11–15), and Robert Tanitch says that "it looks like a great silent masterpiece with a beautifully-spoken, dubbed soundtrack" (1985, 81), suggesting that film and the spoken word are basically incompatible, an issue discussed in Chapter 2 and, later in Chapter 5, in my discussion of Branagh's film of *Much Ado about Nothing*. Jack Jorgens describes the opening this way: "Titles over waves pounding rocky shore at the foot of the castle in swirling mist. Boom slowly in toward castle from dizzying height" (1977, 297). Jorgens neglects to mention the muscular giant, naked to the waist, swinging twice and never missing at that J. Arthur Rank gong. For me, as a teenager in those days, that usually meant a thrilling and often mysterious film to follow. And Olivier's *Hamlet* was no exception. Bernice Kliman notices "the orchestra warming up," at the beginning, "suggesting a play more than a film" (1988, 24). Yes, and Olivier cues us to his artifice by suggesting that his sound track has begun a few seconds too soon. The brief jangle of instruments may also be a wry glance by Olivier (not William Walton) at Strindberg's suggestion that "Life is like an orchestra tuning up and never beginning to play." Davies observes "a screen which brightens slowly to show a visual composition of theatrical properties: a mask, a crown, standards, foils, and spears, a goblet, a dagger, a horn and a drum [props that send] a clear signal that *Hamlet* is essentially a theatrical construct to be played before an audience" (1988, 42). This grouping is assembled a moment before "Laurence Olivier Presents" appears above it. Raymond Ingram notes that "the credits . . . reverse contemporary practice by naming 'The Players' before their roles; this indicates that the film will focus on the art of acting" (1992, 15). Kliman suggests that Olivier "opens up space and moves the audience without losing the theatrical essence of nonrealistic space" (1988, 25). Ingram puts it another way: "Olivier has selected types and lengths of shot that match his perception of what a theatre audience would look at, had it the mobility of the camera" (15).

The film, then, carries forward the overt theatricality of *Henry V* and, in its way, predicts the theater-like qualities of the *Richard III* and *Othello*, the latter indicted by some critics as merely a filmed play. The "effect" of theater is not just a function of the period 1944-64, in which distinctions between filmed and staged Shakespeare were still being formulated and debated, but is clearly Olivier's choice. What distinguishes the film from films of the '30s and Olivier's *Henry V*, and, I would argue, his subsequent Shakespeare films, is the relationship of the set to the action. The "film is in motion," says Roger Furse. "[T]he designer's business is to do everything he can to assist the mobility and flow; *not* to freeze it into a series of orderly compositions" (1948, unpaged; my emphasis). The setting takes on a kind of "personality," beginning with its introduction as a dream castle floating in clouds, and is in this respect like "Hill House" in *The Haunting* (1962), though not actively malevolent.

In the *Hamlet* opening, spectator and director share the same very subjective experience "in space," and perhaps the spectator, at moments, resists the point of view being imposed upon him or her. While it is *not* true that the spectator of a stage play can "look where he or she wishes to look" (although we are told that all the time), it is certainly true that Olivier's camera makes us very aware of its selective presence and movement. Peter Donaldson suggests, furthermore, that "visually, we cannot always locate ourselves quickly or unambiguously [in the film]" (1990, 65). That effect is intentional, of course, even if Andre Bazin overstates the case in claiming that Olivier uses film "to produce *theatre* precisely as [he] feel[s] and see[s] it" (1970, 124; my emphasis).

The opening gives us, as we recall, Olivier's reading of the "So oft it chances in particular men . . ." speech, voiced over the words themselves. The camera booms in on Hamlet's funeral procession on a circular platform at the top of the castle. Horatio stands nearby. This is, of course, a condensation of the *Citizen Kane* approach.[2] The rest of Olivier's film will be a flashback leading to this final procession and ending just before the silhouetted soldiers reach this high stage. Donaldson demonstrates, using evidence from Olivier himself, that the final shot "is the generating image for the film as a whole" (1990, 39).

The "image changes," says Davies, "from the close freeze-frame of the six figures on the highest tower . . . to an identical replication of the composition photographed from a distance in long shot" (1990, 43). These figures, according to Sandra Singer, "appear to be crude little dolls. The 'real' people on the 'real' tower have been replaced by small wooden figures which, in the next moment fade from the scene, leaving only the empty toy tower." Singer's conclusion is "that the scenes that unfold before us do so under the control of an all-powerful storyteller, who manipulates his figures to suit his narrative" (1978, 121). This manipulation is accompanied, of course, by another voice-over, one that haunts the film and its critics: "This is the tragedy of a man who could not make up his mind." Certainly Olivier's "subtitle" for his "essay" has been a filter through which the film has been viewed, so that response has emphasized the camera's entrance into Hamlet's mind in the "To be or not to be" soliloquy, for example, which occurs after the confrontation with Ophelia and, again, at the topmost part of Elsinore. (Zeffirelli puts the soliloquy in the same place in his script, but moves it down to the crypt.) The voice-over seems to make the film "a study of a tortured intellectual in which a great actor plays the part of a prince trapped in the labyrinth of his own mind," as John Collick calls it (1989, 63), twisting us securely into his metaphor of torture and entrapment. Some, however, reject Olivier's description of Hamlet and claim, as Anthony Dawson does, that "Olivier's portrayal itself gave us a caged and vigorous melancholic rather than a contemplative one (several of the soliloquies were cut)" (1988, 154). Parker Tyler suggests that Olivier wanted "to pretend to honor the traditional 'mystery' of Hamlet's hesitation while he patently accepted the quasiscientific Oedipal interpretation" (1949, 529).

We see the battlements from a medium low-angle shot. The castle is shrouded in mist, floating in a zone of its own, a dream castle, vaguely ominous and detached. If it were color, we would think we were entering a medieval fantasy. A soldier moves up a stone staircase. Bernardo and his pike cast a huge shadow against the stone. He pauses as if reluctant to continue. A soldier (Francisco) marches by above. Bernardo's pike appears above the stones before he does, and he shouts his challenge, to be rechallenged immediately by Francisco. The latter's "I am sick at heart" receives unusual emphasis. It comes after a pause and elicits a glance from Bernardo. Horatio is skeptical ("Tush, tush"). "Yon same star" gives way to the melodramatic, in-and-out-of focus beating that accompanies this mist-shrouded Ghost, framed between two pikes. The Ghost approaches and fades as a cock crows, leaving the guards on a suddenly demisted tower. The guards seem to make a prisoner of Horatio between their pikes, until he assents to the story he had scorned. The guards ponder the possible truth of local folklore about ghosts. Anthony Quayle gives us more of the "season wherein our Saviour's birth is celebrated" than film productions usually grant. Horatio, who has been thinking as he listens, smiles and "in part" believes it, suggesting that he wants to cling to his skepticism, regardless of what they have all just witnessed. He remarks the approach of a personified Dawn. Now, on the left of the frame, Horatio commands the pikes as he suggests that they tell young Hamlet of what they have seen. Something is rotten, and the sun suddenly climbs above the wall to touch the faces of the watchers.

The staircase looks very solid. The camera tracks down with seeming randomness, picking up thrones, a tapestry, a door to the outside world—Ophelia's entrance and exit, we will learn—and a big bed below a yawning backdrop. This "symbol," Donaldson says, "in proximity to [a] phallic cannonade, is a kind of declaration of the film's Freudian intentions" (1990, 52). The camera is "rewinding," as we will learn, traveling past symbols—throne, bed, cannons—that it will reemphasize at the ending that these objects have helped to generate, as the procession returns to that high platform against a pitiless twilight. We may begin to notice that Olivier's black-and-white camera can achieve considerable depth, in addition to the flexibility of the-up-and down movements it has already demonstrated. Black and white, of course, is a deep-field medium, as opposed to color, which tends to flatten perspective. We hear voices. Claudius drinks. He tosses the cup to a startled courtier. Trumpets and drums. An ample Gertrude leans beside him, showing no sign of recent grief. On "time be thine" we see Hamlet at last, slumped in a chair downcourt from the throne. We begin to notice Olivier's editing—"persist" for "persever" and "lower'd" for "vailed" (see Dent for the film script). Claudius pulls the power of the court with him as he moves down the long table toward Hamlet. Claudius makes his accusation of Hamlet very public and makes sure that his counselors signal agreement by bowing as he passes them. Gertrude lingers a bit too long in her kiss of Hamlet and a furious Claudius says, "Madam, come!" He is still angry as he says "smiling to my heart" and as he pulls Gertrude from the court, giving her an if-looks-could-kill look. Basil Sydney's subtext as Claudius seems to be, "Damnit all—I have knocked off her husband. Now I have to worry about the kid! Curse Sigmund Freud!" (see Mills 1985, 241–49, for further description of Olivier's performance in the film).

Suffice it that all of this has already happened as we watch the film. Olivier's use of the Oedipal configuration may mean to suggest as well that all of this has happened many times before (see Donaldson 1990, 31-67), and that Hamlet's story is merely a specific manifestation of an inevitable pattern. If so, all men, princes and the rest of us, are characters in an Oedipal sideshow—that is the inevitable "history" dictated from the psyche independently of any external events or circumstances. Neil Taylor nicely captures the relationship between the opening and the closing sequences of the film: "An aerial view of Hamlet's pallbearers reaching the top of the tower . . . provides the opening. . . . [A] companion low-angle shot of the same ascent provides the closing. . . . Between them they establish a cyclical structure which may be read as either regeneration or futility" (1994, 182). I think the evidence comes down solidly on the side of futility.

Max J. Herzberg argues that "on the screen Olivier's version in some ways moves closer to the Elizabethan manner of production than any other post-Elizabethan versions have done. For Shakespeare's theater largely disregarded the conventional acts and scenes in which printed editions of Shakespeare's plays appear; the Elizabethans had a constant flow of action and dialogue that resembles motion-picture technique. The great difference of course is that Elizabethan audiences had to imagine for themselves the backgrounds of scenes; photoplays today can reproduce these with living fidelity" (1949, 4). Olivier's film, of course, does not try for "living fidelity" of scene (cf. Furse 1948, and Donaldson 1990, 65-66), even if language describing place is cut (except in the notorious example of Gertrude's voice-over of Ophelia's melodious cruise down the River Colne). Olivier's Elsinore is, as Robert Duffy says, "midway between heaven and earth" (1976, 149), and the film incorporates what Sheryl W. Gross calls "chapters in a fairy tale . . . a kind of Never-Never Land" (1980, 64, 65). Our suspension of disbelief and extension of imagination—the "contract" we enter into as we encounter a live performance—do not pertain to film, which can make us believe, but which tends to do our imagining for us. Herzberg's comment, however, must be read against zeitgeist. He writes at a time (1949) when Shakespeare on film was very rare, when Shakespeare was *read as text*, and where live Shakespeare was not only a random event but was framed by a proscenium. Olivier's film invites comparisons to theater because its deep-field technique does make "it possible to film long sequences with moving actors and/or camera without losing the focus, [thus] preserv[ing] unity of time and space" (Sheryl Gross 1980, 65). Deep focus also "requires more active participation [on the part of the spectator] than is normally expected of a movie audience" (66).

Mary McCarthy calls the role of Hamlet "Mannerist" (1956, 65) and certainly the play contrasts its techniques with "classical proportion," as represented by the Player's speech, for example, and in "Gonzago." The film itself incorporates some distortion of conventional expectations, in its in-and-out-of-focus responses to the Ghost and in its eerie independent camera which can rove, ghostlike, up and down stone steps and along corridors. The constant movement of Olivier's camera and the time it took for the camera to cover distances caused John Mason Brown to label the film a "travelogue" (1948, 26).

Grigori Kozintsev's film shows us how *far* film can be from the linguistic premises of Shakespeare's theater, as Ingram says: "The film is rooted not in the play's words but in its references: 'something is rotten,' 'sulf'rous and tormenting flames,' 'sweet bells jangled, out of tune and harsh,' and 'o'erhear their conference.' The result is what Shakespeare himself might have conceived had he been a screenwriter" (1966, 17). The film is, as Jack Jorgens observes, quoting Kozintsev, "a cine-poem of stone, iron, sea, and earth" (1977, 223). It begins, as Jorgens says, with "waves wash[ing] though the shadow of Elsinore as a bell tolls. Titles over rock with a blazing torch to the right. Billowing banners of mourning" (300–01). The film is "After the Tragedy by William Shakespeare." The camera pans the wall of the castle and the three opening chords of Shostakovich's somber theme sound. Bernice Kliman picks up the description: "Two horsemen give a signal from below for the flag signifying the death of the king to be flown, and in a reverse shot, we see flag after flag unfurled from the wooden veranda overlooking the courtyard of the castle" (1988, 88).

Hamlet pounds along on a white horse under an ominous sky. He and his three companions thump across the drawbridge. He dismounts and runs up some steps. A huge black flag unfurls as he rushes to embrace his mother, who is weeping. She is "All in black," as Kliman notes, "noticeably well turned-out, with jewels adorning her fingers" (1988, 89). An officer orders cannons to be fired. Workers strain against the seven huge spokes of the wheel that pulls the drawbridge up. Jorgens notes "Gertrude's black-gloved hand embracing Hamlet while the drawbridge and huge portcullis close him in" (1877, 220). The teeth of the portcullis rise as the bridge slowly closes out the light. "The last, slow shots of the drawbridge and moat enclosing Hamlet effectively convey Denmark as a prison," says Kliman (89).

A final streak of sunlight plays against the stone and is erased. We hear a crowd. A soldier beats kettle drums, one on each side of his horse. Claudius's opening speech is read by a soldier from a parchment to the crowd in the courtyard. The black flag behind the soldier is withdrawn. The period of mourning is over. The proclamation ends with "taken to wife." The camera cuts to the inside of the castle, where the king and queen descend from a platform. He says, "In equal scale." Ambassadors stroll past, two speaking in German, two in French, as if to emphasize the cosmopolitan nature of this court. Claudius adjourns to his council room, the queen with him. The king mentions Fortinbras, and has his council look out of a window, where, to martial music, Claudius's army marches out of the castle. It is an allusion to a May Day parade past the Kremlin, a display of power that needs no rhetorical amplification. Claudius deals with Laertes, but when the king looks for Hamlet, the chair is empty. Gertrude and then Claudius pursue Hamlet. He agrees to obey her, and Claudius orders a public celebration. Hamlet walks through the court as his first soliloquy drums through him in voice-over.

"The shots," Kliman says, "are always connected by straight cuts [that provide] no clue about the passage of time" (1988, 91). This camera technique is, as Jorgens notes, in contrast to "Olivier's dreamlike film [where] dissolves frequently link shots" (1977, 218). We begin to realize as we watch the black flags retract in the Kozintsev film that we are experiencing a skillfully orchestrated and total state control of events and their interpretation. Kozintsev emphasizes what he calls "the theme of government," which he finds "very interesting" and which he feels "Olivier cut" (1966, 226). "Kozintsev's *Hamlet*," Collick says, "was intended partly as an antithesis to [Olivier's] psychological reading. [Kozintsev's is] a tragedy of man caught in a climate of political corruption, as opposed to one confronting his inner flaw" (1989, 135), that is, one assumes, his inability to make up his mind.

Kozintsev shows us immediately some of the monumental natural forces that lie under and beyond politics. Olivier shows us "nature" almost exclusively through Ophelia, who can run in and out of landscapes but who is crushed within the stones of Elsinore and must finally float down the river to muddy death. Kozintsev gives a sense of something great and *a priori* around the closed-in construct of the castle. It is an "Aesopian" way of indicting Stalinism. Olivier shows us a single nature—Ophelia's—being drawn into a centripetal vortex that turns innocence to self-destructive nightmare. The dynamics dictated by Kozintsev's Claudius affect many, as in Kozintsev's *King Lear*, where a multitude of peasants gather near the great wall of the fortress to hear Lear's proclamation, and here, in the group gathered in the courtyard to listen to Claudius's announcement, which inaugurates and terminates mourning with a sweeping disdain for human issues but an accurate assessment of how political transition must function. Hamlet has been out of the loop and returns to Elsinore as merely a prop in Claudius's coup. Olivier's camera closes in on Hamlet's mind. Kozintsev's Hamlet is a participant in a politics dictated by a smooth and plausible

King and a Gertrude out of Thackeray, who glances approvingly at a mirror as she utters cliches about "all that lives must die." Narcissism is perhaps an inevitable reflex of tyranny, an effort to benefit from power by imitating it. "The politics of the court," says Kenneth Rothwell, "begin to rival the inner perturbations of the prince" (Rothwell and Melzer 1990, 69), a balance for which Olivier, obviously, does not try. Kozintsev's Claudius is skillful enough to incorporate "nature" into the workings of his court, as Ingram suggests in describing this superbly self-referential film: "The billowing movement of banners is repeated not only by the Ghost's cloak, the curtains in Gertrude's closet and the enveloping mourning veil into which Ophelia is forced after her father's death, but in flames, breaking waves and streaming clouds" (1992, 17).

Of all the *Hamlet* films, Kozintsev's suffers the greatest loss when put on cassette. It is hugely scaled in Sovscope, a seventy-millimeter medium, which makes an epic of the play whether it wants to be or not. Some would argue that the size of screen and conception work better in Kozintsev's *Lear*, which, for example, contrasts the moves and countermoves of a great battle with the intimate reunion of Lear and Cordelia, iron and the clank of arms against the flowing garments and smiles of the captives. Edmund does not understand those smiles, goes into combat still troubled by them, and is defeated. Each film is in black and white, which gives the *Lear* a powerful documentary effect and lends to the *Hamlet* what Kozintsev calls "the cool greys of the North" (1962, 80). *Hamlet*, Kozintsev believes, must, like the screen itself, "convey the enormity of history, and the fate of a man determined to talk with his epoch on equal terms, and not be an extra, with no speaking part in one of the spectacular crowd scenes" (1972, 192. Kozintsev, the maker of films, is hardly an attendant lord himself.

Jorgens remarks a quality that Kozintsev's *Hamlet* shares with his *Lear*, the camera's attention to "a world beyond Hamlet's tragic action which is oblivious to it" (1977, 224). Kozintsev's camera captures the randomness that Auden describes:

> even the dreadful martyrdom must run its course
> Anyhow in a corner, some untidy spot
> Where the dogs go on with their doggy life,
>         and the torturer's horse
> Scratches its innocent behind on a tree.

It is the world we experience as we step over and around the homeless huddled near the steam vents of our great cities as we move briskly toward the snug theatre. Kozintsev's art shows us what we tend to ignore in our pursuit of Shakespeare, but which Shakespeare does not ignore. The film, and the *King Lear* even more, shows us the "history" that formal history does not record, except in a table of statistics.

The Tony Richardson film provides the most close-up *Hamlet* of all. It is a filmed version of a production in London's Roundhouse and was designed to be filmed from the first. Richardson wished to "free the theatre from the tyranny of the proscenium arch and the social habits that go with it" (quoted in Manvell, 1971, 232). And the film succeeds in this goal, as Arthur Knight affirms: "it eliminates all sense of proscenium, and the tatty stage scenery that proved so distracting in, for example, Olivier's . . . filming of *Othello*" (1970, 37). It begins with the credits against a rough, brick wall in the Roundhouse, once a switching station for the vast rail network that converges on London—"a metaphor for the world of the play," says Michael Mullin:

> The brick, the dust, and the darkness form part of this world in the film as they did for audiences in the stage performances . . . the film makes these images predominate, disregarding others— the seas foaming at the foot of the battlements, the russet sky overhead, the images of the Ghost itself, the vision of Hamlet at sea, Ophelia afloat in the stream and many smaller, but no less powerful images conjured up in reading and, in their time, enacted in stage and film performance. (1976, 124)

A jovial Horatio (Gordon Jackson, later "Mr. 'oodsin" of *Upstairs, Downstairs*) joins the guards. He takes his glasses off and blinks before his "Tush, tush," perhaps to suggest that "the characters," as Duffy says, "seem confined by a vaguely visible edge of confusion and myopia" (1976, 151). He is shocked, however, by the Ghost, who is here a blinding light and a series of deep and ominous chords. "The text," says Manvell, "is cut back to the barest essentials . . . to emphasize the impact made by the Ghost" (1971, 128). (See Mullin 1976, 130, for "Cuts in the Text.") Horatio yanks his hat off as he vows to "cross it, though it blast me" and puts his specs back on as the dawn appears as a blank light at an archway. We do get a crow, incidentally, and do not, I assume, have time to wonder how it got here, as the scene blasts on by. This Horatio acts as a Jamesian "reflector," preparing us for Hamlet, as Manvell suggests: "a bespectacled and middle-aged don . . . the friend and 'fellow-student' of Hamlet at Wittenburg University, he prepares us for a mature interpretation of the Prince . . . an academic summoned back home for his mother's marriage" (128) and, based on his colloquy with Horatio, for his father's funeral as well.

The camera cuts to a close-up of Claudius drinking wine, then feeding some to Gertrude. Claudius gets a big laugh on "impotent and bedrid." He is hardly impotent but will be seen shortly conducting state business from his bed, as Gertrude munches grapes beside him. Claudius seems only slightly upset that Hamlet won't join the party. We watch the candelabras and the king depart from Hamlet's point of view, frame-left. Hamlet turns his forlorn face to us as trumpets triumph and a torch flares to the right. His thin voice begins its complaint, "his rough Midlands twang," Mullin says, "making each word new-coined and fresh" (1976, 128). I find the coins dull, however freshly minted. As Mullin also says, "Inevitably, as the naturalistic acting, closely observed by the camera, brings the verse to us afresh, the sweep and cadence of the verse may be lost" (129), as I have found it consistently to be lost in Williamson's performances of Shakespeare. Williamson is "more a peasant than a poet," as Clive Barnes remarked of his Hamlet (1969b). To be fair, however, one must acknowledge the difficulties of applying naturalistic acting techniques to verse drama (see Hornby 1988).

The "neurotic *Hamlet,*" as Duffy calls the film, "deliberately frustrates the spectator's unconscious attempts to impose a spatial coherence on the *mise-en-scene* and establish a perspective drawing the disjointed visual impressions of film into a cognitive unity . . . Richardson, in short, establishes a strategy of visual frustration, and the lack of perceptible depth of field in most scenes communicates what Richardson seems to view as the tragedy's subtext, a contagious inability to penetrate the context and mystery of human affairs" (1976, 150). Richardson's "frequent cuts and soft-focus close-ups completely disorient the audience," says Sheryl Gross (1980, 67). Only Hamlet, Mullin suggests "looks beyond the milling throng to see his fate" (1976, 129). (On Williamson's interpretation of Hamlet, see Mills 1985, 268–82 and Trewin 1978a, 146–48.) Williamson's is an enraged, snarling Prince of Denmark, a Hamlet of the 1960s, along with David Warner. In the 1960s, of course, the sense of displacement in society and alienation from the political process was strong among the college generation, and need not be stressed here. Suffice it that the script provided plenty of opportunity for working from what was more than subtext in the culture and is more than subtext in the script. "Authority" was to be questioned in the '60s. The film launches the interrogation by refusing to provide an architectural buttress for politics, neither the spiraling staircases of Olivier nor the prison-like solidity of Kozintsev's castle. Instead "the production operates [in a] black void . . . Elsinore is like the true Elizabethan court, a collection of courtiers following the king, a network of relations and values" (Neil Taylor 1994, 188), but a network as fragile as a spider's web.

The Ragnar Lyth film begins with "The time is out of joint, oh cursed spite that ever I was born to set it right," written in Swedish and translated into English in a subtitle. We hear laughter (and later learn that it is Claudius's ingratiating laughter, in which he will engage even after he has been given several superfluous stabs by Hamlet). An eye looks from a doorway. Is it Hamlet's? No. It is the eye of the head chef, timing the need for the next course. "Even as the film opens," Kliman says, "we see the spying that is a way of life at Elsinore" (1988, 209). The kitchen help place cherries in the pastry heads that adorn the game hens beneath. A strange wind invades the kitchen, blowing out candles and blasting the pastry heads to the kitchen floor. Silence. The candles are relit. A guard—Marcellus—appears and lights his torch from one of the candles. The screen tells us that this is "The Tragic Story of Hamlet, Prince of Denmark." A cold Horatio, hugging his robe about him, follows the guard's torch through corridors, past a door that creaks open as attendants tug at chains. Another guard joins them. "What, is Horatio there?" "A piece of him." He is skeptical. The procession continues as a clock begins to strike. It grows louder as the group goes up into an attic. Horatio looks down to the catacombs, many stories below and one story ago. There lies the corpse of the former king, arms folded. It is very corporeal. The film gives us a nice contrast between what is going on in the upper floors and Claudius's party below. It is a moment in the play from which Keats borrowed:

> The boisterous, midnight, festive clarion,
> The kettle-drum, and far-heard clarinet
> Affray his ears, though but in dying tone—
> The hall door shuts again, and all the noise is gone.

"Tush, tush, 'twill not appear," says Horatio. The torch flares. The camera follows it upward, as do the eyes of the two soldiers and Horatio. Pigeons flap excitedly and are replaced by a weeping, sighing sound. Horatio sees—what? As Kliman says, "the ghost appears only in the briefest of glimpses while he is speaking to Hamlet in the last scene of act 1, and is sensed rather than seen by the others" (1988, 210). For once then, something (although I found this opening very confusing when I first watched it and was prepared to denigrate the film until I saw the rest, which is uneven but often powerful, particularly in its emphasis on Ophelia). Horatio asks whatever he sees to speak and even goes up a couple of steps to drive his demand home. But the thing evaporates. A soldier grabs Horatio by the shoulders. "Is it not like the King?" Horatio agrees reluctantly. The scholar has been confronted by something beyond his "philosophy." The camera cuts to the throne room, a large and relatively empty space (actually, a room in the abandoned Nobel dynamite factory). Claudius chuckles. Two young men fence. Each gives the other a hit. One of them is Laertes, as we will discover. A man hits a cue ball. A jovial Claudius hefts a bowling ball. A dark figure stands apart, staring out the window, suggesting the "Denmark's a prison" pattern that will be repeated, particularly for Ophelia, as Laertes inhales the light between him and Paris, and the door shuts darkness again into Elsinore. A bell jingles and Claudius gets down to business.

Kliman suggests that Lyth's montage technique conveys "a more powerful sense of knowing the truth than more realistic methods might evoke. [Thus] to analyze the shots is to belie their summative power" (1988, 205–6). That is accurate. The film provides consistent disjunctivity: the time is out of joint, yet a clock chisels its precision upon midnight. Horatio demands speech of something *we* would not ask to speak. Hamlet broods and Claudius chuckles, but Hamlet is not just a self-exiled existentialist and is perhaps less than an exemplification of "the Swedish character [which can retreat] into the role of the aloof, misunderstood exile" (Milton 1993, 436). He is a spoiled brat, rock-or-tennis star, who wants nothing to do with responsibility and who even engages in the adolescent display of trashing his room.

We have here a Hamlet of the 1980s—the man who continues his adolescence into chronological maturity. We also have a postmodernist production, in that what we experience as film audience is not always consistent with what the characters *seem* to be experiencing within the contexts of production—so that disjunctivity exists as our zone of interpretation. The film handles the political theme powerfully, by suggesting the absolute cynicism and opportunism of the citizenry, and benefits from feminist criticism in its portrayal of Gertrude as the power behind a figurehead Claudius and in its brilliant depiction of Ophelia, who is here an agent of discord and dismay that reaches beyond her personal destruction. This is a film that Olivier, had he wanted to, could not have made in 1948. Lyth makes *Hamlet* very much the story of 1984, reflecting an Orwellian perspective on a rotten society.

Zeffirelli, of course, permits us to look down from the parapets onto Claudius's celebration, as Hamlet waits for the Ghost to appear (see Jorgens 1977, 220, on Kozintsev's depiction of this contrast). The view down for Lyth is to the corpse of the former king. And Lyth, it would seem, permits the presence of a night visitor to pervade the kitchen, at least, of the building below. Whatever is on the parapets never comes to the attention of the King, in Lyth or in the script. This king attempts to chuckle his way past the problems he has created for his kingdom. Lyth's opening is not as spare or as nonspectral as Richardson's, but it does, as television tends to and perhaps must, put the emphasis on the viewers, as opposed to the thing seen. It may be that the supernatural, when framed for television, must become merely the psychological (see Dessen, 1986).The Lyth film is among the many productions that exist but that have not become commercially available.

After that intimidating warning from the FBI., along whose parapets walks the ghost of J. Edgar Hoover, Zeffirelli gives us the name of the play in black against a sunlit Elsinore sitting solidly above the begin and cease of ocean waves. The credits come up in white, and we cut to a closer shot of the battlements as Zeffirelli's name appears. The camera cuts to horsemen waiting in the courtyard of the castle and tracks aimlessly. They are waiting for something. We are told that this is "The Royal Castle of Denmark. Elsinore." We hear weeping. The queen approaches a bier. Claudius looks on. We see the corpse of the former king, as in Lyth, before we see the incorporeal version—although Scofield's Ghost is much more human than most and needs no dry ice come from the fridge to tell his story. A hooded Hamlet drops dirt on the corpse. Claudius softly requests that Hamlet "think of us as of a father." Hamlet turns away. The queen weeps. A heavy cover is placed over the tomb. The tristful queen looks up and sees Claudius looking at her down the long length of the tomb. Hamlet sees this exchange of glances. Edward Quinn says that Gertrude's weeping is "one of several instances where a line in the play ['like Niobe, all tears'] is rendered visually rather than verbally, and this one makes it clear who the visual star of this film is" (1991, 2). That is a somewhat perverse viewing of the film, although it permits Quinn to make the point that some actresses playing Gertrude can make, and that is that she be "impressive enough . . . to put to rest T. S. Eliot's . . . charge that the play lacks an 'objective correlative'" (2). But certainly Zeffirelli makes the point that "Hamlet is 'a man who has a terrible problem with his mother'" (Jacobs 1991, 21). Hamlet exits up the stairs, "into the bright dissolving light of out-of-doors, as though [we] witness . . . his birth into the primal visual environment of the film" (Impastato 1991, 2).

We hear Claudius saying "Though yet of Hamlet, our dear brother's death" as we look at the stone walls of the castle. It is not the public announcement of Kozintsev, but it is an inclusive political statement that incorporates those we see as the camera pans across the throne room. As Claudius says "taken to wife," he reaches across and takes Gertrude's hand. Polonius signals and the court applauds. (Olivier's Polonius, Felix Alymer, signaled the court by hitting the fingers of his right hand against the back of his left hand, though he gave an imperative signal to the trumpets to underscore Claudius's naming of Hamlet as heir.) Zeffirelli's room echoes with trumpets and cheers, and Polonius signals that the ceremony is over.

The camera cuts to Laertes entering a library and being asked "what's the news with" him. Claudius and Laertes share a silent joke about Polonius's long-windedness. Claudius gives a jubilant Laertes a kiss on each cheek. A frolicsome Gertrude trips down the castle steps to a waiting Claudius. They kiss at length. Gertrude nods toward a closed door. We'd better do something, she seems to say. They enter a room, Gertrude calling "Hamlet! Hamlet!" Claudius follows with a goblet of wine in his hand. "Now, my cousin Hamlet, and my son." Hamlet, seated, says, "A little more than kin, and less than kind." Gertrude laughs at Hamlet's "too much in the sun." As Claudius sits, Hamlet stands, as if unwilling to accept any equal status with his uncle. Gertrude's right arm surrounds a model of a soldier in chain mail, an emblem of King Hamlet which she embraces unconsciously. Claudius gives his "courtier, cousin, and our son" speech, holds his arms out as if to say, "There!—I've done what I can!" and leaves. The dogs outside, waiting to hunt, yammer excitedly. The problem with this way of doing it is, as Kathleen Campbell argues, "that private rather than public occasions diminish our sense of the king's power. [This] appears to be a conciliatory gesture undertaken at Gertrude's request rather than a delicate public negotiation with a potential claimant of the throne" (1991, 7). The dynastic theme is far less emphatic than in Olivier's "nonpolitical" treatment. Here the Claudius is as little concerned with Hamlet's inability to join the fun as Richardson's Anthony Hopkins. In Richardson, however, Gertrude (Judy Parfitt) also ignores Hamlet, which Zeffirelli's Glenn Close clearly does not.

Close's Gertrude continues Claudius's plea, personally, almost romantically, looking past Hamlet's shoulder with her own vailed eyes at an irretrievable past. Hamlet's "Seems, madam!" is to her alone, and flattens out without its bite at Claudius ("actions that a man might *play*"). Hamlet agrees to obey Gertrude and hers is the commendation of a "gentle and unforced accord"—merely, then, a mother's contentment at her son's acquiescence. She runs down the steps of the inner palace, is helped into a blue robe by a giggling attendant, and races out the door again. Hamlet begins to brood about "solid flesh." He looks out the window. Solid Gertrude is running down the outer steps again. "Things rank and gross in nature possess it merely. . . . That it should come to this!" Claudius leans from his horse to kiss Gertrude. "Satyr!" Gertrude rides off gaily on a white horse, courtiers oohing and aahing, Hamlet still complaining. He shuts the leaded windows, as if on a playmate abandoning him as he stays after school. Gertrude, Claudius and party ride into the deceptive sunlight just outside the castle grounds.

The effect of this opening is of a "return to normalcy" for Denmark and of a reawakening to life for Gertrude, with only a self-isolated prince shading the bright panorama.

The film, of course, has not met with as enthusiastic a response as that which greeted Branagh's *Henry V*. That is partly because, as Max McQueen tells us, "'Hamlet' has always been a tough nut to crack" (1991). Frank Ardolino finds that "so much of the text is cut that we do not experience the full personalities of the characters and their relationships" (1991, 5). In this "telegraphic version," Ardolino says, "the scenes remain isolated and detached because we have not been given sufficient motivation to understand their connections" (6). Edward Quinn criticizes the film for "its neglect of important dimensions of the play. The loss of the opening scene eliminates the threat of war, the rottenness in Denmark and the hint of a sacrificial agent. Fortinbras is cut . . ." (1991, 2; on the problems involved in cutting the opening scene, see Cohen 1989, 9–11). Television versions usually include Fortinbras, partly perhaps because television has been, at least in the United States, the medium of political transition, on which we watch funerals and inaugurations, conventions and computer projections of who's in and who's out. Once the reporter of such events, television now shapes and controls them. Thus, television anticipates the arrival of a Fortinbras and a speech by the new ruler which honors the past before announcing new agendas. Zeffirelli's film incorporates television's thematics in becoming what Ingram calls "a beautifully photographed account of familial lust and hate. This focus is established by replacing Act I Scene 1 with the burial of King Hamlet at which his bloat brother and tearful widow exchange a significant look across the tomb. Her son is disgusted. Zeffirelli has domesticated *Hamlet*" (1992, 18). Richardson had done the same thing, fo course, as Arthur Knight suggests: "between Williamson's modern, uninflected readings, Richardson's unrelenting use of extreme close-ups, and the concentration of the plot upon King Claudius's domestic difficulties, this *Hamlet* often seems like a costumed version of television's 'One Man's Family'" (1970, 37). The effect of "angry young men" collides with the taming tendencies of the techniques whereby the rage is recorded and transmitted. Ace Pilkington says, "It is unfortunate that Zeffirelli, following Olivier in this as in so much else, chose to explain Hamlet with Freud, foregrounding the incest theme" (1994, 175).

*The New Yorker* says of the Zeffirelli film that the "play's alternating rhythms of action and reflection have been flattened to a single tempo, brisk but monotonous" (T. R. 1991, 22). That may be, but if so, it is because that is the "Claudius Rhythm," dictated throughout the film and, with only a few exceptions, capable of incorporating Hamlet within its beat. The tempo is Zeffirelli's acknowledgment of the political theme which he otherwise ignores.

David Impastato defends Zeffirelli's technique by calling it "Baroque . . . fluid, emotionally expansive, sensuously free . . . The camera, like the Baroque frame, seems reactive, improvised—as if unable to predict where the human energy it witnesses might take it" (1992, 1). The film, then, cannot be unified on the basis of an auditor's sense of *Hamlet*, as play or as script, but represents an experience like that of any filmgoer who doesn't know the story. As Zeffirelli says, "the audience sits there in a big dark room, and I have to tell them the story from the beginning, making clear every single word of William Shakespeare" (1990). In other words, "Zeffirelli has a distressingly low estimate of his audience's intelligence" (Pilkington 1994, 168). He anticipates a spectator innocent of even trace memories of his or her cultural heritage, and his mission is "to make this thing accessible to the distracted multitudes. . . . Everything that we do is (designed) to make people forget what has been achieved before us. We impoverish our culture in the end" (Jacobs 1991, 21).

That does not mean, of course, that the result cannot be judged by people who do know the play and the many shapes, guises, and disguises it has assumed as it has confronted the great, modern light-sensitive medium. Zeffirelli does, however, want his film to be judged against other contemporary films, not against other versions of *Hamlet*. It may be that Zeffirelli proves Ralph Berry's thesis that "Hamlet is not . . . a part that demands great acting. But it does demand the essential star quality of magnetism" (1989a, 24). Zeffirelli was attracted, he says, to Gibson's "vitality, his mystery, his sudden changes of color, his humor. We've never had this humor in Hamlet, but it's there" (Jacobs 1991, 21). If Zeffirelli hoped to bring this classic effectively to popcorn people, he would seem to have failed, if Marty Meltz's ear is any criterion: "With only 70 percent of the dialogue comprehensible, it's still a film for the elitist" (1991). If *Hamlet* is taught in the schools, however—and it is—Meltz seems to suggest that there is no link in a student's mind between what happens in class and what happens at Cinema 38½. That means that one *locus* is divorced from another *locus* and that the *plateas*—the teacher's interaction with text and with class and Zeffirelli's intervention in the history of the script cannot usefully contrast with *locus* or with each other.

The script of *Hamlet* moves through time, picking up the shadings of history, its black and white, its deep fields and closeups, its colorations, even, as Pilkington says of the Zeffirelli film, "the blue dimness of distance, the colour equivalent of black and white but with a suggestion that the characters are receding from the audience into a kind of mythic mistiness" (1994, 175). Any production is a reflection of zeitgeist. It cannot help but be and is meant to be, as Barbara Hodgdon argues: "performance acknowledges, in its every aspect, its ephemeral nature. . . . [D]isturbance—one might call it transformation—is just what Shakespeare's texts are about" (65).

Gade's silent film explores and develops the very camera techniques that were making film the powerful medium it was becoming in the twentieth century. Olivier's dark and inward exploration of the deep fields of Hamlet's mind in 1948 contrasts with the technicolor need for a national hero only four years earlier. Kozintsev's anti-Stalinist fable of 1964 looks at recent and ongoing Soviet history from a stance Kozintsev could not have avoided had he wanted to. An effort to free the script from its moment would probably have resulted in an odd and schizophrenic film. Williamson's uncultured snarl is a look back in anger typical of the 1960s, which experienced the bankrupt rule of, for example, a Richard Nixon. Lyth's film offers no hero, again, but does examine Ophelia from the perspective of a feminist critique available in 1984. Zeffirelli despairs amid a culture at once illiterate and ignorant of its past and brings stars who have helped to create the Lethal Terminator XIII expectation to a classic text—along with some superb Shakespearean actors as well. It may be that his film will gain its place by its precise depiction of the marginal characters who surround the great ones—Bonham-Carter's Ophelia, Scofield's Ghost, Bates's Claudius, McEnery's Osric, and Peacock's Grave-digger, the only one I have seen who crosses himself as he says, "rest her soul, she's dead."

Whatever we think of it, Zeffirelli's film has implanted its images into the retinas and memories of our students as surely as the Olivier film did for my generation. It has become *their Hamlet* and it goes forward with them as part of their "history." Time's march invariably transforms the films, fixing them in their times but finding in them "meanings" undreamed of in their conscious composition. The point, of course, is to move from production back to the script and *re*-view the script as an energy that takes *Hamlet* into the future and shows that future what it is. We probably see that reflection only in retrospect.

NOTES

1. For more on Nielsen and the 1920 adaptation of *Hamlet.* see Lawrence Danson, 1993.

2. Like the Olivier film, *Citizen Kane* features a back-lit castle—Xanadu—at the beginning and end. Welles used a similar setting for the end of his *Macbeth*.

# IV

# What Happens to
# *The Comedy of Errors*
# on Television?

Of all the plays in the canon, *The Comedy of Errors* seems the most impervious to television. Although three television versions exist, only one was made originally *for* television—and that primarily because the BBC had determined to do the canon.

The poverty of the modern medium is demonstrated when we consider that *The Comedy of Errors* reaches back to Plautus for its inspiration but has difficulty reaching forward to be incorporated on television. Shakespeare's play has what Douglas Peterson calls an "enframing action" (1995, 38)—the threat to Egeon. Ultimately the threat will dissolve before the recognitions and reconciliations of the ending. The *fact* of an enframing action, whether formal like the Sly Induction or informal like the threats to Hermia and Egeon, is greatly enhanced by the presence of a frame. Shakespeare's stage, however open to its audience, provided a space that was constantly being redefined but that could, over the course of a performance, be defined by who was there at any given moment. That definition also extended to what could happen at any given moment. The presence of the Duke and Egeon or the Duke and Hermia suggested that the scene would partake of some "official" act, as when the Duke condemns or as when the Duke issues a pardon or an overruling of a previous edict. Television, with its "constant present" (cf. Moshinsky, quoted in Elsom 1989, 124), its linear movement, its lack of depth, and its consequent inability to create a frame, is simply incapable of an effect that Shakespeare's stage creates just by being there.

The convention of identical twins—and here we have two sets!—does not translate to the "realistic" premises of television. "[Audience] participation requires only," says Peterson, "that the audience accept the hypothetical situation . . . two sets of long separated identical twins on the loose in the same city" (1995, 38). But that "only" blocks the translation from stage to cathode-ray tube. Although television can incorporate the cartoon, we can readily grasp why *The Comedy of Errors* would not work in that genre. We, and the inhabits of Ephesus, would be observing the same figure. There would be no mistaken identity, no confusion in those misidentified, none of the situational irony and attendant laughter that the stage provides. *Locus* is invariably conservative, says Weimann (1991), but can be challenged by the mechanism and circumstances of production. In the case of *Comedy of Errors*, however, the givens are simply denied by the medium.

Although it might be argued that television's modernist premises are what deny *Comedy of Errors* its ability to translate to that medium, we must remember that none of the comedies in which twins are mistaken for each other or in which a woman disguises herself as a man have succeeded on film, either. One of the best such efforts is Christine Edzard's *As You Like It*, to be discussed later. The Gade-Nielsen 1920 *Hamlet*, in which Asta Nielsen plays Hamlet *as* woman, is also an effective film. She is trapped in her disguise, as Viola might have been had Sebastian not also come safely from the sea. A comedy which insists that we suspend our disbelief cannot succeed, it seems, in a medium which does not ask that we agree to that contract. In other words, at work against this script are issues deeper than those W. B. Worthen describes as "part of how television retextualizes the drama by producing it in its own rhetoric . . . The lack of physical space, the loss of scale, the use of closeup to render characterization intimate, the shifting balance of intensity from public to private scenes, the need to cut the text to accommodate . . . broadcasting conventions, the placement of 'high' art' in the mass media. 'Dramatic quality,' in this sense, is a function neither of dramatic criticism nor of theatrical productions but defines that intersection between the text and the cultural institutions that enable us to produce it meaningfully" (1989, 454). This script presses television to the limits of its ability "to mean," and, indeed, beyond. The problem is in the *platea*, that busy intersection between text and medium. The effort to make *The Comedy of Errors* work on television, however, is instructive, and, in the instance of the two televised stage plays, makes clear how quickly the stage can "date itself," rendering what might have seemed fresh and original at the moment of production very much a product of a zeitgeist that seems longer ago than it is.

It has long been noted that *The Comedy of Errors* is much more than a Plautine farce. Shakespeare eliminates some of the harsher edges of

Plautus and introduces a "psychological" element to the stock characters. That "psychology" is a function of the characters' response to an apparently mad world. But the world of Ephesus is quite sane, indeed rigid in its rationality. It "is not a place of irrationality and dream [as] the Syracusan twins wrongly perceive it to be" (Holland 1992, 177). Its laws, for example, are the inviolate rules that the comic world can sometimes transcend, as in Theseus's overruling Egeus at the end of *A Midsummer Night's Dream*, but that in Ephesus can be delayed but not otherwise extenuated. This world moves literally by the book and by the clock. Neither it nor its characters can allow for chance or coincidence, but Shakespeare introduces precisely those elements to the Ephesian grid. Ephesus does not know that twins have been disgorged into its defined spaces, nor, of course, do the boys from Syracuse know that they are identical to two chessmen already in play on those spaces. Shakespeare makes sure that the timing of events remains exact, even as the playwright's craftsmanship foments greater and greater confusion in the characters. He poises his control of time against their belief that *they* know what time it is. "Here comes the almanac of my true date," says Antipholus S. as, to what will soon be their mutual bewilderment, Dromio of Ephesus approaches. The twins cannot confront each other until the promised end, when "the calendars of their nativity" are reestablished within the flow of a continuity that the characters on stage share at last with us. Until then, some of the characters must construe the events and even other characters as "crazy." Beyond that imputation, however, is their inevitable question: Am I mad myself?

Ben Jonson, Drummond tells us, "had one intention to have made a play like Plaut[us'] Amphtrio but left it of[f], for that they could never find two so like others that he could persuade the spectators they were one" (1925, 144). The master of intricate dramaturgy, who could persuade a character to debate a puppet, had little confidence in the ability of his own audience to suspend its disbelief. Nor did he recognize that it is not *we* but the characters on stage who must exhibit "mistaking eyes" and convince us of their inability to tell one Antipholus or Dromio from another. Nor did Jonson glimpse the psychology behind apparent identicalness. Jonson left it to Shakespeare to be the first to recognize some of the psychological implications of the "double story," particularly the "shadow" aspects to be explored with particular energy by the nineteenth century and early twentieth century in "The Double," "William Wilson," "The Picture of Dorian Gray," "Dr. Jekyll and Mr. Hyde," "The Jolly Corner," "The Prussian Officer," and "The Secret Sharer," to name a few examples.

"Which is the natural man, / And which the spirit?"—what happens to the Antipholi is similar to a "dissociative reaction, in which the amnesic half is represented by Antipholus S. while the conflicting half is represented by Antipholus E" (Johannes Fabricius 1989, 47). The former experiences a regression—"The hours come back"—to an adolescence which pulls simultaneously towards home and maternity and away from home towards matrimony and a new home. Antipholus S. "pursues his future wife while searching for his mother and the past" (Blos 1952, 56), dominated, as Peter Blos suggests of the adolescent, by "two broad affective states: mourning and being in love" (100). The process represents, according to Freud in describing psychoanalysis, "a second education of the adult, a correction to his education as a child" (1959, 268). "Love" is to be achieved, of course, once Antipholus S. contacts the energizing archetype of his maternal being: "how much more bearable it is for a son to conceive the son-father problem no longer on the plane of individual guilt—in relation, for example, to his own desire for his own father's death, his aggressions and desires for revenge—but as a problem of deliverance from the father, i.e., from a dominant principle of consciousness that is no longer adequate for the son: a problem that concerns all men, and has been disclosed in the myths and fairy tales as the slaying of the reigning old king and the son's accession to the throne" (von Franz 1959, 20).

Antipholus E. denies Egeon at the end, but his denial is almost immediately corrected by Antipholus S.'s recognition of Egeon. Antipholus S.'s "sense of having been estranged from a familiar world and sense of [not] having another to hang on to . . . lies at the heart of the adolescent's conflict and crisis" (Johannes Fabricius 1989, 55–56). The signal that tells us that a positive process is at work at last is the Merchant's "By this I think the dial points at five." "We are," says Peterson, "back in the world of time" (1995, 45), a world where the seeming stasis of Shakespeare's comic world can suddenly participate in a future.

The conflict between and within the Antipholi reflects, of course, the conflict between the two cities, each seen by the other as evil. The play must move its characters to that point advocated by Paul in his letter to the Ephesians: "Now therefore ye are no more strangers & foreners: but citizens with the Saintes, and of the housholde of God" (Eph. 2: 19. Geneva version). Into the coincidence that Shakespeare inflicts upon blind Ephesus must flow the grace of God. Coincidence must transform itself to synchronicity. That is the "comic" pattern, here achieved within a perceived dream, or nightmare, as are the results of *A Midsummer Night's Dream* by the young lovers. *The Comedy of Errors* also provides a first glimpse of the rhythm of romance, from storm, shipwreck, separation, from apparent death to rebirth, and to reconciliations of lovers, relatives, and the generations themselves. These may seem "essentializing" or "totalizing" myths, but they are *there*, awaiting what deconstruction may find in the fissures and interstices of the scripts.

That deconstruction, for dramatic literature, is production. But in the case of *The Comedy of Errors*, modern media prove a barrier, as opposed to the challenge that can be overcome in various ways with a script that can be seen as "psychological," as Laurence Olivier saw *Hamlet* or as "realistic," as Kenneth Branagh saw *Henry V* (with the psyche of the king part of the reality depicted).

From one point of view, *The Comedy of Errors* should work on television. For all the talk of the supernatural and for all of the emphasis on exorcism, there is no cosmic intersection here. Therefore the focus is on the psychology of the characters, which invents a thesis of insanity or of the outer mystery to explain what we the audience know to be human interaction. Even when a script does contain a ghost or ghosts, or evidence of nonhuman intervention, television directors attempt to depict a *human* cause. "Such emphasis upon the psychological rather than the otherworldly," says Alan Dessen, "suits prevailing interpretations . . . and sidesteps effects that may strike television viewers as questionable, even laughable" (1986, 12). In addition, television lacks the depth for "cosmic" representations *and* for special effects. Language onstage can convince us that the characters are in a different world from ours, or, at least, *believe* they are. But such language emerging from our own machine into our domestic space tends to lack that potency. Special effects on a large screen in a darkened auditorium also have a power that television is wise not to attempt. Dessen asks, "If the medium is indeed hostile to the artist's original strategy, what kind of interpretative logic or rationale should inform any re-presentation?" (12). Jonson, at least, knew that the twins wouldn't work in a "realistic" medium. Shakespeare, glimpsing greater possibilities for his stage and apparently granting greater flexibility to his audience, shows that *The Comedy of Errors,* although in many ways scaled down to the diminished medium of television, is still irredeemably a play for the stage and our expectations as an audience in the living space where we and the actors work together to create a fiction.

Each of the three available versions is a television production—two are tapes of actual stage productions. In the latter instances, response is complicated. It cannot be just an evaluation of a production on magnetic tape transferred to cassette, but must incorporate a sense of the original site of performance—a stage. But as time takes the production back with it, it becomes less a living thing and more of an artifact.

The Flying Karamazov version, televised on PBS in 1987, was originally presented at the Goodman Theater in Chicago in 1983, and later for the Olympia Arts Festival in Los Angeles in 1984. The televised production was taped during the summer of 1987 at the Vivian Beaumont Theater, Lincoln Center, New York. It tells the story clearly enough and has the virtue of being unabashedly a *stage* production. The semicircular stage is in view as the television production begins, and an occasional upstage camera shows the audience. Indeed, on several occasions the audience is invaded, a la the Olson and Johnson "Hellzapoppin'" shows that older members of the Beaumont audience might have recalled.

During a backstage introduction, a Shakespeare look-alike waves off any connection between himself and the play to follow. Indeed, one of the "tensions" introduced during the production is the question of "authorship." A dramaturge, interviewed at the intermission, says that "Francis Bacon would have been delighted" by the production. Alphonse, the juggling master, suggests that Shakespeare's "text has been cut out of the way of the juggling," a wry glance at the agendas that can crowd in upon any hapless script as it lurches through time. J. Todd Fleming, the dramaturge, claims that he did manage to keep Dromio of Ephesus from becoming "Dromio of Poughkeepsie"—although given the separating expanse of the Hudson River, he might have become "Dromio of Hoboken." As Dromio E. launches into a dying speech, which includes, "Tell Laura I Love Her," "Shakespeare" comes out pointing at the script, then tears it up and strides angrily off. He appears later on the Abbess's "Behold—a man much wronged!" A transvestite Courtezan calls for "a roundel and a fairy song," then quotes from *Hamlet, Coriolanus,* and Jackie Gleason. As the author bows, he is seen from behind. "Bringing up the rear," says the announcer, "is William Shakespeare."

The production does not know whether it wants to be drama or circus. The two elements compete against each other. Adriana and Luciana upstage their first discussion (2.1) with tap routines between their responses. These are not dances that complement the "action," like, say, "Night and Day"—which in its original version incorporates conflict between Astaire and Rogers—or "Fit as a Fiddle and Ready for Love," which is predictably a prelude to romance. The end of the scene, without all the sound and movement, is much more effective in its interplay than is its beginning. Luciana's facial responses to Adriana's questions about her own beauty establish the women as confidantes *and* rivals. But that is a rare parenthesis within the general pandemonium. Later (4.2), Adriana undercuts her speeches with some high-flying baton work. She does the same thing in 5.1 with a scimitar. We admire the skill involved, but we do not hear the words.

"In Syracuse, you wear a tie; / In Ephesus, you juggle or you die," we hear as the Syracusian Antipholus and Dromio change into costumes identical to their Ephesian twins. Otherwise, the characters are constantly juggling. The production even provides some Busby Berkeleyian overhead shots showing the objects flying kaleidoscopically across the screen, along with trapeze work, slack-wire-walking, stilt-walking, acrobatics, knife-throwing, unicycling, fire-eating, belly-dancing, and jump-roping. June Schlueter accurately says that the actors "adeptly pull off their balancing acts, but the linguistic structure of the play sadly collapses. . . . Bring back the text, then bring on the jugglers, and the world of Ephesus could resume its magical shape. . . . [I]n this version it is Shakespeare who is doing the disappearing act" (10–11)—as the production seems to admit. Here is an instance of *locus* being used almost solely at the service of *platea*.

The physical material is seldom integrated into the dramatic, a fact underscored by the "jokes." The text on "How to Tell a Joke" that Antipholus S. and Dromio S. peruse does not help them with all the joking about hair and baldness in 2.2—and that is the "joke." A chicken shot through the door of Antipholus of E.'s house becomes a "fowl intrusion." Every time a character says "say," the company repeats what he or she has just said. The word "bark" summons a stuffed spaniel from the cellarage who says "arf." "As I am a Christian," says Antipholus of S., revealing a pair of Max Baer's trunks featuring the Star of David. Egeon, whose own narrative had been cut, keeps changing his sandwich board. At one point he enters asking that $10,000 be placed in his Swiss bank account. The back side of the board tells us that "Ollie says its okay." When Dromio E. mentions a football, the company shifts into a single wing mode and the band plays the "Notre Dame Fight Song." When Dromio S. says "besides myself," a dummy Dromio is thrust out from behind the arras. As Adriana and Antipholus of E. square off, the troupe hums the "Rocky" theme. Luce attempts to shatter a plastic-foam cup with her voice, then bites it. Dromio S. asks, "Is it Memorex?" When Adriana launches into "Thou art an elm, my husband . . ."—lines apparently written for her by Adriana, who has, in turn, borrowed from Psalms—Antipholus S. asks, "Rod McKuen?" Dromio S. shrugs and guesses "Burma-Shave?"

A production that pulls the inherited *locus* almost entirely into topicality can enjoy only the most fleeting communication, depending as it does on an audience precisely contemporary with its allusions. An audience may "get" the reference to the Memorex ad, in which Ella's tape-recorded voice shattered glass, but is the Burma-Shave rhyme available even to a 1980s audience? The signs inhabited the sides of two-lane roads in the 1930s, when the speed limit was 35 or 40 mph. They disappeared in the 1960s, with the advent of superhighways and the prohibition of billboards. One of their originators, Allan G. Odell, did not die, however, until 21 January 1994, at ninety. His favorite jingle does find a resonance in *Comedy of Errors:*

> Within this vale
> of toil and sin,
> your head grows bald,
> but not your chin.
> Burma-Shave.

The topicality of the production traps it in a too-specific time and place. The pizza-delivery man wears a Mets cap. Where are they now? The drummer rushes off for "the dinner show at El Morocco." The Abbess's word "drugs" evokes a "Just say no!" from three suddenly appearing talking heads. And so on—the juggling veins of rhyming nitwits.

Some good moments do come through. Karia Burns doubles Luce and the Duke with rotund gusto. Pinch (Avner Eisenberg) is a Punch sans Judy, with a head and four skillful arms, two of which double as feet. This is adroitness at the service of dramatic values, however farcical. Antipholus S. and Luciana (Paul Magid and Sophie Haden) conduct a good parody balcony scene. The line "What light through yonder window breaks?" had been interpolated earlier. Alec Willows doubles as Angelo and the Second Merchant: he "actually bisects himself," as John Simon says (1987, 91), the Goldsmith in gold, including hair, effeminate and ingratiating, the Merchant on the other side of the same body, in black, including hair, with tatoos, leather, and thuggish menace. Willows is superb as he makes the instant transition simply by turning to face his alter ego. Each is the other's shadow, and the "doubling" captures the psychological element of the script that is not really reached for elsewhere in the production.

Robert Brustein offers this telling commentary on the production: "About the only thing I learned . . . is that even minor Shakespeare must be acted. [The production seems like] another of those well-intentioned civic efforts to prove to school kids that Shakespeare can be painless. . . . [T]his *Comedy of Errors* is essentially a yuppie phenomenon.

It skirts the surface of experience, offering amusement without involvement, laughter without discovery, technique without depth. . . . I found myself longing for even the most conventionalized presentation of this play" (1987, 28). The "in-group" jokes, for example, could be seen as patronizing, but the audience in the televised version, seems to accept being patronized in return for the self-congratulatory process of "getting" the jokes.

It may be that "straight" television is trapped in the zeitgeist of its emergence—modernism, with its insistence on artistic unity, thematic consistency, and chronological preciseness. An occasional adventure into the surreal—MTV—may simply prove the rule. The BBC version does seem to be a victim of its medium. Not only did major problems occur during the taping, as Susan Willis chronicles (1991, 260–91), but the "realistic" medium apparently called for the same actors as the Antipholi (Michael Kitchen) and the Dromios (Roger Daltrey). As Willis explains, "television is a more intimate, less forgiving medium than the stage; the willing suspension of disbelief is less readily granted" (267). One might amend—if granted at all. Furthermore, if *The Comedy of Errors* "is a less than coherent play [and] is a mixture of unreconciled opposites" (Lusardi 1985, 7), its contact with the normative tendencies of television may result in some reconciliation, but also, and crucially in the single instance we have, can erase much of the interest that (possible) incoherences and oppositions raise.

The issue of the play's genre is resolved by the nature of our laughter. The script exemplifies the Bergsonian criteria whereby an interrupted sequence elicits our laughter. We laugh, for example, when the expectation of a bag of gold is replaced by a rope's end, one of the many examples here of the way the play interferes with the sequences that the characters have set in motion, sequences interrupted by the sudden appearance of the wrong Dromio or Antipholus. If we laugh just at the circumstances—the juxtaposition of gold versus hemp—we are experiencing farce. If our laughter goes beyond that to incorporate the bewilderment of a character, say that of Dromio of Ephesus ("I am in adversity"), then we are responding to comedy. Our laughter can be cruel or sympathetic, and, of course, its nature can vary within the experience of a single production. Whatever its source, it occurs within the conceptual space created by the difference between a character's expectation and what actually happens—when a Dromio, for example, is sent off on a mission and returns to report to the wrong Antipholus. Our amusement at the end of the play can emerge from generic premises: "The fundamental human emotions on which *The Comedy of Errors* can base its claim to be a comedy rather than a farce are the simple and related ones of sorrow at separation and joy in reunion" (Wells 1972, 34). If it is a comedy, we are laughing *with* the characters, who have reenacted our own sorrows and joys.

The BBC production is not funny, except for the business that Charles Gray invents for his Duke. He is called down from his horse by the Abbess's "Renowned Duke!" "Damn! I just climbed up on this thing!" But he has been falling for the Courtezan—"I should get into town more often!"—and is delighted to escort her into the "feast." He thus challenges the rigidity of the class system established in the master (and mistress)/servant structure so firmly in place in the script. His performance is a good example of *platea* challenging *locus,* making use of what Weimann calls "the extra-dramatic 'aside'" (1991, 410). In this case, Gray uses an actor's "authority" to undercut an "authority figure."

But having the same actors in the leads does not allow for "interference of series," as Bergson calls it (1900, 137). We are not amused by the "mistakes" of the townspeople or the twins since they are not *making* mistakes. As Mel Gussow says of the Karamazov Brothers' version, "the Dromio's are instantly distinguishable . . . One would have to be a fool to confuse them—and that fact should say something about the other characters on stage" (1987, 24). They—including the twins, of course—simply refuse to come to obvious conclusions, and that refusal generates the variations on a theme that are the plot. In the BBC production the twins respond seriously to their dilemmas—it is a problem play, not a situational comedy. The distinction is partly a matter of style, partly a question of having a live audience or a laugh track. Even fourth-wall comedy, like *All in the Family* was televised before a live audience. Part of the problem is that the genre decided upon—within television's admittedly narrow range—dictates that the actors are "real," their dilemmas are "real," and that none of this is funny. Television tends to create psychological problems for its characters, as Dessen argues (1986), but one wonders how Jane Howell would have directed this script. Her metadramatic approach, vividly successful with *II Henry VI* might have allowed for separate Antipholi and Dromios, and thus for the kinds of disjunctions that evoke laughter. She might even have built in some version of a laugh track that commented on its own convention—by being silent at moments, for example, and having one of the characters look at the camera as if to ask where the laugh was.

If Egeon's long disquisition at the outset is accompanied by precisely coordinated mime and mixed consort, his speech comes across as having been planned in advance, as opposed to having been rehearsed toward the effect of spontaneity. James Cellan-Jones's approach might work onstage, even if it trivializes Egeon's plight. The stage can absorb the commedia dell'arte conventions easily enough, but on television this opening creates the frictions with the medium that he is at pains to avoid elsewhere. The "ultimate effect of the mime was to distract rather than to support" (Warren 1984, 339). Furthermore, as J. C. Trewin suggests, "Such a piece as the *Errors* is all the better for rising from a basically grave situation" (1978, 47). Here, Egeon's story is drained of a specific gravity that is to be erased by other serious issues at the end.

If the play is not meant to be funny, then the BBC version is very good. Willis suggests that "Approaching the play as comedy meant taking the situation more seriously than simply laughing at the dilemmas. The issues of identity raised by the confusion of twins seemed frightening and even dangerous in the experience of the characters, not just the stuff that chuckles are made on" (1991, 260). One could argue that such a view takes the play too literally and gives the audience no space for response. One might also ask why the seriousness of Egeon's narrative and his present circumstances is undercut at the outset. But this is a *television* audience, which, instead of completing production, as in Aristotle's Final Cause, expects the production to be complete in and of itself.

The production occurs in a sunlit town with a map of the eastern Mediterranean on the pavement. We see a real map just before the transition to color, and again at the very end. The cartography cues the *precision* of things in Ephesus. This emphasis is undercut by the frequent references to a fortune-teller and her crystal ball, but the latter suggest that Ephesus has not yet learned how to measure the future, and that that determination will occur within the unity of our experience of the drama. A Daliesque perspective, seen through one of the arches of the marketplace reinforces Antipholus S.'s belief that he has stepped into his own bad dream. The interior suggests the opulence of upper-class Pompeii, but it is not too busy for television's shallow field of depth. Cellan-Jones permits activity *behind* his speaking characters, however, thus upstaging their lines. Willis tells us that some segments had to be retained simply because time did not permit reshooting (1991, 283–90).

Daltrey gives his Dromio of Syracuse "a small edge of dignity" over the "engaging vacuity" of the Ephesian (Roberts 1984, 4). In fact, Daltrey shows that Dromio of Syracuse is by far the more intelligent of the two, and that Dromio of Ephesus may have become retarded because of the continual beatings he receives from his master. Certainly, the servile crouch of the Ephesian Dromio suggests a constant anxiety, in contrast to the confident smile of his Syracusian brother. Kitchen distinguishes between his Antipholi, making the Ephesian harsher and more sexist: "hot tempered and prone to violence, a response the servant anticipates"

(Willis 1991, 275). The actors try to avoid the problem that Peter Holland isolates in responding to a recent RSC production, in which Des Barrit and Graham Turner doubled the roles: "One of the great pleasures for the audience watching *Errors* is that we know the answer. . . . What we do find, though is that the over-weening confidence with which we begin . . . is shaken in the course of the play. . . . [W]hen both Dromios are played by the same actor the audience's ability to be confused, a confusion that, I am suggesting, the play wants us to undergo, is simply evaded, evaded because the audience comes to follow actor, not role, Graham Turner, not Dromio. . . . The histor[ies] of the actor[s are] replaced by the history of the [single] performance" (1992, 176).

The BBC production, aware of this problem, deals with it in several ways. Cellan-Jones invents "a mirror sequence in the market for the Dromios, so that when Dromio of Syracuse discovers the frame has no mirror in it and that the other self he saw was no reflection, he begins 2.2 full of confusion" (Willis 1991, 267). He has seen Dromio E. also trying on a hat, and he wants to explain what he has seen to Antipholus S., but he is not given a chance. Jeanne A. Roberts notices that "at one moment, Antipholus actually saw 'himself' entering the Porpentine and shrugged his vision off. Such apparitions nicely crystallized the question in the audience's mind—why does Antipholus so resist the very obvious explanation for which he has so long been searching? Openly acknowledging his strange oblivion served to point up the irrational blindness of the psyche in search of itself" (1984, 4). If the subject and the object of the search are the same, one cannot really see the other. And, unintentionally, Antipholus becomes the viewer of television: neither can suspend his disbelief and accept something beyond the givens of a naturalistic medium, whether Ephesus or tube. Antipholus S. closes his eyes and squeezes his nose at this point, attributing his double to a long and confusing day. The production, then, "enhanced . . . credibility . . . without the loss of potential for confrontation entailed in stage doubling" (Roberts, 4) and "made . . . the confusion over identity more realistic" (Pearce 1984, 114). But is credibility the criterion? Or is the need for credibility forced upon the production and its audience by the medium?

In spite of the issues that the production failed to resolve, it achieved some fine moments. The wooing scene, cued by the consort we had heard earlier behind Egeon, is excellent. Luciana's quiet plea for her sister contextualizes Antipholus S.'s awe ("Are you a god? Would you create me new?"), even as she wonders at the lyric voice suddenly coming from her blunt brother-in-law. His thesis of divinity makes some sense of his experience for him, as does a similar attribution by Ferdinand in *The Tempest.* Dromio S. gets the speech about times turning "back an hour" (4.2)—often cut—and makes a mysterious and mystifying moment of it. Warren notices that Adriana's (Suzanne Bertish) "scene with Wendy Hiller's formidable battleax of an Abbess made the brilliant point that strife between mother- and daughter-in-law began instinctively, before the two of them were even aware of the relationship" (1984, 340). And it may be that this sober rendition permits comedy, as Wells describes it—"sorrow at separation, joy in reunion" (1972, 34)—to emerge movingly at the end. We have not been allowed to laugh. Perhaps we can smile as what has been clear to us becomes at last clear to the characters, who have been so implicated in their dilemmas that we have had to respond to them as, if not serious, at least as not funny.

This version, for Roger Warren, "made for a refreshing change from the extraneous gags and music numbers which usually load down productions of the play" (1984, 340). "The Pinch scene and the finale," he says, "were the least hectic I have seen. Everyone spoke very slowly to Antipholus of Ephesus, as to a child, when they thought him mad" (339-40). The Pinch was tall and dignified and did not reappear, singed and smoldering, as he does in the RSC version. Antipholus E. is angry, not insane, and the approach here helps underscore the irrelevance of this exorcism and the phoniness of exorcism generally as viewed by the Elizabethan establishment, which did not want freelancers crowding onto the deity-contacting network. "The power to perform an exorcism is the power to control the supernatural" (Neely 1994). An exorcism overdone, as in most productions of *Errors,* misses the point, which is that exorcism itself is unnecessary. Here *locus,* properly understood, is very much at the service of established authority. That it is a punishment of Antipholus of E., who is himself a scapegoat for the debts and transgressions of others in the play, is true, but he is not possessed by any literal evil spirit. The "exorcism" is often a metaphor for spiritual change, or "individuation," as in *A Midsummer Night's Dream,* for example, but in Shakespeare it must be seen as fraudulent as a specific practice. Shakespeare's application in *Errors undercuts* any belief that the supernatural is actually interfering with identities or relationships. It takes no exaggeration in performance to make the point that exorcism is an unauthentic ceremony, dangerous from an official standpoint to its practitioners. The example of *Twelfth Night*—the response of Toby and Maria to Malvolio after Olivia sends them to look after him, and the scene between Feste/Sir Tophas—makes the point clearly. No matter what is said, Malvolio is a victim of a plot perpetrated by human beings, and of his own narcissism.

The RSC version was taped on a rainy night in Stratford in the spring of 1976 and shown on television on the Arts and Entertainment Channel in 1990. It incorporates the fact of theater, beginning with an audience plunging through puddles toward the Memorial Theatre; shows a "No Cameras" sign (smiling at the television cameras that would be present and at Antipholus S.'s taking a picture of Luciana during the performance); scans the audience many times during the production; and follows them at the end out into soggy Warwickshire. The original production was directed by Trevor Nunn and redirected for television by Philip Casson.

If BBC "over-integrated" through the use of two actors for four roles, the RSC suffers like the Karamazov version from disintegration—in this instance from the imposition of music on drama. Roger Warren points at a crucial problem in this production, assuming that it tries to "emphasiz[e] Shakespeare's distinctive humanizing of his rather inhuman Plautine models" (1977, 177). The problem is that "the director's routines did not help [Roger Rees's Antipholus of Syracuse] develop . . . into a complete characterization" (176). This is particularly true of his solo after falling in love with Luciana: "This can't be me . . . do I exist?" It is badly sung and it stops the action cold. The same routines force Francesca Annis's Luciana and Judi Dench's Adriana "suddenly to switch off their performances of the text itself and concentrate on singing" (176), as in their long duet, "A man is master of his liberty." The protracted song-and-dance number based on "hair" and "baldness" (2.2.70–119) erases the wonderful moment when Judi Dench appears on her balcony and peremptorily commands Antipholus S. to her. J. C. Trewin calls "Dench's jealous Adriana, her glance like a laser beam . . . the best in recollection" (1978, 292)—and that is a lot of recollection!

But things get shallowed-out to the premises of musical comedy, which seldom involves depth of characterization or overcomplexity of plot. In musical comedy, what "plot" there is is a framework for the songs, as in *Anything Goes,* where what everyone knows will be the briefest of incarcerations is a pretext for Cole Porter's plaintive "All Through the Night." "I don't need you or anybody. I got it figured out for myself," says Billy Bigelow before singing "If I Loved You," in *Carousel.* While *Oklahoma!* does include Jud and his "Lonely Room," the issue explored is: Will Laurie go with Curley to the box supper?

Furthermore, the musical depended on singing, not acting, or on great dancing when the voice (Astaire's or Kelly's, for example) is not itself outstanding. The great age of musicals, started earlier on Broadway, of course, than in Hollywood, but was simultaneous from, say 1932 and *The Gay Divorcee* through the 1950s, as Hollywood did its own musicals—its *Broadway Melodies, Big Broadcasts, Goldwyn Follies, Singin' in the Rain,* and *American in Paris*—as well as film versions of *Kiss Me, Kate* and *Guys and Dolls.* Film musicals have disappeared and stage musicals are rare except for Webberizations, revivals like *No, No, Nannette* and *Carousel* or conflations like *Crazy for You.* This was as true in the late 70s as it is today, so that not only are the songs in the RSC *Errors* showstoppers in a negative sense, the genre is already out-of-date by some twenty years.

It follows that the musical format exacerbates the problems inherent in any recorded stage production. It will be at least as trapped in its moment and its conventions as a film or television version, so that it is likely to become at least as much of a record of zeitgeist for us as a production of the script. *Platea* itself, then, detached from *locus,* may become the focal point of our response, as, in several ways, are the musical interventions in the RSC *Errors.* That will happen with recorded versions of past productions, as it must with plays placed exclusively in modern contexts, where we respond to the contextualization but are robbed of any sense of the script's contact with its *locus.* The givens of its inherent " 'glass of fashion,' " as Weimann says, "far from showing 'her own' already-given image, c[an] be quite distorted by a whole set of socially, spatially, and verbally encoded forms of theatricality" (1991, 410), like, in the case of the RSC *Errors,* the musical comedy itself. One irony inherent in the RSC version is that *The Boys from Syracuse* had appeared almost forty years before—in 1938—with songs by Rodgers and Hart like "Falling in Love With Love," "Sing for Your Supper," and "This Can't Be Love." That was probably not as good a score as their *Babes in Arms* the previous year, but the show was done with singers and dancers, and its songs were certainly better than those devised by the RSC (as they no doubt would agree). One point is that if you want to go to a musical, you go to a musical.

In *Errors* all things lead to situations in which *we* know why the characters are confused—until, as Holland suggests above, we become confused ourselves. The game requires speedy play, which the musical interludes deny. Furthermore, although Nunn's "numbers appeared to derive from the text itself, they in fact had the effect of superimposing one medium on another" (Warren 1977, 176). "These interpolations," Warren says, "may have been good for the general morale of the company but they did not seem to me to help the performance of its individual members in any way." The four male actors are not "sharply detailed individuals, reacting to each other and to their situations." What we get is the situation and the blurring of character distinction in the precisely apportioned musical numbers that, for example, each Dromio is given. The songs are "utterly pointless," says J. Fuzier (1978, 75). The one possible exception is the ensemble number in which Antipholus S. sings his puzzlement as he wanders through the myriad greetings he receives (4.2.1 ff.). Here the music coincides with the thrust of the action, which deepens into Antipholus S.'s nightmare. The Pinch "Satan come forth" sequence (4.4), however, just goes on and on. The music is particularly unfortunate for the otherwise excellent Dromios, each a red-headed ragamuffin. Nikolas Grace is a pop-eyed mimic of his Ephesian master. He shows how much his master controls whatever "individuality" he might otherwise have found for himself. Michael Williams (Dromio S.) is a canny operator. The distinction is again a reflection of how each master has dealt with his servant. Mike Gwillym (Antipholus E.) is wonderfully active and inventive in his explanation to the Duke at the end, as is Dench, who runs through her speech in a mind-boggling but comprehensible double time. Richard Griffiths as the hapless Officer, handcuffed to a chair and to Antipholus E. as the latter yanks him hither and yon, and Paul Brook, fat, effeminate, and prone to faint, as the Goldsmith are also splendid. The performances are not enhanced by the imposition of music on situational comedy and excellent actors.

"The best way with *Errors*," says J. C. Trewin, "is to play it lightly, not to batter at the clowning, and to undervalue that sudden lyrical blossoming for Luciana and Antipholus of Syracuse in the third act. . . . However [*Errors*] is done, it has to be brief" (1978, 49, 47). By these criteria the BBC version, which comes in at an hour and fifty minutes, is the best of the three we have. As yet, however, this relatively under-performed script retains its latency, awaiting the imagination that can translate it and its stageworthiness to the magnetic medium of television tape. But the possibilities inherent in its location might make it a candidate for bright realization in the light-sensitive medium of film as well. This, then, should be considered a prolegomenon rather than a coup de grâce.

# V

# Branagh's *Much Ado:*
# Art *and* Popular Culture?

"We *use* [the plays]," says Terry Hawkes, "in order to generate meaning. In the twentieth century, Shakespeare's plays have become one of the central agencies through which our culture performs this operation. That is what they do, that is how they work, and that is what they are for. Shakespeare doesn't mean: *we* mean *by* Shakespeare" (1992, 233. Hawkes's emphasis).

To contextualize the ways we mean by Shakespeare, we might ask— can a filmed version of a Shakespeare play also be "popular"? Must it reflect what Jack Jorgens calls "the anti-intellectual tone of [Zeffirelli's] films" (1977, 88)? Or, as Glyn Maxwell claims, can "popularity genuinely . . . be a mark of artistic achievement" (1993, 18)? Must filmed Shakespeare be "postmodern"—eschewing formerly agreed-upon conventions like "thematic unity," and striving to elicit contradictory responses from its audience? If that is the goal a contemporary director should pursue, Branagh's *Henry V* seems to have been more challenging than his *Much Ado.* But is he constrained to present a disturbingly different rendition of the script, to break new ground in our understanding of what the script is and how it works as it confronts a medium that can move into postmodernist modes (as television, it would seem, cannot, except perhaps in MTV)?

The questions are particularly important when we confront the genre of *comedy.* Is comedy being deployed to support materialistic premises and a *Father Knows Best* authority, as I have argued of *Prospero's Books* (1993b, 163–76)? Or, are the scripts being interrogated so that *locus,* what is presented and represented, becomes something new—and perhaps strange—as *platea,* who is doing the presenting and representing, impacts the ostensible givens of a script. I would suggest that the feminist emphasis on gender analysis is now often part of the *locus,* indeed that it is almost an essential component of a script's ability to do more than present a "standard-received" interpretation in the mid-1990s. The feminist element of *platea*—one aspect of the current culture that is very different from the contexts of the script when it was written—is particularly important if the comedy is to avoid the convenient closure of conventional marriage to which some feminist critics object. The aspect of *platea* likely to interfere with the scrutiny of the script that a focus on gender relationships can encourage is "popular culture." What is being done that is *new* in productions of what we used to call "the Festive Comedies"? What is merely being repackaged?

Recent productions of the comedies suggest that gender criticism is making a difference in how directors and actors view the characters and their relationships. A glimpse at some examples will suggest precisely what Branagh's film of *Much Ado* did *not* do—that is, challenge received opinion. A look at Christine Edzard's film of *As You Like It* will suggest that, while it was not well received, it had the great virtue of doing something new and exciting with the inherited script. Kenneth Branagh's *Much Ado* was indeed a hit with those who also critique the Hollywood film. But the question remains: Should Shakespeare be the generator of meanings in our culture or merely the ratifier of what we think we already know about life, love, and, for that matter, Shakespeare? Is Branagh's *Much Ado* a beneficiary of the tendency that Terrence Rafferty describes: "Hollywood filmmaking has . . . effectively worn down our expectations—has forced us to accept, as a condition of enjoying movies at all, a thin, reductive conception of human behavior" (1994, 109).

When we go to a play, we participate in the fictions, willingly suspending our disbelief, and accepting, for example, that the other characters onstage accept Rosalind as Ganymede. We thus experience, imaginatively and psychically, Orlando's emergence from stereotype and toward a more complete sense of himself and of Ganymede-Rosalind as two androgynous beings who must accept the anima or animus—the contra-sexual minority in each—in order to grow. At the same time, however, we *are* aware of cross-dressing, whether of a boy actor playing a woman playing a boy, as on Shakespeare's stage, or of a woman playing a boy, as in most contemporary productions. In other words, we are aware, as Brecht would have us be aware, that the fiction is a fiction, even if we *do* identify with the dilemma that a character describes to us, if not with the Viola who yields herself to Time's skill in unknotting her problems. Our response is complicated because Shakespeare balances two contradictory versions of drama—the "negative capability"—and forces us to negotiate constantly between the two.

At the end of *As You Like It*, for example, Rosalind appears as boy actor ("if I *were* a woman") offering a hint of homoerotic response *and* a fictional heterosexual promise to the male spectators, embodying the androgyny of the play from which she steps, still wearing a wedding dress, but suggesting that the inner marriage cannot be consummated because she is, after all, a boy. If, as has been speculated, this is the play that was presented to Elizabeth on the eve of Essex's execution in February 1601, then the Epilogue may point at Elizabeth, a virgin queen, whose unconsummated reign is coming to an end. The historicists' research extends the range of Shakespeare's allusiveness without necessarily reducing the resonance of the plays to merely Elizabethan or Jacobean contexts. At the end of Richard Monette's *Twelfth Night* at the Stratford Festival in 1994, Lucy Peacock's Viola came out for her curtain calls in her wedding dress, thereby extending one of the play's final prospects *beyond* the play itself. This moment, while it represented a dramatization of the convention of curtain call, restored gender relationships from the problematized cross-dressing Orsino recognizes to a conventional gender relationship.

In Martin Andrucki's excellent *As You Like It* at Bates College in November 1993, Jaques (Christian Gaylord) was played *as* gay. The only instant when this characterization was obvious was when Jaques put his arms around Ganymede on "I prithee, pretty youth, let me be better acquainted with you." This approach made Jaques's "Seven Ages" speech more than a listing of stereotypes. Since Jaques was alienated from the heterosexual world, all he could do was make it stultifyingly conventional and sneer at it. This subtext lent a rare power to what is otherwise a sequence of clichés, which the play, bursting with androgynous energy, challenges and refutes. At the end, Jaques vigorously rejected "dancing measures." His potential partner, Ganymede had become a woman! Jaques's exclusion from the final festivities and his recognition of his "otherness" nicely balanced the "happy ending." It was happy for some. This Jaques had not merely developed his version of melancholy out of a perverse unwillingness to "see . . . pastime." His stance was a defense against a world in which he could participate only at the edges, as an envious satirist. Andrucki's conception provided the role with a subtext that made Jaques not just a character but a devastating commentator on "comic endings."

Many years ago at The Theater at Monmouth, Malvolio exited at the end of the "Madhouse Scene" (4.2) to a few chords of "O, Mistress Mine" played on a lute. Immediately Sebastian entered, giving himself a reality check: "This is the air; that is the glorious sun." This magnificent transition showed us Shakespeare's intention. Malvolio remains in darkness, Sebastian has stepped into the light of Malvolio's dream.

Olivia has seized the day with a vengeance and is "roaming" with her "true love."

A spritely production by Tina Packard's Shakespeare & Company in April of 1993 at Waldoboro, Maine went even further with the "consciousness/shadow" approach to Malvolio, whose sybaritic daydreams of daybeds become Sebastian's waking experience, by doubling the roles. The process was made easier by the actors' introducing themselves at the outset to an audience of mostly high-school students, while announcing that some would play more than one role, and interspersing the opening sequences of the play (where, as seems to be usual practice these days, Viola's shipwreck preceded Orsino's ennui). Tom Jaeger was an excellent Malvolio in a severe, dark steward's robe, with a wonderfully forced smile, a hilarious savoring of the word "fellow," and a splendid array of obscene gestures for Toby, once Malvolio believed that he had achieved a tangible fantasy (3.4.84 ff.) Sebastian's smile was more natural, of course, and the character wore a loose shirt, cream-colored trousers, and boots, at once costumed like Cesario and free of Malvolio's restrictive formality. Sebastian was what "lies under" Malvolio. The latter had indeed "read" Olivia correctly, even if only in the direction of his own gratification.

The "law of reentry" had to be violated, of course, but the production had introduced itself *as* a play, and the very narrow stage of the Waldo Theater had encouraged a downstage acting style that incorporated the audience, as when Viola asked, "I pray you, tell me if this be the lady of the house," and a high-school student told her. An inner curtain closed in front of Malvolio at the end of 4.2 to facilitate Sebastian's almost instant entrance. Olivia's "fetch Malvolio hither" at the end was to Sebastian. Once Malvolio exited with his angry threat of revenge, Sebastian could reenter to stand with Olivia.

Except for their costumes, Sebastian and Cesario didn't really resemble each other. Sebastian was about six inches taller than she. Our laughter at the end was partly at the characters onstage who could have been deceived into mistaking the one for the other. That, of course, was also an intention of this production—that the awareness of the fictional characters could catch up to ours and thus erase the play at the moment that the fiction on which so much of the plot has been based is also erased. The production, more than any *Twelfth Night* I have ever seen, pointed to Fabian's question (delivered here by Feste) about whether "sportful malice" should "rather pluck on laughter than revenge." Certainly this production emphasized the festive closure, particularly since Malvolio's alter ego was there, Olivia's smiling Count Sebastian.

In a recent review, Peter Holland quotes Molly Mahood's *Bit Parts in Shakespeare:* "the audience must have grieved, as we still do at the death of the child Mamillius . . . Today's spectators cannot, however, share the alleviation of grief which would have come to the play's first audience when they realized that the same boy actor returned to play Perdita." Holland goes on to say that "The consolation derived from a straightforward theatrical event, the doubling, an event untranslatable into the fictional space of the imaginative reading, is none the less real for that. Mahood places the experience of the pain and of its alleviation into the context of performance, of the full and dense and complex experience of seeing the play" (1993a, 4).

The possibilities for creative doubling are many, of course, particularly in the comedies, where the convention will be the more easily accepted for the fact of identical twins and mistaken identity. In the Mark Rylance 1994 *As You Like It* in New York, for example, stereotypes were challenged on both sides of the gender see-saw: "David Dossey, solid as Charles the wrestler early on, is very funny doubling in drag as Audrey the country wench" (Hampton 1994, C-16). I did not see that one, nor did I see the all-male Cheek by Jowl *As You Like It* praised by Richard Corliss: "What should have been mimimalist camp . . . becomes a . . . meditation on mistaken sexual appetites and identity" (1994, 84). The production, says Corliss, "revives one's faith in the theater as a place to weave magic" (84).

The magic, it would seem, is that the spectators are forced to suspend their belief in the absoluteness of their own sexual identities. This all-male world does not return to convention. It cannot. It may be trapped in its own deceptions, but it does not return stereotypic assumptions to us. We must leave the theater pondering ourselves and, if we are to achieve comic endings, we must leave the theater accepting our own potentiality to be, at least psychically, the other gender, and so decipher within ourselves, insofar as we can, the coding of that mysterious other gender. Is it any easier if the other with whom we hope to achieve significance is of the same gender? I doubt it. But these questions push at the circumference of our experience of the comedy. The questions raised by productions like Rylance's and Declan Donnellen's may respond effectively to Kathleen McLuskie's well-known argument that feminism "has little to hope for from a drama in which marriage is a happy ending and the subordination if not the oppression of most women is a necessary element for the continuation of peace and love and quiet life" (1988, 73) and her suggestion that "the text contains possibilities for subverting these [misogynist] meanings and the potential for restructuring them in feminist terms" (1985, 92). I am assuming that feminism at its best tells us something about how the genders relate and, as Jung would have it, relate to each other within the individual psyche.

*Twelfth Night* has become, perhaps suddenly, perhaps gradually, one of the most frequently performed of Shakespeare's plays on stage. The issues of cross-dressing, androgyny, gender identity, and relationships between and within gender boundaries are all reasons for the play's newfound popularity, along with the reasons that have been there all along, as we continually rediscover Shakespeare in our own images.

James Hoban's May 1994 version for the American Renaissance Theatre in Portland was interesting for several reasons, including Hoban's austere Malvolio, in the school of Eric Porter, Michael Denison, and Bernard Breeslaw, that is, a person who really is doing his job well, even if he does have more hope for his future than, for example, Mr. Stevens of *Remains of the Day*. What tipped the balance against this Malvolio with this audience was that Maria despised him. This Maria, roguishly portrayed by Asch Gregory, carried her scenes with dynamism, wonderful use of eyes and facial expression and—how to be politically correct?—she was not beauty-disadvantaged. These performances alone made the production very enjoyable.

Hoban daringly cast women as Orsino and Sebastian. The latter, Michelle Mills, did well with her role, imitating a boy actor and looking enough like Viola that we could suspend our disbelief about the characters who confused them. Christine Millett's Orsino, however, needed to be much more of a duke. A Captain Hook outfit, sans hook, might have made Orsino a comic figure. As it was, while Millet was "masculine," with hair pulled back in a ponytail, severe bone structure, deep voice, and commanding presence, she was still a woman. That Viola disguised as Cesario was obviously a woman is, of course, a point that post-Restoration productions invariably make. But in this instance we could not suspend our disbelief for even a moment and accept Viola's love for Orsino. Being the Duke, he can coerce his locality into collusion with his game. If the love story works, it is because Viola sees through this self-deception to find someone that even Orsino does not know is there. That possibility was not available here, since this Orsino was much more than "not what he seemed," being a woman, or because Orsino never pretended to be a man. Olivia's infatuation worked better—it was woman to woman—and because Stacy Epps's very tentative Olivia was also very vulnerable. Her mourning for her brother was really a protective facade placed before her fear of that "real world" in which her sexuality would be an issue. Part of her attraction to Cesario was that he seemed so nonthreatening to her. At any rate, Hoban did raise the gender issue interestingly, but he introduced problems at the heart of the script's interrogation of relationships, as opposed to illuminating it.

One of the interesting approaches to the script that Hoban introduced—something I have not seen before—was a conflation of the roles of Curio and Valentine. Here, Cesario replaced Valentine as Orsino's chief ambassador and shoulder-to-cry-on. Valentine's "If the Duke continue these favors towards you, Cesario, you are like to be much advanced" was full of animosity. When Cesario asked, "Is he inconstant, sir, in his favors?" Valentine's response was a cynical, "No, believe me." Clearly, he considered himself a victim of Orsino's skittishness. This interpretation provided some conflict where none seems to be available in the script and suggested how isolated Cesario was in the court of Duke Orsino. New Historicists and old could cite plenty of examples of new favorites who were not greeted kindly by other courtiers. Indeed, Shakespeare's *Richard II* and Marlowe's *Edward II* make this conflict central to their plays. Here, Valentine's resentment nicely foreshadowed the plot against Malvolio.

The Summer, 1994, RSC version was extravagantly praised: "Ian Judge's new version . . . produces the kind of collective ecstasy you find only in great comedy. . . . Judge orders his stage beautifully [and] has . . . uncovered the essential Englishness that lies at the heart of [the play]' (Billington 1994d). It was, said Jack Tinker, "as marvelous and memorable a *Twelfth Night* as you are likely to see in many a year" (1994a). But it was hardly a successful exploration of the script. A tiny Viola (Emma Fletcher) dictated a lilliputianization of the Sebastian-Olivia sequences. Judge unnecessarily showed us *Sebastian* coming ashore, confusing those who know the script into thinking that Viola's shipwreck scene was on "re-run" as an elfin Sebastian struggled up the strand. An overly powerful Malvolio (Des Barrit), "a bloated parody of the Droeshout engraving of Shakespeare" (Jackson 1994a), so dominated the Toby-Andrew portions of the play that they were not at all amusing. Barrit "hijacks the whole production," wrote Charles Spencer (1994a). "The acting is bland, placid and ordinary . . . It is a feat to get such actors to give such dull performances," said John Peter (1994e). "Webberish" songs (Jackson 1994a) were meant as entertainment for *us*, the outer audience and so failed in their crucial function as compensatory advice to the inner players—" 'Come Away, Death' is not recognizably a parody of Orsino's self-indulgence, but seems part of the prevailing vaguely 'emotional' atmosphere," Jackson suggested (1994a). The "awful saccharine plaintiveness of the music suggests that this Fool must have been the Johnny Mathis of the Jacobean world," said Paul Taylor (1994b). Richard Edmonds "missed the poignancy of the old tunes" (1994), but with a staff of musicians and composers on hand the old tunes are gone forever from RSC productions. The "Soupy, palm-court-style music" (Peter 1994e), or "Muzak" (Macaulay 1994c) approach denied us Feste's satire and our chance to observe its effect or *lack* of effect on the characters who are the subjects of the satire and suggested that the director had no idea what those songs are doing in the script.

At times the set moved—a staircase trucking in for the nightscene with Toby, Andrew, and Feste, for example—and cut out the final lines of the scene just ending, an effort at filmic dissolves that interfered with language and meaning. The setting was Stratford—Guild Hall and Chapel Street—somewhat like the Model Village at Burton-on-the-Water, wonderfully rendered but unlivable as a stage setting because it simply called attention to itself. For *Merry Wives,* a play literally placed in Elizabethan England—yes. The BBC version created a precise contrast between Olivia's elegant, dark-paneled, Holbein-haunted manor house and Orsino's bright and opulent palace, with a mixed consort playing constantly, and thus was able to explore the differences between two upper-class lifestyles. Peter Hall says, "unless what's on stage looks like the language, I simply don't believe it" (quoted in Ralph Berry 1989, 73), but the RSC version could not go beyond what was an end-in-itself. The set may have reminded some of the *contrast* between remote and removed Illyria and the tourist-trap town where the RSC finds itself. The pace itself suggested the helter-skelter of "an Olde England" (Macaulay 1994c) that boasts a very busy McDonald's, as opposed to the more languorous style of an Illyria frozen in self-deceiving posturing.

Judge did create one superb moment and one very confusing one. After telling her "sister's" history, Cesario stood before Orsino and received a chaste kiss. Cesario then went off on an embassy to Olivia. Orsino backed away in puzzlement: Who am I? What am I becoming? His reaction to the boy Cesario and to himself suggested that Orsino was questioning the easy assumptions about love and sexuality that had put him into the stasis that Feste's song defines. This was an Orsino beginning to surrender to the comic spirit that Meredith's Willoughby Patterne resists and the moment was at once amusing, moving, and convincing. But with the exception of that moment, "the romantic and sexual aspects drift discreetly off into the shade" (de Jongh 1994b). The confusion came at the end. Malvolio exited by suggesting that he had something more to say after "on the whole pack of you!" but had restrained himself. This was powerfully suggestive and it might have worked out had we not seen Antonio, Andrew, and Toby running upstage right to left at the end. Had they been thrown out? If so, what of Toby's marriage to Maria? Then Feste appeared at a door down left, lugging his backpack, being tossed out by Maria. Had Malvolio thrown him out, we would have seen his revenge, indeed intuited in a gestalt the Puritan Revolution that would exile all entertainers. But why Maria? All of this was too much to sort out from a mere series of mimes. Feste's final song, then, was that of the outcast in the rain. It was the only effective song of the night. Festivity was over—and no one would sing at the weddings.

This was another RSC "packaging" of the plays as "tourist-friendly" (Taylor 1994b) vehicles. The RSC is seldom to be taken seriously these days, but cannot be ignored, since its productions *are* "Shakespeare" to those who can afford the tickets. It seems to be a middle-aged crowd at its youngest, so, while the present is dull and unimaginative, the future is very much in doubt.

Christine Edzard's *As You Like It,* produced in Great Britain by Sands Films, and released in October 1992, deserves to be distributed in the U.S. It will serve as a useful contrast to the two available versions, the Paul Czinner film of 1936, with Olivier and Elisabeth Bergner, and the BBC-TV version of 1978, with Helen Mirren. The film was reviewed by Samuel Crowl (1993a). I recommend that review for its sensitive discussion of aspects not treated here.

My problem with the film is in its placement of "Arden" on the concrete of a construction site with Thames bridges in the background. True, such places, in London, Los Angeles, and New York, are the homes of the homeless. We grasp the director's "metaphor." In Mark Rylance's version, Arden was "a junkyard piled with debris, including car tires and a discarded kitchen sink" (Hampton 1994, C-16). But though such treatments come out firmly in the antipastoral tradition, one must ask whether the *script* will support that interpretation.

Television, as we know, demands "realism." But film and stage do not. When we go to a play, we agree to suspend our disbelief. Film's special effects, even something as simple as a dissolve between scenes or a wipe in which winter becomes spring, suspend our disbelief for us. "Pastoral," however, is difficult for any medium, partly because it is not a *genre* but a convention, which ends with Milton (some would argue with Tennyson or Lewis Carroll). Vestiges may survive in the austere New England of Robert Frost or in the sentimentalized forest outside Nottingham, where Robin Hood makes merry and woos Marian, but "pastoral" is a mode, not a location. This fact was brought home by the BBC-TV version of *As You Like It,* which was taped near Glamis Castle,

Scotland, but which was "far too earthbound, too specific for the elusive joys of the Forest of Arden" (Bulman 1988, 174), where "the relentlessly realistic setting . . . [t]he sunny hills of Scotland . . . threw a curious shadow over the play's magical aspects" (Joseph O'Connor 1988, 251), where "seldom have natural settings been used to less effect" (Jorgens 1988, 251). Television may be a "realistic" medium, but it rarely goes on location. Alan Kimbrough suggests that "the location shooting . . . forces some disquieting contradictions between what the characters say and what we see" (1988, 252).

If this is true when the play is produced in a natural environment, it is certainly *more* true when Arden becomes a concrete expanse bordered by a fence built of railway ties. A "literal" location evokes an inevitable literalness in the viewer. References to trees and a forest are indeed disquieting, as are, in a modern dress production, allusions to curtal axes and doublet-and-hose, as is a statement that a sword has been dropped when what clanks to the pavement is palpably a .45-caliber pistol. The site offers no sense of "magic," or of the possibilities of "transformation." It is a dead end, not a transitional "wandering wood" that leads finally back into a conventionally structured society, perhaps a better place after the experience among rocks and stones and trees.

When a play as "conventional" as this is shifted to a contemporary locale, the language either has to be edited and/or altered or it makes no sense. It may be that a "culture" in which song lyrics are merely part of an overall cacophony has lost its grasp on signification. Charles's evocation of Robin Hood and the Golden Age is cut in the Edzard production. But to bring a solitary lost sheep on with Corin is simply to invite unkind laughter. That pastoral is an *un*-Christian mode (see Theocritus) is a factor that Shakespeare exploits in having Duke Senior respond in parallel phrases to Orlando's lines about "better days . . . where bells have knoll'd to church." Those lines are cut in the Edzard script, but Touchstone's "Then thou art damn'd" to Corin is left in. The colloquy is effective here, perhaps the only aspect of Touchstone that works, but it works largely because Roger Hammond's Corin observes Empson's dictum that "the proper tone [of pastoral] is one of humility" (1960, 13). Touchstone is not drawn clearly enough here to "forestall . . . the cynicism with which an audience might greet a play in which his sort of realism has been ignored" (Barber 1959, 232). This is to make a larger point—that the contrasting levels of "love" in the script are not effectively delineated in the film.

Any production of *As You Like It* faces the difficulty that Barber isolates when he says that the play "makes fun of [the] assumptions [of

Lodge's *Rosalynde*]" (1959, 227). What are those assumptions? We probably have little trouble "assuming" the assumptions of "Pyramus and Thisbe," because we witness an inversion of "the willing suspension of disbelief" in the Mechanicals' fear that their play will be taken literally. What we are likely to miss as we laugh at the play-within is its insistence on a grim, red-clawed determinism that makes it bootless to ask mother why she framed lions. The assumptions of pastoral romance are difficult to retrieve unless a production somehow educates us to them. The wealth of notes in a typical RSC program cannot substitute for what the play must do. Nor is it possible for pastoral and its undercutting to be realized on a puddled slab of concrete.

Even if a modern version of the script cannot reconstruct "Arcadia, a pastoral landscape embodied in an ancient and sophisticated literary tradition" (Bevington 1980, 358), this one gives us no sense of a return from a "green world" (see Frye 1957, 181–84) to the world of the court. Crowl says that "surely Northrop Frye and C.L. Barber have taught us that Arden is a metaphor" (1993a, 41). Shakespeare's stage makes its metaphors with a word—"Arden," "Ilyria," "Elsinore." It is infinitely capable of absorbing implied comparisons between unlike things, partly, of course, because our own imaginations participate in constructing the bridges. In a different medium, however, we must for an instant consider the speaker mad who mistakes a bare construction site for a forest. And in this script, we probably want a *contrast* between court and woods. In *As You Like It* one of the primary contrasts is between what Frye calls "the *vegetable* world . . . garden, grove, or park" and "the *mineral* world . . . a city" (1963, 20; Frye's emphasis). Suffice it that the issue of the pastoral mode helps explain why this script, so popular as a stage play, is seldom translated to film or television.

The film has not been well reviewed. Betsy Sherman, for example, says that the "film ends up as damp as the dockside wasteland on which most of it takes place" (1994). Doubling Andrew Tiernan as Orlando and Oliver, she says, "means that in their big confrontation in the first scene, the characters cannot share the screen. Cutting from one to the other dissipates the scene's power" (1994). Russell Jackson says that the "film is a poor representative of the vigour and sense of 'relevance' that modern dress can bring. In the dockside wasteland that stands for Arden the references to trees, streams and deer are allowed to stand and the contemporary social focus is hopelessly vague . . . *As You Like It* is hardly the best vehicle for criticism of present-day Britain, and the suppression of joyousness and sense of recuperation through love makes the choice especially perverse. Paradoxically, this film uses more of the text of its play and captures less of its spirit than other more radically adapted versions of the comedies" (1994c, 101–2). That, of course, is no paradox if we are dealing with *film,* which often is "truest" to Shake-speare in its visualization of what on stage is language.

Edzard's film is not quite that easily dismissed, however. It realizes a splendid moment when Rosalind puts down Jaques, as Crowl notes (1993a, 41). Here, Jaques is not just "the refuser of festivity" (Frye 1957, 218), but one whom festivity rejects. Jaques is not given his final summation of the future of each couple, perhaps because Andrew Tiernan doubles Oliver and Orlando—though that should have been no problem for an inventive camera. Again, however, distinctions are blurred by a huddled, hurriedly-edited finale. Rosalind does not get her epilogue, very effective in the Czinner film, where the camera cuts between Bergner in doublet-and-hose and in wedding dress.

The strength of the film is in Celia Bannerman's splendid Celia, wonderfully able to adapt to life in a construction shack, and Emma Croft's fetchingly boyish Ganymede, speaking truths about love that she discovers as she utters them. In an interesting comment on disguise and "twins," she "arrives in Arden wearing an outfit—jeans, hooded sweatshirt, and black stocking cap—that mirrors Orlando's scruffy attire. She "comes to discover her fuller, richer witty self through the liberation provided by her androgynous escape to Arden" (Crowl 1993a, 41). Indeed, here the post World War II tendency towards unisex clothing really works—as abetted by Croft's winsome performance, "an androgynous dreamboat," as Sherman calls her. The film's "gender-bending kinkiness," says Sherman, involves not only Rosalind's disguise as a boy, but that "she tests Orlando's love for her by encouraging him to fall in love with her male alter ego" (1994). Precisely. The point of her performance and disguise is that she forces Orlando to fall in love with *Ganymede,* pressing her would-be lover through a homoerotic phase before the heterosexual consummation we assume will come in marriage. This is a "test," of course, because Orlando must move beyond the gay persona that Ganymede presents *to* the androgynous, but heterosexual, Rosalind, who waits beyond a persona that represents a partial manifestation—at once true and false, as partial manifestations are—of who she is. Croft's performance comments on Olivia's infatuation with Cesario, a psychic stand-in for Sebastian. "Nature to her bias drew in that," says Sebastian, although, "on the surface," Olivia's falling in love with Cesario seems ludicrous. Thus, in Edzard's film, the "conventional" ending emerges from a profound subtext that goes much deeper than what we are accustomed to calling "Rosalind's 'education' of Orlando," and involves something much more generative than what Sherman calls "kinkiness." The way in which androgyny becomes *active* here, as opposed to merely a Jungian concept, makes the film remarkably rewarding. Given Croft's abilities, "you *can* play a concept."

Another element that comes through in the production is the *cold*. It helps to watch the tape in Maine in February, of course, but the wind whistled up the Thames during the filming, and thus one aspect of the metaphoric Arden was fully realized.

The popular reception of the Branagh *Much Ado* suggests the need for a revitalization of central idea—after the remarkably useful critiques provided by Northrop Frye and C. L. Barber some three decades ago. That reexamination of script in performance along the lines of feminist/gender/identity criticism did not occur in Branagh's *Much Ado*. Should it have—or is it sufficient that a pleasant and conventional rendering be given the public, in hopes that the production will make money and, possibly, engender whatever "interest in Shakespeare" may amount to? That interest probably helps us as teachers, and perhaps we should be unfeignedly thankful.

While Branagh can be seen by some as " 'bold,' " says Michael Skovmand, he is "anti-avantgarde; in fact, far less adventurous than Olivier, with his mix of the cinematic and the deliberately theatrical. But like Laurence Olivier, Branagh is essentially an *adapter*, not an *auteur*. . . . Branagh rummages about in the cinematic special effects supermarket of Hollywood. But Branagh's productions are not governed by a primarily *audiovisual* concept. His approach is that of finding the right cinematic *equivalent* of a primarily *theatrical* concept" (1994, 9; Skovmand's emphasis). "We did not want [the audience of *Much Ado*] to feel they were in some cultural church," says Branagh (quoted in Skovmand, 8), voicing the stereotypic contrast to "popular Shakespeare," what John Collick calls "imperial Shakespeare" (1989, 54). The option between these extremes, of course, is an exploration of the script that doesn't just "tell the story" but that probes the story for its depth and nuances without destroying its accessibility. The option is *interpretation*, a searching of *locus* by a *platea* that incorporates much more than the authority of how "popular culture" may be defined at any given moment.

Leslie Felperin Sharman casts a cold, cultural-materialist eye on the film:

> Branagh's worst problem is imaginative banality—his camera tricks and casting coups are faddish rather than fresh. . . . [He]

has a knack for aping the fashionable mannerisms of today's hot auteurs, like long tracking and stedicam shots *a la* Scorsese and Altman. As in *Henry V,* he makes nodding references to Welles with theatrical lighting, but he has none of the above's sense of timing or elan. . . . [The film] sets itself up as a showcase for its stars, then preens itself smugly while they display their skills at performing Elizabethan prose and blank verse. The camera trots along behind them, weaves among the crowd and wanders around the fountain while they recite their lines, like an awed audience member allowed on the stage but keeping a respectful distance. . . . When Beatrice storms at Benedick after Hero has been denounced, the camera hovers shyly beyond the portal, like a child eavesdropping on its parents rowing. It's as if Branagh were afraid to interrupt Thompson's beautifully polished 'big scene,' demonstrating the kind of respect one expects from a fellow actor and husband, but too obeisant for a good director. . . . Overall, this is an earnest but fundamentally conservative film. With the current debate about the centrality of Shakespeare in the National Curriculum, one wonders if it might even be described as Conservative in the political sense. . . . [The film] neatly falls into line with a tradition of cinematic bardology that unquestioningly upholds Shakespeare as the ultimate emblem of high culture and good taste. . . . [N]o messy attempt is made to subvert, historicize, culturally appropriate or even update the holy writ. . . . Branagh, financially independent yet toeing the Party's aesthetic line, looks much less like the radical revisionist he first purported to be. (1993, 28)

Branagh, then, takes us into the chapel and, simultaneously, into that cultural church that he hoped to avoid in his tour.

Three responses by Ellen Edgerton, Anne Barton, and Samuel Crowl, are more positive. Edgerton says that Branagh's approach is "cinematic, populist, and in some ways intriguingly traditional," that the film is "actually funny" and that the Company's "attitude towards Shakespearean performance . . . [is that it is] to be a revealing, exuberant, refreshing, hands-on experience, not a museum piece" (1994, 43). "Despite its flaws . . . it is perhaps the most satisfying attempt yet at bringing Shakespearean comedy to the screen." It "is an accomplished work of adaptation that clearly confirms Branagh's resourceful perception of the seemingly conflicting demands of cinematic Shakespeare," and it insures that Shakespearean films "will get a chance to be produced and appreciated" (44). The latter assertion, if true, will prove a great benefit to students and to those of us who work in the growing field of Shakespeare-in-performance. But notice the limits that Edgerton sets. The successful candidate is "traditional" (albeit "intriguingly" so) and is an "adaptation." The "conflicting demands" are resolved well within the authority of *locus*.

Barton finds the production "Imaginative, intelligent, and brilliantly filmed" and "likely to make many people—especially the young— understand that Shakespeare can be vital, interesting, moving, and fun" (13). She praises Thompson's Beatrice: "vibrant, spirited, and quick, but manifestly with hidden depths. [Her] beautifully nuanced performance projects in abundance that quality essential to so many of Shakespeare's comedy heroines: a transparent goodness that never becomes sentimental or smug" (12). Barton notes that Branagh transfers "one of the most resolutely urban of Shakespeare's comedies" to a "boldly rural and open-air" setting, thus "obliterati[ng] . . . Shakespeare's carefully structured social hierarchy" (11). "For the fast-moving verbal bawdry of the original, [Branagh] substitutes an equally fast-moving but far simpler visual sexuality. The result, more accessible to modern audiences, is arguably better suited to cinema as a form" (1993, 11).

Russell Jackson disagrees with Barton on this point, stressing Branagh's effort "to accommodate verbal wit [and] the fantasy of happy articulacy. . . . The longer, subtler transactions of the scenes between Beatrice and Benedick may seem less assimilable to the idioms of popular film, but it should be remembered that the range might include (in comedies alone) Woody Allen's best New York films. Few of the cinema versions of Shakespearian comedy so far made have had to deal with this kind of material at the centre of the play" (1994c, 118). Barton is right, though. The film *must* privilege setting over language. Still, the lines can be funny. Woody Allen's "You're so beautiful that I can hardly keep my eyes on the meter," as he and Mariel Hemingway ride a taxi over the Triborough Bridge, is as funny as Leonato's "Signior Benedick, no; for you were then a child," although that line, nicely set up, was cut from the film for some incomprehensible reason. It may be that Allen's films put as much stress on verbal wit as Shakespeare does in the *locus* of *Much Ado*. Branagh's *platea*, however, as conditioned by the demands of color film, is decidedly, perhaps even relentlessly, a visual experience.

Barton notes another exchange that the film makes. Leonard's Claudio is "much less sophisticated and knowing" in this simpler context "than Shakespeare's character." The film Claudio "is meant to be a very young man, barely past adolescence . . . emotionally vulnerable and unsure," a function of "romantic idealism" (11). Suggesting that the film asks us to "forgive" Claudio, Barton finds that "Branagh displaces what is genuinely disturbing in Shakespeare's comedy onto Dogberry" (12). Since, apparently, Branagh did not believe that Dogberry could be funny, he had "to transform Michael Keaton, as Dogberry, into a menacing, sadistic, and profoundly unamusing thug" (1993, 12).

Branagh's Benedick, Barton says, is "credible, interesting [and] in the chapel scene . . . genuinely moving. But in "trying to play Benedick while also directing the film [he] has bitten off more than he can chew." Barton suggests that Branagh's "refusal to address soliloquy to an audience in the way Shakespeare intended . . . cuts [Benedick] off from us, making Benedick seem like a man suddenly talking to himself because he is in a generalized 'state.' " This, then, "is a disappointingly exterior Benedick" (1993, 13).

Finally, Barton objects to the editing, suggesting that "by abbreviating the dance sequences (especially the interminable one at the end) [Branagh] might have found room for more of Shakespeare's text" (13). She suggests that "Branagh's *Much Ado* is significantly better than his *Henry V*. But he will need to take on and master a good deal more of what is challenging and difficult in Shakespeare, while retaining popular appeal, before that frequently made comparison with Olivier rings true" (1993, 13).

Crowl sees Branagh as making a "daring and successful raid into the lush heart of Zeffirelli and Hollywood country" (1993b. 39). He defends the bucolic setting, suggesting that *Much Ado* is less of a "precursor to the problem plays" (39) and more of a "festive comedy" that insists on a "green world" (40). The "tensions of male bonding, the confusions of wooing, and the commitments of wedding" require, Crowl argues, "the green world's liberating, socially leveling spirit" (40). This is to place the script within the tonality and generic assumptions of *As You Like It*, where, while the woman still has much to learn behind her protective facade, it is the man who must be "educated," until he "can live no longer by" the artificial conventions and stereotypic assumptions that block flesh and blood from contact with itself and with another.

Thompson "is the film's radiant, sentient center. Intelligence and wit illuminate every moment of her exquisite performance. . . . The economy with which she allows us to understand her previous romantic entanglement with Benedick . . . is film acting at its most subtle. . . . She also can capture just the right inflection for Shakespeare's muscular prose and deliver it in a rhythm properly suited to the camera (her more busy and noisy husband could take lessons from her on that point)" (Crowl 1993b, 39). Crowl's approach permits him to suggest that "Branagh's Benedick is transformed by her passion [in the chapel scene]. Earlier we had seen his nervous, cocky jester melt into the explosive comic romantic in the gulling scene. Now both of these excessive portraits are clipped, darkened, and matured as we watch his mind absorb and understand the issue that spurs Beatrice's fury. For the first time in the film, Branagh allows his Benedick to look directly into the camera's eye as he honestly confronts his emotional commitment to Beatrice" (40).

Crowl agrees with Barton that Claudio is "an insecure boy whose face is flushed by confusion and embarrassment as quickly as it is colored by the blush of romance," but Crowl is more harsh in his judgment of this Claudio (rightly, I believe). "Claudio's petulant tantrum . . . reestablish[es] what he smugly believes to be the primacy of the male order" (1993b, 40).

Crowl is "fascinated by the lunacy of Keaton's performance . . . a series of Curly and Moe eye-gouging and head-bashing routines from the Three Stooges . . . a cartoon Dogberry like the villains in the recent 'Superman' and 'Batman' films . . . [in] sharp contrast with the crisp, clean playing . . . by the rest of the cast" (40). Nevertheless, Crowl argues that this "*Much Ado* is a marriage, resembling that of Beatrice and Benedick, between Shakespeare and Hollywood. [It is] the most successful translation we have of a Shakespearean comedy onto film and converts all our potential critical sounds of woe into 'Hey nonny, nonny'" (1993b, 40).

The film finds an equally enthusiastic reception in the U.S. popular press, anxious as ever to suggest that "popular culture" is not an oxymoron. Branagh proves them right. The *fact* of the film helps counter those who would eliminate Shakespeare from the curriculum as a canonical, dead, white, European author, in favor of trendy ephemera. An irony, however, is that the Edzard film advances our understanding of how "concept" can be "played," indeed makes Emma Croft the resonant center of a new experience of the script. Can the same be said of *Much Ado*, with the wonderful Emma Thompson clearly "centered"?

In a letter distributed by Samuel Goldwyn, Branagh says that the film attempts to deliver such a

> straightforward, absolute clarity of story line and character that it will enable a modern audience to respond to Shakespeare on film in the same way they respond to any other movie [and] to do so without losing the poetry . . . We decided to approach the film as if no one had ever seen the play before, to present the story as if it were all taking place in the here and now . . . We con-

sciously avoided setting this version in a specific time, but, instead, went for a look and an atmosphere that worked within itself, where clothes, props, architecture, language and customs all belong to the same timeless world. This imaginary world could exist anywhere along a continuum from 1700–1900—a time distant enough to allow the language to work without the clash of period anachronisms, and for a certain 'fairy tale' quality to emerge. (n.d., 1-2).

That the script does not contain much poetry to lose probably makes the translation to a modern medium a bit easier than with scripts more embedded in blank verse. Branagh, however, says much the same thing as Zeffirelli did about his *Hamlet:*

> Nobody knows anything about *Hamlet*, about Shakespeare. They don't know anything. They go there in a dark room and they see something on the screen and they want to know what the story is, and you have to tell them the story from scratch, from the beginning, in a convincing way, using a language that will make clear and accessible every single word of William Shakespeare. (Zeffirelli, 1990)

A script by Shakespeare, one might argue, cannot be "any other movie." For one thing, any other movie would not be discussed in the context of other recent renderings of Shakespeare's comedies, or tragedies. But Zeffirelli and Branagh are unabashedly placing their films in the Hollywood, as opposed to the "art-house," category. *Locus*, then, must be a function of perceptions of the audience that include an antipathy to "cathedral" Shakespeare and an absolute ignorance of so-called "cultural heritage." Whether the latter is a good thing or just a convenient construct of ruling ideologies is another question. It is not attributed by Zeffirelli to anyone who goes to the cinema.

Branagh, of course, takes an unfamiliar script—unlikely to have been taught in high school—and necessarily gives it a local habitation. He has the advantage of not having to project his version of the script against that of an Olivier, Hall, or Brook, or any other *film*maker. His choice of "timelessness" can result, onstage, in a muddy nontime, but here coalesces around the setting and the camera's exploration of it, which many of the film's critics note at length. "'*Much Ado*,'" says Jay Carr, "inhabits a sunny, generous world of psychic daylight, and Branagh finds a heady physical correlative for it in the Tuscan villa where the film unfolds" (1993b). The setting, says Richard Corliss, alluding to the painting-in-progress that the camera picks up at the opening, "brings sunny vitality to an old canvas" (1993, 65). "Mr. Branagh's stroke of brilliance," says Caryn James, "is to turn the camera into an active storyteller. It leads viewers visually through the intricate plot, emphasizes characters' reactions, situates Shakespeare's language in a sunlit world too elaborate to be created onstage" (1993, H-17). "Branagh," says Richard Alleva, "has made *Much Ado* into *A Midsummer Day's Dream*, and the lovers behave as they do because they are dazzled by sunlight, exhilarated and exhausted by heat, blinded by the physical beauty of flowers and flesh, and always at least a little pixilated from being young, alive, and accepted" (1993). The advantage of a set "as removed from the ordinary world in spirit as it is in place" is, says Vincent Canby, that "Branagh sidesteps the whole notion of reality" and thus is able to make "a movie that is triumphantly romantic, comic, and most surprisingly of all, emotionally alive" (1993, C-16).

The film receives largely favorable reviews in the popular press, based on Beatrice and Benedick, Branagh's technique, and the setting. The interpretations of Dogberry and Don John, however, prove unpopular. The general sense is that, as Desson Howe suggests, "Branagh has, once again, blown away the forbidding academic dust and found a funny retro-essence for the '90s" (1993, 53), that is, whatever a "retro-essence" may be.

Jay Carr says that the script provides "the feeling of unhurried inevitability about the coming together of Beatrice and Benedick". The *film* picks up "an added resonance arising from our knowledge that the couple we see pretending to disdain each other is in real life already a couple . . . we wait for the action to catch up to a place we know they already inhabit." Branagh "exposes Benedick's insecurities. Thompson doesn't have to protest so much because she's in touch with Beatrice's security" (1993b). These interpretations can be reversed, of course. In the 1990 Royal Shakespeare Company version at Stratford-on-Avon, Roger Allam played a cocksure Benedick and Susan Fleetwood a vulnerable Beatrice teetering on the edge of spinsterhood. The contrast in valid interpretations suggests the remarkable range of options that this and other scripts offer to the actors. For Bob Polunsky, Branagh is a "somewhat dull-witted Benedick" (1993), and certainly Branagh plays a "developmental" Benedick, as he had played his Henry V—a useful approach for a young actor. For Alleva, Branagh goes too far when he hears that Beatrice loves him: "Trying to establish Benedick's foolishness, Branagh screeches, caws like a crow, does unfunny bits with collapsing chairs. This excess backfires because it keeps us from seeing Benedick's potential, the compassion and true wit that will be released once he becomes a worthy lover" (1993, 24).

"The great thing about their romance," Carr says, talking of the

Branagh-Thompson version, "is that neither has to sell the other; they just have to find a way to let it happen, and it happens in their eyes in closeup—as it should in a film" (1993b). In an interview, Branagh suggests that his relationship with Thompson is a subtext for their Beatrice and Benedick: "it was not difficult for us to use a certain kind of ongoing irony that we use with each other" (Gilbert 1993, B-37). Paul Clark compares Branagh and Thompson with Alfred Lunt and Lynn Fontanne, Douglas Fairbanks and Mary Pickford, and Burton and Taylor and finds it surprising that the current couple's "contagious vibrancy hasn't spread throughout the supporting troupe" (1993). James places Beatrice's line, "I know you of old" in context: "she says this quietly, as if the camera were letting us in on a secret. The line becomes a comment on her unhealed scars from other Benedick skirmishes." Those old wounds explain the Mona Lisa strangeness of her smile as she hears of Benedick's approach. "And after Beatrice and Benedick decide, separately, to love each other," James says, "Mr. Branagh presents overlapping images . . . Benedick is splashing in a fountain; Beatrice is riding on a swing" (1993). They celebrate, separately for the moment, their emotional coming together. For Corliss, Branagh is "charming," Thompson "tart and intense" in a film that "plays like a prime episode of *Cheers*" (1993, 65).

Most of the critics admire Branagh's direction. "His camera is remarkably agile," says Joanna Connors. "It darts in and out of the intimate little groups, or rises high above them, so that watching the movie is like being a spy in the house of love." Connors applauds the film's discovery of physical equivalents for the words: it is "as much about sun and heat as it is about language" (1993). John Lewis, however, believes that Branagh "remains a stage director at heart." In a positive review, Lewis finds the film too "motivated by . . . 'concept'"—too full of devices "more at home on the stage than on the screen," and too reminiscent of "the heyday of Romantic opera" (1993). Jeff Simon, while praising Thompson and Branagh, suggests "that the comedies, in particular, died long ago as theater and were reborn as literature . . . They belong to books, not to the coarser, quicker, more sanguine realm where men and women discourse, emote and cavort. No matter how much inspiration and anxiety Branagh brings to the cause, [he] can't singlehandedly subvert the linguistic and cultural drift of the age" (1993). Simon comes close to making Harry Berger's case in *Imaginary Auditions* (1989) and does seem to suggest that if comedy cannot be accommodated to our "culture," it will exist only in *unread* books. "All the suntanned flesh, American heartthrobs, Italian villas and prancing cameras in the world can't take the . . . subplot of 'Much Ado' out of

culture's attic" (1993). David Sterritt indicts Branagh for "stop[ping]
the story in its tracks for silly slapstick and dreary music interludes"
(1993). Michael MacCambridge, however, says that "this is perhaps the
most accessible Shakespeare film ever. . . . This is Shakespeare for the
'90s: stripped-down verbosity, pumped-up sexuality, keenly rendered
drama" (1993). Sterritt, however, warns against comparing Branagh
with Orson Welles: "Welles was a towering artist with prodigious in-
sights and a steady stream of innovative ideas, while Branagh is just a
talented young man with more energy than inspiration" (1993). Canby
says that "There are times when one longs for [Branagh] to pull back
the camera, not only from the alternating close-ups that turn some of
the Beatrice-and-Benedick exchanges into tennis matches, but also from
the generalized dither of the big scenes" (1993, C–16).

The opening, particularly, proves an attention-getter. "[I]f ever a
film was 'opened' it is this one," says Glyn Maxwell (1993, 18). "Behind the credits," says Canby, "through what appears to be a zoom
lens, Don Pedro and his soldiers are seen as they approach on horseback,
jouncing rhythmically up and down in their saddles in slow motion, as
if anticipating sexual unions still to be negotiated" (1993, C–16). "The
camera cuts back and forth between slo-mo close-ups of the horses' flar-
ing nostrils and women's breasts bouncing up and down beneath their
linen blouses" (Mazer 1993, 14). The "screen is literally awash with
bathing males and females bursting with anticipation. It's an exhilarat-
ing endocrine rush of a sequence," says Steve Starger (1993). The cross-
cutting between the women bathing and the men galloping creates, says
Maribeth Brewster, an "effect that is unabashedly giddy" (1993). Russell
Smith suggests that the "opening sequence is thrillingly mounted, so
much so that the audience is virtually swept off its feet and the rest is
easy" (1993, 5–C). The "screen explodes in a torrent of images . . . and
shimmers with glowing young faces," says Jack Kroll, "voluptuous
limbs, breakneck horsemen. Branagh is showing us that Shakespeare is
vibrant bodies not just talking heads . . . This may be the most sheerly
delightful of all Shakespearean movies" (1993, 60).

The film is associated, of course, with other versions of the moving
image, even with recent trends in the making and packaging of films
themselves, comparisons that Branagh consciously invites with his films
(cf. Pursell 1992 on filmic allusions in Branagh's *Henry V*). *The Hartford Advocate* suggests that the "very villa where the real-life Mona Lisa
lived . . . can't be underestimated: in Branagh's scheme it is vital, a
wonderland midway between Man and Nature, a Garden of Eden in the
here-and-now—a veritable Shakespearean theme park" ("Much Ado
about Dinosaurs," 1993). In an acute analysis of the films of summer

1993, Jay Carr says that "The lastingly significant thing about 'Jurassic Park' is that it finally dissolved the increasingly tenuous line between movies and theme parks" (1993a, B-4). If *The Advocate* is right, Branagh was there first! "Branagh stages the scenes as if he were choreographing something for Fred and Ginger," says Bill Morrison (1993), invoking those black and white theme parks that had music by Gershwin, Berlin, and Porter piped in. As Frank Gukringa points out, however, Branagh's "fresh, bawdy, giddy movie" requires "no one [from] Industrial Light and Magic" (1993).

Starger suggests that "The volleys of merry barbs between Benedick and Beatrice are really elevated variations of the domestic bickering carried on by Ralph and Alice Kramden or Lucy and Desi" (1993). Jack Garner harkens back to the 1950s in suggesting that Branagh's is "the most eclectic cast assembled since the young Marlon Brando joined John Gielgud and Edmund O'Brien for *Julius Caesar*" (1993, 1-C). Marty Meltz, squarely in the film-rating business, gives *Much Ado* three and a half stars out of four, the same constellation awarded *Poetic Justice, In the Line of Fire, Free Willy,* and *Jurassic Park.* The Branagh film, Meltz says "is a delight for discriminating viewers and will not offend the Shakespearean purist. [It is] still a high brow's high but, at that, the most ebullient offbeat film in recent times" (1993a and 1993b). One problem inherent in such praise, however, is that a film *of* its time quickly becomes dated. Against that danger, however, Carr sees Branagh's film as an exception to the tendency of current cinema: movies "no longer feed our dreams. They feed off our nightmares. . . . American movies mostly validate an unhealthy status quo by keeping us anxious, fearful, stupid, apart, constricting our vision to narrowed options based on consumption and aggressiveness" (1993, B-4).

The highest praise goes to Thompson. She "conveys a depth of feeling," says Cary Mazer, "that holds the whole movie together" (1993, 15). Her performance is "definitive," says Alleva. The moment when she demands that Benedick "Kill Claudio" "is," says Alleva, "as great a piece of acting as I ever hope to see on stage or screen" (1993, 23). "[S]he moves through the film like an especially desirable, unstoppable life force," says Vincent Canby (1993, C-16). "Thompson *glows* in a part that seems to anticipate her savage intelligence by several centuries," says *The Hartford Advocate* ("Much Ado," 1993; reviewer's emphasis). Thompson's Beatrice is "a wonder," says Robert W. Butler, "a liberated woman who has seen the posturing and preening of men and has, rather ruefully, decided she'll just have to do without" (1993, G-4). She is "best," says Lawrence Toppman, "when doing what only a great actress can: suddenly changing the mood from buffoonery to pathos and

back again with a few lines" (1993, 3-F). Joan Juliet Buck may over-
state the case a bit when she says, "As played by Emma Thompson,
Beatrice is sharp but also wounded; the unbeatable British actress takes
you where no one else has ever gone before, under the skin of a character in a Shakespeare comedy" (1993, 125).

Mazer notes the inevitable relegation of main plot to the "stars," Beatrice and Benedick, a reduction even more marked in film, where language must be subordinated to image. "Leonard's quivering lower lip
[is that of] an earnest young man so puppyishly in love with Hero that
he's willing to believe the worst about her because he can never really
believe his own good fortune." Kate Beckinsale's Hero, meanwhile, is
perhaps even more of a stereotype in the film than the script makes of
her: "she remains a mostly silent presence throughout the film, an object of transaction in the marital commodities exchange, whose value is
subject to rapid market fluctuations" (1993, 15).

Keaton's Dogberry is "funny all right," says Connors, "but funny-
strange, not funny ha-ha. . . . Three Stooges style slapstick—doesn't
cut it" (1993). Lewis suggests that Dogberry's abuse of his prisoners involves "bruises and blood that give a disturbingly violent coloration to
a scene that would normally focus on Shakespearean wordplay" (1993).
Harper Barnes says that "The only faintly jarring note comes from the
pig-sty Irish accent of Michael Keaton" (1993). "Keaton mugs and
growls through stained teeth and bizarre business, including a Monty
Python trot on an invisible horse," says Steve Starger, "but his Dogberry doesn't quite measure up to the rest of the cast" (1993). "It is
never clear what he's saying," says Joe DeChick (1993), and that in a
role where the character reverses the meanings of his words, so that we
*must* hear what he is saying. "Keaton," says Hal Hinson, "manages to
be unfunny, incomprehensible and out of period" (1993, B-7), though
Hinson does not suggest what period Keaton is not in. "Keaton plays
Dogberry as an utter lunatic," says Clark, "a keen approach bungled in
execution" (1993). "Keaton's appearances stop the film in its tracks,"
says MacCambridge, "altering the tone of nimble, piercing humor to
one of flat obliviousness" (1993). "The thankfully brief portrayal," says
Jack Garner, of Keaton's Dogberry, "seems to have been excerpted from
a Monty Python parody" (1993, 4-C). "Mr. Keaton makes for an annoy-
ing distraction," says Russell Smith (1993, 5-C), or, says Canby, "a
kind of surreal diversion" (1993, C-16). "Michael Keaton makes a
wretched impression as Dogberry," says Sterritt, "and Branagh shares
the blame for clumsy mishandling of what should be the film's most
amusing moments" (1993). It may be that the treatment of the subplot
is meant to suggest that the antics of the aristos have infantilized the

constabulary—as suggested by Dogberry and Verges's imaginary horses. The coming to town of the horsemen has the same effect on the lower officers as the coming of a circus has on the little boys of Mark Twain's Hannibal. Certainly, the cruelty of Claudio and his yuppie friends is reflected in Dogberry's treatment of his prisoners. This is, however, the "concept" of which Lewis complains. It must be *thought about* as opposed to experienced through images. "Keaton's Dogberry," says Maxwell, arguing against Branagh's concept, "is founded upon apparent dementia, whereas the constable's comedy surely functions as the coincidence of sane responsibility far outweighing intelligence and language" (1993). To be fair, R. C. Smith finds Keaton "marvelous" (1993) and Lawrence Toppman says, "Dogberry as Beatlejuice [sic]—who'd have thought *that* would work so well!" (1993, 3-F). A second viewing and discussion with a couple of expert informants suggest to me that Keaton is usually quite audible. The problem, then, would stem from the inability of the film audience to catch on to the game of Dogberry's *reversal* of meanings—"plaintiffs" for "defendants," for example. Such linguistic duplicity is a stage convention that may be impossible to translate to the more literal and certainly less linguistic medium of film.

Reeves's Don John finds no admirers. "Reeves speaks as if English were a language foreign to him, and this version probably is," says Starger (1993). "Only Keanu Reeves, scowling as the duke's villainous half brother, remains inextricably bound to the 20th century," says Toppman (1993, 3-F). "Reeves plays the oily Don John with oily body and oily zest," says Bill Morrison (1993), not intending to praise him. "Reeves, unconvincing as ever in a period role, is the sole clinker in an otherwise splendid cast," says David Baron (1993). To be fair, however, Reeves is "given little more to do than glower and scowl," says Carr, which "he does, like a rock-opera Heathcliff" (1993b).

The editing drew little comment, a fact that reflects the relative obscurity of this script and perhaps that reviewers are recognizing at last that a film relies very little on words even if the script emphasizes a "merry war" of them. Branagh cuts Leonato's "for you were then a child," which is to set up a punch line and not deliver it. Also gone is Benedick's "This looks not like a nuptial." We are meant to absorb the full impact of a yuppie's destruction of a wedding, and it is shockingly done. But without Benedick's wry understatement to release some nervous energy from us, we are unlikely to accept the happy ending. The nasty Claudio has convinced us of the *reality* of the moral space he inhabits. Furthermore, as Maxwell notes, "our actually witnessing the coupling of Margaret and Borachio—which Shakespeare only reports— is no help to [Leonard's] Claudio [who] has not only to convince us that he would sooner believe Don John (whom he distrusts in all else) than Hero (whom he adores) and that he could practically mistake Imelda Staunton's stocky Margaret for Kate Beckinsale's lissome Hero at such close range, but also that Hero could possibly yield her maidenhead to the obviously soapless cur Borachio" (1993, 18).

A negative review comes from Hal Hinson. "Perhaps Branagh wanted to show how similar Shakespeare's work was to modern comedy of manners. But what he has done instead is demonstrate how, in the wrong hands, even Shakespeare can be trivialized and reduced to chatter." In striving for "maximum accessibility . . . the movie feels insubstantial and uninspired. Branagh doesn't seem to have connected very deeply with his material . . . [Branagh and Thompson's] work together is completely sexless and superficial . . . we had every reason to expect more from Branagh than Shakespeare dumbed down for the masses" (1993, B-7). One does have to agree with the "sexlessness" of Branagh and Thompson. The sexuality in the script should play strongly in a performance in any medium, and one wonders whether that lack is a function of a married couple well beyond the tingling anticipation of courtship.

Another strongly negative review comes from Anthony Lane of *The New Yorker*, who agrees with Sharman's and Hinson's indictment of Branagh's superficiality: "The film glances at [the play's darker threads] but turns away to greet the sun; every frame is telling American audiences to book a trip to Italy" (1993, 97). (Indeed, Bob Fenster says that "Branagh has opened up the play, letting us revel in the sunny climes of lyric Italian hillsides that make you want to move to Italy" [1993, D-11].) "When Beatrice nuzzles a bunch of grapes in the opening scene," says Lane, "we know at once that the movie has settled for comic-book pastoral and won't be running any risks" (99). "The camera . . . comes in close to watch Branagh and Thompson swap gibes, but they seem to forget just how close that is, bugging their eyes and throwing off gestures more suitable to the stage; it's the same blaring, in-your-face rush of excess you get when watching opera on film" (97-98). Lane is not alone in this criticism. Daniel Neman says that "the camera work is uneven. For some reason, Branagh films so much of the time in closeup that it feels uncomfortably as if one is watching a soap opera. On the other hand, every once in a while he breaks free and allows his camera to glide and swoop, drawing his audience into a conversation or a dance" (1993). One surmises that the closeups are dictated by the future of the film as it enters the cassette market. "Beatrice and Benedick," says Lane, "celebrate their deluded love in superimposed slow motion: she's on a swing, he's splashing around the fountain. I tried very hard to convince myself this was a parody . . . but no such luck; the film genuinely shares in the joy it should mock" (98). "Branagh thinks he knows . . . how to make the play come alive, when it fact it was never dead. . . . 'Much Ado About Nothing' has the same empty rumbustiousness that echoed through Zeffirelli's 'Romeo and Juliet'—a grim determination to keep up the good cheer. Rarely has the title rung so true" (99).

Lane is claiming that neither the Branagh nor the Zeffirelli film maintains an ironic distance from its content, that is, that the medium itself makes no comment on the script, but merely tailors the script *to* the medium. To put it another way, Lane suggests that Branagh has created no friction between *locus,* who or what is being represented, and *platea,* who is doing the representing (see Robert Weimann 1991). This is to put Branagh in the category of what Jorgens calls "the anti-intellectual tone" of Zeffirelli's films (1977, 88). That placement may be valid. How disabling it is in each case is another question. Must a work of art contain within it its own deconstructive content? Perhaps, if we accept the distinction that Skovmand makes between "Shakespeare on film and movie Shakespeare . . . i.e., the elite notion of art cinema *vs* the popular notion of the movie show" (1994, 8). In the excellent *Much Ado* that came to New York City in 1985, directed by Terry Hands, the Boy that Benedick had sent to get a book (Amy Chang) kept returning with the book as Benedick (Derek Jacobi) scrambled to find cover in the lawn furniture. This was onstage, of course, but the device did undercut, even mock, Benedick's credulity, even if what he overhears is, in effect, the truth. The Boy's popping up complicated our response, so that we were at once laughing at and laughing with Benedick. Branagh attempts to get that response by wrestling with the deck chair, but the effect flows over, for several critics, into mere slapstick and reinforces the film's projection of "good cheer." That the *scripts* contain an undercutting energy counter to "manifest content" is obvious, but how many of the knotty imponderables of a given script can a filmic interpretation bring to the screen?

The point is that Branagh did not mount any subversive challenge to manifest content. For me Beatrice and Benedick, having tumbled to the twin "Gonzagos" presented to them, never emerged from the tender traps to suggest their ongoing self-hoods, the sharp, satiric tongues that are still part of the characterizations, however newly informed by love and redeployed at the service of a loving war of words. Shakespeare's characters retain a kind of integrity down under what happens to them. We know it is Othello, for example, speaking—"Soft you . . ."—even from the far side of tragedy. But does Branagh give us Beatrice and Benedick from the acquired shores of comedy?

The film does convey sentimentality in its use of music. Emma

Thompson gives an ironic reading of "Sigh no more" at the outset, but when the song is later sung it emerges as a static set piece as the camera roams aimlessly over pool and fountain. More important, the sound-track makes no distinction between the indigenous instruments and voices of Messina, and the invisible orchestra that cues us to the possibility that the fellow with the chiseled sneer is up to no good, or that slithers in with echoes of "None But the Lonely Heart" for Beatrice and Benedick. I longed for some hint that the 1940s soundtrack was intended ironically but found it to be merely a sticky "reinforcement" and therefore a containment of any possibilities below the surface in the acting or in the relationship. But, says Mazer, "If Branagh is being ironic in this, then the joke's on us" (1993, 15).

Just in case anyone is congratulating him or herself on being some-how *part* of the process whereby *Much Ado* comes successfully to the screen, I quote Steve Starger: "Branagh must have seen, in the story's two lovelorn couples, an easy route to deconstructing the accretion of stodgy significance built up around Shakespeare by generations of sniffing English teachers" (1993). Sniffing?

One of the healthy signs of transition from New Criticism to current historicist modes is that a film is viewed as part of an economic, political and cultural process. The film, as Sharman suggests, is seen as "taking sides," or, otherwise, as *un*committed because playing it safe. Although my arguments emerge from "conservative" criteria like clarity in the speaking of the lines and coherence in the overall production, I take the more radical side when it comes to "freshness" and "originality"—the qualities that Bogdanov pretends to bring to his productions, even as he masks their imaginative banality with machine guns and the blatting of helicopters. *Platea* can eradicate *locus*. At the same time, however, *platea* can be so implicated in "popular culture" that *locus* becomes about what we "expect" of Shakespeare. Branagh's *Much Ado* meets expectations, but little more than that. Edzard's *As You Like It*, for all its obvious flaws, *extends* our sense of the script by challenging *locus* and discovering something that we have not seen there before.

The Branagh *Much Ado About Nothing*, like the 1994 RSC *Twelfth Night*, comes off as quite conventional. I suggest that we need no more "conventional" versions of this or any script, however. *Locus* needs to be challenged by *platea*, so that useful frictions can develop between what has been received and what is being perceived. That space becomes the site for our response—for our aesthetic, imaginative, and thoughtful reaction to production. That is final cause, of course, and it accounts for as many variations of psychology of perception as there are creatures sitting at a play. We should be knocked off balance by theater, as Peter Brook says (1987). If we continue to be knocked off balance by productions of Shakespeare's plays, then Shakespeare continues to be a dynamic force in our culture and not merely a set of static objects behind the velvet rope of a museum, part of a past but no longer of the present, of interest to curators and those studying to become museum keepers. In other words, the critique coming from the left side of the political spectrum is the one that keeps the plays "alive." It is sometimes strident, sometimes wrong-headed, often oblivious to the issue of Shakespeare as a writer of *plays,* but it also places Shakespeare, as Arnold Kettle said long ago, in "a changing world," and it gives Shakespeare scope to change, even to grow and prosper, within that world.

# VI

## Sorting Well With Fierceness? History Plays: 1993–94.

An examination of a performed segment of a script—in this case, *Henry V*, can suggest the historical shift that has occurred in the fifty years that have incorporated wars less "popular" than was World War II. If any doubt exists that zeitgeist influences *platea* and in fact can be a large component of *locus*, four versions of Pistol's farewell should prove the point. They are: Robert Newton (Olivier film, 1944), Brian Pringle (BBC-TV, 1980), Paul Brennan (Bogdanov, televised live performance, 1989), and Robert Stevens (Branagh film, 1989). Who is the "historical Pistol"? He is defined by the historical moment into which he emerges.

> Doth Fortune play the huswife with me now?
> News have I that my Nell is dead in the 'spital
> Of malady of France;
> And there my rendezvous is quite cut off.
> Old do I wax, and from my weary limbs
> Honour is cudgell'd. Well, bawd will I turn,
> And something lean to cutpurse of quick hand.
> To England will I steal, and there I'll steal;
> And patches will I get unto these cudgel'd scars
> And swear I got them in the Gallia wars.
> (5.1.85–94)

Pistol, of course, never had whatever honor is to begin with, so it is interesting to hear him mourn its loss. This is an unusual soliloquy by a minor character—Hume's in *I Henry VI* and Helena's in *Dream* are other examples—and, in this case, a farewell word from all of the characters we have seen in the taverns since Henry IV's rueful mention of them at the end of *Richard II*. They are all swallowed up in the huge oblivion of time's passage, leaving neither a mark nor a tuppence behind.

The reference to "Doll" (F1) is emended, following Dr. Johnson, to "Nell" in each performance, but permits students so inclined to pursue the textual question and the intriguing speculation that the soliloquy was originally written for Falstaff and then switched to Pistol without the editing that would make the lines conform to what we know of Pistol (see Walter 1954, xxxviii–xxxix). Falstaff's mourning the loss of "honor"—even if he never had it—would have reminded us of his disquisition in *Henry IV Part 1,* his dislike of Blunt's "grinning honor," of his postmortem victory over Hotspur, and of Henry V's reinvocation of the concept in the pep talk before the Battle of Agincourt. There may be, then, a textual reason why Pistol's sense that he has lost his honor strikes us as strange.

These four Pistols prove two basic things: (1) that no "right" way to present even a soliloquy exists, and (2) that the medium conditions the message. We have here two films, one made before commercial television, a televised stage play, and a straight television production. The more performance material we have available, the more able we are to look at smaller moments in production, to learn about the possibilities inherent in the scripts, and to measure the strengths and limitations of the conceptual spaces within which the productions occur. I suggest that our expectation does condition and to some extent control what can occur on any given medium.

In the Olivier 1944 film, made before commercial television, Robert Newton's piratical Pistol considers tossing the coin that Gower has added to Fluellen's fourpence back at Gower, but pockets it instead. Pistol borrows a word from Prince Hamlet by substituting "strumpet" for "huswife." He says "hospital" for "'spital." He looks meaningfully at his sword as he mentions Nell's "malady of France." He decontextualizes the script by substituting "present" for "Galia." We notice that he wears the Constable's armor, scavenged after Henry V has killed the Constable earlier. That means that the film shows Henry V killing his half-brother, Charles de la Bret, but the film does not intend us to dwell on past history. It is 1944 and another perilous invasion of France is about to begin. The Constable had called his "the best armor in the world," and now Pistol wears it. This is another example of the film's economy, in this case, of its self-referential allusions. Pistol has been beaten—by the hilt of his own sword, which Fluellen has taken from him—but he recovers quickly, makes a quick foray through a barn, emerges with pig and rooster under his arms, and gets an actor's exit to the accompaniment of a Prokofieff-like "Pistol and the Pig." The dissolve takes with it part of the wintry landscape and absorbs it into the Magic Kingdom of the next take.

This is a cheerful, self-possessed, resilient Pistol. We have no fears for him as he roguishly makes his way through life, claiming that he is one of the king's "band of brothers." He, too, "will show his scars,/ And say 'These wounds I had on Crispin's Day.'" Although Olivier's film is hardly the blatant piece of propaganda that some critics have made of it, the treatment of Pistol is not disturbing. He is a character in a farce that contrasts but does not conflict with the more sober argument of history. Certainly the film represents what John Collick calls "imperial Shakespeare," and we should not ignore its ideological assumptions, or those of film and television in any zeitgeist. To historicize the Olivier film, however, we should suggest the other ideology and what it was offering for the viewing pleasure of its audiences. Films of the execution by piano wire of the Stauffenberg plotters against Hitler in July of 1944 were being shown to German troops. It is reported that they put their heads on their knees and refused to watch.

The BBC version of 1980, with Brian Pringle, gives us the soliloquy in close-up and extreme close-up. Pringle savors the word "rendezvous." Pistol is a collector of strange words and phrases. Hotspur had used the word much earlier, and perhaps its reemergence here suggests that Pistol is a parody Hotspur, one who survives by cowardice as Hotspur had drowned in honor. Pistol, however, may have learned the word from Nym, who uses it earlier in *Henry V*, apparently to mean "last resort," as opposed to Hotspur's "a home to fly unto." Pringle takes the cue of "old do I wax" and "weary limbs" as he rises achingly to his feet. He has not been cudgeled but beaten by a heavy leak. He is startled out of his bright idea for self-fashioning by an offstage sound of ceremony, and he disappears, cut off by sudden pomp and circumstance. Obviously, he does not count, is not even necessary to swell a scene. And what can we say of this Pistol? The spareness of the TV studio has given him little context, no world against which to demonstrate his small skills and large deficiencies. The close-up technique shows little more than a soap opera character disappearing. The production scarcely raises the issue of whether a character without honor can mourn its loss.

The problem with the BBC Pistol may be generic. "One of the strengths of television," says Elijah Moshinsky, "is the constant present, which is also a weakness if you are trying to build up a narrative structure. In a theatre, the space stays the same when different actors enter and leave the stage, and so a sense of continuity develops through the fixed relationships between the audience and stage. But on television, it's just a constant present" (quoted in Elsom 1989, 124). This televisual Pistol does not have the past he could have fabricated for us onstage and thus is denied both the heroic future he claims he will fabricate for himself with his scars and the probable future his hands will not be quick enough to evade—the gallows. The wash of the studio behind the immediate action tends to erase the larger imitation of an action, the mimesis which incorporates the actors within it—Henry V and Pistol—and to obviate the ultimate issue of time itself, an issue that Shakespeare's stage consistently framed for its audience, with its heaven, hell, and space where fellows crawled briefly between. In its inability to sustain a narrative line, television reveals its weaknesses as "modernist" medium.

Michael Bogdanov's Pistol, Paul Brennan, is onstage, as his voice and the audience response tell us. He has a letter relating Nell's demise, which he pulls from one of his empty holsters. The production uses paper consistently—Grandpre is writing his description of the English when he tears the paper from his typewriter and admits the futility of his image making. And, of course, Henry makes much of his commissions to Cambridge, Scroop and Grey, and of the smaller of the listings of the dead on either side. This Pistol is troublesome in that he wears the tunic of an impecunious marching band and the camouflaged pants of an infantryman. Pistol has stolen part of a Le Fer's comic opera outfit after he has been forced to cut the Frenchman's throat under the pressure of Henry's order to kill all the prisoners, but the irony does not resonate like Newton's audacious assumption of the Constable's armor.

Bogdanov's eclecticism proves, as usual, that he has not looked at what soldiers really wear in battle, or what they wear as veterans. The elevator-operator uniforms worn by the French are designed, of course, to show that, as Zdenek Stribrny suggests, "Shakespeare lays special stress on the fact that the French lords at Agincourt refuse to lean upon their own people and rely solely on their chivalric bravery. Whereas in the English host gentlemen fight side by side with their yeomen as one compact national army" (1964, 89). Montjoy makes the point ex post facto in requesting permission "To sort our nobles from our common men." This Pistol has been forced to doff his Nazi helmet so that he can absorb a blow from Fluellen's billy club. Brennan's poverty-pinched face and complaining Liverpool accent would have been better served by better costuming. But, then, Bogdanov's gimmicks seldom serve his actors well. They are designed to say, "Look how clever *I* am!" The effort to be timeless, by conflating elements of several times, forces us to unsuspend our disbelief beyond anything that Brecht ever intended. Bogdanov's post-modernist undercutting of early modern scripts tends not to be deconstructive—that is, a searching for the margins of the script and the characters who live along those margins, and thus an exploration of issues obscured by a focus on "establishment" Shakespeare. Bogdanov's approach tends towards an obliteration of meanings, whether early modern or post modern.

Pistol's stealing of a life preserver from the troopship taking him back to England proves his compulsive proclivity for theft and suggests perhaps that he, like Bardolph, will ultimately be hanged for stealing something "of little price." An audience cannot dismiss this Pistol too easily, however. His accent points at the troublesome issue of class in Great Britain, and if it is a *Liverpool* accent, it might have even more specifically disturbing echoes. "Liverpool," says Blake Morrison in a recent *New Yorker* article "is the city associated with the Beatles' song 'Penny Lane': 'All the people that come and go / stop and say hello.' And the great refrain of the industrial North is that, while its people don't enjoy the material benefits of the South, they are warmer, more community-minded, stronger on family values. But in recent years images of mutual trust—the back door always open, neighbors minding each other's business, friends who would give you their last shilling— have given way to burglar alarms, glass-topped back-yard walls, and guard dogs. Neighbourliness has been replaced by Neighbourhood Watch schemes; brotherhood has become the surveillance cameras of Big Brother" (1994, 51). If so, then Shakespeare's Pistol, as delineated by Brennan, uncannily captures a postmodern moment. Morrison's article, of course, is occasioned by the murder in Liverpool, in February 1993, of toddler James Bulger by eleven-year-olds Jon Venables and Bobby Thompson.

In the Branagh film, Henry and Fluellen exchange sentimental tears about their mutual Welshness and go off arm in arm, as Henry gestures Exeter to join them. The camera pans to discover Pistol (Robert Stephens) seated, leaning against a tree. "Does fortune play the huswife with *me* now?" It has done so with Bardolph: "Fortune is Bardolph's foe, and frowns on him." Pistol's own motto has come full circle: "*Si fortuna me tormenta, spero contenta.*" This is a Pistol without hope. He has not been cudgeled, though he says he has, but he is isolated, alone, his mates having been hanged or killed in battle. Nym has been killed while robbing a corpse. And Pistol is "cut off" from any welcome home. Here we get the post-Vietnam veteran who also begged at the end of the lane in Elizabethan England, the soldiers that Norman Rabkin describes "returned home to find their jobs gone, falling to a life of crime in a seamy and impoverished underworld that scarcely remembers the hopes that accompanied the beginning of the adventure" (1977, 293). This Pistol has been given only the context of his dissolute friends within which to establish himself. And he fails even there, if only because his friends die in the commission of crimes or are executed because of their crimes. This Pistol learns nothing, but there is nothing he can learn. He can only sit there as a small, ironic shadow cast against the king and his brotherhood and the heroism that Henry politicly undercuts as soon as the necessary victory has been achieved, and against the sentimentality in which the winners among the winners indulge. This Pistol, like many that we see today in the infested streets of our own cities, is below the reach of even the most effective politics.

Simply the thing he is does not guarantee this Pistol his living. No place and means exist for him. Parolles's failure in *All's Well that Ends Well* validates the male code he has failed to meet. Robert Newton's Pistol goes off to an amusing career, not socially sanctioned, true, but not one that disturbs us. He will be safely housed in the hovels of another part of the city. Stephens' Pistol is the by-product of a national purpose. He is discarded once that purpose is achieved, or abandoned for another crafted emergency, or drafted to die in it. He is not given the bright idea of valorizing his wounds, nor does he get an exit. *He* has no way out, but his resonance remains. The thing *he* is subverts the premises of the war in which he has been involved and of the peace which follows that war. Stephens' Pistol will not deploy his scars in the service of a phony heroism. It may be that his cynicism is too deep for any grasp at rationalization. Branagh's editing places the listing of those killed in the battle *after* Pistol's soliloquy, and so the paucity of the English dead becomes ironic. If Pistol is a synecdoche for others, the list should be longer.

Gower suggests of the generic Pistol that he will "grace himself at his return into London under the form of a soldier. And such fellows are perfect in the great commanders' names, and they will learn you by rote where services were done; at such and such a sconce, at such a breach, at such a convoy; who came off bravely, who was shot, who disgraced, what terms the enemy stood on." And certainly Pistol suggests as much at the end of his brief soliloquy. But Branagh's Pistol is edited down toward a very familiar and more contemporary point of view: "I had seen nothing sacred, and the things that were glorious had no glory and the sacrifices were like the stockyards at Chicago if nothing was done with the meat except to bury it. There were many words that you could not stand to hear and finally only the names of places had dignity. Certain numbers were the same way and certain dates and these with the names of the places were all you could say and have them mean anything. Abstract words such as glory, honor, courage, or hallow were obscene beside the concrete names of villages, the numbers of roads, the names of rivers, the numbers of regiments, and the dates" (Hemingway 1929, 191).

The use of camera in the Branagh sequence is simple. That we get no deep-field shooting here and little, if any, in the film, suggests that the film was designed with the cassette market in mind. As Bernice Kliman says, Branagh's "choices [are] more suggestive of tv than of film" (1989, 1). The restricted field of depth also suggests, however, that events that may seem glorious when viewed from afar are really dirty and sordid when seen more closely, and that, as Stephen Crane showed in *The Red Badge of Courage,* a soldier can see what he can see only from where he stands. For the infantryman, no "big picture" exists.

These four excerpts allow us to make a number of distinctions between and within the media. The stylization of the Olivier film tends toward the theatrical in a way we would not accept in a more recent film, as Branagh's blood, rain, sweat, mud, and mist show us. Olivier tends to watch events from a static camera, suggesting a fixed view of history. Branagh's camera moves, arguing no fixed premises and perhaps even a selective view of history, one inscribed by the winners, and then by all-enveloping time, as the ideological camera runs out of film. As the brief Pistol sequence shows, Olivier's style tends toward the cartoon and seems to be heavily influenced by Disney. Earlier, as Katherine pans westward, we expect her to break into "Some day, my prince will come." We notice, however, how neatly the Branagh translates to television. The smaller screen obviously conditions the field of depth that the theoretically larger screen chooses to deploy. Television is all foreground, as the BBC version shows us, but how effective is Pringle's soliloquy directly to us? Anthony Quayle had used the technique earlier, as Falstaff, and in the BBC *Hamlet,* Derek Jacobi had spoken many of his soliloquies directly to us. There, the technique emphasized his isolation from anyone—including Horatio—inside the frame. We were drawn into an uneasy relationship with this manic young man. My own sense is that we reject the too-close intimacy with the BBC Pistol. He leaves us no distance within which to formulate a response, other than a rejection based not on what he says or who he is but on the way he invades our space. That is a very subjective response, of course, but I find the Branagh Pistol, Robert Stephens, the most effective of the four in his bitterness, hopelessness, and lack of self-pity.

Another question, of course, is raised by the Bogdanov production—does the televising of live performance in any way give us a feeling for the energetic continuum that live performance can generate? In the case of the Bogdanov, I find that the answer is no. Other live performances—Papp's *Dream* at the Delacorte in Central Park, Epstein's *Dream* at the Wilbur Theater in Boston, for example—show us an audience watching a play, thus incorporate us into the space of performance. The camera work for the Bogdanov is very awkward, giving us an occasional shot of the entire stage but concentrating mostly on close-ups of the person speaking, as if the play were a series of soliloquies. The groupings may have been effective on stage, but the camera's tendency to be occasionally all-encompassing and often isolating confuses a number of issues that the stage can make clear merely by blocking. We get little sense of the interdependence of Henry's enterprise or, more generally, of the middle distance that Sheldon Zitner claims is the basis of Shakespeare's drama: "what his theatre provided most often was humanity seen not in the all-defining closeup of psychology or at the far and narrowed distance of sociology or through the historical retrospect of montage but in the open middle distance of social relation" (1981, 10). The productions needed a master at televising live performances, like Peter, Dews who directs the television versions of Stratford, Ontario's productions, to make these work *as* television.

Implicit here, and at times explicit, is the necessity for "historicizing" the discussion of any production. We must try to account for the attitudes and assumptions that an audience is likely to bring to a given production when originally presented and when re-viewed today. Some of us can remember the feelings aroused in the war against Nazi Germany and Imperial Japan and the contrast between those feelings and the ones aroused when the United States conducted a war against a Southeast Asian fragment of a country without an air force, and lost the hearts and minds of many of its own citizens until finally it lost the war. Our attitude toward war and toward specific wars is an inevitable component of response that this play and this fragment of script force us to contact and consider. It may be that television has made war less romantic than it once seemed to be—even after Hemingway and Remarque. It is also true, however, that Vietnam was fought by poor young men from the ghettos and farms and, for the survivors, often confirmed and intensified the cycle of poverty that had already begun to close them in. World War II encouraged its survivors in the United States to go on to college, and many did. The percentage of Vietnam veterans taking advantage of the GI Bill is small compared to that of World War II veterans. Vietnam scooped up young men with no defenses against the draft and returned many of them in body bags or drug-ridden bags of bodies. Branagh's Pistol is that veteran as surely as Olivier's Williams, Bates, and Court are the World War II buddies sitting around their foxhole on the eve of battle. Olivier could even give Court the speech on men not dying well that die in a battle, since men before battle do have such thoughts *and* since the battle the next day turns out to be a victory, as World War II would turn out to be for the Allies. The script picks up with remarkable accuracy the emphasis of the moment into which it emerges.

The fact of World War I—the Great War—and its decimation of a generation of European young men; and the poems of Owen, Sassoon, and Rosenberg, and the prose of Robert Graves; the ways in which ghosts from the trenches of the Western Front haunted subsequent memory, as Paul Fussell shows in dealing with "the matter of Flanders"; and Remarque's *All Quiet on the Western Front* did not mean that *Henry V* became, after the Great War, an antiwar play. Quite the contrary, the play was often a nostalgic trip back to a time before 1914-18, before barbed wire and machine guns and the pockmarked muck of the Somme, a time when knights and gentlemen fought and when a battle might be light on casualties—for the winners—instead of producing long lists in small print in *The Times*. Productions of the play after World War I often commented on their times only by inadvertence. The spirit of the play was felt as *supporting* Henry's imperial adventure and reminding England of its former greatness, even as the captains and the kings departed. *Locus*—the script as received—and *Platea* —the script as it might be interpreted as a contemporary *anti*-war play—were fused in the years following World War I by a desperate nostalgia and oblivious sentimentality. The play avoided all history except its own, the English dead at Agincourt somehow erasing the millions who had died near there some five hundred years later.

The Hazlitt/Goddard thesis—anti-Henry and anti-war—tends to come through in production only as a friction that rubs against manifest content. It is a play about winners that may remind us that winners also produce losers. It may be, of course, that, as J. C. Trewin says, "one can see *Henry V* through Elizabethan eyes without being dismissed as a chauvinist . . . Elizabethans thought of King Henry the Fifth as the light by which the chivalry of England moved, [and his] chronicle is a triumphant battle hymn, a salute to national pride symbolized in the victory at Agincourt" (1978, 147). Olivier delivered that text. Its complexity, however, may reside in its showing *how* the winners, Henry and his cohorts and the wily churchmen, control initiating forces. The script can be further deconstructed, as Alan Sinfield says: "*Henry V* can be read to reveal not only the ruler's strategies of power, but also the anxieties informing both them and the ideological representation. In the Elizabethan theater, to foreground and even to promote such representations was not to foreclose on their interrogation" (1992, 127). As with any political discourse, we have to read between and around the spoken lines, and we notice that history is a steamroller that can run out of control. You can get a country into war, but once that dark dynamic is released, and even if you win the war, the results have developed a will, or an insanity, of their own.

One would have thought that the *Second* World War might have produced some reaction against war, even if Olivier's film had helped *win* it for the Allies, but as Patrick Julian suggests, Glen Byam Shaw's version in 1951 featured a "noble, heroic Henry" and cut "virtually all of the Bishop's scene . . . forcing Henry to respond to the arrogance of the Dauphin more than to Canterbury's sly arguments" (1994, 113–14). The French attack on the boys and Fluellen's business of carrying in Falstaff's Page were retained, but Henry's order to kill the French prisoners was cut, "leaving a noble, but somewhat unbalanced picture of the king" (114). Great Britain, after all, retained a "proud sense of superiority . . . until the middle of the twentieth century. . . . As the only great European state to have escaped invasion and internal convulsion, hadn't Great Britain every reason to go on seeing herself as an impregnable and the leader of a world empire?" (Bedarida 1991, 252).

This "official" view was a fantasy, of course, refuted by austerity, boiled cabbage, and a crumbled London. Even when the daydream dissolved, *Henry V* could be seen as a paradigm of, if not inward greatness, at least the inner need of the Royal Shakespeare Company, and, possibly, a reflection of outward anxiety. The years just before the great 1975 production saw "the devaluation of the pound, the withdrawal of British troops east of Suez, further student unrest, a recurrence of separatist violence in Northern Ireland, miners' strikes, and rising unemployment and inflation" (Julian 1994, 118). As Terry Hands, the director of the 1975 production, said, the play "is about improvisation, interdependence and unity . . . essential qualities if the company were to surmount its current difficulties" (quoted in Beauman 1976, 18). And it may be, as Trewin suggests (1978, 147), that the play was addressing the uneasy end of the seventeenth century in similar terms. The play, then, could be seen as a hegemonic and military *locus* that successfully confronted and contained the *platea* of economic, social and political pressures.

The "inscrutability of *Henry V*," says Rabkin, "is the inscrutability of history" (1977, 296). The Branagh film "was created," as Samuel

Crowl brilliantly observes, "in the aftermath of Vietnam and the Falklands, where getting home was more essential than going over" (1992, 172). "Keep the Home Fires Burning" is a stronger theme in the late twentieth century than "Over There" or "So Long, Mama, I'm Off to Yokohama." The Branagh film can be seen as "anti-war" (Corliss 1989, 65, Deats 1992, 285, 292); as reflecting "the complex pro- and anti-war themes" of the play at an historical moment "just when unthinking patriotism and unthinking protest had fought themselves to a standstill" (Schwartz 1990, A-25); or as depicting Branagh as "a literary Oliver North, [who] has deliberately shredded vital documentation provided by the text and the RSC production [in which Adrian Noble directed Branagh in 1984]. . . . [H]is Henry therefore emerges as a familiar figure: the handsome military hero and godly patriot at the heart of an establishment coverup" (Fitter 1991, 260). Hardly an anti-war effort, says Fitter, Branagh's film "whitewash[es] traditional autocracy, and the logic of imperialism. What Shakespeare has demystified, Branagh, persuasively, affably, immorally, has resanctified" (274-75).

To others, however, that sounds like a description of the *Olivier* film: "Olivier's *Henry V* was meant to mobilise the nation and passed lightly over the fact that England is the aggressor in the play, and that the 'real' enemy was not France. Branagh's *Henry V* is, if not a pacifist work, extremely skeptical of violence. What makes the film interesting is its strong emphasis on Henry's conflict between the pressure to lay claim to the French duchies . . . and his 'natural' inclination to peace and his distrust of violence" (Susan Fabricius 1994, 92). In the film, "the words say one thing and the visual experience implies something very different," says Deats (1992, 291). The execution of Bardolph—it was done just offstage in the Noble production—shows, according to Susan Fabricius, that "Clemency towards the enemy is more important than indulgence towards your own people" (94). William P. Shaw *equates* the Olivier and Branagh films: "the two directors have circumvented the play's ambiguities of characterization and theme though tonal distortion or textual deletions. In effect, Olivier and Branagh have adopted Henry V's own political tactic, namely, contriving a virtuous public image to obscure deceitful private behavior . . . Branagh's Henry V is certainly more politically subtle than Olivier's, but he too remains untainted by the deeper political ambiguities at work in Shakespeare's text" (1992, 66).

Jonathan Yardley complains about Branagh's "inability to show why the British triumphed at Agincourt" (1990, C-2). Olivier had shown the French as imbecile or shallowly arrogant, had focused on the discipline and precision of the English longbowmen, and had demonstrated the king's ability to complete his orchestration (or stage management) with a *mano a mano* against the Constable. Branagh's battle scenes, however, "seen in a succession of close-ups," says Vincent Canby, "are chaotic and so exhausting that as the film slips into slow motion it seems to be sympathetic fatigue" (1989, C-19). We can infer that Branagh mystifies the victory or *intends* what Michael Pursell describes as another of the film's contradictions: "Agincourt in the rain [with its] mud and blood-filled puddles that litter the field like shell craters," looks like the Somme in 1917 (1992, 273). "Presenting any event as the Great War is to construct it as negative and futile. . . . Yet by moving that much closer in time [to the Falklands] and in developing the game metaphors [particularly rugby], Branagh strays into potentially destabilizing territory" (275). Branagh's Henry combines "that strange mixture of sincerity and opportunism that characterizes so much right wing discourse" (275).

A final example of the film's *intentional* blurring of "expected" value systems is nicely described by Susan Fabricius: "The topers of [Henry's] youth—primitive as they are—know nothing of treason or hypocrisy [with the obvious exception of the destabilizing Falstaff]. They mean what they say, and so they are young and unspoiled in mind though they are old, debauched, and thievish. The deceitful, noble trio are interpreted by young, strikingly handsome actors, but they are full of double-dealings, and their tongues are false" (1994, 92). Donald Wineke argues that by "foregrounding Henry's betrayal by Scroop, Branagh stresses Henry's isolation, not only from the . . . Boar's Head group, but from his own class as well. He is a king in no man's land, and the spiritual costs of his commitment to his destiny deeply qualify the heroism he displays" (1992, 66). A shrewd essay by E. A. Rauchut suggests how Branagh, by including the oration before Harfleur that Olivier omits, shows "Henry . . . manag[ing] to pull off what, historically, was a terrifically successful bluff" (1993, 39), one particularly necessary since his army was decimated by sickness.

Branagh, says Pursell, in alluding to "popular movies in visually obvious ways, [is] doing more than just popularizing his film text. He is aligning it within our culture and visual obsession with apocalypse" (1992, 270). In doing so, he must falsify the Elizabethan sense of time by creating a "nostalgic" sense of time. Jonathan Baldo cites Christopher Lasch's suggestion that a linear, as opposed to cyclic, sense of history gives rise to nostalgia. Nostalgia is rare in Shakespeare, Baldo argues. It is "one of the aspects of modern memory that seems largely irrelevant to Shakespeare and his culture" (1994, 3). "A culture used to consuming stories about its past in theatrical form, with living bodies bringing back from the dead, as it were, its national heroes and nemeses, crises and triumphs, would be better protected than we are today from the tyranny of nostalgia" (7). "Branagh [in his film version of *Henry V*] takes a play whose orientation to the past is anything but nostalgic and makes it into a modern document in nostalgia, punctuated by the device of the flashback" (7). In Shakespeare's play, "Henry carefully oversees and monitors the national memory, whose possession is nearly as important for a monarch—especially the heir and beneficiary of a usurper—as possession of the throne. *Henry V* is a play about power and remembering, the need for power to control memory and especially to capitalize on the natural tendency to forget. The play's drama about the manufacture and control of national memory yields, in the recent film, to what has become our most prevalent form of cultural memory, nostalgia" (7). "Unlike modern audiences who might watch *Henry V* in a mood of personal nostalgia or nostalgia for lost empire and what [Graham] Holderness calls a 'habitable space' for patriotism in Britain's past, nearly everyone in *Henry V* makes reference to restoring a previous state of affairs" (8).

Branagh's Henry "is a hapless victim of recollection in the film, not the would-be manipulator of the sometimes unruly and refractory kingdom of the past, as I believe he is in Shakespeare's play, where he is shown fighting battles for control of the national memory and in the interests of national unity as well as consolidation of his personal power" (Baldo 1994, 9). "As a result, the King looks like the sad and partly pitiable victim of memory, not its potent sovereign who exercises a vigilant control over the national memory, sustained through sometimes brutal campaigns of forgetting" (10). This treatment "exclude[s] from the film any more vigorous, contestational, questioning, and potentially subversive role for memory" (11). Henry acknowledges its potential subversiveness, of course, in praying that his soldiers *not* remember his father's usurpation.

Baldo makes a strong case, but I would suggest that Henry V's final flashback in the Branagh film, as Burgundy goes on and on about the values of peace (making us understand why war is a viable option to some), is simply a "spacing out"—a flowing in of all sorts of material that Henry has not had time to consider since becoming king. Repression does victimize us, of course, but here the man is only a *personal* victim. His memories do not affect the king, though they may sentimentalize the man. Some would argue that this preoccupation is appropriate to the son of a man who "was thinking of civil wars" at the moment of the son's conception and is *less* than Henry V deserves. The final Chorus shows that both of the king's bodies are subject to the brevity of life itself. Body politic perishes because it has been, as we have seen, a *personal* construct, albeit convincing to those looking on and to a previous generation of critics, with few exceptions.

Proof of the film's postmodernist premises may be that our response to Branagh's Henry can be contradictory, as Michael Manheim argues: "He is the Henry for our time basically because along with his in-genuousness, sincerity, and apparent decency—he is also a ruthless murderer. Branagh's characterization radically divides our sympathies" (1994, 129–30). Body natural may be someone we "like." Body politic is someone—something—else, a construct made necessary by the sunder-ing of sanctity and intangible continuities from the body politic that Richard II had inherited.

Peter Donaldson offers a complex thesis:

[If Branagh's] *Henry V* is more politically aware, more deeply skeptical about wars of imperial conquest than Olivier's, it never-theless presents the king as a great leader whose heroism depends, to a disturbing degree, on his capacity for self-suppression and whose personal growth is fostered by inward assent to the neces-sary evils of politics, war, and courtship. . . . Olivier introduces his audience to the inner workings of Elizabethan theater, includ-ing a tour of its tiring-house and backstage, but does not include his own medium, that of film, in his account of the production of Shakespearean spectacle. Film retains its own, undemystified ma-gic . . . Taking Olivier's suppression of the medium of film as his own starting point, Branagh begins with a modern-dress, Brechtian prologue set in an empty film studio containing the props and sets actually to be used in the film. Even the camera is briefly shown. . . . Branagh emphasizes effort, human agency, force . . . Olivier's authority, in contrast, tends towards the char-ismatic and . . . is typically exercised through the *voice*, with the king positioned at the vanishing point of the image and the camera pulling back to reveal a widening space filled with atten-tive subjects or soldiers . . . for Olivier kingship is inescapably performative. . . . Olivier's *Henry V* does not show the king in the process of development, does not show him growing, but rather shows him performing, acting out of a well established repertoire of skills and competences. Branagh's *Henry V* is a *bildungsroman*, and its view of the king is deeply developmental. [At the end of the Olivier film], Katherine's transformation into the boy actor of the final tableau fuses history and representation, the heroic legacy of Agincourt and the artistic legacy of Elizabethan theater, assimilating both to the wartime image of England as repository of humane culture and courage. . . . Branagh explores dimensions of Shakespeare's play that Olivier's version left relatively untouched—the myth of the king who is also one of his people, whose early experiences provide an intimate link to ordinary life, the king who, though he inherits a crown, must earn his success like a son of the artisan or merchant class making a go of the family business. (1991, 61–71; Donaldson's emphasis)

Olivier's film is framed by the Globe. All we have experienced has finally been "theater." While Branagh refers consciously to his medium, his film has a much more provisional quality than Olivier's, a quality appropriate to the story of a young man discovering who he is as man and as king. Donaldson's contrasts are precisely drawn and show that the same script, as interpreted at different moments in history by different directors, can provide the rabbit and the duck and the shape of zeitgeist that Norman Rabkin discusses in his famous article (1977). In one instance *platea* seeks out and empowers the manifest content of *locus*. In another, whether the film is "pro" or "anti" war, the discrepancy between *locus* and *platea* creates a zone for evaluation that is at least partly a product of the history that has occurred since 1944. At the same time, the contrast between two *platea*s helps us understand and appreciate each. As historians know, history is not necessarily something that moves forward in time.

Two recent papers on Branagh's *Henry V*, by Patricia Salomon (1994) and David Brailow (1994), focus on Henry's oration before Agincourt:

> We few, we happy few, we band of brothers;
> For he today that sheds his blood with me
> Shall be my brother; be he ne'er so vile,
> This day shall gentle his condition.
> (4.3.60–63)

Henry's "band of brothers" speech is problematized—it's what we used to call irony—by Gower's being summoned to Henry's tent after Agincourt. "I warrant it is to knight you, Captain," Williams guesses. No. It is part of Henry's elaborate practical joke on Williams and Fluellen, a plot that argues some wish on the king's part to return to the enjoyable world of Falstaff and the tavern, and *may*, then, validate Branagh's flashbacks. Here, the joke falls flat, and Williams gives an excuse that might have been Falstaff's, had Falstaff been inclined to tell the truth:

> Your majesty came not like yourself. You appear'd to me as a common man; witness the night, your garments, your lowliness.

And what your majesty suffer'd under that shape, I beseech you take it for your own fault, and not mine: for had you been as I took you for, I made no offense. (4.8.50–55)

The script itself gives little evidence that Henry *means* to establish *communitas*, as Salomon suggests. Instead, as David Brailow argues, Henry manages to construct a political entity that *looks like* a king out of the wreckage that Bolingbroke and Richard have cooperated to make of kingship. It may be that Shakespeare shows in Richard that no human being can successfully negotiate the equation between the king's two bodies. Suffice it that Richard's body natural—the willful little boy beneath the robes—sunders the holy metaphor. Henry V is left only with empty form:

Canst thou [Ceremony], when thou command'st the beggar's knee, Command the health of it? (4.1.253–54)

Falstaff had asked at Shrewsbury, "Can honour set to a leg? No. Or an arm? No. Or take away the grief of a wound? No. Honour hath no skill in surgery, then. No." (*Henry IV Part 1*, 5.1.131–33). Yet Henry V can cry, in public, "If it be a sin to covet honour, / I am the most offending soul alive." The old Hotspurian value is still negotiable as rhetoric, but fatal if believed. Public Henry is political Henry. His rhetoric works. But, at best, he can only pretend to be a potential brother. No private or natural Henry exists. As Brailow suggests, Henry has done a superb job of patching together a convincing simulation of a human being. His apprenticeship in the taverns showed him how to outwit the most skilled of adversaries and made for an instant transformation to a mimesis of majesty. He meets a further challenge when the French block his way at Agincourt. His construction of brotherhood and of a prosperous old age for his army becomes necessary. But the emergency past, the words have served their purpose.

As a critic writing in a bygone age has said, "Henry V is not characterized as having much 'inner life.' Any 'personality' independent of the role of king would clash with that role . . . Henry V has allowed the 'personality' he exhibited as Prince Hal to emerge only through the political techniques he mastered as prince. . . . Henry has had to rely on a 'ceremony' that he knows has no merit other than to evoke a predictable response in those assembled around the king. Ceremony creates no links with 'truth,' indeed becomes a necessary falsehood that the man producing it comes to hate" (Coursen 1984, 184–85). Thus Henry's space-out in the Branagh film as Burgundy pontificates. Olivier had provided a visual equivalent of that dull allegory. For Branagh's Henry this has been a gigantic personal venture, calling for absolute management and allowing the king no refuge from kingship, as the campfire scene proves. As the king relaxes for a moment, all that material floods in. Branagh demonstrates the public/private dichotomy, as he did in his first Henry V for Adrian Noble in 1984. Of Bardolph's offstage execution then he says, "I took in the awful sight and found from somewhere the reserves of emotion to carry on, leaving the *man* Henry deeply shaken and the *king* Henry resolved" (Jackson and Smallwood 1988, 103).

Brailow suggests that Branagh attempts to show "a genuine reconciliation of the public and private person" (1994, 3). We see Henry walk off the battlefield with Fluellen and then motion to Exeter to join them. The camera pans to reveal Pistol, sitting against a tree. Branagh's "humanization" of Henry V sentimentalizes the film, not the depiction of Pistol. Those flashbacks are "humanizations" of Henry, even if Bardolph and Pistol are not sentimentalized. A wedge does exist between what we see of the lowlifes and Branagh's response to them. It may be that Shakespeare sentimentalizes Henry in that odd Williams/Fluellen episode, which few critics have dealt with.

The sentimentalization occurs in the depiction of Henry V—his discovery of his humanity and of male bonding, after banishing and/or executing his companions on both the lower and upper levels of the social hierarchy. Branagh takes a step beyond the isolation that Wineke describes (1992, 66). In this, the film is more sentimental than Olivier's. The latter used a fixed camera, and some idealized settings, but it made its theatrical premises absolutely clear by taking us into the Globe at the beginning and by returning us there at the end. But that Branagh permits a repressed past to discover his king is well within the interpretive allowances we should grant to a film director and is one of this film's strongest elements. That the surfacing of the repressed content represents "nostalgia" is an *interpretation,* and valid in that sense, whether one agrees with it or not.

Olivier included Falstaff's rejection—a rich Vermeerian scene in which Falstaff (George Robey), alone and dying, is endlessly listening to Henry's "I know thee not"—Olivier's voice in the mode of public denunciation. Falstaff must be discarded. The King's cause is the Nation's cause and it permits of no self-indulgence, no personal idiosyncrasies, no disabling inwardness. Shakespeare shows the king as superb, given the tawdriness of his entry into war, and the man as empty. Branagh shows the man as full of memories of things past that *do not* intrude in damaging ways. The flashback before Bardolph is hanged is merely a pause before the king nods and the rope pulls taut from the tree limb.[1]

## NOTES

1. See my discussion of the Olivier and Branagh films in Coursen 1992, 146–48 and 170–75.

# VII

# Is Shakespeare's History Our Own?: Onstage in the 1990s.

Even the same production will pull contrasting responses from its auditors, and certainly productions of the history plays in 1993-94 seemed designed to do so. We have entered a phase of postmodernism that has only begun to yield its crafted contradictions. How that is done on stage is one of the subjects of this chapter. The problem, however, is that a single auditor can only speculate about multiple significations as he attempts as accurately as possible to describe his own imaginative experience of the productions. The general question is, How is "history"—the generic history play which may bear a king's name but which shifts its focus from major character to major character as the contest for power continues, and gives us a glimpse of the noncoms and civilians trapped in the struggle—being depicted in 1993-94? "Postmodernism" introduces a set of distinct generic considerations to *platea*, as opposed to the political, "thematic" elements that modernism would encourage. In other words, the modernist director might ask of *Henry V*, "How can I make this play into an antiwar vehicle?" The postmodernist director would ask, "How can I deal with this script so as to evoke conflicting judgments about war and the king even from the same spectator?" Is "postmodernism," which seems to be a superb context for this generically complex drama known as "history play"—as response to the Branagh film shows—working for stage productions?

Yes and no. Yes, if good acting can overcome bad direction. No, if the actors must struggle against the design of the production, or if the design seems to insist on "generalized emotion" projected from the stage in shouting. In France in 1917 soldiers who went over the top were mowed down by the sweep of machine guns. In some recent productions it has been the audience that has been victimized by the charge. People, like dogs, tend to cringe when they are shouted at. If those people are critics, they also learn to snarl. What seems to work best for "history" is an unadorned, even quiet (and therefore thoughtful) approach to the scripts, "undistracted by gorgeous costumes and glittering wargear" (Ranald 1993, 13). What also seems to work is a placement in time somewhere back toward either Shakespeare's time or the imagined time of the historical events themselves. What does not work is obvious contemporizing. The exception to that "rule" and to the minimalist thesis was Richard Eyre's opulent 1992 *Richard III* at the Lyttleton, set in the Great Britain of the 1930s, with a fascist Richard rising and bringing with him eerie shadows of the Duke of Windsor, who would have been king again had Operation Sea Lion succeeded, and of Wallis Warfield shaking hands solemnly with Hitler. It was in many ways a constricted, schematized production, particularly when contrasted with Sam Mendes's spare version at The Other Place, but it was exciting when compared to the gray drabness of many other productions of the season, and it was disturbing when placed against the brownshirts that threaten constantly just beyond the walls of any theater (on these *Richard III*s, see Coursen 1993 and 1994).

Moments that are *too* contemporary cut the telegraph lines from the past and make the plays merely Kottian and therefore even more "temporary" than performance inevitably is. The exciting signal that tells us that "history" is a plan for the future, an insight we share with the characters in the plays, even as, with them, we tend to misinterpret the plan, was not there in the productions that tried to communicate with an audience specifically located in the 1990s. The plays do seem to be eerie predictions of the future or even uncanny allegories of the present—as Barton's *Richard II* in 1972, a meretricious muddle of conflicting styles and isolated effects, seemed to be of Watergate. I can recall the shock waves running over the audience in the Brooklyn Academy of Music as the analogy became clearer and clearer. But what makes the plays powerfully contemporary in production is a firm grasp on their dramatic issues, which are rooted in the 1590s, but which, when explored, echo down the long corridor to our own moment, and back again.

It may be, of course, that we are so jaded by the horrors of civil war, so numbed by the inability of first-world powers to respond effectively, so cynical about our own "leaders" that any effort to communicate a postmodern vision of politics from an old script meets with resistance, as opposed to the shock of recognition that greeted the RSC *Richard II* in 1972 or Michael Kahn's 1969 *Henry V* at Stratford, Connecticut. There, as Agincourt ended, the "dead remain. Henry's triumphal return to London. The Dead become the crowd. Sounds of ghostly cheering" (s.d. quoted in C. Shaw 1994, 10). That production "was a bold and unorthodox theatrical challenge designed to force the audience into individual and national moral self-examination" (Shaw 1994, 10), but it tended merely to evoke outrage: " 'We happy few' is taken to be a demagogue's dishonest bleat" (Kerr 1969); Kahn commits "fatal violence against the essence of this soaring work. The verbal magic is crushed" (A.B. 1969); "filled with . . . self-righteous zeal [Kahn] twists the play every which way, always certain that his little tune is superior to Shakespeare's rich orchestration. The result is frequently a pompous bore" (Zeigler 1969); "to equate our modern view of the carnage of war with Shakespeare's view of the fundamental glory is almost impossible" (Clive Barnes 1969a). Recently, Kahn said, "if you ignore the text or try to subvert the text in order to make another point, then I question it" (quoted in Pressley 1994, D-3.) Those who do not like a particular production tend to know what Shakespeare is *really* saying in the play. It also follows that some people go to the theater for a version of escape in which older values, those of *Our Town,* for example, are perceived to be celebrated. Americans elect presidents on that basis and then wonder why the system has fallen apart when important segments of it have been ignored for twelve years. Shakespeare's history plays show us such collapse—of fundamental principles that underlie social contracts (however hierarchical and antifeminist), of the bond cracking between family members, of sheer opportunism finding language for its justification—but when we narrow that demonstration just to the dimensions of our own perceived present, we lose the position of partial detachment that allows us to see more than the moment, that is, that allows us to see the past, and, in that recognition, to see in that past an after-image of the future. We saw only the present in John Barton's *Richard II,* but in Terry Hands's *Henry V* of a few years later, we saw the imagery of cooperation, as Hands built a production and as Alan Howard's Henry built a coalition. The goal of the coalition was questionable—war—but the trajectory of the production moved toward the wooing of Katherine, and so comic closure did occur, even if within the time frame that Shakespeare's uncomic final sonnet imposed. The future, however, was projected by the production, which was "about improvisation, interdependence, and unity . . . essential qualities if the company was to surmount its present difficulties" (Terry Hands, quoted in Beauman 1976, 18). A production that gets trapped in *our* present has nothing to say—about the past that the play (even as written) depicts or about the future. The history plays are continuums through which we perceive history. The characters in the plays perceive in their past the matrix of the future, even as the past is debated by

Westmorland and Young Mowbray in *II Henry IV* just before the latter discovers that he has no future. We discuss the future as we debate the meanings of the production we have just experienced.

A production of the history plays is a *medium*, both as a live version of a script and as a seer through the dark glass of the past of the rock-eyed shapes slouching out from the production, their hours coming round at last as the plays keep saying they will and as history keeps telling us they have. Even a jingoistic version of the play can reflect its moment, as did the Richard Mansfield *Henry V*, which opened in October, 1900, and represented and retransmitted what Patty Derrick calls "patriotic contagion": "By 1900 the American people seemed to approve of a colonial empire [and] wanted to be perceived as a strong unified force in international affairs after years of divisiveness during and after the Civil War" (1993, 4). By 1917 the United States would enter the divisiveness of the uncivil Great War, whose indiscriminate slaughter had been foreshadowed by Fredricksburg and Petersburg but was different from that fictionalized in 1900 to an audience "ardent for some desperate glory."

For Shakespeare's "history" to make sense as the millennium swings on its huge hinge, we must begin with the sense that the words make in the script. From that starting point, much becomes possible. The sense that the words seem to make will discover its sense in the culture without much stressing from design or director. Without the starting point in the language, however, nothing will be signified, and Shakespeare will sink to banality, to reassure an increasingly desperate elite, as history engulfs them. It may anyway.

Adrian Noble's *II Henry IV*, in 1991–92, one of his first productions for the RSC as its artistic director, began expressionistically with a multivoiced company as many-tongued Rumor, breaking and regrouping, giving "with child" a woman's voice, creating a frightening *Macbeth* rhythm to this beginning. That was powerfully reiterated in the three messengers who came to Northumberland and surrounded him with torches. Morton's mortal word shattered the previous reports along with Northumberland's hope and evoked a choric moan from Rumor. It was a powerful opening that derived from the Shrewsbury of Part 1: "an extraordinary seething, writhing tableau, figures struggling in slow motion for the throne with a woman screaming silently at the horror of war to one side. . . . [T]he woman, dissociated but reacting, brought together all the production's thinking about the place of women in this society" (Holland 1993b, 139–40), "the clash and cacophony of the music and the falling bits of arms and armor seeming to catch something of the futile destructiveness of war" (Smallwood 1992, 342). Rumor reflected war's aftermath.

What was extraordinary about this production was its balance between the two father figures. Falstaff wished he had a son, as his stumble and pause on "if I had a s . . . a thousand sons" (when I have none) and Henry IV, publicly and consistently, wished that Hal were someone else's son. Robert Stephens's Falstaff knew at some point that he would be rejected. According to Alan Dessen, Stephens's "Falstaff sees himself as Hal's substitute father and therefore tries to educate his princely charge after his true father has failed. At the news of Henry IV's death . . . this Falstaff therefore recognized that a place for him no longer existed with Hal or at court" (1992, 478). And, of course, Falstaff does not know that Hal has reconciled with Henry IV and that Henry V has adopted the Chief Justice as "a father to [his] youth." Falstaff's halfhearted boast about the "laws of England" was, then, a "provocative resistance to the received script" (Dessen 1992, 478). Pistol's news had already been undercut by the bells ringing in Gloucestershire. We had heard them begin in London and heard them again rolling over the countryside *before* Pistol's announcement. "[S]hall good news be baffled?" Yes. Here, the news came to Falstaff much as the good news had come to Henry IV earlier: "I should rejoice now at this happy news." But each knew his time was almost up. Falstaff's soliloquy about "sack" had uncannily isolated Prince John as the son he had engendered—particularly since we do not and in this production did not see Hal in any state other than sober. Falstaff's exit from Gloucestershire coincided with the brutal arrest of the Hostess and Doll, the "law and order" London toward which Falstaff was coming. Doll's cry, "bring me to a justice," occurred as Henry V entered.

These rapid transitions made their points simply by letting us experience juxtaposition on stage. Falstaff's plea to the new king was halfhearted, his "king Hal" an oxymoron he knew he was making. His kneeling suggested at once "dignity and the resignation of someone who, like the dead king, knows that he has fulfilled someone else's purpose" (Peter, 1991). Falstaff's "I owe you a thousand pounds" was an assertive effort to acknowledge the debt and thus avoid the repayment of it, as opposed to a unique truth-saying that emerges through the shattered surface of consciousness. Falstaff exited to gaol with apparent jauntiness, arm in arm with Pistol and Bardolph, but the afterimage suggested that they were supporting a Falstaff barely able to move his feet from step to step.

Falstaff almost got an embrace from Hal as the former lay snorting behind the arras in Part 1. Hal hoped for an embrace from Henry IV after their confrontation in Part 1. Finally, after a remarkably powerful and bitter denunciation from Julian Glover's King, punctuated by his forcing the crown angrily down on Hal's head like "a crown of thorns" (as Kallaway 1991, Smallwood 1992, and Paul Taylor 1991 noted), and Hal's eloquent defense, the King gave a long sigh. "My son." He recognized the lineage at last and saw there the entire public-relations campaign that Hal had conducted—the next generation's need to be "wonder'd at" as his father had been "wonder'd at" even in the presence of the crowned king. Father and son embraced. "Henry has to realize here that his son both loves him and wants his crown, that filial love can be sadly and bitterly compatible with ambition" (Peter 1991).

This defining strand of action was carried over to Noble's *Hamlet*, which featured "the arrested embrace"—one of those touches, or *lack* of touches—which good actors use to suggest that the plays are different instants in a *single*, larger moment that is the action imitated. Here, the scene exhausted the king, of course, and the voice coming from the wasted lungs of Julian Glover's king sounded like the voice of Falstaff, coming from the smoke-invaded lungs of Robert Stephens. "This is the first production I have ever seen," said Benedict Nightingale, "in which Hal's reconciliation with his true father was more moving than his rejection of his fake one" (1991). The King laughed—not without humor—when he learned that the room where he first did swoon was called Jerusalem. Laughter devolved to coughing and, by that declension, to a death rattle. Crucially, he died *before* he was taken back to that room, so that he died neither in the Holy Land—whose image, a model of the Sepulchre Church, had been hanging above the play as an ironic reminder of his reiterated "purpose"—nor in that chamber in Westminster named "Jerusalem." Instead, his sons bore him through Shallow's orchards in Gloucestershire. The silent progress of the cortege suggested simultaneously the care that Henry IV had given to keeping his kingdom together and an essential timelessness in the countryside that is prior to politics and superior to any king, regardless of the prodigies (which were reported here) that attend upon the death of a king. Soon the bells were ringing in London, and soon they too would make their resonant progress over the bees and beeves of Shallow's deep landscape.

The coalescing moment of the production occurred when Henry IV, complaining about how many of his subjects were at this hour asleep, stumbled sleeplessly into the Boar's Head and fell into the chair where Falstaff and Doll had been only moments before. Was he, Robert Smallwood asked, "seeking his son in reality or in one of his incessant nightmares"? (1992, 343). The king, said Holland, "was obviously not in the tavern—this was not realist theatre—but the tavern was an echo of so many things for him: a version of the England that he rules, a representation of the anxiety focussed on his son that was preventing sleeping and a perspective and commentary on the political concerns with a philosophy of history in 3.1, all of which justified the simultaneity of space" (1993b, 141). This simultaneity brought to my mind Auden's lines about "suffering . . . in some untidy spot." The Boar's Head had been itself a busy, Brueghelian, almost Boschian, nightmare, for all of the superficial hilarity that inclined to nightmare. One also, however, felt this father's need for the son, and the need that Falstaff felt for a son. The wonderful irony of Henry IV's being there had been predicted by Falstaff who had just turned the tables on Hal—for an instant—by inverting rank and insisting that Hal refer to Doll as "gentlewoman." Falstaff's final turning-of-the-tables on Hal was interrupted only by the knocking on the door with word of further intestine war. Hal angrily threw his drawer's apron at Poins. These moments showed Noble superbly aligning the allegory of performance with what the script is doing underneath.

Toward the end the production linked the scenes in a kind of rapid montage, where earlier, and to my mind less effectively, the approach had been what Peter Holland calls "cinematic theatricality. Elizabethan theatre thrived on fluidity of space, the empty stage metamorphosing with a few words from one location to another. But Noble used a theatrical version of the dissolve on film, the slow fading from one scene to another, to great effect" (1993b, 141). John Peter said, however, that the "play does not need cinematic dissolves: its structure is both firmer and more subtle" (1991).

The son who eluded Falstaff and who was reconciled to Henry at the eleventh (and three-quarter) hour was, as Smallwood said, "an energetic, nervy, unsettling adolescent prince, always on the move, apt to speak unexpectedly loudly or quietly for no apparent reason, constantly surprising . . . jumpy, worried, uncertain of his own wishes or his own feelings, though aware all the time of the inescapable destiny ahead of him" (1992, 344). Those qualities made the scenes with Poins particularly effective—one does not usually pay much attention to them in teaching this seldom- produced script—and lent considerable power to the prince's stillness as the Chief Justice pleaded his case. The new king is already convinced, of course, but, in permitting the Chief Justice to make his case, Henry allows the authority figure to make the case for those listening. He will do the same thing in *Henry V*, particularly in relationship to his claim in France. This prince, however, did not get to play that Henry.

Smaller elements supported the larger here. Philip Voss's Chief Justice found Falstaff amusing, enjoyed bantering with him, and got some laughs that a more stiff-backed characterization will not receive. Doll was attractive enough to be attractive to Hal, so that Hal's scorn of Falstaff might have had a trace of envy in it. David Bradley's dry Shallow and the slow-motion world over which he presided contrasted with the versions of sleeplessness exhibited by the frantic tavern and the haunted palace. Shallow's memory of "mad days" got a big laugh. Nasty Prince John ripped the cross from the Archbishop's neck, then condemned him, whereupon the Archbishop crossed himself in the empty place soon to be empty of a head. This production made clear its worlds, their interconnections, and the people who inhabited them.

Fortunately, the acting in the ART *Henry IV* sequence was excellent. And it must be said that director Ron Daniels moved his actors crisply within the large spaces of the Loeb stage—with one notable exception —and achieved a crackling pace. Like so many productions of Shakespeare, however, this one was fortunate to survive the "bright idea" that Daniels imposed upon it.

The court and battle sequences occurred somewhere along the spectrum from the American Civil War to World War I and featured a confusing medley of hammerlock Springfields, sabers, and .45-caliber pistols, with machine guns punctuating the sound track at Shrewsbury. The king and party wore "Student Prince" outfits, while Hotspur affected a riding outfit out of Frederic Remington. Glendower was a shaman living in a Native America far from the Wild West of Wales. This mishmash was not as insulting as that regularly inflicted on us by Michael Bogdanov, but "concept" made it difficult, for example, to enjoy Royal Miller's (Hotspur) puncturing of Herb Downer's (Glendower) pretensions. Glendower was merely a butt here and was robbed of his lines about musicians hanging "in the air a thousand miles from hence." Native Americans should have picketed outside the theater! The Welsh lady's song did create, as always, a parenthesis of serenity between the plans for war and the civil butchery that ensues.

The tavern scenes were placed in the Jersey City of the 1970s. This was to sever any links between this "world" and previous history and to cut the tavern completely off from the world of the court, that is, between the pragmatic politics that Bolingbroke must now practice after his seizure of the crown and murder of Richard, and the lower world, which is also based on thievery and opportunism and has at its center a prince who has perfected the scheme of invisibility that his father outlines as the basis for *his* career. It is just that Hal, by being seen *too* often, will be "wonder'd at" (as both king and prince say) when he does appear just as his father was. The two historical times do not inhabit the same world, as would, for example, a group of youngsters eagerly awaiting an appearance by Glenn Miller at the Hotel Pennsylvania as their elders soberly watched the ticker many blocks below on Wall Street. The first tavern scene gave us Hal watching *Tom and Jerry* on TV and munching from a box of Cap'n Crunch as Falstaff slept. Lost was the fact that Hal agrees to join Poins's counterplot as part of his own scheme-within-a-scheme to "redeem . . . time when men think least" he will. The crucial soliloquy was undercut by Hal's groping in the cereal box and coming up with a plastic prize. The issue of a prince and power was reduced to that of a boy and a toy.

During rehearsal, dramaturge Peter Scanlan tells us, "director Ron Daniels repeatedly pointed out to the cast [that] there is no way for the characters to know how things will turn out" (1993, 8). The playwright knows where his play is going, but the characters do not, and that is particularly true in a history play, where individuals are subject to events that they may initiate—like the possibility that Bolingbroke returns to England *before* Richard seizes his inheritance—but which they cannot control once set in motion. It is simply not true, however, as Scanlan goes on to say that "The very real possibility exists . . . that the ungoverned Prince Hal will become a disastrous tyrant once in power. . . . There are urgent reasons of state for disrupting any order which will bring the likes of Hal to power" (8). This is to be taken in by Hal, as many are—Henry IV; the Lord Chief Justice, Falstaff, but not Vernon, who twice reports positively on Hal from the wrong side of history and not Warwick, a shrewd political realist who glimpses Hal's purpose. While Hotspur despises Hal on the personal level, the prince is not part of the Worcester faction's negative political agenda. Hal is *not* mentioned as one of the rebel's grievances at Gaultree, as one would infer he should have been from Scanlan's comment. The motive of the traitors in *Henry IV,* moreover, is to depose a monarch who has not rewarded them properly and to replace Henry IV with Mortimer, a motive that reaches powerfully into *Henry V* and to the Yorkist conspiracies in *Henry VI.* Suffice it that, in the *Henry IV* plays, Prince Hal is not a rallying cry for rebellion. "[S]omehow out of this agitation and chaos, by blind intuition and good luck, stability is groped for and, eventually found," Scanlan goes on (9). To make that thesis work, the production does have to destroy Hal's soliloquy, which this one does effectively. Here is a case of a dramaturge rationalizing a director's concept rather than helping him understand the script.

David Bevington struggles gamely to justify Daniels's "bright idea": "the world of the aging King Henry IV [is] an older and more traditional society of stern authoritarianism and of a nation divided against itself. The other (that of young Prince Hal) is a mod world of youthful rebellion, drugs, sexual permissiveness, and the exploration of pluralistic values. These theatrical fictions are technically distant from the immediacies of Shakespeare's history" (1993, 3). Shakespeare's histories, as Moseley says, used his "audiences' attitude to their past" (1988, 79) as part of the energy of response that any dramatist invites. That audience made sense of its present through a dramatic review of events that stood, for them, at about the same remove as the American Civil War does for us. "History" demands some conceptual space within which we can understand and evaluate. The closest that Shakespeare's *history* —and I am not talking about *The Merry Wives of Windsor*—gets to his own time is probably *Othello*, possibly *Love's Labor's Lost*, each set in a locale other than England. That Elizabethan audiences created allegories out of Shakespeare's histories is probably true, but it was between past and present. The present is never allegorical. Time and the history it engenders create the "second" meanings to be discerned in the past, as Shakespeare constantly suggests in these plays. He shows powerful men dictating allegories, of course, as Henry IV does in changing Richard's "the mounting Bolingbroke" to "my cousin, Bolingbroke," a convenient "recollection" that rewrites Icarian ambition as close relationship.

To contemporize one part of a play and to "historicize" another is to create a distracting competition between the two elements, one that *obscures* the competition that does exist between them and that *denies* Hal's decision-in-advance for instant success in the political realm. Hal can read his soliloquy as a "discovery," as David Gwillim did, or as a statement of cold political intention, as Keith Baxter and Gerard Murphy did. However it comes at us, it serves as a filter through which we observe all subsequent scenes. We share Hal's detachment even as we enjoy his game with Falstaff. And that is not an "interpretation." Soliloquies mean what their speakers believe themselves to mean as the words are spoken. In this case Hal knows who he is, who he will be, and how he will get there.

The *point* Daniels is making is a good one. That is, that if authority forbids certain activities, they will break out in wild ways—as repression will do. If, for example, *Romeo and Juliet* cannot be taught because it "encourages" teenage sexuality and because it shows teenagers committing suicide, then teenage sexuality is very likely to run rampant in the society that cannot permit it to be mentioned in school, and teenage suicide is likely to increase in a society that cannot countenance its literary or dramatic representation. Stephen King's novel

*Christine,* filled with the lyrics of teen death-songs, makes the point well. But that is a novel making a point within its fiction, as opposed to a play being radically readjusted to make a point that the script may or may not make itself. The points the script does make are sacrificed to the one that Daniels insisted on here.

The other problem with the punk-rock motif, with its spiky, dyed hair, leather jackets, and chains, is that it does not create a place for Falstaff. He cannot be a debauched nobleman, so he is a street person tolerated—who knows why?—by the denizens of the dive. He has no background against which to project his self-aware self-fashionings, thus must be a victim of a delusional system and of deinstitutionalization, admittedly a madman with remarkable verbal skills, though this Falstaff (Jeremy Geidt) was robbed of such amusing qualifications "as ancient writers do report." Given even a neutral "modern" setting, Geidt's Falstaff, with splendid eye movements and glances to assess his onstage audience and to plan his rhetorical escapes, could have extemporized from a prior career in the long-ago world of Gaunt and Edmund Langley, Duke of York. Kevin Kelly suggests that the punk-rock "idea has weight precisely because it's presented then left alone" (1993). That is fair—we were not blasted from our seats by punk rock. The problem is, however, that the idea once presented left Falstaff in a vacuum. An irony is, I must admit, that this tavern did create space for Remo Airaldi's wonderfully funny Mistress Quickly.

A less blatant setting, moreover, might have permitted us to see that Bill Camp's brilliant Hal was using Falstaff as more than a "foil." Falstaff, who can dissolve "reality" with a word, represents the most formidable of opponents for Hal in a world of necessarily improvised politics. As Bevington says, Falstaff represents to Hal "a means of trying out various roles . . . various identities to see what kind of king he might eventually be" (1993, 13). What Hal *does,* consistently, is to try to trap Falstaff. King Henry V finally shuts the trap (as it were) by denying Falstaff any lines to speak: "Reply not to me with a fool-born jest." This production would have been as fooled by Hal as Falstaff was had not Camp known what Hal was up to.

I suggest, furthermore, that the world of Bolingbroke should remind us of our own Tricky Dicks and Slick Willies and is thus closer to us than are the transitory antics of any subculture. But my statement reduces the script to banality, as this production tried to do by attempting to prove Jonathan Yardley's thesis that "we have become imprisoned by immediacy" (1993, 36).

The best scene in Part 1 was the confrontation between Henry IV and Hal, played in front of the proscenium with only a chair and a glass of water as props for the king. We got our only glimpse of a Henry IV who might have been a Bolingbroke, albeit a pompous one, pumping himself up on "pontifical" and playing at grief. He stood down right while Hal was in the more vulnerable down left position. The king moved toward Hal as the former compared himself to Hotspur. Hal's superb command of rhetoric pulled our attention to him. Hal moved toward the king as the former said "Percy is but my factor." Hotspur was the force that was making them move, a fact nicely captured here in the fitting of action to word. Though the rest of the production could hardly have been played this way and, though this scene benefited from its contrast with other full-stage sequences, it was powerful partly because it was not burdened with a concept. We experienced Hal ultimately controlling the action and thus glimpsed the future. The scene would have been even more effective had we been allowed to watch Bolingbroke's manipulation at the outset. He already knows— though we do not—that his crusade will not occur, but goes ahead with lengthy piety. We learn, however, that Sir Walter Blunt has already informed the king about Holmedon and thus that the latter's opening is a phony. This production took Henry IV's heavily edited opening at face value. His son, Henry V, will develop his own skills so completely that he will convince even the most sceptical of critics that he is indeed "the mirror of all Christian kings." Suffice it that the similarities and the contrasts between this father and son could have been drawn more clearly.

The one actor who needed help was Maggie Rush, whose Lady Percy made confusing pauses in her pleas to Hotspur (2.3) and whose pathos was swallowed up by the large bare stage that Hotspur could dominate easily. The point may be that women are victims of male intention, but Rush was a victim of bad direction.

Some Hotspurs "speak . . . thick" (as Lady Percy says, but did not say here, in Part 2). Miller's Hotspur did, driving out those recalcitrant $w$s with an angry stamp of his foot. This device of characterization suggested that Hotspur should think before he acts as he must pause before he speaks. Here, of course, he was impatient with himself, as he is with the world in which he is an anachronism, a man who should be living back in the time of the Black Prince but is trapped in a politics of expediency. Hal could parody Hotspur effectively, and the payoff for Hotspur's impediment came after Hotspur died upon a struggle with a $w$ and Hal completed the sentence: "For worms, brave Percy."

A lot of the wonderful predawn discussion was cut from the Gad's Hill sequence, but the robbery was conducted like a "happening"—in the auditorium. I lost some lines—"Young men must live" and "They hate us youth," for example—but the trade-off was an exciting sequence that invaded our space. The re-robbery, Hal and Poins brandishing water pistols, was conducted in front of the partially lowered fire curtain. That Bardolph donned a Richard Nixon mask for the robbery was amusing *and* permissible since we are experiencing a farce that parodies Henry's seizure of the crown.

Falstaff's disquisition on honor was splendid, but hollowed out by editing that robbed Hotspur of his earlier, contrasting speech in 1.3. To deny that another world exists—the one in which Hotspur might have been a soldier of the king—is to deny the context against which the more cynical attitude that Falstaff describes can be understood.

The finale featured two armies on either side of the stage—a technique often used at the end of *Richard III*—with each army singing. Hotspur's troops sang "Tenting Tonight," while the king's forces crooned of home and mother. The effect was a prebattle dissonance, presumably intentional. It makes little sense for Henry IV to complain of having "his old limbs . . . crush[ed] . . . in ungentle steel," if he is sitting there in his general's suit. Douglas was at one point surrounded by *three* masked "kings"—a suggestion that kingship is at once an illusion *and* a fact that will survive this effort to destroy it and divide England into three principalities. The final battle was conducted in and around a set of steel picket fences which echoed the many fences that became the sites of slaughter during the American Civil War. Bardolph roamed through the battle picking pockets, a borrowing from Branagh's Agincourt. Part 1 ended with Worcester and Vernon swinging up on the tug of the hangman's nooses.

The actors were the reactionaries here, attempting to unify, integrate, find meaning within Daniels's effort at disintegration—what Kelly calls the "now standard with-it anachronism" (1993). Fortunately, the actors won.

Daniels's *Hamlet*—for RSC—gave us an armored Ghost at the outset and an armored Fortinbras at the end. Hamlet's embassy to the future failed. There we got an effective framing, a concept *surrounding* the inner action and showing us a tragedy neatly absorbed by the status quo. The ghosts of the past entered and took over at Elsinore, easily incorporating the now-dead Hamlet into their agenda (see Coursen 1995 on that production). In *Henry IV*, Part 1 Daniels's simplifying metaphors complicated things for the actors.

Part 2 built from unpromising beginnings to one of the most convincing final sequences that I have ever experienced in the theater. We began with a reprise of the end of Shrewsbury. Henry IV sentenced

Worcester and particularly Vernon with more vigor than he had at the end of the previous play, and gave his peroration against a rising cacophony. The inner curtain rose on a riot featuring a burning Ford Escort. Then Falstaff and the Boy entered for the confrontation with the Chief Justice. Gone, then, was Rumor's Induction and the wonderful scene in which the truth about "Coldspur" comes to Northumberland, Shakespeare's dramatic essay on what happens in the gap between an event and the reporting of that event. Northumberland's line "Let order die" was scrawled on the Escort, a time-saving elision no doubt, but a disappointment, since the seldom-seen sequence was not there to be wondered at.

The "concept" here was to take Northumberland's nihilistic vision and extend it to "the world of the play" and to that "globe of sinful continents," Falstaff. Falstaff *is* the energy that Hal/Henry V must learn "how to handle," as he says, an anarchy as challenging as Hotspur's was in Part 1. The problem, of course, is that *this* Falstaff is just an old bum in the world that Daniels creates around him. While the rustic world of Shallow and Silence is wonderfully convincing, we cannot credit Falstaff's being accepted as "a friend at court," any more than we can believe that Falstaff has been given any charge at all, of horse or of foot. This modernization divorces Falstaff from the world that John of Gaunt describes at length in *Richard II*, of which Falstaff, like Hotspur, is an ironic reminder. Here references to Gaunt tended to be cut, as was Mowbray's long apologia for his father. The latter excision was necessary for streamlining, of course, but symptomatic of the lack of contact with their own "historicity" that each production demonstrated. Mowbray, incidentally, was executed summarily, by gunshots, as he moved angrily toward Christopher Johnson's oily and self-righteous Prince John after the trap at Gaultree had been sprung. Coleville's surrender to *this* "Sir" John made no sense, assuming that Coleville is seeking an enemy captain to whom to surrender, nor was anything made of Coleville's defiance of John, an attitude that probably prompts John's order for immediate execution. A good moment was lost for the sake of emphasizing John's brutality.

The last tavern scene (2: 2.4) did not show that Falstaff turns the tables on Hal one last time by inverting the hierarchy ("I dispraised him before the wicked, that the wicked might not fall in love with him"), thus forcing the prince to praise the denizens of the Boar's Head—that is, "to say that which his flesh rebels against." Hal sets Falstaff up, of course, by anticipating Falstaff's defense ("You knew I was at your back, and spoke it on purpose to try my patience"). The scene should play against the coming rejection, which shows an overconfident Falstaff rushing toward the new king's reassertion of hierarchy. "King Hal" is suddenly an oxymoron, as Falstaff, the last character to say "Hal" is immediately to learn. Clearly, the "dramaturgy" followed the director's cue in the final tavern scene, rather than helping him to inform and enrich the possibilities of the script.

The final sequences, however, transcended Daniels's earlier failures and were splendidly directed. In the crown sequence Camp's Hal pressed real grief past Epstein's histrionic king and gave a convincing demonstration of how much the prince had learned from Falstaff in this analog to the "play extempore" in Part 1. We noticed that Hal wore his gold cross again, earlier merely a piece of jewelery to contrast with his leather and to conflict with the huge cross at which his father had been discovered praying at the beginning of Part 1, now an object that Hal took at more than just monetary value. The king was carried to Jerusalem in a cortege in front of the inner curtain from stage left to right. The curtain opened to Gloucestershire and a wonderful slowdown that fast pacing permits as the old men mused about death and the price of ewes. Falstaff entered to the tune of "When Johnny Comes Marching Home Again," as played by the local high school band. Wart, Shadow, and Feeble were decorated as local heroes. A country festival ensued, the band being fed immediately while the rest sat at a long table upstage under a welcome home banner.

The feast continued as, back in London, Hal confronted the Chief Justice. Camp showed that he already knew what he was going to do but permitted the Chief Justice to make his case, by which Hal could pretend to be persuaded. The stage captured simultaneity superbly here. Pistol brought his news to Gloucestershire—an echo of the Northumberland scene that had been cut—and Falstaff charged on London. Mistress Quickly and Doll were carried off to gaol, a signal that "law and order" had returned to London. The new king appeared up center —the position of power—and marched forward as a long, blue-velvet train trailed behind him. His "I know thee not" was not compromised as his "I know you all" had been. He measured Falstaff's grave as he had measured Hotspur's ("two paces of the vilest earth is room enough"; "the grave doth gape / For thee thrice wider than for other men") and marched off to history. Most of the rejection speech had been delivered down front, Henry V looking straight ahead, with an occasional glance at Falstaff, who stood down left. We, then, the almost six hundred people sitting in front of Henry V, were the kingdom. His was the power. The point was made simply by Henry V's position on stage, by Camp's vigorous delivery of the words, and by the fact that no "crowd" was represented onstage.

This is a great scene, of course. Its strength here was a result of the simplicity of its staging.[1] Again, without a heavy emphasis on a post-modernist *platea*, the *locus*—the human and the political issues in the script—came through from its almost four-hundred-year-old origin, picking up its own resonances as it would with each spectator. On-stage, given actors who understand their roles and relationships, the simpler contexts work best. This is almost invariably true, but it is almost invariably ignored by today's directors. They feel that unless *they* are doing the inventing, they are taking money under false pretenses. Most of them are, as I shall argue in the last chapter.

Falstaff's "Master Shallow, I owe you a thousand pound" was not just a sign that he is so shattered that he speaks truth for once, but also a sentence to fill a silence. He was suddenly one of the old men tossing a few words out this side of oblivion. This was well-done, even if the context for this Falstaff did not allow him to deliver the steely smile that Welles gave to Keith Baxter's king, suggesting that Falstaff could appreciate even in disaster how well his protégé had mastered the lesson. Camp did not wince as Pennington had done in the Bogdanov—as if he just *hated* to be doing this. Camp's Hal had known what he was doing all along, regardless of the cereal box he had been given to obscure his purpose early on. At the end his Henry V was an icon and Falstaff and company were "sweaty, quirky, living people . . . given their orders and left behind" (Saccio 1982, 2).[2] Camp will get a chance to play the King in ART's *Henry V*, which I treat in the last chapter.

Michael Maloney, a tiny Hal in the two parts of *Henry IV* for RSC two seasons ago, did not go on to play Henry V. The actor selected was Iain Glen, touted as the RSC's first star since Kenneth Branagh: "It's been a long time coming but the RSC have finally gotten themselves a new star. In one leap, Iain Glen has written himself into theatrical history, with the most stunning Stratford debut since Kenneth Branagh burst upon Stratford's stage in, strangely enough, the self-same play" (Woddis 1994a, 5). While the production was enthusiastically reviewed by some and did strike an effective sequence on one of the two nights I attended, it was a weak effort, even if one avoided comparisons with the 1984 Branagh version, directed by Adrian Noble, or the superb 1975 Terry Hands production, with Alan Howard.

Comparisons with the Branagh film (1989) were inevitable, however. Tony Britton, as Chorus, entered as a World War II veteran—an officer in a good regiment, his tie proclaimed—limping, cane in hand, as if past the Cenotaph, with poppy in lapel, M.C. and "theatre" ribbons on his military overcoat. This was an anachronism integrated confusingly into the production when Chorus helped Henry up with his cane during a lull at Agincourt. This Chorus was hardly "outside of history" as Gary Taylor's program note placed him. What made Chorus unmistakably Branaghian was his control of the main light switch at the outset and at the end, when he pointed at the tableau of the signing of the Treaty of Troyes on "*this* acceptance" and threw the switch, making the moment perpetual in history—in defiance of the words he had just spoken. The traitors going for their weapons as they were arrested, the gap in the wall at Harfleur, through which fire flared, Henry's exhaustion when the French capitulated there, his lifting of the Boy, the long anthem after Agincourt, Henry's emotional overflow when talking about being Welsh with Fluellen after the battle—all were imports from Branagh.

The staging was otherwise eclectic. Chorus stayed on stage for part of the first scene, as if the inner play were somehow his creation, as opposed to a narrative that points at his *mis*construction of it. Henry's royal red robe stood in a bank of poppies behind a velvet rope. Henry doffed his friar's habit and put the robe on to receive the French ambassador. Poppies were planted during the battle of Agincourt at the side of the stage, which by this time had been raked for the battle scenes and would remain elevated until the English had sung their "Te Deum." Several times characters created a bright upstage tableau while other things were happening downstage. Falstaff's death was described below Henry's heroic pose, sword held high. Pistol's soliloquy occurred while Gower and Fluellen gazed across the peaceful vineyards of France. The effect was of stained glass in a cathedral, with light looking down towards darkened corridors where, as at old St. Paul's, the goings-on were hardly pious. Perhaps the effect also glanced at anti-war poem like Owen's "Dulce et decorum est." Before the English left for France, swords dropped to them on wires from—God?—and during Agincourt pieces of armor ("all those legs and arms and heads, chopped off in a battle") hung over the stage, as a rain of poppy blossoms—blood?—fell on the rattling struggle below.

"[P]ictures do not add up to a point of view," said Michael Billington (1994c). The "scenes," said Irving Wardle, "arise from the opportunities of the moment rather than from any coherent view of the play" (1994b). The confusion of styles was augmented by the English troops pounding swords on metal scaffolding before Harfleur, drowning out whatever Henry was yelling, the sound of horses galloping through the shouted French speeches before Agincourt, and the inexplicable songs that rose, for example, behind the Boy's soliloquy about his cowardly companions (2.3.28 ff). The production employed *thirteen* musicians.

The editing was bizarre. The extensive feudal system that the King *might* have set up in lieu of his French war (1.1.12-14) was cut, so that the automatic modern analogy with what "we can and cannot afford" was gone. The full explication of the Salic Law was silly—the English peers clearly needed far less legalism to convince them. Henry had already memorized the translation of "In terram Salicam . . ." and had the passage describing Edward III's defense against "the Scot" marked in a book, for immediate reference should that subject arise. Henry's telling lines about "The slave, a member of the country's peace, / Enjoys it, but in gross brain little wots / What watch the king keeps to maintain the peace, / Whose hours the peasant best advantages" (4.1.275) were cut, as was his second threat to kill prisoners (4.7.58-63). Gone as well were the foreboding last three lines of Grandpre's marvelous speech ("Description cannot suit itself in words . . ." 4.2.51 ff), which leaves one beat open for response to his suggestion that "there's something here that doesn't meet the eye." Here, it did not matter, since the speech was shouted from up center. Grandpre could have been shouting lines from *Coriolanus*. The last lines of the speech as edited were "the knavish crows / Fly o'er them, impatient for their hour." Soon we heard crows indeed above the English, as if Grandpre's prediction were *true*, instead of the variation on overconfidence the editing made of it here. Why leave in Burgundy's long disquisition (5.2.23-67), which makes even the onstage English impatient? Are we meant to be amused by them, while being bored ourselves? The Chorus to act 5 was cut, but alluded to shamelessly in the program as evidence for dating the play. Chorus's allusion to Essex would have been another distracting anachronism, and so the material was permitted to drop off into an expensive footnote.

At the outset Canterbury put his own cross around Henry's neck ("Gracious lord, / Stand for your own") to endow the war with the Church's blessing, if not necessarily with sanctity. Henry took the cross off after his "God of battles" prayer, left it in the dirt, then said, much later, "O God, Thy arm *was* here!" The sequence before battle was clear—Henry listened to Williams's argument while seated somewhat apart from the campfire and moved toward Williams to respond—something the soldiers did not expect. The speciousness of his counter-argument was obvious—the son about his father's business was Henry, not the soldiers. Henry then came close to recognizing his own culpability in his soliloquy, avoided it by shouting, "I am a king that find thee," and then shifted the blame back to "the fault / My father made in compassing the crown"—that seeking for precedent that occurs so often in this group of plays and in the *Henry VI* sequence. Here, while it was a negative instance, it avoided the more immediate issue Williams has raised: "if the cause be not good, the King himself hath a heavy reckoning to make."

That was an effective line on the first night I attended. On the second night the company was having a difficult time. A prop kept falling from the conference table in 1.1, Cambridge blew his line about "the gold of France," and the timing—that crucial element one notices only when it is badly off—was badly off. Henry tended to whine. His specific anger at Williams was more unseemly than before. He looked at Williams's glove, and the latter became "every fool" who made the king insecure with his questioning. This was just an angry and arrogant Henry, as opposed to one approaching a truth he dare not acknowledge. Linal Haft, playing Fluellen, seemed to sense the problem that evening, but increased it by shouting out words at inappropriate places: "as touching the *DIRECTION* of the military discipline," "keep his word and his *OATH*." The results of these "new readings" were disquieting. Almost lost in the tumult were Daniel Evans's quiet and endearing Boy, and Gwynn Beech's strong Dauphin, a contrast to the usual effete treatment of the French prince.

Glen may well go on to celebrity, but this role was hardly "This star of England." His "mock," "mock," "mock," punctuated by a bounce of one of the tennis balls—another "mock"—seemed to promise a sense of humor, as did his faking out the French ambassador with a mock toss of the tennis ball. But the humor never resurfaced. Apparently, it was lost during the episode with the traitors. Henry permitted Scroop to hold a dagger to his throat, creating a powerful mime of simultaneous treason and containment. Henry refused to pardon them: "God quit you in *his* mercy" (emphasis not mine). The "joke" with Williams was a vicious manipulation that found Williams on the point of execution until the King apparently changed his mind. That sequence shows, of course, that practical jokes are no longer in Henry's province. The last use of "Hal" had been Falstaff's oxymoron "King Hal" at the end of the previous play. Here, however, the King's rage was abated only just in time, and Fluellen's potentially amusing line about Williams's shoes was cut. The wooing was interminable—"irrelevant and never-ending" (Dudgate 1994), and the only laugh came on Henry's "I will not part with a village of it." His "Shall Kate be my wife?" was a shouted threat to the French, which merely emphasized that all of this was politics and that, even in his wooing, Henry had not been trying to decontextualize himself into some version of humanity. Playing "against the text," Henry's speech before Agincourt was quiet, a story around a campfire, at precisely the moment when we might have expected him to raise the dynamics to at least a fortissimo. It was a relief *not* to be shouted at, but here, the conversational tone played against meaning. It was "sincere but wan," said Chris Peachment. "Quite why the troops stiffen their sinews and summon up the blood is a mystery" (1994). Howard delivered the lines while walking among his men, inspiring even Pistol into a sense of momentary brotherhood. In the current production the speech represented an odd implosion. The speech at Harfleur is, of course, rant, but it is a prelude to the greater speech on the eve of Agincourt. Having encouraged his troops to imitate the action of the tiger, he can now talk them past the battle to honored old age, but at some point he has to take his foot from the soft-pedal. Suffice it that this was a Henry who had never played Hal (as Alan Howard had done, for example) and had not honed his skills against the formidable Falstaff. Indeed, for Glen to claim that Hal-Henry "has always shrugged off his responsibilities" (quoted in Senter 1994, 8) is to be taken in by the negative public relations that Hal conducted when he *was* Hal.

It may be that the production's "brutal realism" (Doughty, 1994), the display of an actual battle at Agincourt and an onstage killing of prisoners—Henry forcing Pistol's sword across Le Fer's throat—was meant to be a "deeply moving lament of pacifist persuasion," (Woddis 1994a, 5). I found the sound, fury, rattle and noise *de*sensitizing. It was as if more pictures from Bosnia, Somalia, or Rwanda were emerging. After a while, inevitably, the pictures, like anything repeated too often, lose their power to evoke a human, or humane, response. Another anti-war sermon, if that is what this was, can meet only cynicism in a world of wars without causes and causes without wars. Jack Tinker felt that the production conveyed a "pervading spirit of jingoism" (1994b), while John Peter found "the point [to be] that war is neither glamourous nor just a bust-up for skinheads [as in Bogdanov's 1989 production]" (1994a). In a production as deafening as this, however, it was difficult to discern intention. It "leaves most of the big questions unanswered," said Billington (1994c). Such emptiness is inevitable when a director attempts to make a play say something other than whatever it might be saying without his blundering intervention.

Some critics insisted that Glen is "one of the most significant stars the troupe has recruited in a decade" (de Jongh 1994a), and even that Glen was as good as Branagh had been in 1984: "an older, more chilling and equally powerful scourge of the French," said Michael Coveney (1994a). The "central relationship," said Stephen Wall, "is between [Henry] and his role, and it's because Iain Glen negotiates the tension so intelligently that his director Matthew Warchus is able to reclaim the play for the stage so effectively" (1994, 18). From whom—Bogdanov?

Others demurred. Glen, said Tinker was "out-bellowed" only by Clive Wood's Pistol (1994b). Repeatedly, said Wardle, Glen "goes through the same emotional cycle—from pious modesty to wrath and then to tears—with increasingly mechanical effect" (1994b). He established "nervous intensity," said Alastair Macaulay, "[but] he has as yet no stillness" (1994). He "began to dwindle," said Benedict Nightingale, "into an earnest evangelical preacher, a Billy Graham of the battlefield" (1994b). Robert Hanks felt that "Glen suffers from being too much on one note—all sinews and straining jaw, with tight smile or fierce psychotic stare" (1994b).

For me, the production was a loud, indiscriminate muddle of effects and styles that promises little from any of its major participants.

That Katie Mitchell's production of *III Henry VI* was one of the more successful versions of history among those that I am considering here was not just a function of the script's relative underexposure in the theater and classroom. The virtues of the production lay in Mitchell's minimalist approach, which insisted that the actors themselves scale down to a quietness that verged at times on absolute passivity. This was a self-contained version of Part 3, a notable omission being Henry's blessing of Richmond (4.6.68 ff).

The production was the culmination of a sequence we did not witness, where simultaneous rises and falls occur (Cambridge as narrated; Mortimer versus York; Joan versus Margaret; Cade versus Iden, and York), where desertions and changings of side are frequent (Fastolfe, Burgundy, Clarence, spirits deserting Joan, crowd deserting Cade, and "wind-changing Warwick"), where witches are burned (Jordain and Joan), where rank and station are topsy-turvy: where York is a "yeoman," Joan a "high-minded strumpet," where Cade can claim his midwife mother was "a Plantagenet," where Suffolk falls to "an obscure and lousy swain," and a king takes "a beggar to his bed." No principles underride the characters or their actions. Oaths are a matter of the moment, and conflicting precedents emerge to serve the naked agendas of ambition. The many asides tell us "the truth," and it is often a cynical and self-serving truth that the asides deliver. The images of the cosmos are of "comets . . . Brandish[ing] crystal tresses in the sky," and "malignant and ill-boding stars." The earth is a jungle inhabited by "devilish spirits," serpents with "forked tongues," and "wolves . . . gnarling." All of this culminates in Part 3 with the murder of Rutland and the taunting of York at Wakefield, the murder of Prince Edward at Tewksbury, and the murder of King Henry in the Tower. The product of this terrible disorder and the fomenter of more is Richard of Gloucester, a "foul, indigested lump," as Clifford calls him, "an indigested and deformed lump," as Henry calls him, "like to a chaos," as he himself says, "or an unlick'd bear-whelp."

Out of this tumultuous progress of characters and events, Mitchell crafted a quiet and coherent narrative that would have been easily the best Shakespeare production on any of Stratford's stages during the summer of 1994, had it not been for one grisly miscalculation which I will describe after detailing the production's strengths.

Seats at The Other Place are on three sides of the stage on the ground level and in the gallery. The site of the action was a square of bark fragments below a wooden wall on which was painted a peeling portrait of St. George. Both Yorkists and Lancastrians knelt to St. George before this or that battle, suggesting that George was neutral or nonfunctioning. Up left was a roadside shrine to the Virgin, to which characters now and then knelt. The *real* kneeling was in the huddles that the plotters of both factions formed as they crafted their sudden tactics. The production began with York entering up center and looking down at Henry's Bible with a smile. Obviously, it was open to Matthew 5:9, "Blessed are the peacemakers." York came downstage, took the throne, and was there confronted by Henry. The parley before York (2.2) repeated the pattern, but reversed the positions of power—Henry and party were downstage as Edward, Warwick, and the Yorkists entered. The stage itself reflected the seesawing of control, as downstage entitlement surrendered to upstaging agendas. This configuration paid off at the French court (3.3), when Warwick faced Margaret, who stood at the side of Lewis's upstage throne. She and Prince Edward were dismissed and "st[ood] aloof" (s.d.) as Warwick moved into the zone of power. When word of King Edward's marriage arrived, Warwick and Margaret read their letters on either side of Lewis and "let former grudges pass" to the laughter of an audience by now conditioned to vows that had been repeated so often that they had become nonsense syllables and to the physical shifting that signalled a rebalancing of power. Warwick was then left alone for the soliloquy that ended the first half of the production.

This was a very quiet production, blessedly underplayed to ears deafened by the bellowing of Toby Stephens as a Coriolanus overpowering the hapless Swan, and the roaring of Iain Glen and Clive Wood as Henry V and Pistol in the main house. Even if Henry VI was so underplayed as to appear to "confuse . . . otherworldliness with unconcern" (Nightingale 1994e) and Clifford so soft-spoken as to be no menace, Mitchell's approach encouraged some wonderful moments and enforced the "irony of so much violence, hatred, and perjury in an age of faith"

(Gore-Langton 1994). Indeed, Mitchell might have interpolated Henry's lines from Part 1: "I always thought / It was both impious and unnatural / That such immanity and bloody strife / Should reign among professors of one faith" (5.1.11–14). "[T]hese warlike nobles retain some residual memory of Christian idealism," said Michael Billington, "which they constantly violate" (1994e). Irving Wardle put it another way: the production showed a "gang of male youths on the make [and a] king who refuses to join in" (1994c).

Mitchell's attention to detail drew and rewarded similar attention from the spectator. The sequence of Warwick's farewell, if scanned, leaves two beats unuttered: "and save yourselves, for Warwick bids you all / farewell, to meet in heaven . . ." [Dies]. The two-beat "or in hell" was not spoken here, but could be heard in the pause that good direction provided. Clifford embraced Rutland, apparently accepting his plea for life, and then plunged his dagger into the boy's back. "Richard even plants a desecrating kiss on the dead [Clifford's] lips" (1994a). Such actions prompted Nicola Barker to call this "an erotic war . . . not a phallic one" (1994). Margaret beautifully set York up as an oath breaker as she crowned and uncrowned him, creating a powerful justification for her immediate command for his execution (1.4.96–108). Here, Ruth Mitchell's haughty control was as powerful as the sexual frenzy that Peggy Ashcroft employed with York or the icy imperviousness of Julia Foster, who clipped off syllables with delight at her virtuosity. Moved by York's lament, Dugald Bruce-Lockhart's Northumberland was scorned by Margaret as he gestured for a pardon. As other characters had been, York's body was carried out by a chorus singing a "Kyrie Eleison." His chorus included his three sons who remained onstage for the next scene (2.1) and their meeting with Warwick. Later, Clifford was lugged off unceremoniously, no flights of music choiring him to rest. At the end, Queen Elizabeth held her arms out to receive her son from King Edward, but he retained the male baby and exited. She had done what she was supposed to have done and thus was no longer needed. The final chorus was the lament: "O God, why dost thou turn from me, / And smile on the cause of my enemy?"

The editing found King Edward getting "*Et tu Brute*" from Q1, the stuttering prophet Exeter unnecessarily speaking lines at the end of 1.1 from Carlisle's prophecy in *Richard II* (4.1.138–45), and a Priest warning before the Battle of Wakefield, "Remember men you are but ashes, / And to ashes shall return." Immediately, ashes seemed to tumble from above, but these turned out to be snowflakes manufactured for the battle. In an effective touch, Mitchell had the scene between Lewis and Margaret (3.3) spoken in French—until Warwick's entrance at line 43.

That this sequence was clear attested to the production's careful establishment of Margaret's motivation.

Moments that did not work included the son/father, father/son sequence (2.5). In each case the survivor cradled a rose—a white for the son and a red for the father, a metaphor for the physical body. But this was just plain silly—perhaps was meant to be? — and undercut an important segment in Henry's quiet assertion of an alter ego against the prevailing insensitivity. When Lady Elizabeth Grey appeared before King Edward (3.2), she appeared but as the most abject of poor widows. He had to be the horniest man in Christendom to be attracted to her. His subsequent rape—his cross hanging down into her mouth—tried to make up in physical action what the scene lacked in emotional dynamics, but did not.

The grisly miscalculation was Tom Smith's Gloucester, who, alone among the characters, spoke with a Yorkshire dialect—"Fooot, were it further ooff, odd ploook it dune"—"with his mouth open, outward sign of inward retardation" (Francis 1984, 33–34), and often with his finger in his mouth. This drooling, headlobbing, bald Richard was plausible neither to the onstage characters—his family would have kept him locked in a northern dungeon and shoved a bowl of cold porridge into his cage once a day—nor to us. The pleasant aspect here was that Smith ruined only the latter part of this production—completely wiping out Henry's final speech (5.6. 35ff), for example. The thought of his going on to become Richard III was not a present danger. A question on this Richard was submitted to Adrian Noble in writing but was headed off by Stanley Wells in the latter's tame interview with Noble at the International Shakespeare Conference on 26 August 1994. This was a Richard "without wit or intelligence [who] chews his finger meanly, even when it's clad in armour" (Macaulay 1994). What was gained, asked John Gross "by cropping his hair like a skinhead, or equipping him, alone of all the Yorkists, with a thick Yorkshire accent"? (1994). Nothing. Much was lost.

Here was a fragment of *platea* that almost completely undercut the *locus*. A subtle interrogation of politics and war, powerful because of its intimacy and our proximity to what was being said, with meanings neatly expressed simply by stage blocking, was suddenly destroyed by this lout. I felt somewhat the same when Andrew Jarvis played Richard in the Bogdanov production in 1989—how could any, even disordered society, permit this obvious psychopath to wander freely about? Part of Richard's skill—as shown by actors like Olivier, Ian Holm, Ian McKellen, and Simon Russell Beale—lies in his ability to convince us that he can seem plausible to those inside the play he frames for us. Anthony Sher was an exception to this rule of thumb, but he was so powerfully intimidating that plausibility was not an issue. While Mitchell's Richard was *meant* to inhabit an extreme opposite position to the preternaturally mild Henry, the former did not conform to the rest of the production. This one goes on tour to the provinces, so the point is hardly local. Otherwise, the production provided "a sense of political clarity [and] of power shifting to and fro between small, close-knit groups" (Peter 1994c), of "the pain, the pity and the violation of divine law inseparable from civil tumult" (Billington 1994e), and "a salutary sense of unpurged unease" (Taylor 1994a). If Richard, however, was an allusion to contemporary hooliganism, the reference represented an unfortunate intrusion on a spectator's enjoyment of this seldom-heard play and certainly a demonstration on the limits of "intertextuality." The old play was "speaking for itself" very well at the point at which the contemporary world interrupted.

Michael Kahn, who directed *Richard II* in the fall of 1993, says that Richard "relishes power and, yes, misuses it, but . . . comes to understand in defeat that the possession of power itself has the ability to destroy one's own humanity" (Knapp 1993, 7). That is a standard view of Richard, it would seem, although Richard's recognition, if it comes, emerges primarily through the devastating irony with which he undresses kingship and Bolingbroke in the deposition scene, as opposed to his soliloquy in prison, where, Kahn, says "he is stripped to his essential being" (quoted by Knapp, 7). That is probably true, but the inference that Richard understands himself is refuted by his soliloquy, in which he misconstrues the Gospel (it is the "rich man" who cannot enter the kingdom of heaven) and in which his wishes still lean toward being king again. One can say, whose wouldn't?—but Richard never grants that power has destroyed his own humanity, only that he wasted time.

It is more promising to see the sequence *as* sequence—*Richard II* as a simple tragedy of a fall from greatness complicated by the necessity that the survivors face in picking up the pieces, *Henry IV, Part I* as a play that combines that fruitless project with festival elements as a prince bides his time before Lenten kingship comes, *Henry IV, Part II* as a more satiric play that combines an elegiac drift with the brutal politics of one prince (John) who looks bad doing them and another (Hal) who looks good, and *Henry V* as a culmination of the sequence, ostensibly heroic but also bereft of anything but a temporary contact with positive cosmic forces, if that, at Agincourt.

This is Robert Bennett's thesis. He argues that the four plays "depict different temporal conditions which a society must pass through in a single cycle of its history" (1987, 61). Bennett combines the cycle theory with linear teleology in which each "stage describes a different relationship between man and time and, by extension, between man and God. Each play has its own zeitgeist, reflected in its dramatic mode, and the plays in succession . . . reflect definable stages of time [and] the order of the plays charts the process of time" (67). Richard's murder of Gloucester and seizure of Bolingbroke's inheritance "undermine . . . the very foundations of his power. Bred in the slow pace of formal time, Richard finds himself totally inept at managing the new order of secular, business time which his actions have ushered in" (69). *Henry IV, Part I* "operates according to . . . secular or immediate time" (70). *Henry IV, Part II* represents a "daringly unconventional hodgepodge dramatic structure and . . . pervasive use of deflation and anticlimax [which] convey the image of man bereft of the dignity, wisdom, and strength needed to control his fate" (73). It is a time, says Bennett, of "characters whose names reflect predictable and risible stereotypes, frozen personalities governed by their humors" (74). It is a time of apparent aimlessness in which Hal grows restless as he awaits a moment he knows will come but which he cannot coerce into reality—thus his understandable anticipation of kingship as he exorcises the crown before Henry IV dies.

I disagree with Bennett's argument that Shakespeare grants Henry V's England an "initial sacramental" zeitgeist (67). Shakespeare has already written the *Henry VI – Richard III* sequence and thus knows that the long exploration of the ramifications of Richard II's deposition and murder had yet to occur and was only delayed, at best, by Henry V's brief reign. As Richard's murder of Gloucester and seizure of Gaunt's estate had to work itself out negatively for him in the play that bears his name, his blood would cry like sacrificing Abel's into the next generation and the blood shed there would beget a seemingly endless sequence of murder and retribution at places like Wakefield and Tewksbury and more than once at the Tower of London, all of this culminating at Bosworth Field, seventy years after Agincourt. In other words, I tend to agree with Alvin Kernan's suggestion that the world after Richard II opens out to a zone wherein "Man no longer expects the future to repeat the past but stands on the edge of great vistas of time and lives in the historical process of endless change" (1970, 274).

It is, however, important to try to discern a theme or tonality for *each* play in the sequence, lest they blend together in a muddle, as did the *Henry VI* plays in Noble's *Plantagenets* for RSC several seasons ago, and as opposed to the mishmash of styles and periods that Bogdanov and Daniels present as their version of postmodernist "history." This is not to take a position on the "unity" or "disunity" of the tetralogy (see Berger 1991). It is to say that a thesis like Kahn's—that *Richard II* is "about power" (Knapp 1993, 7) is unlikely to go very far in translating a script into a successful production. Whether we agree with Bennett or not, the plays have to be seen in some relationship with each other. The thrust of Hal's career is central to the middle two, even if he is decentered in *Part 2*. Even if Shakespeare's history is not teleological, the two *Henry IV* plays are. They aim at *Henry V* and ask us to watch Hal prepare himself for kingship and also ask, What kind of a king is *this* Hal likely to be, given the options available within the framework of the play that bears *his* name, as king.

It is a question that Iain Glen, for example, did not ask himself. He had not *been* Prince Hal and therefore sprang, full-blown and isolated from his dramatic heritage, into the overpowered Memorial Theatre. At some point, Adrian Noble decided that Michael Maloney would remain a prince. Julian Glover was thus permitted to be a powerful Henry IV, perhaps preventing Maloney from going forward to *Henry V* or perhaps given such emphasis because Glover would be the only king in this truncated series. He wandered *into* the tavern with his insomnia and, after his death, was carried through the countryside. For better and for worse, his experience incorporated his kingdom, and the rejection of Falstaff seemed almost a final reflex of Henry IV's influence, rather than an early instance of a new king's long apprenticeship to political craftsmanship. For Alan Howard, Hal was a prelude to a consummate if extemporaneous career. For Bill Camp, his rehearsal as Hal led to the *Henry V* which I discuss at the end of this book.

How time is defined—or undefined—how zeitgeists compete within the same time, in tavern, court, or on battlefield, how different concepts of history, of honor, love and justice jostle with each other as reflected by characters in the same script, how the lack of sanction "in this new world," how the breakdown of continuity and the conflicts of those competing for power which are the heart of any history play are depicted—no matter what pious rationalizations and sanctimonious evasions the characters provide—these are questions a director must ask and answer for his production. What conceptual space, what physical space, are his actors to inhabit? The questions are more difficult when sequences are involved, because they do probe the issues of unity of sequence, and of distinction between the elements of the sequence. The problem for history plays is augmented by the fact that, in public at least, the characters are seldom speaking the truth. That ironic edge must always be conveyed to an audience perhaps numbed by it in their contemporary politics. It is probably *not* a good idea, then, to permit the *platea* to reflect too much of our own political scene. That might be to render *locus* contemptible through familiarity and to erase its uniqueness, its taking us to another time not stultifyingly analogous to our own.

A conflated script does not answer the questions—or, if it does, it delivers an answer that says the questions are not important since the two parts of *Henry IV* can be made one. The designer, Loy Arcenas, says, "We're striving for the epic . . . The stage is . . . a huge arena in which events are played out. Within that space four immense architectural elements, different shapes, a bridge, will combine in various ways to create different locations, interiors and exteriors. Very big spaces will be created with very simple elements" (quoted in Allen 1994, 6). The stress on "epic" is frightening, of course, particularly since *Part 2* could be described within the generic assumptions of epic degeneration, but the flexibility that Arcenas predicts might accommodate the several mixed modes of these two plays. The conflation may inevitably be a trivialization of issues raised in early-modern England through late-medieval history, since so much context, contrast, and commentary must be excised to pull some seven hours down to four. If that is the case, the questions raised at the end of the 1590s merely become cliches for us, more dull evidence of Shakespeare's alleged "universality."

The thesis behind this *Henry IV* is fairly straightforward: "Shakespeare portrays a country and a people at a crossroads of power: the feudalism and divine right of kings in *Richard II* give way to capitalism and Machiavellian politics in the *Henrys*" (Baker 1994a, 1). "Henry is the traditional king," says Kahn (quoted in Baker, 10). It has been argued that Henry IV, as Bolingbroke, negotiates a neofeudal arrangement with those who support his claim against Richard (see Coursen 1984). It is the only *premise* of power available to him, other than the sheer numbers of men he musters. The argument made by dramaturge Baker and director Kahn is similar to that of Graham Holderness (1985) —that Richard espouses an absolutism, symbolized by the sun, against the barons' insistence on a system of reciprocal responsibilities and obligations. Such a thesis can support a production of *Richard II*, but it tends to leave the two *Henry* plays looking too much like our world for comfort: "It is a curious time of transition. . . . The post-modern, post-Cold War world anxiously awaits the coming of a new millennium. So we find in Shakespeare's great history, *Henry IV*, a strange modernity, and recognize our own condition in this sixteenth-century play and its portrait of the threshold-state of Henry's England . . . How, in perilous times, does one govern? Shakespeare challenges us by asking not what kind of a person a leader must be, but rather, what kind of leader leads best?" (Baker, 1, 10). Perhaps, but Shakespeare shows us the king that Henry IV *must* be—a monarch responding to the emergencies that he (with Richard's cooperation) has set in motion. The question the two plays ask is about Prince Hal. And the question consistently raised, since Henry IV's complaint about his "unruly son" at the end of *Richard II* is, What kind of king will this prince be? Each production answers the question in a different way, of course, and much depends upon what we observe in the tavern scenes and on how the new King, not Hal, deals with Falstaff in the final scene of the *II Henry IV*. Baker tells us that "in *Henry V*, [n]o vestiges remain of the young prince" (7). That is radically untrue—the King's facility in trapping the traitors shows what Hal learned from Falstaff, and the effort at the practical joke on Williams and Fluellen is an embarrassing excrescence of the career of the prince—but irrelevant to *Henry IV*, except in its vision of a Hal who is *not* preparing himself for kingship. We know he is doing just that from his first soliloquy in *I Henry IV*. The question, of course, is, What is the thrust of *this* Hal?

Fortunately, Kahn's *Henry IV* was better than some of what was said about it in advance. In "historicizing" a production, it may be helpful to look at the various documents surrounding it, if only to discard the verbiage in favor of the performance. Anne Barton (1972), for example, contributed a brilliant essay for her husband's gimmicky and unconvincing *Richard II* of the early 1970s (see Coursen 1992, 140-46). Kahn conflated the two parts of *Henry IV*, with an intermission after the first part and a streamlined second part that rushed toward the rejection scene. The production lasted four hours, but they were hours well spent, and the performers received a standing ovation at the end. They did seem, however, to be *one* play, a result of an editing and cutting of a lot of the Gloucestershire material, which gives the second part its unique tone, and an excising of many of Falstaff's soliloquies, particularly in Part 2, where his cynical discussion of his gulling of Shallow and his disquisition on the two princes were gone.

The quality of Kahn's production and the considerable challenges he met and overcame, however, allow the critic to be more than forgiving, indeed to step back in admiration at the ability of ART and Shakespeare Theatre to produce such convincing and powerful versions of English history. Kahn, particularly, is to be praised for not forcing the material into "relevance," regardless of the prose produced to promote and elucidate the production. And, blessedly, Kahn did not strain for "postmodernism" with these two plays. The avenue back *into* history was not blocked by concept or theory, and thus the way was open for our evaluation of "final cause," which, in the case of the history plays, invariably insists on some response to "current events," however defined and interpreted.

The chief victim of the pressure and pace of this condensation, though, was Hal. Derek Smith played him as very young. His "I know you all" soliloquy was delivered as if he were sharing an adolescent prank with us. That is to trivialize a cold and calculated statement of intention that we are, I am certain, meant to take with us as we follow Hal's career to "I know thee not." To undercut *locus* with a *platea* that tells us that Hal is young or that he is really a good guy is, I assert, to undermine the characterization. "Popularity" is something the politician courts—as Bolingbroke is said to have done in *Richard II*—but we, the audience who know more than anyone else on stage, are not meant to like the *character*. Smith was given a postmodern "bowl-on-the-head" haircut, which usually makes its modish wearers look imbecile because it makes eyeballs look protuberant. Hal was permitted "modern" clothing—a silver shirt and, later, a suit with buttoned-up jacket. These anachronisms of detail were meant to show that he was "the man of the future," that he "knows what time it is," or will be when he gets to be king. One of the great ironies of *Henry V*, of course, is that its motivating agent cannot finally control the time he so effectively "redeemed" in the first moments of his kingship. "We are time's subjects," as Hastings says, and as Joan K. Andrews reiterates in a perceptive program note (1994, 27).

The production, as Lloyd Rose noted accurately, "focuses most strongly on the predicament of a king's son . . . unable to please his stern father" (1994 D-1). But the speed with which events went by gave Hal no time in which to mature. It was almost as if "unity of time" were being observed. Thus the gradual process whereby Hal becomes Henry V was blurred into a fast-forward. The transition is signaled by the new king's "know [ing] how to handle" Falstaff (as Hal says) by denying the fat knight any words at the coronation procession: "Reply not to me with a fool-born jest." Here, Henry V knew what he wanted to do, but he was not as coldly certain as, for example, Bill Camp in the ART production of 1993. Camp had fuller scripts and separate productions from which to emerge as king. Derek Smith's Henry made the rejection a bit more spontaneous than the script suggests it is. Henry may not know when, exactly, Falstaff will arrive, but the king has rehearsed his response as prince. "I know you all" will become "I know thee not." And as he measured Hotspur's grave—"two paces of the vilest earth"—so he provides a dimension for Falstaff's: "the grave doth gape / For thee thrice wider than for other men."[3]

That this new king knew how to handle his misleaders was demonstrated by his rejection of *Poins*. Poins had arrived and lined up opposite Falstaff, the former certain that he had replaced the latter as Hal's favorite. He may have done so, but the new king gave his lines "I have turned away my former self; / So will I those that kept me company" to Poins. This brilliant blanket rejection was rendered somewhat awkward by Henry's having to break from the processional format and wander unceremoniously back along the route he had taken—back into a time he now despises. While that movement is understandable conceptually, it detracted from Henry's march into the future here. The move combined with some emotional strain in Henry's voice to make the rejection perhaps more personal than political. The king is using Falstaff (and here, Poins) to read a speech of sober intention to all of England. The point was underlined by the bringing in of Hostess and Doll, Peto and Gadshill bound and under arrest as part of the general roundup of the usual suspects, although the earlier arrest of Doll and Hostess had been cut. Shallow, Boy, and Poins fled before the Chief Justice reappeared to arrest Falstaff. Henry V's "personalization" of the speech undercut the point he was making and confused what is obviously his intention to have Falstaff put into prison. While the Fleet was considered a mild punishment—it is where Hal had spent his time for striking the Chief Justice—it is well within the "ten mile" limit Henry V has set. Falstaff is forced to break the law.

Smith's emotional treatment of this cold and effective finality muddled the ending. Here it was a function of youth and inexperience which seemed to be a result of the conflation of the script. Thus the sense of Hal's impatience with the passing of time, particularly in Part 2, and *our* sense that Hal is ready to be king—regardless of Henry IV's doubts—was undercut. To see this young king becoming Henry V in his own play was possible, though, in that Kahn left in a portion of the scene in which Henry listens to the Chief Justice's argument and then agrees with it. It is what Henry V will do with the Archbishop—let an elder statesman make a case that the king already agrees with, which permits the king to pose as a reasonable person acquiescing to good persuasion. In each case, the king gets someone else to make *his* argument—one, a speech in favor of law and order in England and, another, a long brief on the legality of an invasion of France.

A neat touch here was to shift a scene that some stage directions claim is "a room in the Prince's house" (see Humphreys 1991, 49) to the palace, as Hal, it seemed, tried to adjust to the life that is to come. He was bored and drinking tea. Poins slipped in with a welcome flask of some thicker potation. Then Bardolph and the Boy appeared. Hal was "at home" and planned with Poins another strategy against Falstaff. One of the points here was that Hal cannot be king until he is. He resisted the "low transformation," however, and the scene showed him emotionally ready to accept the position that would go with the palace. The finale was strengthened by two superb tableaux. The first found Falstaff, Shallow, Boy, et al. on one side of the red carpet, Poins on the other. From upstage, Henry V's glittering procession was suddenly illuminated. It came toward us in silvery splendor—silver, "pale and common drudge / 'Tween man and man" being the Lancastrian mettle. At the very end, Henry V stood on the bridge that came down from time to time above the stage and everyone else below him, upstage, for a magnificent instant, the living and the dead and the banished, showing from whence this king had come. And, insofar as Henry had broken "through the foul and ugly mists / Of vapours that did seem to strangle him," he did seem to have risen from the dead. This Hal, however, will move more tentatively into a full-fledged Henry V than will Camp's more mature Henry. Smith will have to think what it has meant to be Prince Hal. Camp learned that much as he went along.

Two other effects of conflation inhibited the production. Pace is essential to Shakespearean production, but here Kahn went too fast at times. I could accept the elimination of Rumor and of the wonderful first scene of Part 2, in which the "nature of news" is dissected. Part 2 began with 1.3, in which the Archbishop of York meets with his co-conspirators. They stood on the bridge, with Henry IV sitting darkly on his throne, below right. As the Archbishop said "The commonwealth is sick," Henry coughed. As the conspiracy exited, Henry went into "How many thousand of my poorest subjects are / At this hour asleep!"—lines from 3.1 that were at once ironic and appropriate, in that a powerful, not poor, group of subjects were at this hour awake and plotting Henry's overthrow. At the very beginning, we had seen Henry IV looking at a pile of corpses, with hanged men above them, so that we began with a haunted king, "shaken and wan," and could predict that more than one person "bears hard" these slaughtered men, as the Archbishop of York does his brother's execution by Bolingbroke at Bristow, lines left in here. Thus the seemingly endless sequence of political murders that elicit revenge was introduced and repeated, preparing us for the appearance later of a justice seeker. It is the role Bolingbroke had assumed at the beginning of *Richard II*.

After the opening of Part 2, the production then went back to Falstaff's confrontation with the Chief Justice. This editing, I assume, posed no problem for most members of the audience. Some of the leisure of Gloucestershire was eliminated—the counterpoint of the first scene of Act 5 was cut, and thus we lost one of Falstaff's soliloquies, as we had lost his disquisition on the virtues of sherris-sack, and on his soldiers in Part 1 (4.2). In the ART version the ironic celebration of returning "heroes" and the slow drift of the scene into a starlit dusk made a wonderful contrast with the brisk business being conducted in London. Again, I doubt that the deletions were a problem for most of the audience, although I had to sort out the blending of Mortimer and Mowbray, since "Mortimer" became a character in Part 2.

Other difficulties included a new scene's crashing down upon the previous scene. Henry IV, for example, was interrupted by the descent of a bridge for the first tavern scene. Even mad Pistol—played gloriously by Daniel Southern as a "skin-walker" exhumed from an old play—was upstaged by a man staggering onto the bridge from a whore's room with his pants down. The editing occasionally eliminated some of Shakespeare's verbal linkages. Hastings's shallowness in sounding the bottom of the aftertimes and Falstaff's seeing "the bottom of Justice Shallow," moments that comment on the prophecies and false predictions that web through these plays, were gone. One had to agree with dramaturge Christopher Baker that "it is easy to forget how the two worlds are linked" (1994c, 25). John's cynical "God, and not we, hath safely fought today" would have indicated the *lack* of contact between the world of the play and any encompassing dispensation. The quickness of the production did not absorb all pauses—moments in the tavern scenes provided some intentional randomness which played against wild spurts of chase, thus giving the surrounding political and military sequences their different drummer—but Henry IV should pause after "Bear Worcester to the death" and *then* say "and Vernon too." Why leave in Vernon's reiterated admiration of Hal if not to emphasize the irony of the king's order? Vernon has seen Hal better than anyone else—including Henry IV—indeed is the first character, other than Hal himself, to predict what Hal will be as king. That is a minor point, admittedly, but the production's attention to detail makes it worth mentioning here. Falstaff's satire of military values in his description to Shallow of how effective the soldiers *Falstaff* has selected will be was missing.

The only major problem in the script as delivered was in the final tavern scene (2.4). If the script leaves out Doll's "What says your Grace?" and Falstaff's amused "His Grace says that which his flesh rebels against," we out there in audience land are bound to miss the point. Falstaff has turned the tables on Hal one more (and one last) time by inverting order and forcing Hal to elevate the denizens of the tavern to rebut Falstaff's excuse that he "dispraised [Hal] before the wicked."

Henry V will correct this inversion, as he demonstrates with the Chief Justice and with his so-called "misleaders," but here he is bested in the context of what he cares most about—good government and a precisely structured hierarchy. Falstaff's line about "how men of merit are sought after" comments on his own triumph within the scene just ending. As king, Henry will seem to be "democratic" in his oration before Agincourt, but he will revert to form in receiving the lists of dead on both sides and in claiming that "it was ourself thou didst abuse" to Williams. In other words, if that final tavern scene is left in, it has to be *understood*. Other things were not here, of course, and I missed Falstaff's capture of Coleville and the latter's defiance of Prince John, which, I think, motivates John's order for Coleville's execution. But for the most part the editing was skillful and made a long and complicated production seem short and exciting without a surrender of nuance or complexity.

Production values were superb. Loy Arenas's metallic set moved on tracks and pulleys so that it could become prison like—particularly in the Northumbria scene in Part 2—and could open out to David Leong's precisely choreographed battle sequences. According to Norman Allen, "the entire Battle of Shrewsbury is played out onstage over the length of two scenes. Leong has broken the action down into two major battles, five skirmishes, and five individual fights, making a total of 12 separate units to be choreographed" (1994, 7). That definition was there in the battle sequences, but they came off, fortunately, as bloody, dirty scuffles. Hal, for example, was armed with sword and dagger, Hotspur only with sword. It was the counterpunching left hook of the dagger that nailed Hotspur.

After Henry IV's nightmare glimpse of the bodies on which he had risen to kingship, the court entered liturgically, with crosses echoing the dull glint of the set. The northern faction contrasted with Lancastrian silver, the former wearing brownish red and, for the most part, red hair. This was flaming rebellion from perhaps a primitive place, if that is what the animal fur on their costumes was meant to convey. Hal's tiger tights linked him with the rebels, appropriately in one sense, since he seems to resist authority within the world of the play; even we know early on that he will assert his authority when he has it to assert. The background was often a gray, abstract sky, reflecting a Lancastrian reign that was "neither right nor wrong." Occasionally, as when Falstaff rose to complain about having his pocket picked, it was dawn. The long, slow slant of a falling sun played against the three trees in Shallow's orchard. The set made for a "curiously timeless production" (Pressley 1994b, D-3), but the "eclectic" costumes, said Roy Proctor, served no "discernible [or] expressive purpose . . . beyond depriving the production of a flavor, any flavor" (1994). When asked what the setting of the play was, Kahn said, "I have no idea" (quoted in Pressley 1994, D-3).

The acting was without exception excellent, and although doubling occurred, the consistent quality of so large a cast was remarkable. Edward Gero's Hotspur crumpled the letter from the unknown defector, threw it to the floor, and spoke to it as if it were a person he despised. This action was repeated as Pistol threatened to shoot the ruff he had torn from Doll and tossed to the tavern floor, and as Hal tore his apron off and discarded it angrily at the end of his masquerade as drawer. I had hoped that the courtier whom Hotspur satirizes in his excuse to Henry IV would be onstage during that amusing diatribe, or that Hotspur had picked out a courtier as an "example" of what he scorns. That action would have set up other sequences in plays where almost no one likes anyone else. One exception—Hotspur and Kate (Caitlin O'Connell)—was played out with the gusto of the first confrontation between another Kate and Petruchio (as Bob Mondello [1994] noted). O'Connell's complaint about Hotspur's post-traumatic-stress disorder (see Shay 1994, 165 ff.) was particularly powerful. The carryover of her character from Part 1 to her actually striking Northumberland in Part 2 was one validation of the combining of these two scripts. Hotspur's problems with diction centered on the letter *d,* which Hal captured in his parody, "give my roan horse a d-d-d-d drench." Emery Battis's Glendower dangerously mocked Hotspur, though with a different letter: "A virtue that was n-n-n-never seen in you."

Ted van Griethuysen's Henry IV did not dominate the sequence (as Julian Glover had done in the RSC productions) but balanced the effort to be king against the attempt to convince Hal to be the prince the king wants him to be. The precision of this performance paid off powerfully when, at the end, he recognized Hal as "*my* Harry" and placed the purloined crown back on his son's head. David Sabin's Falstaff kept the character's tendency to overplay under control, so that Falstaff fitted into this world believably, mocking it even as he yearned for its conventional rewards. The key to Sabin's performance was a matter-of-fact "modern" tone of voice that balanced Falstaff's more absurdly grandiloquent boastings and pronouncements. This controlled Falstaff could out-do Hal at almost any moment, with the exception of the coda to the "play extempore"—"I do, I will"—and the ending that Hal has predicted and that this Falstaff glimpsed and then forgot. Floyd King's Shallow posed as an intelligent man but undercut himself by forgetting what the next word might be in the most simple of utterances. He was not suffering from a speech deficiency but from a gumming of the synapses. He had no trouble "recalling" his youth, however, and he packed his bags in record speed and rushed after Falstaff, saying "London! London!" Smith's Hal showed us that his response to the "death" of Falstaff at Shrewsbury flowed from Hal's grief at having killed someone he wished could have been his friend in Hotspur. Hal's promise to lie for Falstaff, one assumed, emerged from Hal's recognition that he must submerge again, having come out (like the sun) briefly to dispatch Hotspur. Here, Falstaff, as in the rejection scene, served the purposes of Prince-King.

## NOTES

1. For the strategies employed by many recent directors of the history plays on the British stage, see Barbara Hodgdon (1991). For a discussion of the Hands production of *Henry V* see Coursen 1992, 140–78.

2. For a review that goes into even more detail about the mishmash that this production presented to its audience—though the response is surprisingly neutral, indeed the verdict is that the productions are "coherent"—see Dorothy and Wayne Cook, "*Henry IV, Parts 1 and 2.*" *Shakespeare Bulletin.* 12/2 (Spring 1994): 14–15. They find Falstaff "neither fish nor fowl" because of his being cast as "part guru, part clown" (14), but do not discuss Falstaff's being torn from the historical and aristocratic context which helps him re-invent his character as he scripts himself and assigns parts to others as he goes.

3. Those familiar with my *Performance as Interpretation* (1992) will recognize my attack on "Director's Theatre," particularly as directorial approaches obscure the issues in the admittedly "generically unstable" history plays. Those familiar with my *The Leasing Out of England* (1984) will recognize my analysis of the *Henry IV* plays, rendered in far greater specificity there than here. On the possible ways of performing the executions of Vernon and Coleville see my "Vernon and Coleville" (1990).

# VIII

## "Truth, a Pebble of Quartz?": *Hamlet* in 1994 I: Shakespeare & Company and Orlando

In *"Hamlet:* Entering the Text" Michael Goldman suggests that the question, "How does a person relate to the text?" as asked by "contemporary criticism" is "full of a kind of adolescent despair" (1992, 449). Goldman offers "drama" as an "illuminating general case of the encounter with writing" (449). The "negotiation" between a person and a text is similar to that between an actor and a script. "What the actor does, what the script means, can't be determinedly fixed by either, but each exacts a commitment. . . . [I]n the dynamism of performance, script and actor become inseparable" (450). The script becomes "inseparable from what the actor is saying and doing now." We "go to the theater instead of staying home and reading the play [because] acting realizes a specific life at the moment of performance" (451). That is another way of saying that a play is a play, but it is also a way of saying that Harry Berger's concept of "imaginary auditions" (1989) is just that—a concept, at best an encounter between person and book. Plays, says Goldman, are "especially responsive to the interplay of scriptedness and improvisation in life, particularly to junctures where one mode gives way to or becomes questioned by or mingled with the other" (451). The Ghost gives Hamlet one script, he makes himself another. Hamlet and Gertrude confront each other, scripts in hand, as it were. Hamlet may make a nasty reply—"I shall in all my best obey *you,* Madam"—but Claudius provides its subtext for the court. The official version is that it is "a loving and a fair reply." In other words, Hamlet's effort to impose his scenario on the first scene in the court can be seen to be effectively countered by Claudius. These dynamics are the immediate trigger for Hamlet's fragmented first soliloquy.

We no doubt sympathize with Hamlet. Later, though, Claudius may make a direct appeal to *us* with his prayer, while Hamlet stands nearby talking of damning him. In the latter instance—hardly the only way of staging that scene, of course—our own "scriptedness" can be jarred into an uncertainty eased only later by Claudius's plotting with Laertes. Any "drama will reproduce this interplay to some degree . . . great drama often takes special advantage of it" (Goldman 1992, 452). "*Hamlet* regularly reenacts the basic scene that takes place when an actor prepares or performs a part, the moment of . . . entry into the text, the moment of the actor facing a script . . . contemplating or testing its ambiguities and demands and the consequences of beginning to play it." When Hamlet looks at Yorick's skull, he "is looking at past, present, and future simultaneously" (453). When "Ophelia's body is carried in [Hamlet finds that] his lady has already come to the favor of death" (454). Hamlet's admonition to Yorick has predicted a moment that also looks at past and present and which cancels a future that the queen, as she tells us, had scripted. "Hamlet seems unusually concerned about fixing texts"—giving the Player some lines to read, telling the actors to read no more than is set down for them—but Hamlet also displays "an anxiety about letting texts unfold," as in the "commentary that threatens both to disrupt and to anticipate the action" of "Gonzago" (454). *Hamlet*'s concern with texts—their fixity and their instability—is also the actor's situation, because "insofar as it is concerned with *performance,* the relation between actor and script is one of unstable exchange" (455; Goldman's emphasis). While the actor "must follow" the "commands" of the text, "by entering into the text he modifies it irrecoverably. So Hamlet must follow the commands of the Ghost, a script which entails a chain of improvisations" (455)—i.e., "howsoever thou pursuest this act . . ." At the outset, Hamlet "is deeply suspicious of anything that smacks of theatricality" (456), but "the play charts [his] journey from depression to involvement to action and death as a coming to terms with the theatricality of life" (457). "In *Hamlet* we have the opportunity to watch another group of players discovering, while they act, that they have become pawns in a dangerous political plot" (458).

In Ron Daniels's production for RSC in 1989, the players had apparently been banished to the provinces for producing a subversive play and suddenly found themselves, innocently but dangerously, presenting another. Goldman points out that the Zeffirelli film showed "the actors' bewilderment and apprehension as they discover that their performance seems to be creating an unforeseen script of scandal and subversion. To put on a play that throws your sovereign into a rage is not a good career move, and they know it" (1992, 458). Goldman cites the Essex rebellion of the spring of 1601, which would have been on the minds of the audience of the original *Hamlet* and which "remind us . . . of the interweaving strands of meaning, of implication and result that reside in an ostensibly single dramatic event" (459). Goldman suggests that "we entertain the idea of a relation between text and reader that is more like the relation between actor and script. . . . [T]here is in this notion of entry into the text room to account for our stubborn sense that there is life in literature, our sense of a process that isn't adequately pictured as a mere proliferation of signs, a mere adding of other texts to the text—any more than the actor's contribution to a play could be replaced by another text. It is, like good performance, an addition of life to the text, a life that is responsive to the text and inseparable from it" (460).

Goldman is talking, of course, about *metaphor*, the means whereby two unlike things join in a problematic and often uneasy relationship, but the way unlike things, actor and script, become that third thing that makes all the difference.

After meeting Nils Bohr in 1930, Robert Frost thought about metaphor. Bohr, of course, had enunciated the "complementarity principle" a few years before, which claimed that experimenting in one area of a system erased the prospect of exploring another aspect of the same system. The wave-particle duality is an example. Frost said that "In carrying numbers into the realm of space and at the same time into the realm of time you are mixing metaphors, that is all, and you are in trouble." When Frost asked Bohr about this contradiction, Bohr said, "the action of the individual particle is unpredictable. But it is not so of the action of the mass. There you can predict. That gives the individual atom its freedom, but the mass its necessity." Two unlike things —freedom and inevitability—join their unlikenesses into something that is neither one but is more than each. The "proper poetical education in the metaphor," Frost suggests is to "know the metaphor in its strength and its weakness." Truth or a pebble of quartz?—for once, then, something.

*Hamlet* has its complementarity principle, for to look at one aspect is to cast another into darkness. Like metaphor, "It is a very living thing" and is perhaps the best example of what Frost calls the "Greatest of all attempts to say one thing in terms of another . . . matter in terms of spirit, or spirit in terms of matter" (Frost 1930, 1028). One of the ways in which *Hamlet* works is that while we and Shakespeare may have the end in view—we, even as we experience it for the first time, he, even as he wrote it—it is "not set like a trap to close with" (1032). Or, since it *is*—with the evil party falling into the trap he has set for the revenger (as Helen Gardner [1963] shows *must* happen in this genre) and two would-be revengers falling too—it could be made to seem "written that way, with cunning and device" and simultaneously something "believed into existence, that be[gan] in something more felt than known" (1032).

The metaphor known as *Hamlet* has it both ways—an ending planned by a villain and dictated by a sub-genre and a play that commences in feeling and that creates an unspoken "third" entity out of the "silence" of the "rest." It is *platea* that believes the already existing script into existence.

The script continues to be remarkably capable of exciting and original interpretations, of making metaphors between it and contemporary audiences, that is, of challenging *locus* with *platea*, which is what the players may have done—they at least challenged the boy actors, and lost—and is what "Gonzago" is supposed to do. The script carries with it a remarkable ability to poise "what and who was represented in the dramatic world" against "who and what was *representing* that world" (Weimann 1991, 409) against each other in ways that permit the latter, *platea,* to assert its authority powerfully so that the *locus* communicates to an audience within a remarkable variety of times, places, and languages.

If Hamlet is "less a man than part of the discourse" (as postmodernist theory would have it), then other characters move into slightly more independent positions than they were when considered in "Hamlet-centric" analysis or, as often in the New Criticism, as merely subjects of Hamlet's point of view. Claudius becomes more than modernist productions tended to make him. Basil Sydney, Olivier's Claudius, was a nasty hermit crab, while Anthony Hopkins, in Tony Richardson's production, was an almost absolute sensualist. By pressing Hamlet back into "the discourse," Claudius can emerge as a "mighty opposite," particularly if the script used is F1, as in the Ashland version that Barry Kraft prepared. Ophelia benefits in much the same way, as feminist critics, like Carol Thomas Neely (1981), Anna Nardo (1983), and Elaine Showalter (1985) look at Ophelia as a character in her own right, rather than as a scripted victim who frets and wails her hour on the stage. Some Ophelias in 1994 dominated their moments, not just as "reflectors" (in the Jamesian sense) but as subjects of their own tragedies and certainly without "any hint of the creepy ethereality that tends to dog the character" (Maupin 1994, A-2) The Oedipal energy that Olivier deployed (with an Eileen Herlie younger than Hamlet) reached its culmination, perhaps, when Derek Jacobi virtually raped Claire Bloom in the 1980 BBC production. It seems to have dropped away from current notions about the play. In 1994 the dysfunctional families of Claudius and Polonius tended to reflect each other within the scripts, and that notion echoed even into the scene in Gertrude's closet, which certainly depicts a dysfunctional family, among other things. Current productions are uneasy with the supernatural and either normalize the Ghost, à la television, or eliminate him as much as possible. The ways in which the script opens into mysteries beyond, above, and below the visible world seems not to be something for which modern directors reach. The political dimension also proves troubling to directors and it is often eliminated as much as possible or rendered in modern terms. Today's *Hamlet*s, in North America at least, tend not to suggest monarchy with any conviction, and today's Hamlets tend not to be particularly princely. That trend can be traced back to the 1960s, to David Warner's "rebel sans cause" and Nicol Williamson's snarl of a Hamlet, looking back in anger, in Tony Richardson's production.

The point, however, is, What *is* there in recent productions, and what is it within the script that keeps the play so vividly alive on stage, even as some argue the primacy of *King Lear* (cf. R. A. Foakes 1993a) as the play of our post-World War II era? The answer is provided by Russell Treyz, Director of the Orlando Festival *Hamlet,* who says, "If you go back to the text, everything is new. And this time we're working on it with these specific people and in this specific place and for this specific audience. That's what's exciting about live theater—that it is different every time" (quoted in Maupin 1994, A-2). In other words, *platea* can serve as an energy that can constantly renew *locus.*

Productions of 1994 proved the director of one of them wrong. Richard Monette said, "to act Hamlet is to act Everyman, for there is a part of Hamlet in us all. The actor as Hamlet gets to play everyone, all at once. This is indeed holding a mirror up to nature" (1994). No. The actor as Hamlet plays the role at a specific moment in time, putting himself in Hamlet's circumstances and letting the metaphor between those unlike things, human actor and character in a fiction, fuse within himself. He holds his unique mirror up to a moment in time. Even the meaning of the moment in the production and of the moment in history is inevitably subject to debate, so that "nature" is problematized, subject to "the form and pressure of the time" and of the "indeterminacy principle," which alters the precision of measurement itself and therefore some of the authority measurement might claim. It is truer, as

Margaret Atwood says, that "Hamlet himself—Hamlet the character—has kept his secret . . . He is elusive; he mocks our efforts to pin him down. And so we go to see him again and again, wondering which of his selves he will be this time, and which of our own selves he will speak to" (1994, 25). As postmodernists would argue, different mirrors were held up at different moments in different places to even a different person, conditioned as that person was by immediate and distant previous experiences of the play and changed as he or she was during the four months within which he or she saw the plays. The mirror, which is itself an ambiguous reflector, had become a kaleidoscope. But Hamlet remained five distinct metaphors, each requiring a different deciphering, and each decoding reflecting the subjectivity of the reflection—thought and image—that went on within the spectator as he pondered the mirror the production had held up.

It was possible, within a few months of 1994, to experience five different versions of *Hamlet* and to submit each to the same interrogation in radically different ways. The productions that I examine here were "contemporary," although none was set in "the present." They were contemporary because of the specificity which Treyz stresses. "A good *Hamlet*," says Geoff Chapman (1994), "should always be a thriller." The versions of 1994 were thrillers. They also included what Chapman calls a "good *Hamlet* . . . one that creates a convincing character out of mortal despair, a survivor offering a laser-sharp portrait of deep insecurities, a bitter witness of events as well as a glamorous hero and a man who can deliver spine-shivering rage, suspicion and contempt while battling indecisiveness and the tussle between duty and right and private, painful emotions. That's asking a lot." It was, though, what we got in these productions—particularly in those that decentered Hamlet a trifle to give us a stronger Claudius than usual and a more central Ophelia than usual. The "thriller" aspect was facilitated by the scale of the staging of three of the productions—Shakespeare & Company played in different spaces as they toured, using only a set of five arches to be erected on various stages, while both the Stratford, Ontario and the Ashland productions occurred on other than the main stages of those festivals, Stratford's in the Tom Patterson, a converted ice rink, and Ashland's in the six-hundred-seat Angus Bowmer. The Regent's Park version was up against the closing bell and the shutting of the iron gates.

Shakespeare & Company's touring *Hamlet,* directed by Kevin G. Coleman, was a heavily cut version designed for secondary school students that ran for one hour forty-five minutes, including a fifteen-minute intermission. A lot of the inherited script was missing: the opening scene, Pyrrhus and the players, the first half of Hamlet's "guilty creatures" soliloquy ("Oh, what a rogue and peasant slave"), Laertes's rebellion, Ophelia's second mad scene, the first half of the graveyard scene (Clown and Yorick), Fortinbras, and, it follows, the "all occasions" soliloquy. Surprisingly, Rosencrantz and Guildenstern were kept, with Alyssa Lupo, who played Gertrude, doubling awkwardly as Rosencrantz.

To cover the gaps, one of the actors offered brief synopses of the action. I am not sure whether I was confused by the narrative itself or by the presentational technique. Why, after Ophelia has said, "I shall obey, my lord," must we be told that "Ophelia is an obedient daughter"? One moment that did work, because daring and "dramatic," was Horatio's interruption of his reading of Hamlet's letter to tell us what had happened before—that is, that Hamlet had discovered the king's commission, altered it, and sent Rosencrantz and Guildenstern to their doom in England. This was the "narrative hook" technique, used by fiction writers, who stop the story at a crucial moment in order to contextualize that moment. The program provided descriptions of the eighteen scenes into which Coleman had divided the script. The houselights were up for the first half of the production so that people could refer to the brief outlines. They did. The lighting also created a sense of inclusiveness. We shared the same space as the actors instead of watching them up there behind the proscenium. There was a strong feeling of rapport with the actors and with what they were trying to do.

Given six actors playing eleven parts, Coleman decided to acknowledge his audience, indeed to create soliloquies from speeches that in the script are delivered to someone onstage. "Who should 'scape whipping'?" Hamlet asked, gesturing at the audience. He indicated the audience again on "sitting at a play" (as Branagh did in his 1993 RSC production). *We*, the audience, were the ones who had approved of Gertrude's marriage with Claudius at the outset, and, later, as Claudius mollified Laertes, we were the "general gender" who loved Hamlet. Claudius, the uncharismatic Machiavellian, reproached us because we did not love him. At the end, of course, we were the "mute . . . audience" that had witnessed these events. Ophelia's "so affrighted" speech was a soliloquy—and powerfully so—until Michael Marlow's Polonius blundered in, upstaging the words and draining the scene of the energy that she had created. Hamlet's anticipation of "Gonzago" ("like the murder of my father"), his taunting of the King ("a knavish piece of work"), and his description ("a murder done in Vienna") were all soliloquies.

2. Design by Cedric Gibbons for *Romeo and Juliet*, 1936.

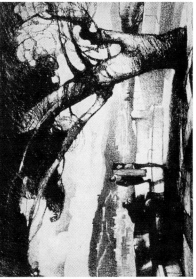

3. Design by Cedric Gibbons for *Romeo and Juliet*, 1936.

1. *Romeo and Juliet*, MGM 1936. Leslie Howard: Romeo. Courtesy of Turner Entertainment, Inc.

4. Leslie Howard, *Hamlet*, 1936.

5. Laurence Olivier, *Hamlet*, 1949. Courtesy of the Rank Organisation Plc.

6. Still from *Much Ado About Nothing*, directed by Kenneth Branagh. Top (L to R) Don Pedro (Denzel Washington), Benedick (Kenneth Branagh), Beatrice (Emma Thompson), Leonato (Richard Briers), Antonio (Brian Blessed), Hero (Kate Beckinsale) and Claudio (Robert Sean Leonard) celebrate their wedding. © 1993 Renaissance Films PLC and The Samuel Goldwyn Company. All rights reserved.

7. Damian Lewis as Hamlet and Pamela Miles as Gertrude (with background Ghost) in The New Shakespeare Company's *Hamlet,* Open Air Theatre, Regent's Park. Photo courtesy of Alaistair Muir.

8. Shakespeare and Company *Hamlet* directed by Kevin Coleman. Tom Jaeger, Hamlet; Alyssa Lupo, Queen Gertude. Photo courtesy of Lezlie Lee.

9. *Hamlet.* Directed by Russell Treyz. Orlando, 1994. Hamlet: James Helsinger. Ophelia: Suzanne O'Donnell. Photo courtesy of Michael Glantz.

11. Richard Howard, Ashland, 1994. Photo courtesy of David Cooper.

10. *Hamlet.* Directed by Russell Treyz. Orlando, 1994. Paul Kiernan: Horatio. James Helsinger: Hamlet. Photo courtesy of Michael Glantz.

12. Stratford Festival. *Hamlet,* directed by Richard Monette. Stephen Ouimette as Hamlet. Director Richard Monette. Courtesy of the Stratford Shakespearean Festival Foundation of Canada.

13. Hamlet (Richard Howard), Ophelia (Dawn Lisell): Oregon Shakespeare Festival's *Hamlet,* directed by Henry Woronicz. Photo courtesy of David Cooper.

14. Linda Alper: Rosencrantz. Richard Howard: Hamlet. Jonathan Toppo: Guildenstern. Ashland, 1994. Photo courtesy of David Cooper.

17. *Henry VI.* Directed by Katie Mitchell. Stratford-on-Avon, 1994. Jonathan Firth as Henry VI. Courtesy of the Royal Shakespeare Company.

15. *Henry IV.* Directed by Ron Daniels. American Repertory Theatre, 1994. Bill Camp: Hal. Jeremy Geidt: Falstaff. Photo courtesy of Richard Feldman.

16. *Henry IV.* Directed by Michael Kahn. Shakespeare Theatre, D.C., 1994. Derek Smith: Hal. Sheira Venetianer: Doll. David Sabin: Falstaff. Photo courtesy of Carol Pratt.

18. *Henry IV, Part 1*, directed by Ron Daniels. Bill Camp, Will LeBow, Benjamin Evett, Nathaniel Gundy, Jeremy Geidt. Photo courtesy of Richard Feldman.

19. *Henry V*, directed by Ron Daniels. Bill Camp, James Farmer, Michael Janes, Jeff Breland. Photo courtesy of Charles Erickson.

21. Simon Russell Beale: Edgar, RSC, 1993–94. Courtesy of the Royal Shakespeare Company.

20. *King Lear*, directed by Adrian Noble. Simon Russell Beale: Edgar. Robert Stephens: Lear. David Calder: Kent. Ian Hughes: Fool. Courtesy of the Royal Shakespeare Company.

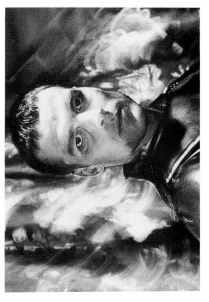

22. *Henry V*, directed by Matthew Warchus. Stratford-on-Avon, 1994. Iain Glen as Henry V. Courtesy of the Royal Shakespeare Company.

The production had opened with a masked and golden-robed mime of "Gonzago"—the nap, the entrance of Lucianus, the murder, and the wooing (in which Gertrude played coy for a while, then took the initiative by grabbing Lucianus-Claudius's hand)—so that we were meant to re-create the offstage performance of "Gonzago" within the production itself. Gertrude read the prologue to "Gonzago," and Claudius, not having heard any of it yet, asked Hamlet whether there was "any offense in it," then shrugged, took Gertrude's hand, and went offstage to see the play. While I am not sure that this audience knew that a memorial reconstruction of the opening mime was required of it, the scattering of the inner audience in the aftermath of "Gonzago" was powerfully chaotic.

Hamlet's "To be, or not to be" was delivered center stage, with the five other actors stationed in each of the five freeform arches of the set. The effect here was to include all of them and all of us within Hamlet's general analysis of the human condition. Indeed, Claudius, down right, winced and put his hands together as Hamlet said "Thus conscience does make cowards of us all," a nice foreshadowing of Claudius's paralysis during the prayer scene. The soliloquy linked up with the later scene through Hamlet as well, since it is *lack* of conscience—the wish to send Claudius's soul to hell—that stays his sword. The "To be, or not to be" was undercut, however, by Polonius's mugging from under the second arch, midstage right, and his tapping of his finger against his belt. Gertrude's promise to Hamlet that she will not reveal what he has told her was also a soliloquy, delivered after Hamlet had dragged Polonius out. She did not desert Claudius, however, and her drinking of the wine was just that, not an effort simultaneously to save Hamlet and to test Claudius. Since Claudius was standing close enough to take the poisoned chalice from her, one had to wonder why he did not.

A metadramatic approach to the script, demanded by the number of actors, could have been employed even more extensively. At moments I could not discern the "style" of the production. Still, several scenes benefited from relative completeness—permitting the contrapuntal rhythms so characteristic of Shakespeare's scenic design to establish themselves—and from Coleman's imaginative staging. Hamlet's confrontations with Ophelia and Gertrude, for example, mirrored each other. The blocking was not precisely the same, but Hamlet's physical violence and verbal rage linked the scenes indelibly. Some Oedipal energies may have been at work in Hamlet's sexual attack on each woman, but what came through in each instance was Hamlet's anger at what he felt was a betrayal of him and, in the latter scene, of his father. He ripped the locket from Gertrude's neck and the locket from his own to make his comparison, then pressed the miniature of King Hamlet into

Gertrude's palm. The Ghost had entered, actually touching Hamlet with his sword, as if to protect Gertrude from being raped. Wearing armor for the closet scene, the Ghost was at once furious with Hamlet for his delay and for his treatment of his mother and hopeful of a glance from Gertrude (as in recent productions like that of Ron Daniels for RSC and ART and Michael Kahn's for the Shakespeare Theatre). The Ghost had previously hung his head in sorrow as he described his "seeming-virtuous queen." The closet scene, blessedly, had no bed—one of the few productions since Gielgud's in 1936 without that seemingly obligatory queen-size.

Perhaps the finest scene in this production involved Ophelia, who mimed her drowning up center accompanied by Lupo's elegant description. Ophelia wore a white shawl on her right shoulder over her blue gown, the shawl an emblem of the river in which she drowns. Ophelia gave an enigmatic half smile as she considered the serenity of her cruise down that river. Gertrude said "old lauds" (Q2)—praise be!—as opposed to "old tunes" (F1), so that the moment blended word, mime, and subtle music to create a religious resonance. Ophelia's drowning is, after all, a precisely configured disjunctive analogy to baptism. When Laertes and Claudius put the shawl over Ophelia's head, it became a shroud with a hint of wedding dress. Gertrude's "sweets to the sweet . . . Hamlet's wife" reminded us that the second scene of the play had linked a funeral with a marriage, a marriage that has led in its sinuous way to another funeral. Ophelia was carried in. Laertes placed a rose on her body—we were the ones who would "lie howling"—and Gertrude said farewell. Ophelia then rose up and exited—a ghost—as the final scene began.

The production could have been driven more in the direction of "opening up" the script, as in the work of Ralph Cohen's Shenandoah Shakespeare Express. Against that imperative, however, is the apparent obligation to "tell the story," and here it was often thinly told, the scenes scarcely penciling in the narrative, with the editing of individual speeches often confusing. Hamlet, for example, told the Ghost to "Go on—I'll follow thee!" but there was no movement. Had Hamlet said these lines to Horatio? Perhaps—meaning "I'll catch up to you later." The Ghost conflated, "bear it not . . . Taint not thy mind . . . The glow worm" into a confusing mishmash. Hamlet told us that he would assume an "antic disposition," but some narrative about Hamlet's pretending to be mad might have helped us. Hamlet, at the end, began to "prophesy" but told us immediately that "The rest is silence." This editing made him sound like the dying Hotspur. It may be that the meter of the speeches was disturbed or that meter was retained while meanings jostled frictionally against each other without transition.

The early sequences suffered from the absence of any fragment of the first scene. Horatio's frightened "Where, my lord?" does not have much impact if we have not observed Horatio's initial encounter with the Ghost. Cohen's approach with Shenandoah Express is to leave some portion of each scene within his edited scripts. Watching Shakespeare & Company's production felt like watching a Q1 production, which provides a precis of the play but eliminates complexity and sometimes clarifies ambiguity. Coleman says in his program note that it "is the retelling of the deeper story, the 'feeling story' that touches the listener [and has] the power to recreate an experience in the listener . . . to capture us and bring us more alive" (1994). That "deeper story" did come through here, but only fitfully.

A moment that did not work in Coleman's production was Hamlet's "killing" of Polonius. Since Polonius had been in full view, up center, during the scene, Hamlet had to turn around to stab him with a backhand. Polonius fell into Gertrude's arms. Here we had to unsuspend our disbelief since neither Hamlet nor Gertrude could know that Polonius was dead. We had to wonder why she did not shout, "Quick, call 911!" Here the actors were reading lines against a fiction that we had to recognize as completely fictitious. Even the hint of an arras and a vigorous thrust by Hamlet would have resolved this problem.

Tom Jaeger's Hamlet was young, attractive, and necessarily vigorous within this "activated" script. At times he tended to shout. He read his soliloquies clearly and briskly, thus without the sense of discovery with which Mark Rylance, for example, energized those words in the RSC production of the late 1980s. He did smile as he remembered how "loving to [his] mother" his father had been, returning for an instant to that idyllic moment. His "imagination was as foul" as the possibly "damned ghost"—Vulcan's stithy being cut. "Hell" breathed out "contagion to this world," making it a hell at midnight. Hamlet's "antic disposition" was "acted"—not the exploration of a zany, half-mad vein of Hamlet's character. Hamlet's plea to Ophelia that he be remembered in her "orisons" was generic, since she had not been given a book by Polonius. Jaeger's decisions, however, were the product of this production, which rocketed along, without any potential pauses or complexities. It was the Claudius rhythm—rapid, pragmatic, shallow.

The women were splendid. It was they who conveyed what Coleman calls "the deeper story." Jayne Ogata's Ophelia, tall, shy, fragile as a porcelain statue, was clearly crazy about Hamlet—love as a prelude to madness. She precisely outlined the beginnings of her surrender of sanity as Polonius lectured her about "springes to catch woodcocks." Ophelia was sure that Hamlet loved her. Suddenly her father was questioning her own grasp on "reality." The quiver on the right side of her mouth suggested that "reality" itself was becoming equivocal for her. Alyssa Lupo's sensuous Gertrude obviously believed that all kings look alike in the dark, but she was sensitive to Ophelia's position as Polonius read Hamlet's love letters to Claudius. Lupo took the letters out of the men's hands and returned them to Ophelia. Later, Hamlet tore the letters up and flung them at her ("I loved you not!"). At the end of the scene she crawled around the floor to retrieve the scraps. Polonius could find nothing to say to her and stumbled off after Claudius. Ophelia's victimization at the hands of the male world was vividly rendered.

Given this vast and complicated script, the size of the cast, and the apparent imperative that it be delivered to a young audience in under two hours, Coleman's production was a remarkable achievement. The crowd at the Waterville Opera House on a chilly (thirty-five degrees Fahrenheit) late April evening—many of them school children—gave it a rousing ovation. Afterwards, many of the young people gathered around the board that held the actors' photographs to reidentify them. That was a very good sign that the production had succeeded.

Russell Treyz mounted a stunning, fast-paced *Hamlet* for the Orlando Shakespeare Festival. It featured a brilliant Hamlet in Jim Helsinger.

The Walt Disney Amphitheater, backed by Lake Eola, seats one thousand spectators and, on a cool night in late April, created a superb sense of "interactivity." As the natural lighting of the outdoors dropped, the stage lighting came up, and we looked in on an increasingly lethal Elsinore. Crows flew out from under the lip of the semicircular stage arch as the trumpets and kettle drums announced the entrance of a new king (1.1 was cut). This unplanned migration conveyed a steel-blue prediction to the twilight.

For this production, projections coordinated precisely with lighting cues made huge pictures on the upstage panels. "Hamlet" appeared over the photograph of a castle before the play began and during the intermission. While the play was in progress, giant photos of walls, parapets, dimly illuminated great halls, and stony corridors stood grainily behind the action—the implacable hardness against which the characters smashed, evoking the inevitable graveyard. These images became more indelible as darkness tumbled around the audience so that we became more focused on the action. Because the photographs had the quality of old silent films, the production was subtly updated to an historical moment close to our own, even though doublet and crown, rapier and dapper were the mode of performance. The mounting thus made a strong appeal to our imaginations and to our need to participate in the building of the fiction.[1]

Helsinger's Hamlet consistently used a subtext of "discovery" and convinced the audience that the character was exploring his dilemma and was often surprised by what he found. When Helsinger broke a wooden sword (a player's prop), he looked at us, half-amused, half-disgusted with himself: "This is most brave." We laughed with him. Since "brave" suggested bravado in 1601, as opposed to courage, he ironically conveyed the older meaning of the word. Hamlet's first soliloquy was cued by offstage celebrations. It was Claudius who represented "too, too sullied flesh" and his court that showed "rank and gross." To pursue the Ghost, Hamlet wrested Marcellus's sword from him and used it to threaten his companions ("I'll *make* a ghost . . ."). He later used the sword to insist on their swearing. The guards were reluctant. They are, after all, Claudius's guards, not Hamlet's. I have never before seen that point made in production.

"To be, or not to be"—given its sudden but always potent Q1 placement—was delivered to us, so that as Hamlet swung his eyes and his arms around the amphitheater, we were the victims of the law's delay, the insolence of office, the spurns that patient merit of the unworthy takes. The antique generalizations came alive as Hamlet insisted that we apply the words to our own lives. This was the style described by W. B. Worthen as "psychological motivation complicated a degree of openness to the theatre audience, the post-Brechtian compromise between 'realistic' and 'theatrical' characterization" (1989, 450), that is, a way of making even this hackneyed *locus* suddenly brought alive by its *platea*. Hamlet almost did commit suicide with his dagger during the speech; his contemplation and rejection of self-slaughter enforced his peculiar blend of optimism, enthusiasm, cynicism, and fatalism. He chose to continue to live even if he also accepted his negative critique of life itself. The moment represented a minicatharsis for the audience and readied us for Hamlet's later acceptance of his own death. The ancient concept of the tragic hero as scapegoat was vividly present.

Hamlet's antic disposition incorporated a handheld jester's puppet, which Helsinger manipulated skillfully. One of the roles that falls to Hamlet is that of jester, a position apparently untenanted since Yorick's death years before. Helsinger's use of his puppet set up his later animation of the jester's skull in the graveyard. In the prayer scene, "This physic" was accompanied by an upward jab of the sword that

Hamlet was, for the moment, refusing to employ. His almost immediate dispatching of Polonius was an impulse carried over from the previous scene. Helsinger's response to the death of Polonius was a moving blend of sadness—he recognized Ophelia's father—and anger —he knew a prating knave as well. Hamlet refused Gertrude's attempt at an embrace after the closet scene, so that we got no uncomfortable Oedipal resonance here. Although upstaged by the Gravedigger's cataloging of bones, Helsinger's work with the skull was splendid. His hand provided a lower jaw as Yorick told the lady to paint an inch thick.

This Hamlet was attentive to the relationship Michael Pennington suggests is the key to the role: "Hamlet's purest and most distinctive encounters [are] those with his audience" (quoted in Brockbank 1985, 119). Helsinger was the most inventive and spontaneous Hamlet I have seen since Mark Rylance's antic version for RSC in the late 1980s. In addition, Helsinger conveyed some of the nastier aspects of Hamlet, as Derek Jacobi did some fifteen years ago in both his Old Vic and his BBC performances.

The production's major weakness was David McCann's Claudius. McCann's concept was good. He presented Claudius as a lightweight, surviving through a constant trick of personality. He rolled his eyes around to see whether his latest speech or action had found favor with his immediate audience. When puzzled, he looked to Gertrude for a cue about what to do. She was the power in Denmark, Claudius *her* choice so that she could stay queen. This Claudius would have succeeded in Elsinore had it not been for Hamlet's obstinate challenge. That Hamlet's challenge was potent was demonstrated by the many in the court who flocked around him in the opening scene, literally upstaging the new king.

McCann's Claudius had three good moments. After "Gonzago," Claudius held the "light" toward Hamlet, as Patrick Stewart does in the BBC production. Thus the king retained control of the scene. After the nunnery scene, this Claudius showed clearly that the official verdict on Hamlet was "madness" and that "in great ones" it required supervision. And, after the graveyard scene, he made certain that it was Gertrude's "son" and not his who had caused such a ruckus. But McCann ranted and raved through the prayer scene, hiding from us as he hid his insecurities from his court. He outdid Herod and spoke more than was set down for him with his "Hail Marys." He missed the opportunity to use the continuum that Helsinger had opened up with the audience and to permit Claudius's uncharismatic character to become at least sympathetic by acknowledging us, even by appealing to us. If he had paused, for example, and looked at us on "my crown, mine own ambition, and my queen," sharing with us the need for what he was afraid to lose, the moment would have captured us emotionally and intellectually. Since the attempt at prayer was downstage right—and Hamlet's competing soliloquy delivered from behind Claudius—the opportunity was there for an unforgettable *coup de theatre*, indeed a momentary reversal of our ostensible point of view. Admittedly, Claudius's soliloquy is in the "fourth-wall" tradition, but no rule insists that it must be. To indict McCann is probably to blame him for a director's decision.

The "Gonzago" sequence, which can be seen as the climax of the outer play, was perhaps this production's most controversial aspect. The Player King spoke his lines about oaths and lost purposes *to* Gertrude, making the play-within an attack on her and setting up her "The lady doth protest too much" as a precisely focused instant. "Gonzago," however, was a victim of Lucianus's ineptitude as actor. He did all the things Hamlet had told him not to do and, at a critical moment, had to glance at the script that he had tucked into his belt and thus introduced, unwillingly, a kind of Brechtian "alienation device" just at the crucial moment of the play-within (and, possibly, of the outer play as well). The "play-within," then, ended "within itself," draining the moment of any tension and removing from it any sense that it could have entrapped Claudius into confessing his guilt or pulled Hamlet into its dramatic continuum (as the script suggests does occur). Thus, we could not "tell whether it is Claudius or the Prince who has prematurely sprung the mouse-trap" (Styan 1978, 82). The trap imploded. The "play-within" became a commentary on what Claudius later calls "bad performance."

Most of Treyz's decisions were effective. Claudius at the outset insisted that Gertrude discard her locket with her former husband's picture on it for a locket containing a miniature of Claudius. Hamlet picked up the rejected locket and thus set up the closet scene. McCann was good as Ghost, more upset at Gertrude's betrayal than the loss of his crown and, as is the style with Ghosts these days, hurt that Gertrude did not acknowledge him during his foray into her closet. Ophelia read her letters *to* Gertrude and Claudius. As Hamlet later used the skull, he made his book "read" itself to Polonius, by opening itself as it spoke of "weak hams." Ophelia was onstage when Hamlet asked Polonius "Have you a *daughter?*"—as if a delighted stranger had just met Polonius and had just recognized the younger woman as his daughter. Some guards could see the Ghost and some could not, suggesting that many in Elsinore never learn what is going on and that we, as audience, are in a position at once more privileged and vulnerable than some of the spear carriers. The players were delighted to be invited to stay at Elsinore—they were in for cold, hungry nights otherwise. Claudius and Polonius entered *as* Ophelia spoke her soliloquy about sweet bells jangled, thus avoiding the problem of their delay before Claudius's "Love!" or "Love?" Claudius looked out to the place where Hamlet had exited, then turned, once Ophelia had finished. Horatio, clad somewhat as a Puritan and proving more than just a straight man, was truly Hamlet's good friend. Rosencrantz and Guildenstern, looking like Cavaliers, were merely old fraternity brothers.

Horatio, indeed, was a rival to Ophelia. Hamlet seemed not about to let love interfere with friendship. Suzanne O'Donnell's Ophelia was tiny, snub-nosed, angry at Polonius, but powerless. The gifts that she longed to redeliver to Hamlet were a ploy to get him back. It almost worked, but as to embrace her he inclined, he spotted Polonius blundering out from behind an archway. The rest was excoriation. The mad Ophelia was smeared with mud, as if she had been playing on the banks of the river that would soon claim her.

This was, then, a production that gave great attention to detail and, it follows, achieved freshness of vision. Only an occasional stale idea appeared—Claudius and Gertrude in bed for ambassadors and Polonius, for example, a scene on which Anthony Hopkins and Judy Parfitt set their seal twenty-five years ago.

The ending, though, was an unfortunate mishmash. Gertrude's ostentatious realization that she was poisoned attracted a lot of premature attention. Claudius crept up behind Hamlet with a dagger, and Hamlet turned just in time to dispatch him. Claudius then staggered about, stumbled upstage, fell into his throne, only to be carried out by several suddenly available attendants. Why? And why erase the one death that makes a difference in the play and to this audience for whom Hamlet has been so important? The scene *has* a rhythm dictated by various focal points—Gertrude and the drink, Laertes's confession, Hamlet with the cup, Hamlet dying, Horatio eulogizing, then negotiating with Fortinbras, Fortinbras dictating closure for Denmark and assuming his own kingship.

The BBC version is a model of how the scene works—albeit in a different medium. Here it was a muddle and a hollowed-out conclusion to what had been an energetic and convincing version of this difficult script.[2]

The actors were miked. While miking tends to mellow out the voices, denying them crispness, it was necessitated by the size of the space and its openness to the sky and the landing pattern of the Executive Airport. The audience was splendid—attentive and knowledgeable. I overheard several people talking animatedly about this production and others. The Festival may be in the Walt Disney Amphitheater, but it is on the other side of town from all that stuff and is eminently worth the visit.

## NOTES

1. The set itself included eight panels, each five by seven feet, of crystalline plastic designed to pick up rear projections. Sixteen slide projectors controlled by computer held nearly two hundred slides of the *Hamlet* backgrounds. The process is described in Maupin (1994, 14).

2. See my *Watching Shakespeare on Television* (1993a, 113-25) for a discussion of how the ending is treated in television versions of the script.

# IX

# "Seems, Madam?": *Hamlet* in 1994 II: Stratford (Ontario), Ashland, and London

Two versions of *Hamlet* in 1994 benefited from other than main-stage space, achieving intimacy and spareness while avoiding the need for spectacle or overamplification, from a slight decentering of Hamlet in the direction of Claudius, and from an emphasis on Ophelia as a significant character in her own play, or at least as a character capable of developing her own conception of who she is and where she is, even if that insistence must be carried out within madness. Thus the productions avoided what Mangan claims: "The whole play . . . seems structured precisely" to do, that is "reflect kaleidoscopically a variety of images of Hamlet" (1991, 140). Instead, the productions reinforced Bernard McElroy's thesis that "a satisfying production of *Hamlet* depends on the subtle and difficult business of realized character relationships even more than on brilliant individual characterizations" (1989, 96). If McElroy is correct, current productions will tend to focus on relationship, to the possible detriment of elements that may well be in the *locus*—the circumferences of dynastic and eschatalogical issues with which the script implicates its relationships.

Contemporary directors seem uneasy with the supernatural element in the play, perhaps because television's ubiquity has destroyed our sense that the supernatural can "play" as anything other than the psychological (see Dessen, 1986). The authority of that aspect of *locus* seems incapable in the late twentieth century of working out a successful negotiation with the authority of *platea*, Directors are also unsure about the political aspects of the play these days—either eliminating them as much as possible or including them in an obligatory, often awkward way. It has now been over thirty years since the United States watched numbly as its own political transition followed a script set down almost two hundred years before. The *trauma* of sudden changes in leadership, which Horatio and Fortinbras understand very well, does not seem to emerge from contemporary productions. An exception was Ron Daniels's 1989 production for RSC, in which a Fortinbras, armored as the Ghost had been, took over at the end in the name of the ancien régime. Hamlet (Mark Rylance), ambassador to the future, had failed. Tragedy became history. In the 1993 Adrian Noble production for RSC, Hamlet (Kenneth Branagh) marched directly to Valhalla, where his father awaited him—an ending that fitted Noble's "concept," but that was totally at odds with the modern prince that Branagh had crafted out of the full text. In speaking of her 1938 uncut *Hamlet*, Margaret Webster says, "Behind the facade of familiar things moves the spiritual and emotional conflict of the play" (1961, 161). If the larger rhythms that surround the play—cosmic and dynastic—are reduced in production, the "inner play" tends to become domesticated, the story of failed families. It is that, of course, but is not *only* that. Hamlet as *Prince* of Denmark is a threatened character these days. The "inner" play remains intense. The larger implications that circle the domestic interior have been diminished.

Richard Monette's *Hamlet* is the second version of the play that Stratford, Ontario, has essayed in recent years. It contrasted vividly—and positively—with the previous version.

In 1991, David William directed a production with Colm Feore on the Festival stage, notable for one striking and one awful moment. The interval came just as Hamlet raised his dagger over Claudius and said, "Now, might I do it, pat," so that we were left for fifteen minutes to ponder the downward descent of the blade. It was a melodramatic method of bridging the interval. When Claudius, after "Gonzago," demanded light, Hamlet aimed a flashlight at the king's face. We had in no way been prepared for the introduction of this technology, since the costumes seemed 1840ish. As one critic said, "I could not believe that this outlandish stunt was actually taking place" (Newell 1991, 32). The moment did *not* "incriminate" Claudius, as the program (*Hamlet* 1991, 16) claimed, but it did incriminate director and production. It was "an 'exhibition' of the play" (Newell 1991, 31), as opposed to an exploration of or a challenge to the inherited script, "utterly conventional [and] overlong" (Steele 1991, 25).

As the flashlight suggests, the production did not understand its own conventions. William introduced a cardinal, in long red gown, in the opening scene, apparently to show that the pope sanctioned Claudius's reign *and* new marriage. Why this would have been necessary in nineteenth-century Denmark, as opposed to the pre-Lutheran Elsinore that Shakespeare gives us, was not clear. The cardinal also appeared in the final scene to compete with Hamlet in giving very different last rites to Claudius. The *payoff*, though, would have been at Ophelia's funeral, where both conflict (Laertes) and collusion (Claudius) with the Church could have been depicted powerfully to show the fissures and disruptions that have become epidemic in Elsinore. Instead, "four captains" bore Ophelia to the grave, no cross going before, no hint of rites reduced, no ceremony at all—so that Laertes's "What ceremony else?" had no context. One learns to resent directors who do not pursue their own ideas to what could be once-in-a-lifetime experiences almost as much as one resents the directors who substitute their own ideas for those still living in the scripts.

Alex Newell called Feore's an "overly romantic . . . Byronic Hamlet" (1991, 32). This approach is predicted by the program notes. They are almost all from the nineteenth century, with the exception of a note from Granville-Barker to the effect that as long as man does not understand himself, *Hamlet* will continue to fascinate us: Blake and Coleridge, Dostoevsky on the mystery of man, Stark Young, another exception to the ancient critiques but not to their conclusions, claiming that "the very essence of Hamlet is that we could never understand him," and Tolstoy on Pierre: "He was suffering from the anguish men suffer when they persist in undertaking a task impossible for them—not from its inherent difficulties, but for its incompatibility with their own nature." Goethe is, surprisingly, not quoted. The "continuity of human experience," as William calls it (*Hamlet* 1991, 13) may involve the transmission of incomprehensibility from generation to generation but that does not help the script of *Hamlet* to generate meanings in the last decade of the twentieth century.

Feore's Hamlet broke down, hands to head, upon remembering his father as "a man," and was, fortunately, called from his posturing by Horatio's "My lord, I think I saw him yesternight." Whatever happened here, Feore did not follow Derek Jacobi's advice to imagine oneself in Hamlet's position and work from there. This was all externally "understood," it seemed, and might explain why Feore found playing Hamlet "surprisingly fun" (Yungblut 1991, 10). Feore did not give us Burton's irony—the precarious balance between optimism ("a special providence") and nihilism—or Jacobi's cynicism—"I am dead, Horatio," meaning don't bother with me, I am trash—or Rylance's anticness —turning the skull so that it could view the duel, or Kevin Kline's insistence that Rosencrantz and Guildenstern actually lie on the floor to view the "brave, o'rehanging firmament," or Branagh's icy author-ity—threatening Osric with the rapier as Hamlet said, "I'll play this bout first"—or Jim Helsinger's invention—"Have you a *daughter?*" incredulously to Polonius, with Ophelia on stage, as if a Falstaff meet-ing a fertile Shallow these many years later.

The production *almost* came alive through Leon Pownell's Claudius, a nervous ruler who kept talking in the second scene because, like Macbeth after his murder, he *had* to. Later, alone at center stage, lit like a Rembrandt portrait, he moved quietly into his "offense is rank" soliloquy. He almost had us!—but began melodramatizing his plight. The hinge of sympathy that might have made this man almost "tragic" swung back toward the freeze-frame of Hamlet's uplifted dagger.

The lines tended to be well-read, though Hamlet rushed past his po-tential "antic disposition" and thus made his subsequent behavior simply baffling—though it was not particularly antic. "I *am* thy fa-ther's spirit," said the Ghost (John Hampere), as he should, since he is not disguised and knows that the devil hath power to assume a pleas-ing shape. Shakespeare knew that "I am" is an iamb. "That he should weep for *her?*" Hamlet asked, as he should, since the emphasis is on Hecuba's inadequacy as "objective correlative," and not on the appro-priateness of tears (which is what you get when Hamlet emphasizes *"weep"*). The ending featured a Fortinbras and army in more modern uniforms than those of Elsinore, suggesting that "modern man" is tak-ing over after the midair collision between medieval and renaissance value systems has seen both spiral fatally to earth. Fortinbras (John Devorski) said "Take up the body"—singular, as F1 suggests. That made sense. It was Hamlet who was carried off and Hamlet's was the "body" with which Fortinbras was reinforcing his "rights of memory." We *did* need a more powerful Fortinbras and a sense that the moment into which he marches quivers with danger. The point about "body politic" that Hamlet has made disjunctively earlier ("but the King is not with the body") can be communicated to the attentive observer *if* the ending includes the negotiation between Horatio and Fortinbras, *and* Fortinbras's quick grasp of how to begin his own reign.

For all of that, the 1991 *Hamlet* was a failure. And, in spite of the 1994 production's *failure* to observe any of the signals outlined in the previous paragraph (there was no Fortinbras), it was a success. This in spite of some other problems in the dramaturgy.

The Ghost, for example, appeared in military uniform, uncovered. Yet Horatio told Hamlet that the Ghost "wore his visor up." Hamlet wandered into the second scene as if in search of the executive men's room, canceling what the scene seems to show—that is, that Claudius has an agenda set up that includes a prince who is present, however inappropriately attired. If not, then Claudius's "Now, our cousin Hamlet . . ." must be much more spontaneous than it was here, and that is not easy, since so much of what Claudius does in the scene until Hamlet refuses to cooperate has a rehearsed quality. Hamlet dispatched Polonius with the dagger that he had carried in after not killing Claudius. Yet Gertrude informed Claudius that Hamlet "whip[ped] out his rapier" to kill Polonius. Rosencrantz did not tell Claudius about the arrival of the players, so that Claudius's "give him a further edge, / And drive his purpose into these delights" was cut. The Machiavellian's cooperation with the agency of his potential demise was gone, then, as was this script's mirroring of "Gonzago" and the final scene, planned by Claudius but, invariably in revenge tragedy, a trap for the villain.[1] Since no dumb show occurred, Ophelia's "What means this, my lord?" and Hamlet's "miching malicho" made no sense at all. Without Hamlet's narrative to Horatio about his turnabout at sea, Horatio had to utter the unwieldy line, "So Rosencrantz and Guildenstern go to their deaths!"—which was not said with the appalled surprise that was necessary to elicit Hamlet's rejoinder ("Why man, they did make love to this employment!"). Gertrude said "fair maid," not "sweet maid." Without Fortinbras, the ending found Horatio holding the crown up to a beam of sunlight, as if "Heaven will direct" Denmark. But the excising of Fortinbras did not erase the question, What happens now? That we live in a different polity does not make our feeling for the transfer of power any less keen than that of the Elizabethans as Elizabeth kept refusing to name her successor. If Fortinbras is at least mentioned, he need not appear at the end if Hamlet emphasizes "He has my dying voice" and if we hear drums approaching. This is what Joseph Papp did in his 1982 production.

But with the exception of the deletion of Fortinbras, none of these problems mattered. That they did not was a function of other small points made well, of relationships between characters made clear to us, even if misunderstood *by* the characters, so that the emotional dynamics of this Elsinore were powerfully evoked, and of the fluidity and flexibility of the stage.

The Tom Patterson Theatre is shaped like the Swan at Stratford-on-Avon. The Patterson is a converted hockey rink and does give the spectator something of a hockey fan's view of the action. The seating is on three sides around the long apron. The auditorium does not rise nearly as high as the Swan's. An upstage platform allows for "proscenium" effects and has four steps down to the apron. The space permits a lot of interchange between "staged" effects and observers on the lower area. Claudius, for example, delivered his opening oxymorons to the court from the upper platform, then, after briefly kissing Gertrude, descended to shake some token hands on "For all, our thanks." Lucianus entered *through* the audience gathered for "Gonzago," even walked, leprous distillment in hand, within reach of Claudius. He pulled all eyes with him into the dramatic space. "Gonzago" was played on the upper platform in front of a bronze model of a wind bent cypress. Behind the stage was a triptych of mirrors, suggesting that the play was an infinite regress into a past that reflected different things to spectators in the present. A mirror up to nature*s*. Hamlet's identification with the players was announced by his having whitened his face—an actor and jester, of course, and an "antic." The word also means "skull." (Jacobi actually donned a skull mask from the players' prop chest as the court entered for "Gonzago.") Stephen Ouimette borrowed a cloak from the Players's chest and was intentionally histrionic during part of his "rogue and peasant slave" speech. Having upstaged his own play—as Jacobi did—Hamlet watched Claudius rise, drop his goblet clatteringly to the floor, and ask for light just as Hamlet commanded a black out. The point seemed to be that Hamlet was insisting on what he saw at that instant, making what he took to be Claudius's betrayal of guilt indelible to all eyes. Hamlet had torn the mask from the actor playing Lucianus, but *had* he unmasked Claudius? Horatio seemed to agree with Hamlet's interpretation, but the evidence for us, the outer audience, was inconclusive, as it was for all others in the court. The tree remained onstage for the next scene, so that Claudius's "a brother's murder" and his mime of the pouring of the poison was conducted in the lost orchard of the Ghost's narrative.

The ultimate point of the staging, of course, was that "staged" events flow into their spectators and resonate there in various ways, as was happening to the capacity audience at the Patterson. It helped that a thunderstorm rumbled through Stratford during the performance—a synecdoche for our experience and its clarification.

This Hamlet was furious at Gertrude. His first soliloquy was aimed at her emotionally and physically, at the point at which she had just exited. Jim Helsinger at Orlando had aimed the words at Claudius, but both Helsinger and Ouimette vivified Michael Mangan's description of the speech: "The ability of language to give order to thoughts and emotions is challenged from below by a pressure of thought which is beyond its normal capacity" (1991, 131). Later, in the closet scene, Ouimette's Hamlet attempted (as Branagh had done) to force one of the lockets into one of her nether orifices. Gertrude was carefully coiffed, her wavy hair looking like that of a '30s movie queen on the cover of *Silver Screen* (well, if Kate Smith were there depicted). She had made a simple adjustment to Claudius—"All kings look alike in the dark"—and only *his* face, or "picture in little," had to be replaced on the souvenir tea sets hawked outside the castle walls. She was indeed the "matron" that Hamlet called her, and she was content with a new husband and a continuing role in Denmark. Hamlet's disquiet troubled her, however, and she made more than a pro forma request to keep him at Elsinore. Hamlet, in turn, did convince her to abandon Claudius. Her explanation to Claudius after Polonius's death was an excuse. Hamlet's had not been a "brainish apprehension." She recognized a kind of premeditation that went even further than Claudius's shudder that "It had been so with us had we been there." Her response to Laertes's insurrection was on her own behalf, we inferred.

Claudius was a successful Harold Stassen, calm, unruffled, moved only by "Gonzago," and moving only in his effort at prayer, which "even evokes sympathy for this least sympathetic of characters (which in turn adds shades of meaning to Hamlet's decision not to kill him)" (Kirchhoff 1994). The transition had gone well, Gertrude being helpful in this enterprise and *part* of the goal, but secondary to the power that Claudius had achieved. After his failure to repent, he hollowed out completely. He was angry at Gertrude for telling Laertes of Ophelia's drowning because the report subverted his effort "to calm his rage." The fight at Ophelia's grave was the fault of *Gertrude*'s son, not Claudius's. He was willing to conduct further plotting over Ophelia's very grave—part of "last night's speech" being transferred to that place in this script. His line became, "Laertes, was your *sister* dear to you?" When the letters were brought in, Claudius read the one from Hamlet to Gertrude, then gave it to the sailor for delivery to the queen. How much more effective would it have been for *this* Claudius to retain that letter—and its mystery—and dismiss the sailor empty-handed! At the end, once Gertrude had drunk the drink, Claudius strode to her, through the sword fight, as if to say that he was sorry, but also to manage her inevitable collapse: "She swoons to see them bleed!"

*Feeling* had flowed to the younger generation—Hamlet was a baggy-eyed young man who, as the script suggests, didn't get much sleep and Ophelia was a virgin on the brink of consummation. The irony was that Hamlet lashed the sensitive Ophelia for his own outrage at Gertrude's betrayal. Ophelia became the stereotypic "my lady" who painted an inch thick. Hamlet slapped away the gifts that Ophelia wanted to redeliver. He saw nothing in this scene—not Ophelia, and certainly not the spies. The nunnery scene was an extension of the one that she had described to Polonius and certainly uncalculated on Hamlet's part—not an exhibition of "antic disposition" but a blind rage. Still, Claudius was right. Hamlet was acting here under a compulsion that caused his speech to "lack . . . form a little" while still staying on this side of "madness." But that insight surrendered to what Claudius recognized must be his official position: "Madness in great ones must not unwatch'd go." The sequence can be played as a perverse love scene, of course, but here we saw Hamlet rejecting his *natural* ally. Horatio is a friend, but not "passion's slave." Hamlet lacerated the person most *like* him—Ophelia, giving his excoriation a terrible sense of inevitability, coming as it did from his repressed self toward something in him that he recognized and loved—Ophelia. She needed that recognition and love for her own completion as well.

In her madness, she assaulted Claudius, the source of sexual disturbance in Elsinore, the primary agent of her mental destruction, as Lalla Ward did more mutedly in the BBC production of 1980. Sabrina Grdevich did a Lacanian thing in inspecting the place where Claudius's trouser legs joined. Hamlet had made much of "*country*" and of the "O phallus" "between a maid's legs," and now Ophelia had her revenge, forcing the king to respond to her, to look on as she invaded herself on "By cock." "How long hath she been *thus*?" Claudius had to ask. Ophelia mimed pregnancy on "We must be patient," the "we" being *women*. Claudius was her *de*flowerer. Claudius was also, it follows, a "stand-in" for Hamlet. Ophelia was a stand-in for Denmark. She was not "lost," as Terry Doran said, "but lost-in-progress, showing signs she might somehow be brought back from the abyss" (1994).

Although Claudius was a considerable figure here, at the center of production was Ouimette's prince—always under control, physically and vocally, as character, seemingly open-eyed to all that was motivating him, but fatally blind to the ways in which his narrow interpretations controlled him—his indictment of Ophelia for what he perceived *Gertrude* to be, his insistence that everyone see Claudius's guilt just as he obscured it from view, his willingness to be challenged by an Osric he scorned. In the latter instance, after "How if I answer no?" Osric took a step toward Hamlet on "I mean, my lord, the opposition of your person in trial." Osric was suddenly Laertes's alter ego, and Hamlet surrendered to Osric—a telling "touch."

"To be or not to be" was given its early Q1 placement—one that makes sense with this script and that is proving popular with directors these days—*and* was delivered in a freeze-frame to Polonius. After it, Polonius said, "Fare you well, my lord," and Hamlet said, "These

tedious old fools." But "fare you well" was not tedious, nor was it inappropriate to what Hamlet had just been saying. Who was the fool
here? Hamlet's enlistment of the Rosencrantz and Guildenstern he had
just interrogated *against* the Polonius bringing word of the players'
arrival was brilliantly conducted. In having seen through one plot,
however, and immediately developing another—"Gonzago"—Hamlet
underestimated the power lined up against him, which *includes* Rosencrantz, Guildenstern, Polonius, *and* the king. It was fascinating to
listen to Oiumette failing to understand what Hamlet was saying, or, if
not failing to *understand,* refusing to let his emotions and imagination
flow into what he understands. This Hamlet remained convincingly
incomplete, disjoined. He could not see Ophelia—or Gertrude, for that
matter—yet he could "mistake" Polonius intentionally for a "fishmonger" and project his own confusions about relationships, gender,
and himself upon Claudius in sneeringly saying, "Farewell, dear
mother."

Polonius contributed to our understanding of the inner misunder-
standings. He did care for Ophelia. He also liked Hamlet, in contrast to
most Poloniuses—Eric Porter, Patrick Godfrey, and David Bradley, for
example—and thought that Hamlet's "buzz, buzz" was quite funny. He
also enjoyed Hamlet's "weasel," even though he knew that *he* was the
weasel. Still, he believed that Hamlet was a star not contained in his
daughter's zodiac, and out of such misprisions is tragedy formulated.
Monette gave us the Reynaldo scene, "which restores to the play, still
reeling from its ghostly visitation, the proportion and accent of the
humdrum world where Hamlet's 'strangeness' will be so inevitably
misinterpreted" (Webster 1961, 160), and which reflects "the rational
and pragmatic world of the court (and the 'normality' of its everyday
life, to which Claudius needs so desperately to return)" (Mangan 1991,
131).

The scene showed Polonius's losing track of what he was about to
say. We also got a lot of the Pyrrhus speeches, which were powerful in
and of themselves, enhanced with vivid, "theatrical" lighting—a narrative inset, a sudden and vivid transport to the water-worn stones of deep
mythology, a different way of telling a story than a play is, and thus a
pause, a circling, a reiteration within the pressure of the drama itself.
The Pyrrhus speeches show that drama can be interrupted—by Hamlet
in turning the speech over to the Player, by Polonius ("This is too
long!") by Hamlet again ("Mobbled queen"), and by the wedging back
into time that the inset itself is. The sequence prepares us—if anything
can—for what happens at "Gonzago," also an effort to open backward
into time. The interruptions, including that of Polonius of himself,

have the "consequence" of driving against the play, creating a rhythm that Terry Hawkes (1985) compares to jazz, making the larger play something called *TELMAH*. A good director leaves that material in, precisely because it is less "relevant" than other aspects of this vast and complicated script. Such material, though, creates the illusion of an extemporaneous event and keeps reminding us that, for the characters, all of this is, as the current cliche has it, "not a dress rehearsal."

Monette kept suggesting that but for this small decision or that, this slight misunderstanding, this minute over or under emphasis or that, things might turn out differently. He signaled cross purposes by slanting light at angles across some scenes—a very effective technique when the audience is seated above the stage, as at the Patterson. And it was "purposes mistook" that made all of this, at last, inevitable, even though the story was told anew on the Patterson stages. Thus the production was "responsive," as Goldman says, "to the interplay of scriptedness and improvisation in life, particularly to junctures where one mode gives way to or becomes questioned by or mingled with the other" (1992, 451).

Critical response was positive, suggesting that Monette's concept of "almost no set [and not] quite rehearsal dress, just a uniform which will allow the actors, and the audience, to focus totally on the text," had been successful (Quigley 1994, 7). The critics applauded what Stewart Brown called "a minimalist chamber production, with the emphasis on words, subtly enhanced by the low-register organ-and-percussion music of Louis Applebaum, the sound designs of Evan Turner and the sometimes stark lighting of Kevin Fraser" (1994), what Terry Doran called "a conversational mode" (1994), what Jamie Portman called a "spare, brooding production . . . aided immeasurably by Louis Applebaum's highly dramatic music and Kevin Fraser's spooky lighting design" (1994). Monette, said Ian Gillespie, "par[ed] away all extraneousness," so that the characters did not resemble "the shouting cartoons that often stride across the Festival stage. [The production was] austere, yet expansive. Minimal, yet majestic" (1994). The "spartan simplicity keeps distractions away from Ouimette's lonesome Dane in the eye of this whirling story," said Lawrence DeVine (1994). Indeed, one critic said "This *Hamlet* has the feel of a *Macbeth*" (Kirchhoff 1994). "Monette," said Robert Reid, "brings us back to the power of the words themselves" (1994), an evaluation supported by Alex Suczek: "eliminating distracting production values facilitates the appreciation of this intricate play of words and ideas" (1994).

The critics found the story more clearly told than I did. "One is never at a loss in following what is happening and why" (Donal O'Connor,

1994). "One of the virtues of Monette's production is the clarity of its narrative line and the meticulous definition of certain key moments" (Portman 1994). Ouimette, said Geoff Chapman, gave "as glintingly clear a treatment of this weighty part as I've encountered for eons . . . [His] intelligent presence, . . . mocking and measured, showed up the vital cleavage between society's public face and private demons, so that losing the expansive aspects, the chance to underscore the doom facing and oppressing the residents of Elsinore fortress and removing the Fortinbras scene, which takes away the political context, are not crippling . . ." (1994). Some, however, discerned trade-offs for the spare script and production values. This production, said Dennis Armstrong, was "more Jacobean than Elizabethan. Gone is much of the introspection, the poetry, the mellifluous idylls on love [and] life. . . . In its place we have murder and mayhem and a sense of irony [and a Hamlet] given to ingenious and brave action rather than doubt and misgivings. This *Hamlet* is more about revenge than about being and nothingness" (1994). And without the props and postures of monarchy and the external threat from another country, the production became for some a domestic drama, in which Ouimette forgot "that he's playing a prince" (Coulbourn 1994), and in which Gertrude "looks and acts more like a suburban mum than a queen" (Kirchhoff 1994). "The scaled intimacy of the stage [does not convey a] sense of elevated illusion, or specifically of kings and queens and princes. . . . King and Queen dilute to father and mother, or, even more familiarly, to mom and step-dad" (Doran 1994).

The Grave-digger (William Hutt) had the best metaphor for what this production did. He held the skull toward Hamlet. "Who's do you think it was?" Don't you recognize him? (*We* recognized the Gravedigger, of course, as Polonius, a doubling that James Cairncross had also accomplished some twenty-five years ago in Robert Chetwyn's production.) Grave-digger, of course, comes at us with vast experience of "*his* trade" and, clearly, can tell one skull from another. It must be identified, though, for Hamlet, and then the past flows in, the bone becomes flesh. But the flesh has long been bone and mephitis. Recognition comes. But Yorick has long been dead, and it is too late for the "fair Ophelia," who is even now riding though the deepening tide of tombstones in Elsinore's graveyard. Hamlet did not recognize her earlier. He thought she was Gertrude. And that made it too late for him. If we were to see the play in Oedipal terms, we would say that he never had a chance. If so, Monette and Ouimette dramatized a long denouement brilliantly.

The outcome here was determined by Hamlet's abrupt closure of "Gonzago." The *"Mousetrap* may, for some, implicate Hamlet in a plot on Claudius's life," argues Douglas Green, "but it may, for Hamlet, reenact the Oedipal scenario that seems to fascinate him. If Hamlet seeks a rationale for revenge, he has not found one. . . . As has often been noted . . . the image of the theater exposes the hero's own confusion of play-acting with acting, of stage acting with action on the world's stage" (1992, 32. On the premature ending of "Gonzago," see Speaight 1970, Styan 1978, Woodhead 1979, and Coursen 1992). Green goes on to say that

> Hamlet isn't really interested in action . . . he is interested in returning to the scene of the crime(s). . . . It is no wonder he is so violent in the closet scene with his mother; he has just had her incestuous infidelity . . . re-enacted in the players' performance. . . . [H]is own latent fascination with the re-staged crime and lust contributes to the overt Oedipal quality of succeeding scenes with his mother, as well as his inability to kill Claudius; after all, the king has done no more than Hamlet, in a Freudian scenario, has himself wished. . . . If in the *Mousetrap* scene Hamlet has been seeking evidence of the guilt of Claudius (and perhaps Gertrude) through the 'identification process' of theater but has managed only to implicate himself, then what are we to make of our own identification with the hero? (1992, 33)

Green evokes the familiar Ernest Jones (1948) thesis without indulging in the thesis-serving simplifications that mar Jones's analysis. One could argue that Hamlet's interruption of "Gonzago" is dictated by Oedipal energy—the father-figure has been killed but the alter-ego father has yet to gain the wished-for woman. Hamlet is then faced with an opportunity to kill the "real" alter-ego father, does not do so, and, naturally, puts an Oedipal charge into his killing of Polonius (the sword he has put "up" leaping unbidden into his hand and through the arras) and castigation of Gertrude. The Ghost appears to reassert a proper "conscious" structure, but it is too late for that! Green's suggestion that Hamlet likes to revisit the scene of the crime might remind us that the speech he requests of the player features the murder of yet another recumbent father-king, Priam.

Robert Weimann's concept of "appropriation" suggests that Hamlet appropriates unto himself a range of inconsistencies. As his advice to the players shows, Hamlet tends to see a dramatic text in essentialist terms. It is an inviolable text that is "set down." It is not amenable to extemporaneous expansion. But Hamlet's narrow view of "the purpose of playing" ignores his own interpolation of a dozen or sixteen lines and his own role as chorus, critic, narrator, and, finally, interrupter of the play he has commissioned. Hamlet's disquisition to the players reveals, Weimann says, a "tension . . . between poetic theory and theatrical practice" (1985, 280). The "rupture as well as the interaction between what is shown and what is meant (what 'passes show'), between what is presenting and what is presented, are central to the whole relationship between the play and the play within the play" (282).

It could be argued that Hamlet, insisting that his play-within imitate precisely what *he* wants it to mean, denies its meaning to Claudius. This "profound crisis in representivity . . . has a lot to do with the rupture, in Hamlet himself, between what is shown and what is meant, and his related capacity for both dissociating and associating his own feigning and his 'I know not seems'" (Weimann 1985, 282). It may be that the return to the scene of the crime in "Gonzago" elicits from Hamlet the psychic guilt ("presently they have proclaimed their malefactions") that comes from Claudius in his aside before the nunnery scene and that spills out in the prayer scene, but does *not* come as public confession during "Gonzago." The latter is one of the enticing possibilities that *Hamlet* holds out and denies—in this production a possibility overtly canceled by Hamlet himself. In appropriating all mimetic meanings to himself, Hamlet erases the possibility that "a speech" might give a "smart . . . lash" to Claudius's "conscience" and move him "to speak with most miraculous organ," perhaps because, as Hardison speculates, "Hamlet lacks faith in his own strategy and spoils the play's effect by his interruptions" (1969, 6). Thus *Hamlet* becomes, generically, a tragedy.

Green extends his argument to our inevitable "identification with Hamlet [which] implicates the audience (whether Elizabethan or twentieth-century), since each generation recasts the confused hero in its own image" (34). Green maintains that "the play's providential finale absolves both characters and spectators of guilt" (1992, 34). If so, "Why does the drum come hither?" Green's skillful problematizing of "Gonzago" ends up taking the outer play at Horatio's valuation of Hamlet. Monette gave more to Claudius than some productions do. When no king came in to take the crown that Horatio lifted at the end, while I missed Fortinbras, I thought of the king Denmark had just had—Claudius.

It follows that I expected *Claudius* to encourage the play-within in this production, and that I picked up some of the Oedipal energy that

Green discusses. I was following the story that I thought was being told but, quite possibly, was pursuing my own critical and psychological narrative. Others will derive another story. DeVine, for example, found it "unFreudian" (1994). The production made the "case for a *Hamlet* of multiple viewpoints" (Hawkes 1985, 332). *Hamlet* quivers with possibilities—a script descending a staircase, throwing out angles and planes of meaning that include flesh and bone and fragments of soul, an explosion in a shingle factory where the shingles are words, words, words and "the matter" is finally between the performance and the individual spectator. That this one detonated Oedipally for me may be a result of what I saw from where I was in the mirror held up to "Gonzago"—a Player Queen, a boy actor, protesting perhaps too much in a voice about to change, about to be consummated in maleness even as Hamlet argues its temporary virginity, or femaleness: "Pray God your voice, like a piece of uncurrent gold be not cracked in the ring." This Hamlet made bad currency of Ophelia because he believed that his mother was a whore. Thus, in her madness, Ophelia cracked her own ring.

The Ashland *Hamlet* capitalized on a last-minute directorial change —from Adrian Hall to Henry Woronicz, which, in turn, meant that Woronicz gave up the title role to Richard Howard, just as rehearsals were beginning. Since the "theme" of the production had already been determined to be "the time is out of joint," since the set showed a palace in transition, and since the costumes were eclectic, all of this off-stage transition actually fed into an energetic and at moments powerful production. Some critics felt that the last-minute changes at the top affected the production negatively, and there is some truth in that. Discussions in and around Ashland suggested that the production was very "controversial"—the word used exclusively—and people were observed walking out, or were *un*observed in the auditorium after the interval. The competing Shakespeare plays were a spectacular *Tempest,* marred by a totally inaudible opening scene, some questionable editing —Claribel's aversion to marriage, "all whores and knaves," "hereditary sloth," and the invasion of Cupid were gone, "excrement" was substituted for "siege"—but enhanced by a sparkling Miranda (Corliss Preston) and a lyric Ariel (B. W. Gonzalez), who abandoned its body at the end and tinkerbelled off, free in a convincingly ahuman way in a zone where no flesh and blood had been or could go, and an opulent and absolutely empty *Much Ado About Nothing.*

Placed against the two productions in the larger Elizabethan Theater, the *Hamlet* in the more intimate, six-hundred-seat Angus Bowmer had to be "controversial." The script itself offers probably more room for interpretation—that is, for the imaginative interaction of actors with language and for spectators with actors—than probably any other in the canon. The actors playing Hamlet, Claudius, and Ophelia worked out detailed and original interpretations of their roles. Barry Kraft edited the playing script from the First Folio text, meaning that a Q2-conditioned ear heard some words for the first time ("kinde Life-rend'r-ing *politician*," and "Rosin*crane*," here a childhood nickname that Hamlet remembered with pleasure). Neither set nor costumes were in the "received-standard" mode. Indeed, a detailed *exploration* of the script, lasting for three hours and twenty minutes (minus fifteen for the interval) was bound to tax the attention span of the most willing of spectators. This was not, however, caviar for the general. The production rewarded attention. On the night I attended, the audience was rapt.

The set featured scaffolding covered by heavy, opaque plastic, construction lamps, and huge statues wrapped in plastic and bound in ropes. The only recognizable statue was a huge head of Julius Caesar, up center. Two chairs were deployed as thrones. Clearly, Claudius and Gertrude were redecorating the palace, getting rid of all those monumental reminders of a former reign. Woronicz stopped short of insisting that all the principals wear hard hats. The set "portray[ed] the limbo of an interregnum, between drastically different styles of leadership" (Woronicz, paraphrased in Kent, 1994, 12). We knew that the transition would not be made, since a fascist flag, black letters on a white background with a red frame, was center stage as we entered. It said "Fortinbras." Before the opening lines, a rising cry of "Fortinbras!" came from the darkness, and a brief spot illuminated a small man in uniform and red beret. As guards in Elsinore prepared to see a ghost, we glimpsed the result of all the "carnall, bloudie, and unnaturall acts . . . accidentall judgements, casuall slaughters . . . death's put on by cunning, and forc'd cause [and] purposes mistooke, Falne on the Inventors heads." Thus the play was a retrospective examination of how a Fortinbras gets to rule. This approach achieved one brilliant moment much later, but fell short of what it might have accomplished. It may be that the original concept, which was to have something to do with Bosnia, was dropped. That was fortunate, but trace memories of that bright idea remained to haunt this production. The distant bust of Caesar, visible almost constantly from the second scene on, predicted Fortinbras, of course, but also served as the terminal point of the *almost* infinite regress of power politics, since it was "Imperiall Caesar, dead and turn'd to clay," or, in this case, to stone.

It was *Fortinbras* who explained to Hamlet—in a snippet borrowed from Q2—that the Norwegian army went to gain "a little patch of ground." The two princes met, then, without knowing it. At the end, however, when it had been so carefully prepared for, Fortinbras did *not* recognize the dead Hamlet as the young man whose path he had crossed near some misty fjord. Nor, unless I was nodding, did Fortinbras employ F1's "Take up the body," a singular usage (as opposed to Q2's "bodies") that shows how quickly Fortinbras has picked up Horatio's cues about "Whose voyce will draw on more." Hamlet's body and the ceremony that Fortinbras will create around it will consolidate the latter's "Rites of memory in this Kingdome," enhancing "body politic" so that the king will be with the body. Fortinbras was given an up-center position on the scaffolding above the littered throne room. It was the same spot from which Hamlet, in command for an instant, had outlined his plans for "Gonzago." Otherwise, the ending did not exploit what the production had prepared us for—the potentially powerful *and* subtle interchange between Hamlet II's ambassador to Norway, Horatio, and Fortinbras, humanized for an instant even as he becomes king by his realization that he had met Hamlet, each young prince then, as now, going in a different direction. His recognition of Hamlet would have cued Fortinbras's "For me, with sorrow, I embrace my Fortune."

Another problem in the production, again perhaps an excrescence of prior concept, was the treatment of the Ghost. In the first scene it was a flashing light that moved more quickly than human guards. Fine—the Ghost in Gielgud's 1964 production was a gigantic shadow against the bare, backstage bricks. One did have to wonder how the Ashland Ghost could be said to have worn "his Beaver up"? When Hamlet confronted it, along a section of parapet whereon the guards had been charmed into a spell, it had become an armored ghost, though with ropes around its shoulders, like its shrouded likenesses in the throne room. Then, letdown of letdowns, the Ghost appeared for the closet scene, again in medieval armor, on a platform, downstage right. The grouping—Hamlet and Gertrude were also downstage right—reminded us of similar earlier family configurations: Claudius, Gertrude, and Hamlet, Polonius and Ophelia, and the Ghost and Hamlet during their first meeting. This use of the stage was valid enough, but predictable. What Woronicz had prepared us for was the use of the huge, pinioned statue stage left (where ghosts come from) as Ghost. It would have taken some subtle adjustments in lighting and in the direction from which the Ghost's "Do not forget . . ." came. The use of the statue would have simultaneously made the Ghost powerful *and,* just possibly, a "coynage of" Hamlet's "Braine" (though hardly a "bodilesse Creation").

Again, as with Fortinbras, the production got us ready for a moment that did not come. In this instance the production would have completed Woronicz's sense that "Hamlet's father is the old: the chivalrous, the courtly; Hamlet's uncle is the modern: the wily diplomat, the conspirator" (paraphrased in Kent 1994, 12). It follows that Hamlet is the "postmodernist," constantly deconstructing, and failing when he *becomes* modernist—that is, on insisting that a work of art contain only a single, univocal meaning. Hamlet's failure with "Gonzago" means that the production must become postmodernist, that is, permitting of more than one interpretation. That statue was an opportunity missed.

One very good moment *did* occur in the Ghost sequences—tiny, but worth mention. Marcellus (Joe Hilsee) was scornful when he said to Horatio, "Thou art a scholler. . . ." The line translated to "So you didn't believe me! Let's see whether your learning will do you any good in *this* situation." The line, then, was similar to the Boatswain's "Use your authority!" to Gonzalo, during the opening storm in *The Tempest*.

The anachronism—the Ghost in armor in an otherwise vaguely contemporary setting—was disconcerting only because it was not made to make any sense. Ron Daniels, in his 1989 RSC production (but not in the ART revival in the United States) linked both Ghost *and* Fortinbras by putting them in armor. Fortinbras's takeover at the end showed Denmark falling back in time to the red-clawed world of Beowulf. Here, the Ghost at least had the merit of making no comment on Bosnia, but was, while he was on, a character in an old play that was making no sense even on its own terms.

I cite these shortcomings to suggest how much this production invited us to *notice* details and conditioned us to expect that smaller points would be developed intelligently into larger—how much energy remained *latent* here. For the most part, the production and its values realized themselves powerfully. Some critics felt otherwise, one suggesting that the production was "tedious" and that the "staging . . . work[ed] at cross purposes" ("Inconsistencies" 1994), and another that "the play is muddled by a lack of direction, or the absence of a point of view . . . the stage is cluttered with concepts that are left undeveloped" (Juillerat 1994). "Just as the audience begins to identify with one production style," said Al Reiss, the production "switched to another . . . This 'Hamlet,' so overdone, holds a funhouse mirror up to nature" (1994). "In the ocean of possible interpretations available," said Barry Johnson, "it floated without special commitment to any one . . . the production has the feel of a show caught in the middle" (1994). The last statement is accurate—the question is whether *Elsinore*'s being "caught in the middle" worked for the audience, as it seems not to have done for most reviewers.

With the possible exception of the closet scene, the staging was very well-done. The down-left area of the stage was underused—though Laertes and Claudius plotted there (as they should—down left is the place of plots). One superb moment occurred as Gertrude described Ophelia's drowning. Gertrude stood down right, pointing off in the direction from which she had entered. Claudius and Laertes stood on a line above her. This staging forced us to follow Gertrude's arm to that brook and allowed us to visualize the moment that she described, making an otherwise ornate speech vivid and moving. It was Ophelia who was drowning, not some mythical lady in a pretty pastoral poem.

Susan Wing suggests that a dignified Ophelia strengthens Hamlet's role. Wing asserts that the Nunnery Scene is a precise prelude to Ophelia's mad scenes. Ophelia goes to both nunneries in madness—she is the virgin bedded by her fiance and then the whore, discarded because she has come prematurely to that bed. Wing shows that the part of Ophelia is not "written." A script in which the part was somehow complete as words on the page would be a bad script. The words are there to be deciphered toward an interpretation. "I shall obey, my lord," need not be abject or tear struck. It can be angry and can even raise a warning eyebrow from Polonius, if he hears the reply. Its placement as the last line in the scene suggests that Polonius could already have swept out. A rebellious Ophelia can become rebelliously insane, almost in the "I'll show you!" tradition of adolescent anger. Zeffirelli privileges the character. Just after Ophelia calls for her coach, she is viewed from a low-angle shot, black-rimmed eyes burning with rage. Around her head the inner keep of the castle forms a gigantic crown. She becomes Queen Ophelia of Denmark, a madwoman ruling a superficially sane kingdom. In Raynar Lyth's 1984 film, Pernilla Wallgren's Ophelia, seeking "the beauteous majesty of Denmark," bursts into a ceremonial occasion, forcing both king and queen to attend to her. She is that which had been repressed exploding into the smirking civility of the garden party, an instability at the heart of Elsinorian politics that breaks through at the most unsuitable of moments—as insanity will do. This is Ophelia as Banquo's ghost. In the Richardson film, Marianne Faithfull's Ophelia is a voice from the grave, a version of the Ghost of King Hamlet, a pale-faced jester who anticipates the skull. To this favor she has come. Later, we know why this Ophelia is being buried in Yorick's grave.

The part is completed by the electrochemical reaction between script and actress. Ophelia must go mad, but the way she gets there and the nature of her madness itself must be variously interpreted. I would defend Olivier on just one aspect of his Ophelia. She is the only character in the film who is viewed in contact with nature. We see her running in from a bright out-of-doors to be trapped and maddened within the walls and corridors of Elsinore. I would suggest that Olivier sees her as being alienated from that external power and from her own nature by the stones and shadows of the hollow world in which she becomes trapped. In fairness to Bennett, his Ophelia flirts shamelessly with Claudius (Patrick Stewart) during the "St. Valentine's Day" scene, making things not just politically but personally uncomfortable for the king and recognizing in him the source of the sexual disturbance in Elsinore that has made her its victim. This interpretation hardly redeems Lalla Ward's performance but might have been powerful with a more "sexually advantaged" Ophelia.

In another 1994 *Hamlet,* not otherwise worth examination here,[2] Asch Gregory created a remarkable Ophelia. She went to her father after Hamlet's appearance in her closet to prove, at last, that she was right about Hamlet's love for her. Polonius agreed—"I am sorry," he said, and again, "I am sorry" (pause for emphasis). But then, as Ophelia rested her case, Polonius drew only the political conclusion to his error and insisted on dragging her off to the king. Having proved her point, Ophelia was suddenly implicated in a political plot of which she wanted no part. Gregory's mad scenes were powerful because she was finally insisting on who *she* was and what *she* knew. She could do so, however, only by abandoning a public persona and the future that persona granted her—if not to be queen, at least to stay alive. Her identity and grasp of reality had been driven inward so that her songs and distribution of flowers emerged from a concentrated core of inviolable selfhood. That is usually madness—or something equally dangerous. Gregory had pulled back—literally and figuratively—from the falseness imposed upon her. In her madness she moved intently *into* her role, brow furrowed as she phrased her sense of what was "right" and insisted that others play the roles *she* assigned to them. It was a rare instance where I looked forward to the mad scenes and wished that the rest of the production had used the Ophelia as a way of calibrating characterization. Ophelia had a concept of who she was and a vivid sense of how Elsinore was distorting her identity. She resisted to no avail. Others accommodated—also to no avail—and their placement in proximity to or at a distance from the Elsinorian norm of subterfuge, espionage, and hidden agendas could have defined the production concept.

Dawn Lisell's Ophelia at Ashland was as good as Gregory's, but Lisell charted a reverse course toward extraversion, showing how remarkably varied the role can be when confronted by intelligent actors.

Lisell was not running *to* Polonius after the closet scene, but *away from* Hamlet. She was surprised and not too happy to encounter Polonius, but did tell her story. In the nunnery scene Lisell tried to play against the lines—saying one thing to Hamlet, another to the listeners behind the arras. "Remembrances" were not objects she was returning to Hamlet, but their love. "There, my lord" was supposed to sound like, "here are those things you gave me," but Lisell pointed to where Claudius and her father hid. Hamlet, instead of being grateful that she was confiding in him, grew angry at the presence of eavesdroppers and played the rest of the scene for them. Ophelia's "At home, my Lord," was extraordinary. She was saying, "I have already told you where he is, but I will play this scene with you, knowing we have an audience." Lisell let out an agonized cry when she realized that her effort to communicate with Hamlet—that she still *loved* him in spite of the reports he had received to the contrary and in spite of her apparent rejection of him—had failed. Since her love could now emerge only in her grieving soliloquy, it was not just a conventional listing of what Hamlet had lost but a remarkably powerful expression of her own loss.

In the mad scenes Ophelia played the roles she had been denied "in life," and parodied in a little-girl's singsong the stereotypic persona imposed upon her. Her "dove" was her father's spirit, flying off to some conventional "rest," but her "We must be patient" was an imitation of gruff Polonius. Resentment flowed in, as the animus, the contrasexual element that had been repressed in her, took over. Lisell stepped neatly into the role of Fool, vacated years before by Yorick and, only yesterday, by Hamlet. Hers was not conscious jesting, of course, not "ambiguity of personality, the conscious assumption of different roles," but "the disintegration of personality, which is madness," as Sidney Thomas says in distinguishing between Hamlet and Ophelia (1943, 6). The mad scenes here were eerily like those that Lady Macbeth plays, before the murder of Duncan, and, much later, at the beginning of act 5. Ophelia's "Pray love remember" and Laertes's "thoughts & remembrance fitted" echoed potently against her earlier "Remembrances . . . That I have longed long to re-deliver."

This was another Ophelia who had chosen to play down by the river, as her muddy gown suggested, so that her being allowed to drown was explained in advance. (Someday, a production will show a Gertrude, ambitiously at cross purposes with Claudius, or Claudius himself signaling to a henchperson that Ophelia be done away with.) This production did show Claudius explaining to a distraught Ophelia the necessity of Hamlet's banishment to England. Hamlet looked at her briefly, perhaps apologetically, as he said, "At Supper."

Gregory's Polonius (P. Michael Bourgoin) cared for his daughter deeply, but blundered. His love could not save Ophelia. Sandy McCallum, the Ashland Polonius, was a tough survivor of regimes, his face made ugly by politics. He gestured as he spoke to Reynaldo on the word "carp," making a hook of his left index finger and dragging it abruptly past his mouth. He knew how to catch fish, was a "fishmonger"—a retailer of carp—but impervious to his own sharp destiny. *His* reiterated "I am sorry" meant merely that he was now more determined than ever to be right, and motivated his confident assertions to Claudius about the cause of Hamlet's "Lunacie." It was a brutal Polonius who doomed his daughter. No matter who he is, Polonius presses Ophelia into a pattern alien to whoever she is. But who she is and where she goes in her madness is remarkably open to choice, as Lisell, in developing roles from the fragments of her psyche, and Gregory, in assigning parts made up of her own fragmentation to spectators, brilliantly demonstrated.

The central contrast in the Ashland production was drawn between Claudius and Hamlet. Lawrence Hecht was a large, confident king, unruffled, perhaps the most debonair Claudius since Alfred Drake in 1964. This Claudius showed the king's remarkable skills in diverting energies that threatened him—from Fortinbras to Laertes. Very little bothered him. Here, it was not so much Gertrude's "prayers" but Claudius's easy overconfidence that kept Hamlet at Elsinore and permitted the Ghost to contact his son. Like Patrick Stewart, Hecht could be amused by Hamlet. "Madnesse in great Ones, must not unwatch'd go," Hecht said blithely. He knew that Hamlet wasn't mad, but he was dictating the official line for Polonius to promulgate. Claudius was angry at Hamlet after "Gonzago," but even more scornful of himself as he tried to pray. He was modern man recognizing that the cosmic rhythms of an older order still pertained, regardless of his temporal power as king. "May one be pardon'd, and retaine th' offence?" he asked God with a sneer and paused for a reply. He knew there would be none, but he shared his joke on himself with us. "There is no shuffling," he said, looking at us as he pointed up—which is exactly the way to read that line. The effort at prayer humanized him for us and, more than that, involved us in his contradictions, and our own. He did not perceive Hamlet as a threat until he realized "It had bin so with us had we beene there." But even that insight did not shake him for long, and he appeared at the duel as, again, a commanding and amused monarch. He *did* care for Gertrude, who seldom left his side (even after the closet scene) and died with her name emerging with his death-sigh.

She is almost invariably attended by a lady-in-waiting, but here Claudius performed that mourning duty. The First Folio makes Claudius more of a "mighty opposite" than does the Second Quarto, and this production permitted the king to live up to Hamlet's description. One believed, as I think one should, that Claudius *almost* made it at the end. But not quite.

If ever a Hamlet *should* have returned to Wittenberg, it was Richard Howard's Hamlet. Tall and ungainly, Ichabod Craneish, he was unprincely, except insofar as the upper classes learn to play games with a confidence that knows no pressure. Pressure in life? Plenty. But never while playing tennis or squash, or, in this instance, while dueling. Like the occasionally sensitive upper class person, this Hamlet attempted to introduce a different way of looking at things to Elsinore and almost succeeded when his old friends, the players, showed up. After seeing the Ghost, Howard did act wacky on occasion—effusively greeting Guildenstern when the latter said, "The Queene, your Mother . . . hath sent me to you." Howard drew part of his characterization from Yorick, explaining that Hamlet's "antic repartee, as it would be with Yorick or any good fool, is the truth." Furthermore, Hamlet "finds a great deal of freedom in behaving strangely" (1994, 1). The antic disposition is a way out of the dilemma of having to "hold [his] tongue." Howard could have gone even further in the antic direction, since he does sight gags and comic routines very well. (Jacobi linked up with Yorick by donning a skull mask from the players' prop chest to "be idle".) Howard read that sequence of early seventeenth-century clichés ("To be . . .") with one interesting variation. "To sleepe No more" is usually read with a full stop at the line ending, after "sleepe," though F1 has no punctuation. Howard read it without punctuation—that is, "no more to sleep in a human sense." His next emphasis should, I think, have been "And by a sleep, to say . . ."—in other words, death is *not* sleep, or, if it is, we have to change the definition of the word. The emphasis was not there—or perhaps my ear was not—and so the contrast with the easy cliches of Lady Macbeth, Octavius Caesar, and John Donne was not there either. Howard's "Rogue and Peasant slave" speech was his best—he pounded his own cloak, which was Claudius, "making the cloak act," as was said of Ellen Terry, reminding us of our own futile tantrums in the face of the insolence of office, and getting a laugh as he raised his head, looked at us and said, "What an Asse am I." Howard completed the line about the recorder—"yet cannot you make it" (which is then given a period in F1) with a bleep *from* the instrument. (Years ago, Sam Tsousouvas played a couple of brilliant cadenzas on the instrument and handed it to an angry Guildenstern.)

The Rosencrantz and Guildenstern scenes were complicated by Rosencrantz's gender. *She* (Linda Alper) was a very attractive "city girl," in contrast to a more sheltered Ophelia. Rosencrantz was now Guildenstern's girlfriend, but had been Hamlet's. The line "My Lord, you once did love me" was moving and created a web of tensions that touched Ophelia, of course, and that made of Guildenstern a man very quick to surrender to jealousy and consequent hatred of Hamlet. The poignancy of Hamlet's sending Rosencrantz to *her* death was strong here—partly because we had met her and knew of her ongoing love for Hamlet and partly because her death meant nothing to Hamlet. The closet scene was vocally violent, but not particularly sexual. Howard handled Gertrude's "What shall I do?" brilliantly. His "Not this by no meanes that I bid you do" translated to "Damnit, Ma, if you don't know by now, how the hell can I tell you?" Thus the convoluted directions he gave made perfect sense. At the very end, Howard gave Horatio a reason for not drinking the rest of the cup. Hamlet did not, like most Hamlets, wrest the cup from Horatio's hand, but saved his friend's life with all that business about telling Hamlet's "story." That subtext made Horatio's "sweet Prince" much more than a pro forma eulogy. The interchange between Hamlet and Horatio at the end was nicely anticipated by Horatio's cuing Hamlet earlier, allowing Hamlet to continue with the Pyrrhus speech.

Gertrude (Katherine Conklin) was elegantly coiffed—a woman from a Breck Shampoo ad—and tailored, a Nancy Reagan without the venom. This Gertrude had found her man in Claudius. One assumed a lack of humor, social grace, even some boorishness in her former husband—no matter what Hamlet may say of his father. Her happy "I shall obey you" to Claudius, as Ophelia is about to meet Hamlet in the hallway, contrasted with Ophelia's earlier, frustrated "I shall obey my Lord," pointing the difference between a woman who is content in her marriage and one who is restrained by a patriarch *from* contentment. This Gertrude was not, as T. S. Eliot suggests, an adequate objective correlative for Hamlet's rage. Quite the opposite. Conklin's character eased comfortably into her superficial awarenesses about Hamlet's "fathers death" and her "o're hasty Marriage" to Claudius. It was precisely because this shallow and extraverted Gertrude felt so little that her introverted son felt so much. This Gertrude also helped us believe in Hamlet's love for an intelligent and sensitive Ophelia.

Howard exhibited an "uncanny flair for staying in the moment," said Steven Winn (1994, E-3) and so did the production, creating a constant "present" for us and even forcing us to wonder not what will happen next, but how it will happen. "Every new Hamlet," says John

Gielgud, "must link the strands of the play by an individual, original attitude, and tell the story anew for the audience. He must try to experience the progression of the play and not think which scene he needs most to worry about. He must . . . not know what is coming next, and really live the part every night" (1992, 43). Howard did this. The story was old but the way of retelling it was new, "genuinely fresh," as one of the few approving critics said (Stutzin 1994), "keen and absorbing," as another said (Winn 1994). The production probably gained far more than it lost from the change in directors. Barry Johnson complained that the production "fails to make a particular point" (1994). The point it makes is complicated—we cannot leave politics to the politicians, as the criminals who perpetrated Vietnam made clear to us, *but* when we, the nonpoliticians, "get involved," we make a considerable mess of things. A Fortinbras, in uniform and special-forces beret, is always waiting in the wings.

*Hamlet* at Regent's Park was the first production of that play at a theater noted for its annual *A Midsummer Night's Dream*. This was the first outdoor *Hamlet* I had ever seen—other than a 1603 Quarto production in the yard of the George Inn in 1992—and it was a delight to watch members of the audience turn to find the cloud that Hamlet pointed out to Polonius. It was backed like a weasel.

The set was a sixteen-gauge steel structure that blocked the playing area's linkage with the real foliage of the park—all out-of-doors looking darkly in on *Hamlet*. It was "an abandoned brown hulk" (Hagerty, 1994), "a huge piece of ghastly '70s sculpture" (David Clark 1994). One set of steps, however, descended to a point lower than the wall between the steps and the audience, so that the Ghost, descending, disappeared on "All my crimes full blown," and reappeared as he reached the stage level. The instant gave us a sense of the Ghost's power to appear and disappear and come again. Otherwise, all this metal rusting under a blistering London summer provided an occasional metallic clangor that caused a character to turn and see a portal just closing, taking its mystery with it as it echoed. Suzi Feay found the set "brilliantly effective" (1994b).

Damian Lewis, fresh from drama school (Guildhall), brought to his Hamlet the qualities of several recent princes. He was an awkward young man—except when he dueled—who really should have been in school but had been told he must be prince. Hamlet explores among other things the discrepancy between his own abilities/inclinations and his public role as crown prince, *both* roles remarkably complicated by the Ghost's visitation and the seemingly contradictory injunctions in which the deeply private and the vital public aspects of Hamlet's being must participate. Lewis, tall, carrot-topped, thin-shouldered, bony-faced, needed more of a sense of humor, perhaps more of the ironic attitude he displayed only fleetingly, as when, standing in the sun down right on a hot afternoon, he said that he was "too *much* in the sun." The extra element in the pun got a laugh for the first time in some 393 years. Otherwise, it was all a bit serious. We needed more of Hamlet laughing at himself, as Jacobi did so well, or perhaps more of Hamlet observing himself, backing away from his more extreme postures and pronouncements and telling us that *he* knows that "this is most brave." Lewis, however, superbly *underplayed* his initial response after the Ghost exited (1.5), attempting to "behave rationally" while emotionally in turmoil. Paul Taylor summed up his experience thus: "though the alfresco loveliness of Regent's Park on a glorious evening seems a far cry from Hamlet's sterile promontory and could well be a distraction, Lewis's performance makes sure you see the thematic wood for the trees" (1994c).

Lewis had thought about the part. "Not this, that by no means I bid you do" was excited, voyeuristic. On "hoodman blind," he groped Gertrude in a private part, suggesting the blindness of what he perceived to be her game of sexual roulette. His strongest soliloquy was "how all occasions": "even for an egg shell" was whispered incredulously. He paused to consider when Osric proposed the match with Laertes, his hesitation an objective correlative for "how ill all" was about his heart. He knelt to Laertes in asking pardon, an action that made his defense for the psychopathic killer who happens to be himself seem sincere. "Silence" became "sigh lence"—the half-regretful, half-grateful expiration of a final breath.

The soliloquies were delivered against a freeze-frame of other characters. Paul Taylor found that the technique "emphasis[ed] the production's weaknesses . . . the quality-in-balance generally evident—Lewis's Hamlet intensely alive, the rest of the show relatively inert" (1994c). "Too, too solid flesh" was projected against a court caught in midexit. It might have been more specific. Hamlet might have indicated Gertrude on "Niobe," even gone to her and pointed in scorn. As it was, he stayed downstage, a placement that neutralized the decision for stasis and suggested only that nothing moves while Hamlet is thinking. More effective was his "Rogue and peasant slave," begun in the players' cart while they became statues around him, continued downstage, and completed back in the cart, so that he was surrounded by "these players here" as he described his plans for them. The choice for freeze-frame was interesting, but it might have been put to better use—to permit

Lewis to develop the detachment and sense of irony missing in his performance. While Taylor's analysis is accurate, the staging concept could have been used to make Lewis's performance even more "alive."

Inevitably, Lewis attracted almost all of the critical attention, most of which was positive. An "edgy, passionate Hamlet," said David Clark. "The play's shortening makes him seem more decisive than usual" (1994). Michael Billington found Lewis "highly exciting . . . With his height, flaming red hair and black loosely-bound scarf, he looks a little like Rothenstein's painting of Gordon Craig's Hamlet" (1994a). "He makes no particular play between *piano* and *forte*," said Alastair Macaulay, "he employs no great contrasts of speed during his soliloquies . . . is still shifting in his way of addressing the audience—and yet one attends to him" (1994). "To Hamlet's antic disposition, Lewis brings a splendidly intimidating levity which can shade into the potent expression of spirtual disgust," said Taylor (1994c). According to Macaulay, Lewis was a Hamlet "both romantic (frozen in melancholy, vivid in action) and modern (playing at crude aperies in his 'madness,' sardonically rude)" (1994a). Indeed, Lewis's "simian impersonations" (Billington 1994a) looked like the antics of bored fourth formers at an all-male prep school and drew Ian Shuttleworth's ire: "there's no place in the prince's 'antic disposition' for impersonations of a chimp" (1994). His "antic disposition," said Feay, "smacks more of a callous undergraduate mocking a spastic than of heartsick distraction" (1994a). Billington "missed the character's quiet irony and the humane stoicism Branagh brought to the latter stages of the play"—in an uncut version. "But this is a recklessly dangerous Hamlet whom you can well understand Claudius wishing to dispatch on the first available boat to England" (1994a). Michael Coveney felt that Lewis lacked "the modern, punkish, sardonic quality this role now seems to demand" (1994b), but Coveney gives no examples of actors who have played that Hamlet. Alan Rickman? Jeremy Kingston found that Lewis "presents a striking figure with his flaming red hair and black frock coat . . . and in repose his silhouette has a haughty grace. But he hits a note of loud-voiced frenzy at an early point and seldom budges from it" (1994). I found Lewis's range more varied than did Kingston, particularly in contrast to the earsplitting shouting of Iain Glen and Toby Stephens as Henry V and Coriolanus, respectively, at Stratford.

Paul Freeman (Claudius) was an actor playing Claudius. "Everything" he did told us, said Macaulay, "with emphatically actorish deliberation" that he was an actor "of the old school—a school so old that one thought it was dead. . . . I cannot believe in [his] characterization . . . for a minute" (1994a). Claudius *did* need a court, having only the Polonius family to thank at the outset. The players should have been enlisted as attendants. This Claudius was effectively insecure at the outset. He began to approach Hamlet but switched to Laertes ("Now, Laertes, what's the news with *you*") to "warm up" for the more difficult assignment of this postcoronation business meeting. Freeman's effort at prayer, however, was loudly histrionic, an approach that never works. What did work was Hamlet's standing right over Claudius to deliver the competing soliloquy ("Now might I do it") while swinging the sword over Claudius's head ten times. We had been conditioned by the freeze-frame so that our disbelief could remain as suspended as was Hamlet's intent. Claudius's "It had been so with us" was a line delivered by an actor who had memorized it, not the discovery of a character who has just avoided six inches of fatal steel.

But Claudius stared Hamlet down as the latter played with "mother" and "father." The King's steely smile said, "No more games," and Hamlet broke off weakly on "For England." Here, Claudius exerted pressure against the usual reading of the colloquy, in which Hamlet gets away with insulting Claudius and we laugh at the king. Why did Freeman not bring more of this strength to Claudius? After "Gonzago," for example, Claudius seemed in control, if angry at Hamlet. Suddenly he panicked and shouted "Give me some light!" Why? After the interval we got a reverse-angle shot: Claudius entered another room, having exited from "Gonzago" and completing his previous line with "Away!" The court followed in disarray behind him until Hamlet and Horatio were left alone onstage.

Pamela Miles's attractive Gertrude took an anti-Claudius line after the closet scene, setting up her defiance about the chalice. She began to become unhinged in an Ophelian way. She picked up Ophelia's flowers after the second mad scene and "became" the drowning woman she described, explaining how she knew by a kinesthetic re-creation of what had been told to her. She might have taken this line further and sung "Sweets to the sweet," recalling Ophelia's earlier distribution, but Faith Brook had done that years ago in the Robert Chetwyn production (with Ian McKellen). Miles's through-line was her rejection of Claudius. A fine moment occurred when Laertes shouted "The King! The King's to blame!" Claudius, cradling the dying Gertrude, pulled away. She turned to indict him with a final gaze.

An Ophelia played straight in the mad scenes, with manic swings between childish obliviousness and screeching grief, is excruciating, to say nothing of "lachrymose" (Feay 1994a). Here, a talented and attractive young actor (Rebecca Egan) needed more help from the director than she got. The scenes were conflated, with Gertrude's "I will not speak with her" followed by the entrance of Laertes, a sleight-of-line that argued Denmark's disorder and set up Ophelia's "My brother shall know of it." He was there, hearing of it, but invisible to her, played by a young actor, Guy Burgess, destined for a splendid career. Egan's Ophelia did lead Laertes into a brief waltz to "And on his grave rained many a tear." The moment parodied their earlier dance, just before he left for Paris. It was chilling to be reminded of an instant of mutual happiness and youthful pleasure in this court of death. This is the first Ophelia I have seen who rose from her grave—a space below a panel down left—for her curtain call.

The Ghost was played conventionally, in armor, which made sense of "he wore his beaver up" for a change and did not clash with the Dickensian flavor of the rest of the costumes. This was the Ghost that Michael Kustow calls for: "precise, firm and genuine" (1964, 144). Kenneth Gilbert doubled as Ghost and First Player, the latter brought in standing under a sheet in the players' cart and unveiled with startling effect. He wore a beard and thus looked exactly like the Ghost. But on "Comest thou to beard me in Denmark," Hamlet pulled the beard off. It became "a tawdry theatrical prop" (Paul Taylor 1994c) that suggested the wispy line between illusion and reality and that the line is often a function of perception. The Ghost, too, has been an "illusion." For a moment Hamlet did not know where he was or whether there was any there there. One payoff of this doubling did not occur here. That is, that Claudius recognize his brother during "Gonzago," as in Ron Daniels's production of the late '80s. One might assume, then, that the Regent's Park player king looked like the former king only to Hamlet. If that was the case, this Hamlet was doing some projecting and *might* have been doing so during the closet scene. The Ghost entered stage right, behind Hamlet, who had Gertrude pinioned, but Hamlet perceived his presence before he saw him. Had the pressure of an extremely Oedipal moment forced Hamlet to hallucinate his father's interference? The possibility was there, an exercise in point of view worthy of *The Turn of the Screw.*

The editing followed Tim Pigott-Smith's dictum that "in reducing the play specifically for this theatre, I have also tried to recapture some of the thriller element that the revenge play held for Elizabethan audiences" (1994, 11). Feay expressed a more cynical view: "This version has been so brutally cut to enable white-wine swilling punters to get out of the park before locking-up time," with the result that "Hamlet whirls in a vortex of displacement activity rather than being stalled and gloomy" (1994b). Whether a stalled and gloomy Hamlet is a preferable option to a frantic pace or not, this production did rush past the moments in the script that question actions taken and untaken. "Gonzago," for example, was reduced merely to the dumb show, so that the play-within became another instant in the pell-mell play-without, as opposed to a significant "inset" (see F. Berry 1965) whose controlled, if "old-fashioned," artistic premises and clearly understood, if aphoristic and sanctimonious, moral grounding, hold a mirror up to the outer play. This *Hamlet* tended to be a long "chase scene," where the length of the chase diminished the thrill. For Shuttleworth, "it makes sense to heighten the 'thriller' element by way of compensation [for] the diminution of the play's tragic force" (1994), but it might be argued that the diminution was a *product* of the heightening. For Kingston, this "reading of the play . . . lacks the sense of doom [and is] as a whole, unsubtle and unexciting" (1994).

One result of the editing was that, as Feay accurately noted that "the cruel twist which dispatched Rosencrantz and Guildenstern is dispensed with, and Hamlet re-emerges from what seemed like certain execution with no explanation" (1994a). This sequence was no problem if one automatically filled in the narrative but might have troubled someone for whom this was a "first" experience, as Regent's Park often is for the younger members of its audience. We heard Polonius asking to be "left alone to find the depth of this" and agreeing to accompany Hamlet to England. His voyage was canceled, of course, and Hamlet was led off, bound in ropes, unaccompanied by Rosencrantz and Guildenstern, who presumably had gone off in search of Tom Stoppard. The choices leaned toward F1: "cast thy nightly color off," "wild and hurling words," "all we wail for," for example. Hamlet's "To be" got its early Q1 placement, and the Grave-digger got "a great soaker" from Q1.

Pigott-Smith is right to say that "no theatre in London . . . reproduces so closely as Regent's Park the conditions in which the play was originally performed" (1994, 2). It was for that reason that I chose to attend a matinee. Some critics appreciated this aspect: " 'This most excellent canopy the air, look you . . .' It makes a difference when you can see the firmament Hamlet is talking about" (Macaulay 1994a). "The lighting man (God) has contrived a jokey day-lit ghost scene and progressive murk to the final dark duel," said Feay, who went in the evening, when sunfall lingers above the summers of the northern hemisphere. "It works" (1994a). By "nightfall," warned Michael Billington, " 'the air bites shrewdly' in Regent's Park as much as in Elsinore" (1994a).

Astonishingly, however, critics complained about the "historicizing" of *Hamlet*. "To play the first scene in broad daylight . . . was to make . . . nonsense of the soldiers staggering around and blindly demanding each other's identity [and of a Ghost] forced to walk abroad at this all-too earthly hour . . . It hardly wings us effortlessly into the rank, claustrophobic atmosphere of Elsinore," said Jack Tinker (1994c). The "production's biggest enemy is daylight," said Shuttleworth (1994). The "daylight . . . militates against the somber mood of the play in the early stages," said David Clark (1994). Critics brought up on film and accustomed to all of the technical facility that Shakespeare's stage lacked have forgotten what Michael Hattaway points out: "What was seen on the stage was never to be taken for reality: Elizabethan drama-tists expected their audience to be always conscious of the distinction between signifier and signified" (1989, 51). As Lois Potter says, "dark-ness was metaphoric at the Globe . . . The peculiar horror of Othello, often blunted in productions with overatmospheric lighting effects, is that we are forced to watch in helpless clarity as the hero walks blindly, in his private darkness, over a precipice" (1975, 187).

For me, it was a joy rather than a chore to suspend my disbelief as I watched a *Hamlet* returned to daylight for perhaps the first time since 1601.

Earlier, I suggested that the scripts usually work when they are placed back in time. Ralph Alan Cohen's Shenandoah Shakespeare Express makes an effort to re-create a sense of the playing conditions of Shake-speare's Globe—the lights are on, the audience is visible, and, if it is dark, the actors must grope around the stage. This is the way Cohen directed his 1994-95 *Hamlet*. The guards in the opening scene found each other by sound and touch. The payoff came later, and it was bril-liant. Claudius exited from "Gonzago" with "some light"—a candela-bra. Polonius took the *other* candelabra off to Gertrude's closet. When Hamlet arrived, he looked at that candelabra and assumed that Clau-dius had brought it there and that he was behind the curtain. "Nay, I know not. Is it the King?" was a question within an assumption. Then Hamlet (wonderfully played by Thadd McQuade) picked up the can-delabra and held it over Polonius for a disappointed "Thou wretched, rash, intruding fool, farewell!" Here, the "metaphor" was that people cannot see. It was imported effortlessly from the fact of darkness, both exterior and interior, imputed to a time when candles and torches supplied the only light. And thus a brief moment in the script was su-perbly "illuminated" for an audience that, then as now, had to be con-vinced that the characters onstage were wrapped in several versions of darkness.

Good productions of the script show how potent a metaphor it still can make with those "unlike things"—a contemporary company and a contemporary audience. Most recent productions, however, are not only "domesticated," they tend to *reflect* "society" rather than use the script to explore it. In other words, we now realize that very few of us either grew up in "functional" families or made one available to our children. Assuming at least two dysfunctional families in *Hamlet,* what is unique about the old-king, new-king, uncle-father-aunt-mother, or the absent-mother in the Prime Minister's family tends to lose the political element in favor of how these configurations compare to the non-nuclear, upper-middle-class family today. The challenge is to explore the script, not just to "make it compare." In the ways that count, *Hamlet,* Hamlet, and what happens in *Hamlet* are incomparable, or, if comparable, they are so only when their own terms are understood in a specific production as opposed to a generalized "culture." A careful exploration of the script will create its own analogies, without a production's reaching for them.

It may be that a postmodernist director will want to employ for emphasis and as structuring device the theories that Joseph Meeker puts forth in *The Comedy of Survival* (1980), which, as far as I know, has not been noticed by scholars or theater practitioners. Meeker argues that "comic man" chooses to survive, as Pistol and Parolles do, and as Falstaff does at Shrewsbury by playing dead and therefore mimicking the behavior of animals. Most species, even predators, do not kill within the species, nor do they execute their kind for antisocial behavior. Man does, partly because he has a memory. And man can kill his own species if he dehumanizes it—"How now! A rat?" In *Hamlet* prior history confronts the prince, and "inherited cultural morality tells him that murder in his situation is proper and appropriate. Somewhere within him, however, is a force which resists and looks for alternatives. He creates redirections with his mind when his instincts fail to supply them. Hamlet is an anomaly among heroes because of his strong aversion to lethal violence, although his evasive behavior would seem perfectly normal if it were observed in a wolf" (69). One might argue that Brutus, Othello, and Macbeth are also averse to murder and, in the former two instances, ritualize it so that it will seem a sacrifice, as each says.

Hamlet becomes tragic hero at precisely the moment that he fails as comic hero—that is when his redirection of murderous anger cancels the play-within with "verbal mockery" (Meeker 1980, 66), indeed, when he reduces the play to "murder on the mental plane" (Goddard 1951, 369. See Coursen 1976, 89–167). In comedy, some contrivance—the "nightmare" Oberon induces in Titania, Orlando's wooing of "Rosalind," the eavesdropping scenes in *Much Ado,* for example—changes individuals and thus helps create a better society. Although Meeker does not make the argument (Goddard does), the crucial moment in *Hamlet,* his thesis would suggest, comes when Hamlet merely reformulates aggression into spoken daggers. He does not "modify [his] behavior to agree with the ecology of the world" (Meeker 1980, 135). Instead, he tries to insist "that the world be rearranged to suit [his] desires" (135), which are that Claudius be both punished *and* sent to hell, as Hamlet makes clear more than once. The "ecology" of Denmark is set, it seems, within a larger frame, of heaven, hell, and purgatory. Through "Gonzago's" possible operation, Hamlet has cleared a space that might open into that potentially saving dispensation, if the play contacted the troubled soul of Claudius—the microcosmic subparticle of the purposive cosmos. Hamlet, however, reverts to existential habit and denies himself, Claudius, and the kingdom the comic possibilities of the play he has commissioned. Hamlet's dilemma is thus phrased as an effort to behave as a member of the species ("kind") while fulfilling a culturally invented mission—revenge. "Gonzago" is his only chance to resolve the apparent contradiction. A production emerging from this premise would show, according to Meeker, that "Adaptation to environment is more than just a defensive technique of survival in [dangerous circumstances]. It is a creative ethic which requires that all . . . imaginative powers be directed toward encouraging a more durable equilibrium among the various forms of life" (135). We hear Hamlet's "brain" provide the answer. We watch Hamlet cancel the potentiality of the answer he has given himself. The allegory of the play, set in a late-medieval zone where all of the Dantean supernature pertains, is not Meeker's, but the imperative of the "creative ethic" applies to both worlds. The placing of the two worlds together in production could create a metaphor that projects the energy of the script into the future. Meeker contextualizes Hamlet convincingly within the issues of the late twentieth century, without falsifying the nature of Hamlet's problem as the character grappled with it at the beginning of the seventeenth.

Even as we "place" Hamlet in our times, however, another challenge for directors and actors will be to create convincingly for an audience a *Hamlet* that restores the supernatural and dynastic elements to contemporary performance. Certainly the latter aspect is available to our history. R. A. Foakes suggests one way in which the political element might be explored as a prologue to future productions: "Hamlet's last gesture is to vote for Fortinbras, who, as Peter Hall said, will make a good military dictator; and the play does not decide between a corrupt government by consent on the one hand, and on the other, a military government by force. Such a reading would, of course, have to be fleshed out, and it would be a contemporary interpretation; but then I take it as axiomatic that no other kind is possible. At least it might help to release the play from the burden of Hamletism" (1993b, 13).

A recent Dramaten production by Ingmar Bergman, wherein Horatio is shot at the end, would seem to be a step towards the radical *platea* that Foakes outlines. According to Robert Brustein, it

> prophesies the nightmares of the future [and] radically alters our understanding of Shakespeare's play without altering its shape, thus vindicating and somehow even purifying the basic tenets of classical reinterpretation. [It is] an oddly liberating experience [through which] you are permitted to absorb the soul of the tragedy as expressed through its racing plot, psychological relationships, social arrangements, and metaphysical overtones. . . . By demystifying the verse [which was in Swedish], this production makes the play a theatrical rather than a lyrical experience, restoring its intellectual and emotional surprise . . . it helps to reinvent the meaning of catharsis for our time . . . Bergman's *Hamlet* is the first production of the 21st century — a daring probe into tone, mood, and theatrical techniques of the future." (1988, 28–29)

The "second" production of the twenty-first century, a daring probe through the iron arras, occurred in Rumania just before the fall of Ceausescu, indeed is said to have contributed to the tyrant's tumble. There, as Joan Montgomery Byles reports (1991, 25–26), we discern a strong challenge to *locus* by *platea,* as opposed to some comforting confirmation of the numbness of the spectator.

This script's power to be *subversive* is probably stronger than that of *King Lear.* The latter expresses its own subversiveness, as Peter Brook demonstrated with his bleak productions of the 1960s. *Hamlet* can be more easily "contained" than *King Lear,* no doubt, but for that reason alone holds an explosiveness, an ability to decenter and disturb that its further history on stage will demonstrate.

The other missing element—that of the supernatural—will come again when directorial and spectatorial imaginations coincide to create a dramatic continuum that permits the Ghost to revisit the glimpses of our too-diminished expectations. It may be that merely a probe into Shakespeare's time, that is, a return to the relatively simple context that Shakespeare gives his Ghost—as in the Regent's Park production and also in Cohen's Shenandoah version—is all that is required. Alan Dessen describes a minimalist approach, as essayed by the five-actor ACTER company in 1993:

> with no special effects possible, the actors built skillfully upon their own resources and upon the playgoer's imagination. In the

cellarage scene, the Ghost . . . delivered the "swear" lines while seated in view but "offstage," but Hamlet, Horatio, and Marcellus "heard" the voice as if it came from beneath the stage and reacted accordingly so as to convey the strangeness as forcefully as I have ever seen. The opening scene was equally successful. This Ghost was preceded each time by a blast of cold (as signalled by the actors); at its second departure, the two sentries tried to stop it with their imaginary weapons, but it literally walked through their blows in eerie, magical fashion . . . (1994, 7)

Such a stylization, if not carefully controlled risks the laughter that the ghost at the banquet scene in *Macbeth* sometimes elicits. But in the ACTER production, the superiority and therefore mystery of the ventriloquist and invulnerable Ghost was imparted, and the audience, like the inner watch, paused to consider a moon-glimpsed mystery for which our "philosophy" cannot account.

It is perhaps too easy to blame television for the domestication of "the outer mystery" and for the reduction of a time of breaking of nations to brief summaries between commercials. If history is spiraling, as Yeats would have it, into antithesis, where materialism is to be veiled in the piety of fundamentalist movements, then television can be only a pale reflex of that inexorability. Theater, however, can be more, and it remains for the script of *Hamlet* to show us how.

### NOTES

1. Helen Gardner (1963) demonstrates that the would-be solver of his problem (whether it is revenger or villain) almost invariably falls into the trap he has set for others. This applies to Hamlet and his "Mousetrap" and to Claudius and his staging of a sword fight.

2. American Renaissance Theater, Portland Performing Arts Center, Maine. Directed by James Hoban. 28 June to 3 July 1994.

# X

## "You Would Be King of the Isle?": The Tyranny of Design: 1994

    Confronting us on the stage as we walked towards it was a stunning rendition of what I took to be the blasted heath which opens *Macbeth*. Real trees were in evidence, as well as shrubbery and a three-dimensional rocky terrain. The effect was so startling that we stopped for a moment in wonder.

    "Isn't it remarkable?" Miss Terry remarked. "Sir Edward Burne-Jones does a great many of our productions. Sometimes I think the public comes here just to look at the sets."

    —Nicholas Meyer, *The West End Horror*

Leonard Tannenhouse argues that "given that the existence of the theater depended on serving the interests of monarchy, it is . . . likely that dramas were staged to remain constant to their purpose of authorizing the monarch in the face of a new political challenge" (1986, 156). If Weimann is right, however, Shakespeare's scripts—*locus*—were susceptible to challenge from *platea*, that is, a conservatively constructed script could be presented subversively in a specific production. That is true, for example, of the players in *Hamlet* as they present "Gonzago," though they are unaware of the *platea* dimension inherent in that old *locus*. What seems to be happening in the larger English theaters today, however, is that meaning is being defined by the design of the production, which tends to serve only the box office (*if* that) and which subverts the inherited script only unintentionally, by interfering with whatever the words may be trying to communicate to an audience in the late twentieth century. "Authorization" has become an autonomous, free-floating authority willing to shell out some fifty dollars for a single ticket and to join with a thousand or more other similarly inclined authorities to hear a play on a given evening. That is, to *see* a play, or perhaps just a set. It has all become an elite enterprise in Great Britain dominated by the necessity to deliver a production as pleasant and reassuring as was the 1994 *Twelfth Night* treated elsewhere on these pages. Were one "psychologizing" the process, one would be inclined to describe it as the presentation of an "image" to the kind of narcissistic audience that Christopher Lasch defined years ago (1978). If "perception is reality," we have two "realities"—stage and audience mirroring each other and thus both parties frozen in some version of "mirror stage," and unlikely to disengage unless it is the *theater* that breaks free from symbiosis and thus liberates its audience.

Suffice it for this discussion that production values are dictated by a set constructed before any actors show up to rehearse. When someone years from now asks, "Whose History?"—the answer will be "The designers'." The evaluation of this "historical moment," if 1994 is any criterion, is unlikely to be positive. Directors and designers, like some New Historicists, tend to "dismiss the notion of the author having shaped his materials with a coherent moral and aesthetic design" (Vickers 1993, 259). They make little effort to interpret that design. Rather, they substitute their own design, which is often incoherent and which often drives whatever the play might be saying into competition *with* the design. In that case, the play seldom wins.

In his magnificent new book, *Looking at Shakespeare*, Dennis Kennedy contrasts English-speaking productions with those of the European continent:

> The distinctive strain of Shakespearean representation in our time, a tension between a decentering aesthetic and the desire to retain the plays as touchstones of traditional western culture, has produced uneven results. . . . The postmodern suspension of the past inside the present [results from Brecht's] realization that the rapidity of change and the increase in knowledge in the modern world have forced us to see history in a new light: not as a finalized past but as a process in which the new continuously transfigures the old. Though many recent British and American Shakespeare productions have slighted public themes, social issues have remained vital to Shakespeare in Europe, both east and west. (1993, 302–3)

In London and Stratford in 1994, the results were worse than "uneven." If postmodernism was at work it produced a muddle, drowning language and meaning, as in the Royal National Theatre's *Pericles*. If "tradition" were the touchstone, it produced a *Twelfth Night* that brought before us a quaint olde Stratford that would have been better served *by* the early music, as previously discussed. Another approach was to suggest that Shakespeare's scripts can be placed anywhere in history, in late eighteenth- or early-nineteenth-century France, for example, where, indeed, the setting did transfigure the old script, which in this instance was *Coriolanus*. The only "social issue" that mattered to the big theaters of London and Stratford was that of selling tickets. As Adrian Noble said in 1994, "The desire to be popular is a noble desire." A 10 percent drop in RSC audiences, he said, would result in an instant two- or three-hundred-million pound deficit. A secondary issue for RSC was avoiding the look of immediately previous productions of the same script—*A Midsummer Night's Dream*, for example. The overriding factor in these productions is that they are *designed,* often in absolute defiance of what the script still may have to say and certainly in conflict with the idea that a set is a space where actors can work. The exceptions—Adrian Noble's *King Lear* and Sam Mendes's *The Tempest* —both lucid, moving and basically traditional productions, were the ones where the set at least permitted the actors a downstage area relatively free of obstructions.

   Noble's *Lear* used a design that at times looked like a war of amoebas as seen under a microscope and, at other times, a great planet that cracked open as Gloucester was blinded. The planet dripped sand— "like some portentous planetary hour-glass" (Brodie 1994, 4)—or perhaps seeds ("all germens spill[ed]"). The upstage also had a hill from which entrances "from a distance" could be negotiated, and a metal wall on which the bodies of Goneril and Regan were produced at the end. With some accuracy, Sheridan Morley suggested that Noble's approach was similar to "1930's Hollywood directors like George Cukor [who went] heavy on the narrative and light on the individual interpretation of character" (1994a). Certainly, Cukor's *Romeo and Juliet* was weighty with setting and "historical accuracy," as opposed to Zeffirelli's film and its gesture towards contemporary relevance. Ward's amoeba/ planet background was a simple-minded microcosm/macrocosm contrast, which, while disconcerting, did not inhibit some very good actors. Some critics applauded the background, one, at least, reading gestalt there: "the amoebae are really eerie, mobile faces. The effect is ominous and unsettling, fitting for a scene [1.1] in which Lear's decision to divide his kingdom creates a new age of unreason" (Geckle 1994, 10).
   The way all this stuff got there, though, is disconcerting. The sheer pretentiousness of the process is revealed by what the director and the designer have to say. "I have never started," says Noble, "with 'I want to do this play like that.' I work a lot with the designer *and sometimes with the actors,* on this occasion with the designer, trying to find a

physical manifestation of one's thoughts and feelings about the play and thereby you explore the thoughts and feelings in great depth. The process of design is actually the process of revealing, making manifest the inner architecture of a play" (Brodie 1993, 3; my emphasis). What we understand here is the a priori nature of design. Time is short. Actors cost money. Everything, then, is "set" by the time they show up for rehearsal. It is doubtful that this process saves money, as is the claim, but it is indubitable that the actors inherit a space on which they must sink or swim. What was designer Anthony Ward doing before the actors arrived? "We went down to some scrap heaps, my assistant and I, and pulled out lots of things we thought were interesting and there was this one thing in particular which was the top of an oil drum, the metal, rusty top of an oil drum, that we wedged into the model box and that looked fantastic in as much as it was like the base of a vast great planet. Adrian looked at it and said, 'Well, it's the moon, isn't it?' That is the whole big deal of how you relate on stage" (Brodie 1993, 3a). It is?

The next step, Ward tells us, "was to find a way to represent the civilized, internal world" (Brodie 1993, 3a). "It was a question," he continues, "of dividing the stage and deciding what the geometry of the space was going to be that would allow the natural world and the civilized world to exist together and to exist separately. So that is why I've got this huge steel cornice that completely cuts the two worlds in two. I saw it as something to do with classical architecture." A steel cornice has something to do with classical architecture? We can perceive here that the design is not emerging from anything *in* the script but that it is diverging *from* the script and becoming very threatening to "meaning," or perhaps becoming splendidly "postmodern," i.e., a set that *conflicts* with whatever the lines may be, so that set and script become separate fractions that do not add up to any single meaning and therefore encourage a disparity of responses to the production, all of which are valid, however diverse.

Another aspect of design was the paper map that covered the stage and gradually got ripped up. "The entrance to the hovel is created by cutting a hole in the floor which is still covered with the paper map. Beneath the paper, the floor is red like a wound" (Brodie 1993, 4). Ward explains, "This is not realistic, it is not meant to be a real shelter. It is using a language, a theatrical language in a sense. We are only setting up broad strokes. So what Edgar does is to rip the centre of the heart of England and we are left with this wound" (4). Not at all—what Edgar did was to rip up the map to reveal a heart—not to wound a heart. But then, as Benedict Nightingale asked, "How gratuitously editorializing can RSC decor get?" (1994c).

The RSC production pack reaches its point of no return, however, when it says that "The order and reason of the civilized world is felt to be restored [in 4.7] as behind a gauze four musicians in exquisite 18th century court dress play beautiful, contrapuntal music. Lear wakes up believing himself in heaven" (Brodie 1993, 4). Why eighteenth-century dress, we are not told, though critics surmised that the production depicted "the hell of madness in the Age of Reason" (Nathan 1993). That Lear, "bound upon a wheel of fire," his "own tears scald[ing] like molten lead," believes himself in heaven is a thesis that even those who see Lear as continuing in his perverse ways after he awakens in 4.7 do not maintain. Clearly, he believes that *Cordelia* is in heaven, that he is in hell, and "in torment in these flames," as Dives is, perceiving Lazarus in Abraham's bosom in the passage from which Lear's nightmare of damnation and salvation emerges. But farewell the production pack, not all of which is to be blamed on Noble and Ward.

The production that emerged from this radically unpromising "plan" was excellent and deserves placement alongside the Lears of Wood, Cox, and, to a lesser extent, Briers, which competed with each other in 1990 (see Coursen 1995 for a discussion of those productions).

Michael Billington "kept wondering when Lear was going to start" (1993), as did other critics. At the outset, Geckle said, Lear "appears to be a congenial, rather weary patriarch" (1994, 10). Sheridan Morley added that Robert Stephens "must be the only actor in the world to have played Falstaff more angrily than he plays Lear" (1994a). The "great rage had never been there to start with," said Wardle (1994d). The trajectory of Stephens's performance was toward madness and the compassion that Lear found within himself as a lifetime of defense mechanisms was erased. He had lived with Horneyian "bargains with God." He failed in his final effort—the love test, when Cordelia refused to play the "game he has just invented" (Nathan 1993), which was but a variation on the game he had been playing all along. He found himself deserted by Cordelia, and Fool and whatever gods there may be, but discovered compassion down there below the ripped layers of rationalization. Almost every reference to "heart"—and one was surprised that there are so many in this script—was a reference to Lear's heart, as indicated by his holding his hand over it or by another character's gesture —"thy sweet heart," said Edgar, touching Lear's chest. The point was partly that the organ was failing, but also that "heart" as metaphor was coming alive. The effect of this Lear was inverse to what we expect— from a John Wood, for example. Stephens gave us an implosion. The "poor, naked wretches" speech was "all the more piercing for being delivered quietly," as John Gross said (1994b). The quiet reflected the depth. Stephens explained his strategy to Liz Gibney: "Acting is a matter of tricks. So what will be the trick with Lear? 'Not to start getting techy too soon,'" Stephens said. "'The first act is huge. If you really let go in that, then, phut—there's no where to go'" (1993, 11).

Beyond insight and the madness it brings was the insight that madness brought, as piercingly enunciated in the meeting with Gloucester. "I was . . . everything," Stephens said, pausing so that the word evoked "nothing" and led to his pointing at his chest on "ague-proof." His hand smelled of mortality because it had been held down "beneath" which was "all the fiend's." "Are you there with *me*, now?" he asked Gloucester, not so much universalizing his own experience but recognizing that he and this bleeding blind man somehow inhabited the same physical and emotional space. Lear's disquisition on justice was superbly done, his voice dropping down to "whore." His voice cracked on "crying hither" and he made a sweeping gesture with his arm in the middle of "great stage . . . of fools."

The Gloucester scene was the terminus of a great performance. The reconciliation scene was not moving, perhaps because Lear was trundled in lying in a modern hospital bed and therefore the moment was "institutionalized." The going off to prison scene showed Cordelia inexplicably giving in to all of Lear's rhetoric, even breaking away from her guards to run to him. For that sequence to work, she needed to provide *some* resistance to his reappropriation of her and her "kind nursery." The cogent feminist criticism of McLuskie and others makes it impossible for us to accept with equanimity Cordelia's surrender to the agenda she had resisted earlier. Lear seems to have learned nothing, but does that mean that Cordelia must now cooperate with his ignorance? Here, yes, and the production seemed to emerge from 1950. It refused to tell us that Lear had, with some modifications in attitude, merely "resume[d] the shape [he had] cast off forever," so it told us very little once it arrived beyond Lear's madness. The king, says Ralph Berry, "has created a system that is his own identity" (1993, 69). If he *re*-creates such a system as he goes to prison, Cordelia's acquiescence trivializes the entire experience of the play—for her, for Lear, and for us. It may be, however, that she was one of the victims that Russell Jackson describes: "Abigail McKern's Cordelia was . . . prickly, a bit bossy, and certainly her father's daughter. In a less grandly symbolic staging the subtleties of some of the performances and in particular the elegance and lyricism in the anger and pathos of Stephens's Lear would have shown to better advantage" (1994b, 339).

The ending was hokey Noble. At the end of his *Hamlet,* he had Kenneth Branagh go up left to be initiated into Valhalla by Papa Hamlet. This may have validated Horatio's eulogy in some way but it falsified the martial, heavily political ending that Shakespeare wrote. Here, Lear apparently had one of those light at the end of the tunnel experiences. Down right, cradling Cordelia, he stared into an expanding cone of light—"Look there! Look there!" He pulled at Cordelia and died. In his white shirt, Lear resembled the central figure in Goya's "Execution of the Defenders of Madrid." Paul Taylor saw there "a last-minute vision of a benign heaven opening its gates to him and Cordelia that comes across as a piteous illusion" (1994e). David Murray called it "a cruel final vision" (1994). I am convinced, however, that we were meant to accept A. C. Bradley's "unbearable paroxysm of joy" thesis (1904) as interpreted by reports of "near death" experiences. I, like Clive Hirshhorn, was "left . . . completely unmoved" (1994). Part of the problem was that, assuming that Cordelia was "icy [and] charmless" (de Jongh 1993) and "unsentimental" (Nathan 1993) at the outset, she had lapsed into the standard Cordelia mode at the point of her reappearance and thus this *Lear* became a play we already knew, as opposed to the specific and detailed exploration that Stephens was making of it during the vast middle sequences.

Two elements of the production helped Stephens develop his Lear. David Bradley, in a characteristically intelligent performance, made his Gloucester a dry-voiced, tentative man who tried to think before acting. He was reluctant to act even then, and was thus a contrast to the impetuous Lear, to whom thought came too late and came, of course, as feeling. Bradley showed, however, that his own speech about "ruinous disorders" had merely created a context into which to fit Edgar's "treachery." "I serve *you*, madam," he said to Regan—Gloucestershire apparently having been part of the slice of the West Country ceded to Regan and Cornwall. "That's true . . . too," said Gloucester, as if to say, "in addition to the pain that I am experiencing within the existential coordinates of human life of which you speak in general terms."

Ian Hughes's superb Fool was gagged in the opening scene, from which he is usually absent, and served only to mark out the chunks on the map that Lear designated. Thus Cordelia and Kent were *forced* to speak unless truth was to be silent. The Fool sang well and accompanied himself with counterpointed irony on his mandolin. He knew the meanings of words—pointing at his foot on "goest," for example, which means "walk" here. The Fool later gave Lear a paper crown—a glance at Margaret's crowning York at Wakefield, effective nonetheless in marking the contrast between what Lear had given away and what he now had. The Fool later pointed at Lear in admiration as the latter castigated Regan: "Age is unnecessary." "He *does* make a great fool!" Hughes seemed to say. And Lear proved the point when he pointed at

Kent in the stocks and said "Follow me not!" topping the Fool's jest about "cruel garters." "Let me not go . . . mad," Lear had said, realizing the particular fate that was to be his. Later, on "I *shall* go mad," he exited arm in arm with the Fool, as he had with "noble Burgundy" much earlier. Once Lear switched allegiances from the Fool to Edgar, the Fool picked up the knife with which Lear would have "anatomize[d] Regan" and exited to commit suicide "at noon."

One other excellent decision was to have some of Goneril and Regan's lines spoken as soliloquies or asides—"How in one house / Should many people under two commands / Hold amity?" and "This house is little; the old man and's people / Cannot be well bestowed," for example. These moments were very arresting, as unsympathetic characters appealed to us for understanding and fulfilled Michael Hattaway's designation of soliloquies as "rhetorical acts, speeches delivered directly to the audience in an effort to persuade them to see the play from the player's point of view" (1987, 78). Here, the quick asides contrasted with Cordelia's opening commentary. "Even as we listen to an ongoing conversation, we are made privy, through asides, to observations concealed from other stage figures," says Jean Howard. Cordelia's asides, by their "brevity and understatement [clash] with the fulsome hyperbole of her sisters," whereas the asides employed by Goneril and Regan *reveal* their earlier hypocrisy. In either case, the "disparity between asides and dialogue alerts the audience to potential conflict and projects our attention toward the future. We wait to see when—and in what way—that potential will be realized" (1979, 346). Thus this production deepened the experience of the script for its audience. Russell Jackson, however, said that the asides made the onstage groupings "resemble . . . operatic ensembles" (1994b, 336). He found Goneril, Regan, and Edmund oversimplified in a Wagnerian *Konig Lear* at the service of "grandly symbolic staging" (339).

Mendes's *Tempest* had less negative design to overcome than Noble's *King Lear* and was, with *Lear,* one of the two successful productions of the RSC London-Stratford season. Even then, however, Alec McCowen, who played Prospero, suggested that there is nothing that even a lead actor can do against the tyranny of design: "I spend quite a bit of time standing up a ladder at the back of the set, watching the action I've planned unroll—people tell me it's a marvelous image, but sometimes I do find myself wondering quite what I'm *doing,* trying to climb a ladder in this long, heavy robe. Sometimes designers take actors' lives in their hands!" (quoted in Elgin 1993, 14; Elgin's emphasis).

The production began with Ariel swinging a lantern, which summoned wind, storm, and the pitching decks of a ship. The lines, how-

ever, emerged clearly—unlike the opening scene of Ashland's version
where sound effects obliterated the Conradian contrast between the
perceptions of mariners and landlubbers. McCowan's Prospero stood
above it all, behind a scrim. Ariel stood midcenter, and the Boatswain
was down front, shouting orders. A hierarchy descended toward us, the
audience, which was also the sea and, at the end, of course, the ultimate
authority to which Prospero prays. The opening neatly articulated the
issues of theater and the issues beyond theater by placing characters onstage so that they told us who we were. And we "are in turn simply
another group of players in a larger play, and . . . the physical theater
in which [we] sit is not final reality but simply another stage on which
a longer play is being enacted before an unseen audience" (Kernan
1974, 1).

The production, then, placed the script within a context far removed
from postmodernism, with its suggestion that the attitudes of art are
almost (but not quite) nihilistic, and back within premises that argue
that plays create a community of response that shares a single experience even if the evaluation of that experience breaks down into myriad
singular responses. Prospero then became a storyteller, with Miranda
sitting to his left watching the various characters appear as Prospero
named them from behind an upstage screen. This was, says Russell
Jackson, "the only play in the main house [Stratford] to be presented
with direct appeal to the text's own theatricality, sustained by its opportunities for metatheatrical devices and ideas" (1994b, 345).

Both Stephano and Trinculo were Prospero "offshoots"—the former
an uncontrolled megalomaniac—"a mad parody of Prospero himself"
(Billington 1994g)—the latter a failed ventriloquist from Yorkshire with
a look-alike puppet. The payoff with the puppet, of course, was when
Ariel said, "Thou liest," and poor Trinculo thought that his wooden-
head had come alive, as in various modern versions, from Pinocchio's
wish to be a real boy, echoed in *The Tempest* by Cupid, and more ma-
lign manifestations. Trinculo emblemized the equivocal nature of "illusion" and the fragility of "theater." The tricksiness did not necessarily
evoke a parallel psychological response, particularly from James Hayes's
impassive Antonio. David Troughton's Caliban, however, a Boris Kar-
loff imitation, was afraid of Trinculo's puppet—as if it were another of
Prospero's spirits sent to torment him.

The central concept was developed in Prospero's cardboard pop-up,
picture-book theater, which became a life-sized proscenium for the
puppet-show masque. This was a very "theatrical" and "stagey" sequence but was a splendid way to integrate the masque, which is often
difficult to present, with the idea of theater that dominated the play. In

the masque, of course, Cupid must be dissuaded from his venereal attack on the betrothed couple. In this masque, the "sunburnt sicklemen of August" turned out to be Caliban and party, having infiltrated illusion as a cover for their ambush. We watched a simultaneous creation and stripping away of fictive layers that demonstrated at once the "reality" of theater—the action behind the mimesis—and the nothingness there as well—not even "a rack" of elegant but insubstantial cloud "behind." For Paul Taylor, however, "Prospero's eventual image of life and theatre dissolving into one another" was undercut by "Mendes' playfully illusionistic approach" in which "All the island's a stage from the outset" and thus the final "perception is pre-empted" (1994e).

A bit of staginess that did not work was Ariel's dispersing of the banquet. Rather than a "sea-nymph," he appeared as Banquo's ghost—blood-boltered—to remind the "men of sin" of their crimes through a physical manifestation of them. This allusion to the denial of a eucharistic feast to "notorious evil-livers," as the Communion rubrics have it, which also pertains to the "solemn supper" in *Macbeth*, was valid enough ideationally, but finally only proved the old adage that "You can't play a concept." The Antonio-Sebastian conspiracy, meanwhile, was very much underplayed—indeed, lazily performed, as if a function of almost suicidal boredom. Sebastian made a point, however, at the end when he took the crown that Stephano had appropriated from the various items that Prospero had put out to deflect Caliban and confederates. "Or stole it, rather," Sebastian said. Again, the production's constant contrast between "reality" and "stage property" was underlined.

Simon Beale's Ariel was a stiff, angry-eyed, pajama-clad Mao holding within this shape a yearning for some ahuman version of freedom —a state beyond the "freedom/service" paradox that the play keeps asserting. It was "the best Ariel" that Michael Billington had "seen in a lifetime's theatregoing" (1994g). Benedict Nightingale, in a review that concentrated on Beale's Ariel, wondered, however, "if you had been jammed in a tree by a witch for 12 years, would you be quite so rude to your rescuer on your very last day of employment? . . . would you act like that if your rescuer was . . . McCowen's . . . benign" Prospero (1994d)? But Ariel's "smoldering impassivity" (Farley 1994, 13) could also be attributed to Prospero's threats to do worse to Ariel than Sycorax had done. At Stratford, Ariel spat in Prospero's face at the end, making some point about colonization, perhaps. In London no spitting happened. It would have been against whatever the ending was saying. "My Ariel chick!"—are you still here? Prospero asked, in lines rearranged for this emphasis. "To the elements—be free!" I have set you free—go! Ariel, having yearned for the moment, seemed reluctant to accept it. He had not received much reassurance in his quest for "love," and he had come close to being human in talking of *"your* affections" to Prospero, so he vacated a kind of emotional vacuum for whatever vacuum he would henceforth inhabit. He looked back as if on a zone like a dream or a memory from childhood—an uncompleted space that must remain incomplete. It was a moving ending that then asked us, through Prospero, to respond to it.

In the 1995 Shenandoah Express production, directed by Jim Warren, Philip Lortie's Prospero said, "Please you, draw near," *to* Ariel (Thadd McQuade), who refused. Now Prospero's charms *were* all o'erthrown. He had no place to turn but to that outer god to which he prays, the audience.

"Prosperos today," says Ralph Berry, "are, and have long been, unfailingly angry, disturbed, bitter" (1989b, 35). It was a relief, then, to escape from the John Wood version of Prospero to one who might be considered "old-fashioned"—calm, controlling, even underplayed, and speaking the lines with a sense that they are "high poetry"—in Alec McCowen. Prospero was decentered, the fragility of theater placed in the forefront, and thus Prospero became a kind of Ronald Colman explaining Shangri-la to Jane Wyatt. The joy of watching this Prospero may have stemmed from his refusal to "tap . . . one of the mysterious themes of our time, the legitimization of anger" (Ralph Berry 1989b, 136), certainly a theme that Kent in Shakespeare's time also tapped (cf. 2.2.68).

For critics, however, conditioned by the recent trend, this Prospero was inadequate: "having abdicated the driving forces of rage and revenge for a kind of melancholy irony, McCowen finds it hard to exert real authority over this band of exiled misfits and the result is a *Tempest* with no real eye of the storm" (Morley 1994b). It is doubtful that Prospero has revenge in mind at all, except as an option he had discarded at some point during his twelve years on the island (see Coursen 1969, 1976 and 1986). "Prospero has been voice-coached out of existence" (Billen 1994). The "stress on Prospero as meta-theatrical manipulator, frequently seen atop a ladder, diminishes his own sense of buried grievance" (Billington 1994g). The "play needs to be alive with Prospero's sense of grievance and hunger for revenge. This McCowen does not manage" (de Jongh 1994c). "This Prospero is so much master of himself that he robs the play of half its tension" (Macaulay 1994e). "McCowen's tetchy Prospero is . . . dispiritingly low-key" (Hanks 1994a). "He seems to need reminding that it was this detached attitude that precipitated his exile in the first place" (Farley 1994, 13). Paul Taylor called

McCowen's "dapper, donnish" Prospero "damagingly under-driven" (1994f). Sara Abdulla, however, found McCowen to be "a generous and attractive Prospero," infused with "warmth and humanity," with "no room in this reading for the customary megalomaniac: indeed his omniscience seems a wholly acceptable consequence of his superior moral fibre in comparison to the rest of the island's inhabitants" (1994).

Indeed, the extreme position that critics would wish upon Prospero was inhabited by Mark Lockyer's Stephano. Charles Spencer found that it was "the undertow of sadness that makes this *Tempest* so moving. . . . McCowen's . . . dry pedantry and sense of repressed grief [is] deeply affecting. [At the end] Prospero seems an old and broken man, courteously begging release from the heartache of this cruel and unfathomable world. It's a chilling moment, as if Shakespeare himself were finally admitting both bafflement and defeat" (1994b). Perhaps, but we, the audience were the sea from which Prospero had come, and the gods to whom he prayed at the end, and it is we who had to "fathom" his meaning in our response. This was a Prospero who asked for "final cause"—our willingness to complete his fiction, to make it whatever "reality" we could or would—and that was the powerful point of his understated Duke.

One of the few problems with this production was Mark Lewis Jones's sappy, falsetto Ferdinand, lucky to be compared to Caliban at all. As I had in watching David Troughton's Cloten opposite David O'Hara's incomprehensible Posthumus a few years ago in RSC's *Cymbeline*, I was rooting for his Caliban against this Ferdinand, but to no avail. The alacrity with which Miranda at the end began inspecting "such people" as inhabited this "brave *new* world" got a big laugh, perhaps because Ferdinand suddenly had competition that might prove insurmountable. "With [Lewis] as her benchmark of mankind, we can well understand Miranda's wide-eyed joy when she beholds the other men on the island" (1994). "A chap who quacked around like [Ferdinand] would leave a Miranda as spirited as Sarah Woodward wondering if she hadn't made a mistake spurning Caliban's advances" (Nightingale 1994d).

It is tempting to argue that Prospero was engaged in the psycho-game that William Watterson describes. Having "enjoyed the . . . satisfaction of enslaving Caliban's rowdy masculinity" (forthcoming, 3), Prospero "welcomes the arrival of Ferdinand since it gives him another opportunity for compensatory dominance and filial subjugation. . . . Ferdinand draws his sword against the patriarch only to be disarmed by the latter with a stick. Prospero then makes the young man's 'weapon drop' . . . Prospero's symbolic emasculation of his son-in-law is the kind of petty sadism born of homosexual envy" (7), or perhaps, as I would prefer to argue, of Prospero's repressed incestuous desire. At the very least, Prospero gained in this Ferdinand an adoring foot-licker, not only in Prospero's power but forever in Prospero's debt.

*Coriolanus*, at the Swan, featured banners below either balcony proclaiming "Unity or Death" and "Liberty and Equality," and, upstage, a version of Delacroix's bare-chested, musket-toting Liberty carrying a white banner. To whom was she surrendering? Who was following her to this capitulation? A shattered brick wall in front of this vehemently yielding woman completed the set. I admit to being immediately offended by this launch into—where?—Revolutionary France? If so, "irritatingly" so, said Charles Spencer (1994a). "None [of] this fits," said Michael Coveney, "and all of it is fussy and distracting" (1994c). The "evening bristles with needless anachronisms . . . the analogies that keep intruding are false ones," said John Gross (1994a).

I kept trying to rationalize the upstart but skillful Napoleon with the aristocratic and uncontrolled Coriolanus. Was this the Napoleon who had, though indifferent to religion, agreed with Voltaire about the people's need of it? No. Was this the Napoleon who conspired with Tallyrand and Fouche to kidnap and execute the duc d'Enghien? No. Was this the Napoleon whose addiction to licorice is said to have done him in? Not that I could tell. "Thacker's transposition . . . creates more confusion than clarity and renders the first hour almost incomprehensible" (Review of *Coriolanus* 1994). The "French revolution," said John Peter, "is quite the wrong setting. The clothes and the furniture suggest that we are under the late Directoire, with the Consulate about to arrive, but politically and historically, this is an entirely different situation from Republican Rome" (1994b). Furthermore, as Paul Taylor noted, "there was no real attempt to convey the comparative primitiveness of the rival Volscian society, a politically much less evolved unit and one in which, by a bitter irony, Rome's hero is not the misfit he has become at home" (1994d). "Thacker implies that Shakespeare is endorsing popular fervor," said Michael Billington, but as "Brecht discovered, you have to rewrite the text if you wish to make the play a sustained critique of a disposable hero" (1994f). As Ralph Berry astutely points out, Rome's citizens are not a mob, but, instead, observe the "civilities of [a] debating society . . . by no means the raw episode of class war that it might at first appear" (1993, 99).

Thacker does, indeed, write another play. It convinced Irving Wardle: "The fact that [Coriolanus] turned against his country and the other [Napoleon] lived on to become its emperor only reinforces the show's intention: to awaken a sense of alternative possibilities and acknowledge that a prodigious individual can sometimes derail the forces of history" (1994a). Perhaps, but a disjunctive analogue is difficult for an audience to make and to sustain during a production. Even more difficult is one play wrestling with another on the same stage. It can be done, of course, as Stoppard's empty and pretentious *Arcadia* demonstrated at the Haymarket.

Still, bad wombs have produced good productions. This one, though celebrated by many of the critics, failed because it did not observe what Peter Holland calls the Swan's "visual dynamics [which are] less the work of the set-designer than of a redefinition of actor-audience relationships outside the established traditions of British theatre. The activity of looking at Shakespeare in the Swan is radically unlike that in any other major theatre in its sense of audience communality, in the possibilities of spectacle and in its closeness of contact between actor and playgoers" (1993a, 3-4). And that failure was only partly a result of the imposition of a set upon the Swan's space. Certainly the space is set for spectacle, as productions of *King John, Titus Andronicus, Doctor Faustus, The Jew of Malta,* and *Tamburlaine* have proved. The Tribunes actually did use the audience as "crowd" and, indeed, plebeians were placed in the aisles and balconies. And it was we whom Coriolanus banished. But Toby Stephens, "permanently in heat," speaking with "generalized derision" (Wardle 1994a), was so earsplitting that the production was a physically uncomfortable experience. It is true that he did have to shout over the almost constant "music" that Thacker chose to deploy, as if the presence of Coriolanus were itself a cosmic disturbance. His quiet return to Rome and Virgilia was moving and showed the balance that the production might have achieved had the director deigned to watch and listen from a spectator's position.

Caroline Blakiston's Volumnia, effective in her early tutoring of her son before he encounters the plebeians, was inadequate when she persuaded Coriolanus not to attack Rome in the famous climax. The scene was "curiously muffled" (John Gross 1994a). She was "slightly hysterical" (Coveney 1994c), perhaps simply because the prevailing atmosphere had forced her performance in that direction. If the scene worked at all, it was because Stephens was so young and we could therefore believe that a mother could dominate him. As Wardle says, however, "Present him as a boy . . . and there is no belittling immaturity" (1994a). Suffice it that it is a scene which Volumnia must dominate, which Blakiston did not, but as, in different ways, Irene Worth (opposite McKellen in Peter Hall's 1984 National Theatre production), Barbara Jefford (opposite Charles Dance in the Barton-Hands production of 1989-90), and Judi Dench (opposite Kenneth Branagh in Tim Supple's 1992 version at Chichester) did. Those may be three tough acts to follow, but this production failed at precisely the point where numbed ears might have tried to be forgiving.

The ending did work. Barry Lynch's small but powerful Aufidius asked for help in lugging Coriolanus's body away. The Volscians ignored him. He was left with the weight of his rival's corpse on top of him and the weight of his treachery forever with him. Amid the generalized roaring, Philip Voss delivered a suave, sybaritic, and finally heartbroken Menenius. He showed brilliantly how this wonderful space can work to establish that actor-audience relationship for which the Swan is designed.

Noble's *A Midsummer Night's Dream* on the main stage was a postmodernist nightmare. A very unfunny Quince and Company, featuring Des Barrit as a serious amateur actor (one assumed) as Bottom, were dressed in contemporary clothes, Barrit being a motorcycle rider. The rest of the play occurred at another time. Still, the discrepancy was not overly confusing. The young lovers entered and exited through many doors, perhaps borrowed from the RSC *Comedy of Errors* of a few years back, while lightbulbs—many of them—dropped from the skies to create "the woods." The swing on which Hippolyta swung at the outset was borrowed from Peter Brook, and the fairyland lights and the sparklers at the end from Peter Hall. The "ghastly red room" (Nightingale 1994a) was Noble's own invention, as was the gigantic upside-down red umbrella in which Titania and Bottom snuggled. Mary Poppins, The Travelers Insurance, "Pennies from Heaven," and "down a chimney up" were some of the irrelevant allusions that the umbrella summoned. The male lovers wore the same outfits, so were not differentiated and thus "seem under characterized" (Billington 1994b). Hadyn Gwynn's Helena was consigned to that embarrassing clinging-to-Demetrius's legs business as she played "spaniel"—instead of speaking the speech scornfully, satirizing her role as rejected lover, as the rest of the scene suggests she might. We were meant to laugh at her willingness to be victimized. Rhoda Koenig suggested that "too much of this performance was done with knees and elbows" (1994).

Hippolyta and Titania and Theseus and Oberon were doubled. The problems of the court couple had dissolved in the dream they had experienced—an old device, and a misreading of Jung. Dreams do not resolve problems but suggest how consciousness can work toward the kinds of useful attitudes that move a person on his or her unique path of "individuation." It would have been possible here for Theseus to say rather lamely, "My hounds are bred of the Spartan kind" after Hippolyta's flagrant allusions to deep mythology (hunting with Hercules and Cadmus), for Theseus to be relieved when his debate about "the story of the night" is interrupted, and then quite confident in his relationship with Hippolyta when, just before the play, he recalls his kinsman Hercules and his coming in conquest from Thebes. The process would have shown that the working out of the issues between the duke and his Amazon *were* process, as love is, and that some issues, as those between a rationalist and an intuitive, are best left harmoniously *un*resolved. Dreams impose responsibility, not solutions. Dreams deliver compensatory imperatives to consciousness. But the postdream Theseus and Hippolyta merely spoke their lines, discovering nothing in them and perhaps explaining why Maureen Paton found it an "oddly empty evening" (1994). It is no wonder that Jung is scorned as "essentialist," when a simpleminded interpretation of Jung is thus offered to a theaterful of intelligent auditors.

This was an ill-designed and shallowly conceived production, apparently afraid of Caird's successful but badly over-elaborated version on the same stage a few years ago. A couple of commendations must be given, however. Daniel Evans was a splendid Flute/Thisbe, who very quietly dominated his character's few moments. Stella Gonet was not helped by her tarty, red-feathered dress—why was any love-juice necessary for Titania?—but she neatly linked her roles by denying (a) Theseus her battle-won body and (b) Oberon her vicariously-conceived baby. Her Titania was committing a kind of reverse hubris in wishing to be mortal, so her punishment, though grotesque, was comprehensible. Gonet did her best to suggest the "very considerable differences" that John Russell Brown argues exist between Hippolyta and Titania (1974, 133). Gonet and Alex Jennings spoke the lines beautifully, so, as Nightingale said, the "solution for those oppressed by [the set] is simply to close your eyes and listen" (1994a). Still, I would assert in the face of postmodernist tendencies that sensory insult *or* deprivation should not be a product of a production of this script.

The seldom-seen *Pericles* was seen but not heard at the Royal National Theatre. Gower entered in a piano on which Pericles later pounded. Gower narrated energetically, having no choice, since the noise level was almost consistently high as musicians insisted on making contemporary and therefore irrelevant sounds across whatever the lines were trying to say. This Gower consistently emerged from the action and thus was never a detached storyteller. Indeed, he doubled confusingly with Leonine. The primary impediment to our understanding what is a difficult story to tell, however, was the huge circular platform, which revolved like a fairground ride, totally obliterating, for example, Thaisa's negotiations with Simonides in act 2.

Unlike Terry Hands's version, where, as he explained, "We were more aware of what is done in each place, than of the place itself" (quoted in Ralph Berry 1989b, 24), we got place itself—the random travelogue that the script might seem to be at first sight. It followed that Ceremon as healer and bringer of "still and woeful music" (3.2.90) was in no way that I could discern linked up with Marina and her "music" (5.1.79). Antioch featured ball-like characters out of Wonderland, who melted for no apparent reason into their rotundity. Tarsus was a land close to the sun. Its costumes smoldered. Pentapolis was a polar region. One expected Sonja Heine to dance in at any moment, arms held out daintily as princess of the frozen waters. Thaisa, however, was a decidedly African queen.

Gerald Berkowitz describes this postmodernist patchwork more completely than I do and responds to it more favorably, but does say that, at times, "the production was violating its own rule-violations" and that "[a]t the center of all this was, unfortunately, not much" (1994, 31). The lack of discernible transitions, emphasized by Gower's incorporation into the scenic design, suggested that Pericles was undergoing a phantasmagoric nightmare, but such a thesis merely confused the issue, since no allegory underlay the dream. Things had gone beyond confusion by the time Gower's chorus to 5.2 should have arrived, but that potentially clarifying moment was excised.

A moment that did work was the reconciliation of Pericles and Marina. On the evening I attended, Marina was movingly played by understudy Jennifer Scott-Malden. She was not undercut with irrelevant sound although she was placed up left for this scene, a place from which communication is difficult. She overcame this blocking and was splendid in her delight at Pericles's hearing "the music of the spheres" (5.1.228), music that she, it seemed, did not herself hear. The final scene was played for laughs.

John Peter claimed that this "strange, thrilling and utterly original production . . . gives unity of style to an almost impossible play" (1994d). My own sense was that it was a designated lack of unity that made the production impossible. That—and the noise level which in British theater these days seems to derive from the amplification of rock concerts or perhaps in response to the deafness that rock audiences now bring with them to the theater. "Pericles," says Trevor Nunn, "is a journey from the bestiality of Antiochus's court to the temple of Diana. It is a metaphysical journey, rest only comes with self-knowledge" (quoted in Ralph Berry 1989b, 26). There being no self-knowledge to be gained from the production, relief came only with a walk across Waterloo Bridge above the tide filling in under a cooling August evening.

A final bizarre example will suggest how a total disregard for *locus*, in this case, a virtual replacement of *locus* by a director's and a designer's *platea* can render the script incomprehensible. In this instance —the ART *Henry V* in early 1995—the effect was intentional.

One of the tenets of postmodernism is "multiple signification." Spectators of a production may legitimately disagree about what it signifies. Is Kenneth Branagh's 1989 film of *Henry V* antiwar, prowar, a blend of attitudes that amounts to neutrality? The film arranges the inherited script so that it does not make a univocal point. Postmodernism is not to be confused with incoherence, however. What was the point of Ron Daniels's *Henry V* for the American Repertory Theatre in Cambridge, Massachusetts, in early 1995? The answer would be irrelevant were it not that this production was highly praised, was sold out night after night, and received standing ovations.

The incoherence was "by design." Set designer John Conklin says that "In *Henry V*, we did the most extreme distance chronologically between the French Court and England. [The French] are foolish in that history has passed them by; they're no longer able to survive in the world of Marines and modern technology. It's historically true they could not cope with technology. The English had longbows, which were like machine guns. They're like the Poles in World War II, charging Panzer tanks on horseback" (quoted in Cooper 1995). The French and English, then, inhabited different times, and the French—five unarmed men on horseback—were no match for three times as many English armed with automatic weapons. But this is to do violence to *locus*—the inherited script and what is incontrovertible in it—and to render some of the lines about fearful odds that the production retained into nonsense.

It is true that the French misread the lesson of Crecy, *failed* to attribute the English victory there to the longbow, and so set themselves up for Agincourt. It is also true that Ethiopian tribesmen attacked the armored columns of Granziani and Badoglio with spears in late 1935. It is true about the Polish uhlans of September 1939, and true that an army without an air force could defeat the United States in Southeast Asia. But these battles between anachronistic armies *did* occur sometimes within the same culture. To use them as a pretext for making the inherited script say something it does not say is illegitimate. The French may have relied on the old-fashioned method of a charge of armored horsemen. The English may have been similarly stupid at Balaclava, but neither army was the product of a lost tribe discovered on a remote archipelago and thus immune to Western concepts of change.

Daniels gave us a number of choices for when Agincourt occurred—at some moment corresponding to wherever the French may have been, World War I, World War II, Vietnam, Desert Storm. The answer, then, was that it did not occur. Not only were the odds gone of which the inherited script makes so much, but so was any sense that the play's defining moment could have happened. Daniels created a nonworld that did not ask us to suspend our disbelief but forced us to disbelieve. The experience was like watching a dull variety show. But that subgenre has its disconnectedness built in. Here the director and designers had to work to "unlink" and render inarticulate the script of *Henry V*, but they did so with stunning completeness. Pistol's "songs," for example ("Bear him to the burial ground"), were extratextual, emerged from yet another time and place (the Negro New Orleans jazz tradition?) than the several apparently depicted in the play, and slowed an already slow production. But it wasn't Pistol's fault. The project was deeply flawed at its conceptual heart, yet emerged, as I shall suggest, with remarkably self-congratulatory tones and with a built-in defense against anyone—like me—who found the production just plain bad.

The ending of Daniels's *II Henry IV* had seemed to promise a powerful Henry V. The new king, splendid in royal garments, rejected Falstaff with a brutal coldness that told us what Hal had been doing all along. He had been hiding out as a punk rocker, and had learned from Falstaff "how to handle" (*II Henry IV* 2.4.309) his adversaries. The king showed how well he had mastered his lessons in dealing with his former enemy, the Chief Justice, and then in denying Falstaff his primary weapon, words ("Reply not to me with a fool-born jest").

I was absolutely convinced that Camp's Henry V would prove a powerful leader and that Camp's study of kingship would be eminently worth observing and evaluating. What we got was a crew-cut, chubby young man who, apparently, *had* been that punk rocker, not paying attention to the mastery he had been achieving through Falstaff, not aware, it seems, of the devastating impact of his transformation. Daniels cut the churchmen's lines that describe the instant coming of "consideration like an angel" and the "wonder" of the change (1.124–69). It seemed that Henry had been thrust suddenly and unexpectedly into a position he had never wanted, as opposed to the prince we have watched in training for this kind of improvisational kingship from the first. What do I do now? Henry seemed to be asking himself as he stared down at the huge map of the Channel and France. He had made up his mind, of course—the Salique Law exposition was a joke. The options he had at the outset—the establishment of a huge feudal system with him as liege lord (1.1.11-14) and "a thousand pounds by the year" (1.1.19)—were cut, so that the production went immediately for the simplistic version of events that the Chorus offers. Thus Camp was robbed of his own background as prince and of the complexities of decision making that go into that opening sequence with Chichele. I thought that Camp would hit his stride at some point, but he never did. His hoarse voice lacked range, his chief mannerism was an exhausted rubbing of his brow, and his speeches made little sense. Since he was costumed as either a full general or a soldier in fatigues, his speech on "ceremony" was incomprehensible. There had been no ceremony.

The production did reflect what the program notes called "The unwavering focus of *Henry V* on war" and provided no other point of view. Thus, when we got to the wooing scene, we took Henry at his own valuation, as opposed to recognizing that he was turning disadvantage—his poor French, his soldiery—into advantage. That ability to translate shortcoming into strength is one of his primary traits. We watch him acquire the technique from Falstaff. Knowledge of his character's ability and where it comes from gives an actor something to work with *behind* the lines.

The deepest problem, however, was the treatment of the French. "Whereas the English are very much these mud creatures," said Daniels, "the French are sky creatures" (quoted in Graham 1995, B-30). This is as if Daniels—or J.R.R. Tolkien or Frank Herbert—were making a fiction, not Shakespeare, as if the contrast between the English and the French, a "given" in the script, must be driven to a *reductio ad absurdum*. "We're looking at these French creatures as very beautiful creatures," said Daniels, "very wondrous creatures. They walk on shoes that are 1 foot high, they ride these beautiful horses" (B-30). The French did walk around on high shoes and later were pushed around on wheeled platforms, from which they played chess or rolled dice on trays held high by servants. Later they pranced inside toy horses from *Equus*. The "ideas" go back at least to John Barton's *Richard II* (1972), where Bolingbroke and Mowbray appeared inside horses for the trial by combat and where Northumberland (the "ladder") grew into an eight-foot upstage crow. The contrasting English, muddy, fatigued, and in fatigues, of course, came straight from Michael Bogdanov's *Henry V* and *Macbeth*. Yet, to one critic, the "staging . . . was strikingly fresh" (Lehman 1995, 15).

But it was not the staleness of the concepts that made me angry. It was the deeper incoherency of the entire enterprise. Suffice it that the French and their fillies sank out of sight to loud sounds (music, one supposes). But what was sinking them? Were they melting into puddles of hubris? Sinners in the hands of an angry St. Denis? It may go without saying that Grandpre's wonderful speech—in which he almost defines the indefinable quality of that English army—was cut down to just another of the overconfident lines that the French shouted at us from their various perches. Bogdanov had his Grandpre rip his dispatch from his typewriter, recognizing that "Description cannot suit itself in words / To demonstrate the life of such a battle / In life so lifeless as it shows itself" (4.2.51–3). Daniels's French *should* have been asking what those funny looking tubes were in the English hands. As Rambures should have noted, they did not look like crossbows. The Allies were asking a similar question in France in late 1944 when the Me 262—the first operational combat jet—was introduced. But that was in late 1944, when suddenly a fighter that flew a hundred miles faster than the 51 or 47 was in the air, an anachronism, yes. But the 262 was not flying in the nontime or antitime in which this production took place, where M-16s went up against a liberated merry-go-round.

The exceptions to this mishmash were moments almost worth the expense of spirit and waste of time that the rest of the production entailed. Henry read his threat to Harfleur through a tannoy. The loudspeaker amplified the threat and made a metaphor with "hostage situations." What was he doing? Reminding his men about what war is really like, thus getting them ready for Agincourt? Warning them *not* to become outlaws, like those he must hang for being "[un]gentle gamesters"—thus anticipating Burgundy's "savages / That nothing do but meditate on blood" (V.2.59–60)? Getting rid of some of his own frustrations in a sour, self-condemning speech? Distancing himself from his men at a time when he looked and acted like little more than an NCO? Trying to bluff Harfleur into surrendering to an exhausted army (as Branagh seemed to be doing)? It was a moment full of possible meanings, about which reasonable people could disagree. Henry's army, insulted, glared at him angrily. His brother, Gloucester, refused to salute him after the speech. I neither represent nor condone that kind of talk, Gloucester seemed to be saying.

A tiny moment that also worked was a version of "Te Deum Laudamas" in cadence count (e.g., "Sound Off, One, Two . . ."). This was a brief commentary on how religion subserves national policy, as the Archbishop had done earlier.

Yet a third instant that worked was Katherine's listening to Henry's Harfleur speech in translation on her Atwater Kent. Her crash course in English was motivated—by fear? Fascination? Awareness that she was one of the prizes this irresistible conquerer would gain? We could not be sure, nor could she, until time revealed her motive to her in the wooing scene. There she leaned in for another kiss, and Camp drew back on "Here comes your father." This borrowing from Branagh got the evening's biggest laugh.

Daniels claims that Henry "learns . . . the terrible cost" (quoted in Graham 1995, B-30) of his policies. To try to make that point Daniels left in much of Exeter's mawkish speech about the deaths of York and Suffolk. The speech balances chivalric values against the slaughter that Agincourt really was, but that contrast had already been made, however awkwardly and stupidly. In this production, the speech was meant to tell us how much the *English* had lost, as was Henry's bursting into tears when he read the tag on Davy Gam's body bag. The "terrible cost" has been on the French side of the equation, a fact the script makes clear but that Daniels attempted to avoid by cutting "None else of name; and of all other men / But five and twenty" (IV.8.104-5) and by eliminating the subsequent attribution of this miracle to God (IV.8.105-11).

Another distressing and untenable resonance was Daniels's insistence that "part of the process Shakespeare is investigating [is] the demonization of the enemy" (quoted in Graham 1995, B-30). The play cannot be made to reflect "demonization." The English don't demonize the enemy—Exeter makes that clear in singling out the Dauphin for particular rebuke (2.4.117-26). The French insult the English, but with the grudging sense that their women prefer the lusty English (cf. 3.5.27-31 and 4.5.12-16)—as Katherine seems to. The French know that the English have "mettle" (3.5.15) and will "fight like devils" (2.7.147). The latter simile does not represent demonization, however, any more than Henry's "imitate the action of the tiger" (3.1.6). Indeed, the French view the English in the context that Daniels applies to the *French*, that is, that the English rush into danger heedlessly, not like "a hawk" (3.7.15), admittedly, but like "Foolish curs that run winking into the mouth of a Russian bear, and have their heads crushed like rotten apples" (3.7.139-41). One might argue that Henry demonizes Scroop, comparing his treason to "Another fall of man" (2.2.142), but that is because Scroop seemed so full of "The sweetness of affiance" (2.2.127), not because Scroop was an enemy demanding demonization.

Daniels got hold of an idea and applied it to a play where it does not work. Does Hamlet denigrate Claudius, describing his uncle in terms that the play itself will not support? Yes, and the contrast between Hamlet's point-of-view and the Claudius *we* experience was one of the strengths of Daniels's late-1980s production for the Royal Shakespeare Company. Do Malcolm's forces demonize Macbeth? Indeed—and not without cause. It did seem at times that Daniels's French *were* a fantasy invented by the English because they needed an enemy—as we are currently inventing Islam and our own poor as enemies, with enough terrorist bombings and drug-related murders to feed the process. But the French here, if a fantasy enemy, were composed of the easy pickings of daydreams.

In the great RSC production of *Henry V* in the 1970s, Terry Hands and Alan Howard broke the play down into performance units. Howard could not remember Grey's name in the line "And you . . . my gentle knight" (2.2.14), but came up with it on "though Cambridge, Scroop, and . . . Grey" (2.2.58). The soldier Henry "enlarged" was right there onstage and became the MP who arrested the explicitly sober Scroop. Even Iain Glen, in the overwrought RSC production at Stratford in 1994, made a point when he said, "*God* acquit you in his mercy" (2.2.166) to a Scroop, who appealed with a gesture to Henry. That meant *I* do not forgive you. Here, the Constable's "*whore's* manship" (3.7.53), was one of the few instances of an emphasis that illuminated what was meant. Hands doubled Scroop and Williams, Grey and Bates. Daniels doubled Grey and Williams, Cambridge and Bates. Hands's doubling subtly raised the question of treason versus loyalty, as I have argued elsewhere (Coursen 1992, 144–45).

Daniels's doubling did not link 2.2 with 4.1 ff. The blocking of the scenes was somewhat similar—each developing on the narrow edge of the front-stage area, Henry down front center for the first and down right for the second. Each scene, however, got a very perfunctory reading. Neither scene in this "postmodernist" production was meant to remind us of the other. The doubling, then, was merely a matter of convenience, not a technique. That Daniels's Williams was a first lieutenant, a platoon leader, and thus an *inhabitant* of the social plane on which Henry lives further confused things. The Boy at one point was an USAF staff sargeant, a fact that, again, pointed at the production's intentional effort to refuse to tell us who was who, what was what, and when any of this was happening. The more we noticed, the more confused we were meant to be.

What does "Convey [him] with safe conduct" (2.2.298) mean if the French ambassador then walks off alone? What does it mean to us when we hear that the King has ordered "every soldier to cut his prisoner's throat" (4.7.9–10), when we have seen the prisoners shot down in a spatter of automatic weapons fire? Why upstage the Chorus at the beginning—Henry appeared as the Chorus says "Suppose" (19)—and at the end, when the cast slithered in for its curtain call behind the final words? In the latter case the obliteration of the words may have made us believe that the bright young couple down center was destined for all good things. Suffice it that no one concerned with the production has ever sat in a theater and thus experienced the ways in which movement behind a speaker erases what is being said.

"Shakespeare is not owned by the critics or the intellectuals or the academics, but by the man on the street," says Daniels (quoted in Graham 1995, B-30). That is more or less what Bogdanov says to rationalize his ownership and to make certain in advance that any criticism can be dismissed as "elitist." The man on the street will not have seen other productions, of course, so he *is* likely to accept Daniels's staging as "fresh," when it is really a collection of bad ideas culled from other directors. The man on the street, however, is not going to pay forty-five dollars a ticket for ART productions, and, if he did, he would learn that all the bad things that are said about Shakespeare are true. We are told that "Through his challenging, contemporary productions, Daniels hopes to return Shakespeare, and the theatre in general, to those for whom it was originally intended—regular folks" (Graham 1995, B-30). That is self-serving nonsense. He wants no such thing. I would advise Daniels to have a look at what companies like Shenandoah Shakespeare Express and ACTER are doing. They, without the pompous cliches, are putting exciting and coherent versions of the plays in front of students. Daniels is serving a more obscure, personal cause—ego, perhaps—perhaps megalomania.

If, as one critic of this production argued, "stage directors supply concepts and images to make up for [the public's inability to] follow Shakespeare's language," then, indeed "acting becomes almost irrelevant" (Dyer 1995). If language and acting are irrelevant, so is Shakespeare. Let Daniels call his play "Having Fun with Anachronisms: A Perverse Reading of *Henry V.*" Whatever Shakespeare's script still may have within it to communicate was distorted and unintelligible in this version. If directors and designers do view their task as the supplying of concepts and images that replace language and acting then Shakespeare has no future.

# XI

# Conclusion: "What, Out of This, My Lord?"

Dennis Kennedy isolates what he calls the "two distinctive properties [of]" postmodern approaches to Shakespeare production: "The first is a clear preference for the metaphoric over the metonymic, which parallels the movement away from Brechtian or other political uses of the texts. The second is a transhistorical or anti-historical use of eclectic costuming and displaced scenery, creating, through irony, a disjunction between the pastness of Shakespeare's plays and the ways we now receive them" (1993, 266–67).

A clash occurs between these elements of *platea,* when a production becomes a specific metaphor. If, for example, *Richard III* becomes a metaphor for Great Britain in the 1930s, as in Richard Eyre's production with Ian McKellen in 1990, the costumes and scenery become very specific and the setting very elaborate, insisting that we accept a precisely delineated "pastness" and, probably, a political commentary on an England at the moment that Edward VIII was departing.

Kennedy's term "metonymic" suggests a linking of ideas within the script that can be communicated from the *locus* without much encouragement or pressure from the *platea*-dimension. That means that the script was, until recently, much more of a "self-contained" system of signs than it is now. Recent productions of *Macbeth,* as I have noted (1995), do not reach for what used to be called the "holy supernatural" element (cf. Knights 1947, 37), a metonymic energy that some would argue is irrefutably *there* in the *locus.* But no, whether it is Bogdanov drowning the play under the chop of choppers, or the Buttonhole Theatre exploring the subtleties of a failing relationship played out against a political background, or Katherina Thalbach using the script to draw a brutal political cartoon, the play is not being explored for meanings that a director assumed were there as recently as the late 1970s.

Trevor Nunn's wonderful production *did* depict good versus evil—a praying Duncan against a fascist Macbeth who could pass a chalice around as he talked of cutting throats. The ending of that production —an exhausted Malcolm (Roger Rees) taking over with little conviction—may also have suggested that the positive supernature had been itself expended in the struggle against its nemesis. The metaphoric approach was illustrated in the excellent Haworth production (1995), directed by Stephen Rayne, in which Lady Macduff (Irma Inniss) spoke both her lines and those of her precocious son, imagining a future for the baby she held in her arms, giving him language that articulated her own view of her absent husband and of the world's inherent treachery. The effect was poignant, of course, because that child was destined never to learn to talk. The "unlike things"—mother and son—fused themselves in the mother giving her first and last lesson in language and meaning.

One of the current favorite models for Shakespeare is Chekhov—as if the scripts can go back into the past only a little ways, or as if "pastness" is available to us only when we can remember having breathed on the same earth as that now-gone generation of our grandparents or great-grandparents. A production of *The Merchant of Venice* is reviewed as employing a "Chekhovian approach to the play as a series of self-exposures" (1994, Shapiro 33). A *Twelfth Night* is condemned because of its "Chekhovian pace" (Coursen 1995). A *Hamlet* is seen as Chekhovian (Billington 1992, Spencer 1992). In the latter instance, however —the Kenneth Branagh *Hamlet,* directed by Adrian Noble—the production showed vestiges of a former dispensation in its characters' inability to touch each other. The "arrested embrace"—the thought of holding or the wish to hold another—was a constant physical action, or *in*action here. The physical failure or inability emerged from a sense of the world's divorce from positive action, from the supernatural sanctions that endow mere human activity with "meaning," or metonymic resonance. As Dr. Murray Cox said in the program notes for this production, "one of the thematic threads woven in many colours and of various textures [in the play] is that of defective ceremony" (1992, 14). That is old-fashioned criticism, of course, but merely because something is noticed in the script and phrased in a quaint way, as in this case a recurring motif that becomes thematic, does not mean that it is not there because not signaled to us in trendy phrases that suggest what has been found in a context either of the early seventeenth century or the late twentieth. It is still possible for a *production* to discern and communicate theme, though by metaphoric means, as in the use of "the arrested embrace" to signal the absence of a basic contact, lost to the world of Elsinore as it seems to be *almost* lost as "meaning" in Shakespeare's scripts.

That does not mean that productions must inhabit some "timeless" zone or that they must move into the ahistorical area that Kennedy mentions. It may mean that some productions, like many that I deal with in the final chapter are merely the words "dressed up" to resemble some version of adulthood, or that are hopelessly trapped in immediately former times—Ibsen is the playwright whom Cox adduces to exemplify the "theme of the dead not letting go of the living" (1992, 14). It may also mean that productions of Shakespeare's plays are *superior* to whatever contemporary criticism may be doing at its given moment and may even be superior to the means of reproducing them as plays. Since so much Shakespeare criticism ignores production and denies the concept of script, production can only ignore what is irrelevant to it. But production itself is subject to limitations, particularly when a conceptual space like television cannot expand to incorporate dramaturgy that Shakespeare's stage could accommodate with ease.

The issue of the production's "detachment" from context that Kennedy mentions—the eclectic costuming and indeterminant zone of action—can force us to concentrate on what is being said. Usually the eclectic approach domesticates the issues, rendering them personal rather than dynastic. But the narrowing of the scope does not necessarily drain the production of power. It focuses it, implodes it. This is the effect of productions by Deborah Warner, Sam Mendes, Katie Mitchell, and often of productions *not* on the main stage at Stratford, Ontario, and Ashland, Oregon. The problem with eclectic productions is that, with all ranks and statuses represented by the same uniforms, we cannot tell who is who. If the effect is to egalitize the scripts, then their exploration of status and power is itself blurred. They are not "modern drama" except at dazzling moments—as when Hamlet questions Polonius about clouds—and do need some informing contact with their times. That is where the meanings *were*. To communicate what the meanings *are* we have to retain some contact with that generative moment, if only to keep *A Midsummer Night's Dream* out of the sandbox that the word "desert" communicated to a director who did not ask a simple question.

But much more than that, of course, because the translation of the issues of the plays into the "metaphoric" mode that Kennedy sees as one of the essentials of postmodernist Shakespeare depends on grasping what the other side of the metaphor—that *first* unlike thing—is. Two unlike things—the past and the present—become a third: not necessarily the future, but an enriched present. That means that Shakespeare is our contemporary even as we insist that he is his own contemporary. The *fusion* of unlike things into a new entity—the way Shakespeare's stage worked and the way *our* minds work—is neatly expressed by W. B. Worthen as "a concentration of psychological motivation complicated by a degree of openness to the theatre audience, the post-Brechtian compromise between 'realistic' and 'theatrical' characterization" (1989, 450).

That is to give the actor his style and the key to his sense of relatedness and relationship. It is not, however, to suggest how the postmodern stage shows the crumbling of kingdoms or the melting of empires into Tibers or Niles, or how that stage shows us ghosts come from the grave or how evil lurks visibly on the horizons of human intention. The problem is, simply put, How does a world saturated with commercial messages driving at us from all the media accommodate a world view, or a combination of zeitgeists that could—along with Shakespeare's unique genius—create these scripts? The *locus* is there and will be there. The *platea* is, nowadays, largely the function of a director's craft and imagination. And it is to those capacities that we look for ways in which to see the *locus* anew and so renew it as it hurtles into a millennium awaiting its opportunity to explore these scripts and to show us what we mean by them.

# Credits for Stage Productions

*II Henry IV*. Presented by the Royal Shakespeare Company at the Memorial Theatre, Stratford, and at the Barbican, London, 1991 and 1992. Directed by Adrian Noble, assisted by Colin Ellwood. Designed by Bob Crowley. Costumes by Deidre Clancy. Lighting by Alan Burrett. With Linda Bassett (Mistress Quickly), David Bradley (Shallow), Anthony Douse (Lord Bardolph, Silence), Rob Edwards (Poins), Julian Glover (Henry IV), Denys Hawthorne (Northumberland), Ian Hughes (Prince John), Bernard Kay (Hastings), Paul Kiernan (Morton, Warwick), Sylvestra Le Touzel (Lady Percy), Christopher Luscombe (Travers, Francis, Feeble), Michael Maloney (Hal), Joanne Pearce (Doll), Gary Powell (Westmorland, Fang), Scott Ransome (Gloucester, Peto, Wart), Clifford Rose (Scroop), Ken Sabberton (Snare/Davy/Shadow), Valerie Sarruf (Lady Northuberland), Robert Stephens (Falstaff), David Terence (Beadle, Mouldy, Coleville), Phillip Voss (Chief Justice), Bill Wallis (Bardolph), Albie Woodington (Pistol), Angus Wright (Beadle, Bullcalf).

*Henry IV*. Parts One and Two. Presented by The American Repertory Theatre, Cambridge, Massachusetts, November 1993 to January 1994. Directed by Ron Daniels; Associate Director, Steven Maler. Sets by John Conklin. Costumes by Gabriel Berry. Lighting by Frances Aronson. Music/sound by Bruce Odland. Dramaturgy by Peter Scanlan. Remo Airaldi (Mistress Quickly), Mark Boyet (Thomas, Gadshill), Bill Camp (Prince Hal), Thomas Darrah (Bardolph), Herb Downer (Glendower, Douglas, and York), Alvin Epstein (Henry IV), Benjamin Evett (Vernon, Pistol), James Farmer (Bullcalf, Coleville, and Snare), Jeremy Geidt (Falstaff), Nathaniel Gundy (Page), Christopher Johnson (Prince John, Ralph), Karm Kerwell (Mortimer, Fang, and Wart), Will LeBow (Westmorland, Chief Justice), Robert McDonough (Peto, Feeble), Royal Miller (Hotspur, Warwick), Vontress Mitchell (Francis, Shadow), Phillip Munson (Poins, Davy), Todd Peters (Humphrey, Mouldy), Maggie Rush (Lady Percy, Doll), Noble Shropshire (Worcester, Gower, and Silence), Jessica Walling (Mortimer), Kevin Waldron (Mowbray), Jack Willis (Hastings), William Young (Northumberland, Shallow).

*Henry IV*. Presented by the Shakespeare Theatre, Washington, D.C., 20 September to 6 November 1994. Directed by Michael Kahn. Designed by Loy Arcenas. Lighting by Howell Brinkley. Costumes by Tom Broeker. Fights directed by David Leong. Dramaturgy by Christopher Baker. With Emery Battis (Glendower, Chief Justice), Joseph Culliton (Blunt, Hastings), Franchelle Stewart Dorn (Mistress Quickly), Zachary Ehrenfreund (Prince John), Edward Gero (Hotspur, Mouldy), Davis Hall (Vernon, Warwick), Eric Hoffman (Bardolph), Steve Irish (Douglas, Gadshill), Floyd King (Francis, Shallow), Caitlin O'Connell (Lady Percy), Shannon Parks (Lady Mortimer), Sean Pratt (Mortimer), David Sabin (Falstaff), Michael Santo (Worcester, Silence), Derek Smith (Hal), Ted Sorel (Northumberland, Archbishop of York), Daniel Southern (Westmoreland, Pistol), Ted van Griethuysen (King Henry), Sheira Venetianer (Doll), Craig Wallace (Coleville, Poins).

*Henry V*. Presented by The Royal Shakespeare Company at the Memorial Theatre, Stratford-on-Avon, first performance: 2 May 1994. Directed by Matthew Warchus. Sets by Neil Warmington. Costumes by Kandis Cook. Lighting by Charles Edwards. Music by Mark Vibrans. Fights by Terry King. Sound by Paul Slocombe. With David Beames (Exeter), Gwynn Beech (Westmoreland, Dauphin), Tony Britton (Chorus), Nigel Cooke (Nym, Montjoy), Monica Dolan (Katherine), Kevin Doyle (Ely, Bourbon), Ken Dudley (York), Steven Elliott (Cambridge, Gower), Daniel Evans (Boy), Iain Glen (Henry), Tim Griggs (Warwick), Linal Haft (French Ambassador, Fluellen), Ewan Hooper (Canterbury, Grandpre, Burgundy), David Hounslow (Bardolph, Williams), Adrian Irvine (Court, Orleans), Colin Jarrett (Gloucester, Scroop), Joanna McCallum (Mistress Quickly, Alice), Janice McKenzie (Governor of Harfleur, Isabel), Anthony Naylor (Grey, Constable), Liam O'Callaghan (Erpingham, Charles), Sean O'Callaghan (Clarence, MacMorris, Le Fer), Quill Roberts (Bates, Berri), Clive Wood (Pistol).

*Henry VI*. Presented by The Royal Shakespeare Company at The Other Place, Stratford-on-Avon, from 27 July 1994 and subsequently on tour. Directed by Katie Mitchell. Designed by Rae Smith. Lighting by Tina MacHugh. Music by Helen Chadwick. Movement by Paul Allain. Fights by Malcolm Ranson. With Nick Bagnall (Thorpe, Messenger), Dugald Bruce-Lockhart (Northumberland), Declan Conlon (Montagu, Tutor, Father), Jonathan Firth (Henry VI), Chris Gardner (Exeter, Keeper), Jamie Hinde (Clifford, Hastings), John Keegan (Warwick), Liz Kettle (Lady Elizabeth Grey), Ruth Mitchell (Queen Margaret), Lloyd Owen (King Edward), Stephen Simms (York, Lewis XI, Mayor of York), Tom

Smith (Gloucester), Jo Stone-Fewings (Clarence), Tom Walker (Prince Edward), Tam Williams (Rutland, Lieutenant, Son).

*Hamlet.* Presented by Shakespeare & Company at the Opera House, Waterville, Maine, 22 April 1994 (1994 Touring Production). Directed by Kevin G. Coleman. Set by Robert Boland. Costumes by Arthur Oliver. Fights by Jonathan Croy and Brian Crawford. With Michael Burnet (Laertes, Guildenstern), Tom Jaeger (Hamlet), Alyssa Lupo (Gertrude, Rosencrantz), Michael Marlow (Polonius, Horatio), Jayne Ogata (Ophelia, Osric), and Adrian Swift (Claudius, Ghost).

*Hamlet.* Presented by the Orlando-UCF Shakespeare Festival at the Walt Disney Ampitheater, Orlando, Florida 1 April to 1 May 1994. Directed by Russell Treyz. Set by Karen Cox. Costumes and choreography by Sandria G. Reese. Lighting by Michael A. Reese. Sound by Steve Rogers. Music by Keith Koons. Fights by Rick Sordelet. With Jonathan Brownlee (Rosencrantz), Allison Daugherty (Player Queen), William E. Dobbins IV (Reynaldo, Priest), Jim Helsinger (Hamlet), Celia Howard (Gertrude), John Jezior (Player King, Fortinbras), Jack Judd (Polonius), Paul Kiernan (Horatio), David McCann (Claudius, Ghost), Suzanne O'Donnell (Ophelia), Russ Oleson (Guildenstern), Nick Rodriguez (Bernardo, Sailor), Scott Sophos (Voltemand, Osric), Patrick Stretch (Laertes, Lucianus), Paul Vogt (Marcellus, Grave-digger), and others.

*Hamlet.* Presented by the Stratford (Ontario) Shakespeare Festival at the Tom Patterson Theatre, 1994. Directed by Richard Monette. Design by Debra Hanson. Music by Louis Applebaum. Lighting by Kevin Fraser. Sound by Evan Turner. Fights by John Stead. Stage Management by Nora Polley. With Tim Barker (Marcellus, Priest), Kevin Bundy (Rosencrantz), Steve Cell (Bernardo, Lucianus), Antoni Cimolino (Laertes), Jonathan Crombie (Guildenstern), Peter Donaldson (Claudius), Sabrina Grdevich (Ophelia), Roland Hewgill (Player King), William Hutt (Ghost, First Grave-digger), David Jansen (Prologue to "Gonzago"), Tom McCamus (Horatio), Robert O'Driscoll (Second Grave-digger), Duncan Ollerenshaw (Reynaldo, Player Queen), Stephen Ouimette (Hamlet), Douglas Rain (Polonius), Janet Wright (Gertrude).

*Hamlet.* Presented by the Oregon Shakespeare Festival at the Angus Bowmer Theater, 1994. Directed by Henry Woronicz. Scenic design by William Bloodgood. Costumes by Deborah M. Dryden. Lighting by James Sale. Music/sound by Todd Barton and Douglas K. Faerber.

Fights by James Newcomb. Dramaturgy by Barry Kraft. With Linda Alper (Rosencrantz), Michael Behrens (Lucianus, Fortinbras) Katherine Conklin (Gertrude), Don Donahue (Reynaldo), Kirsten Giroux (Player Queen), Lawrence Hecht (Claudius), Joe Hilsee (Marcellus, Osric), Richard Howard (Hamlet), Dawn Lisell (Ophelia), Sandy McCallum (Polonius, First Grave-digger), James Newcomb (Laertes), J. P. Phillips (Voltimand, Second Grave-digger), John Pribyl (Horatio), Davon Russell (Captain), Yumi Sumida (Cornelius), U. Jonathan Toppo (Francisco, Guildenstern), Tyrone Wilson (Player King, Priest).

*Hamlet.* Presented by The New Shakespeare Company, Regent's Park, London, 15 July to 10 September, 1994. Directed by Tim Pigott-Smith. Designed by Tanya McCallin. Fights by Peter Woodward. Adapted by Tim Pigott-Smith and Roger Warren. With Richard Addison (Marcellus, Captain), Carl Antony (Lucianus, Fortinbras), Cameron Blakely (Rosencrantz), Jonathan Broxholme (Bernardo, Priest), Guy Burgess (Laertes), David Collings (Polonius), Oliver Darley (Francisco, Player), Rebecca Egan (Ophelia), Paul Freeman (Claudius), Kenneth Gilbert (Ghost, Player King), Dominic Gray (Guildenstern, Second Grave-digger), Simon Harrison (Osric), Rupert Holliday-Evans (Horatio), Damian Lewis (Hamlet), Pamela Miles (Gertrude), Lewis Rae (Reynaldo, Player), Kate Seaward (Player Queen), Tim Stern (First Grave-digger).

*King Lear.* Presented by the Royal Shakespeare Company, Stratford-on-Avon and London, 1993–94. Directed by Adrian Noble. Designed by Anthony Ward. Lighting by Alan Burrett. Music by Shaun Davey. With Simon Russell Beale (Edgar), Raymond Bowers (Doctor), David Bradley (Gloucester), David Calder (Kent), Christopher Colquhoun (Captain), Janet Dale (Goneril), Simon Dormandy (Cornwall), Tim Hudson (Burgundy), Ian Hughes (Fool), Mark Lockyer (Oswald), Abigail McKern (Cordelia), John Normington (Albany), Jenny Quayle (Regan), Christopher Robbie (Curan), Nick Simons (Old Man), Robert Stephens (Lear), Owen Teale (Edmund).

*The Tempest.* Presented by the Royal Shakespeare Company, Stratford-on-Avon and London, 1993–94. Directed by Sam Mendes. Designed by Anthony Ward. Lighting by Paul Pyant. Music by Shaun Davey. With Simon Russell Beale (Ariel), Joanna Benyon (Ceres), David Birrell (Adrian), David Bradley (Trinculo), Mike Burnside (Boatswain), Paul Greenwood (Alonso), Peter Grimes (Francisco), James Hayes (Antonio), Christopher Hunter (Sebastian), Mark Lewis Jones (Ferdinand), Mark

Lockyer (Stephano), Alec McCowen (Prospero), Sian Radiger (Iris), Christopher Robbie (Master), Clifford Rose (Gonzalo), David Troughton (Caliban), Sarah Woodward (Miranda).

*Coriolanus.* Presented by the Royal Shakespeare Company, Stratford-on-Avon, Swan Theatre, first performance: 18 May 1994. Directed by David Thacker. Designed by Fran Thompson. Lighting by Alan Burrett. Music by Adrian Johnston. With Caroline Blackiston (Volumnia), Monica Dolan (Virgilia), Kevin Doyle (Nicanor), Alan Faulkner (Senator), Colin George (First Senator), Linal Haft (Velutus), Ivor Hill (Young Martius), Ewan Hooper (Brutus), David Hounslow (First Watch), Colin Jarrett (Second Watch), Griffith Jones (First Volscian Senator), David Killick (Cominius), Barry Lynch (Aufidius), Tanya Moodie (Valeria), Anthony Naylor (Titus), Jeremy Pyke (Young Martius), Kenn Sabberton (Adrian), Toby Stephens (Coriolanus), Philip Voss (Menenius).

*A Midsummer Night's Dream.* Presented by the Royal Shakespeare Company, Stratford-on-Avon, first performance: 28 July 1994. Directed by Adrian Noble. Designed by Anthony Ward. Lighting by Chris Parry. Music by Ilona Sekacz. With Desmond Barrit (Bottom), Alfred Burke (Egeus), Howard Crossley (Snout), Kevin Doyle (Demetrius), Daniel Evans (Flute), Emma Fielding (Hermia), Robert Gillespie (Starveling), Stella Gonet (Hippolyta, Titania), Haydn Gwynne (Helena), Ann Hasson (First Fairy), Alex Jennings (Theseus, Oberon), Barry Lynch (Puck), Toby Stephens (Lysander), Philip Voss (Quince).

*Pericles.* Presented by the Royal National Theater, at the Olivier Theatre, London, first performance: 19 May 1994. Directed by Phyllida Lloyd. Designed by Mark Thompson. With David Burke (Simonides), Selina Cadell (Helicanus), Anna Pons Carrera (Daughter, Diana), Henry Goodman (Gower, Leonine), Douglas Hodge (Pericles), Kathryn Hunter (Antiochus, Ceremon, Bawd), Lennie James (Thaliard, Lysimachus), Toby Jones (Second Fisherman, Lychorida, Boult), Sam Kelly (Cleon, First Fisherman), Susan Lynch (Marina, Third Lord), Anastasia Mulrooney (Messenger, Third Fisherman), Patrice Naiambana (First Gentleman, Pander) Andrew Price (Escanes, Second Gentleman), Joy Richardson (Thaisa), Jennifer Scott-Malden (Marina, Second Lord), Richard Wills-Cotton (First Lord, First Servant), Tom Yang (Dionyza, Knight).

*Henry V.* Presented by the American Repertory Theatre, Cambridge, Massachusetts, February to March, 1995. Directed by Ron Daniels. Designed by John Conklin. Costumes by Gabriel Berry. With Remo Airaldi (Quickly, Governor of Harfleur, Le Fer), Jeff Breland (Jamy, Court, Salisbury), Bill Camp (Henry V), Leonore Chaix (Katherine), Miles Chapman (Bedford), Robert Colston (Westmorland, Gower), Thomas Darrah (Canterbury, Fluellen), Alvin Epstein (France), Benjamin Evett (Bardolph, Montjoy), James Farmer (Grey, Macmorris, Williams), Jeremy Geidt (Chorus, Ely, Erpingham, Burgundy), Georgine Hall (Alice), Ben Halley, Jr. (Pistol), Michael Janes (Cambridge, Bates, York), Randall Jaynes (Scroop, Grandpre), Josh Karsh (Gloucester), Michael Edo Keane (Constable), Jeremiah Kissell (Dauphin), Will LeBow (Exeter), Ajay Maidu (Boy), Jean-Paul Pentecouteau (French Announcer), John D. Thompson (French Ambassador, Orleans), Kevin Waldron (Bourbon).

# Works Cited

A.B. 1969. *"Kahn's Henry V." Christian Science Monitor,* 16 June.

Abdulla, Sara. 1994. Review of *The Tempest. What's On,* 20 July.

Allen, Norman. 1994. "Epic Simplicity: The Design of *Henry IV." Asides.* Shakespeare Theatre, Washington, D.C.: 6–7.

Alleva, Richard. 1993. "Beatrice Forever." Review of the Kenneth Branagh *Much Ado about Nothing. Commonweal,* 18 June, 23–24.

Andreas, James. 1995. Letter to author, 15 February.

Andrews, Joan K. 1994. "We Are Time's Subjects." In *Henry IV* Program. Washington, D.C.: Shakespeare Theatre.

Andrews, Nigel. 1994. Review of Branagh *Much Ado about Nothing. Financial Times,* 26 August.

Ardolino, Frank. 1991. "Three Reviews." *Marlowe Society of America Newsletter,* 11, no.1: 5–6.

Armstrong, Dennis. 1994. "Stratford's *Hamlet."* 96FM, 6 June.

Atwood, Margaret. 1994. "Was There Life Before Hamlet?" *Stratford Festival.* Stratford, Ontario: Stratford Festival, 25.

Auden, W.H. "Musee des Beaux Arts." *The Collected Poetry of W.H. Auden.* New York: Random House, 1940.

Baker, Christopher. 1994a. "Kingdom in Crisis." *Asides.* Shakespeare Theatre: Washington, D.C.: 1, 10.

1994b. "The Story of Three Kings." *Asides.* Shakespeare Theatre: Washington, D.C., 6–7.

1994c. "A World of Lies." In *Henry IV* Program. Washington, D.C.: Shakespeare Theatre, 23–25.

Baldo, Jonathan. 1994. "Memory and Nostalgia in Kenneth Branagh's *Henry V.* Paper presented at the annual meeting, Shakespeare Association of America, Albuquerque, New Mexico.

Ball, Robert Hamilton. 1968. *Shakespeare on Silent Film.* London: George Allen and Unwin.

Barber, C.L. 1959. *Shakespeare's Festive Comedy.* Princeton: Princeton University Press.

Barker, Nicola. 1994. Review of RSC *Henry VI. Observer,* 14 August.

Barnes, Clive. 1969a. "Kahn's *Henry V." New York Times,* 9 June.

1969b. "Williamson's Hamlet," *New York Times,* 2 May.

Barnes, Harper. 1993. "Much Ado About Something." Review of the Branagh *Much Ado about Nothing. St. Louis Post-Dispatch,* 18 June.

Barnes, Howard. 1936. Review of the MGM *Romeo and Juliet. New York Herald-Tribune*, 21 August.

Baron, David. 1993. "A Mix of Wit and Laughs." Review of the Branagh *Much Ado about Nothing. New Orleans Times-Picayune*, 18 June.

Barton, Anne. 1972. "Note." In *Richard II* Program. London: Royal Shakespeare Company, 1972.

———. 1993. "Shakespeare in the Sun." Review of the Branagh *Much Ado about Nothing. New York Review of Books*, 27 May, 11–13.

Bazin, Andre. 1970. *What is Cinema?*. Berkeley: University of California, Press.

Beauman, Sally. 1976. *The Royal Shakespeare Company's Production of "Henry V."* Oxford: Pergamon Press.

Bedarida, Francois. 1991. *A Social History of England: 1851–1990*. London: Routledge.

Benchley, Robert. [1928] 1994. "Enter the Talkies." Reprinted in *New Yorker*, 21 March, 100.

Bennett, Robert B. 1987. "Four Stages of Time: The Shape of History in Shakespeare's Second Tetralogy." *Shakespeare Studies* 19: 61–85.

Berger, Harry. 1989. *Imaginary Auditions: Shakespeare on Stage and Page.* Berkeley: University of California Press.

———. 1991. "On the Continuity of the *Henriad.*" In *Shakespeare Left and Right*, edited by Ivo Kamps. London: Routledge.

Bergson, Henri. 1900. *Le Rire.* Paris: Lycee Henry IV.

Berkowitz, Gerald. 1994. "*Pericles.*" Review of RSC production of *Pericles. Shakespeare Bulletin* 12, no. 3: 31.

Berry, Francis. 1965. *The Shakespeare Inset.* London: Routledge and Kegan Paul.

Berry, Ralph. 1989a. "Hamlet and the Audience: The Dynamics of a Relationship." In *Shakespeare and the Sense of Performance*, edited by Marvin and Ruth Thompson. Newark: University of Delaware Press.

———. 1989b. *On Directing Shakespeare.* London: Hamish Hamilton.

———. 1993. *Shakespeare in Performance.* London: Macmillan. 1993.

Bevington, David. 1980. *The Complete Works of Shakespeare.* 3ed ed. Glenview, Ill.: Scott, Foresman.

———. 1993. "Ron Daniels's Production." *ART News*, November, 3, 13.

Billen, Andrew. 1994. Review of RSC *The Tempest. Independent on Sunday*, 17 July.

Billington, Michael. 1992. "First Night." *Guardian*, 21 December.

———. 1993. "*King Lear.*" Review of RSC *King Lear. Guardian*, 22 May.

———. 1994a. "Al Fresco Neurosis." Review of Open Air Theatre *Hamlet. Guardian*, 16 June 1994.

———. 1994b. "Design for Dreamers." Review of RSC *A Midsummer Night's Dream. Guardian*, 5 August 1994.

———. 1994c. "Henry, Portrait of a Simple Hero." Review of RSC *Henry V. Guardian*, 12 May.

1994d. "Hits with Myths." Review of RSC *Twelfth Night. Guardian,* 27 May.

1994e. "The Power, the Pain, and the Pity." Review of RSC *Henry VI. Guardian,* 12 August.

1994f. Review of RSC *Coriolanus. Guardian,* 26 May.

1994g. Review of RSC *The Tempest. Guardian,* 15 July.

Bilson, Anne. 1993. Review of Branagh *Much Ado about Nothing. London Sunday Telegraph,* 29 August.

Blos, Peter. 1952. *On Adolescence.* New York: Free Press.

"Boy Meets Girl—Just 340 Years Ago." 1936. Review of MGM *Romeo and Juliet* (MGM film). *Literary Digest,* August, 20.

Bradley, A.C. 1904. *Shakespearean Tragedy.* London, Macmillan.

Brailow, David. 1994. "The King's Two Bodies: Branagh's *Henry V.*" Paper presented at the annual meeting, Shakespeare Association of America, Albuquerque, New Mexico.

Branagh, Kenneth. n.d. Letter, courtesy of Richard Bornstein of the Samuel Goldwyn Company.

Brewster, Maribeth. 1993. "Much Ado Branagh." Review of Branagh *Much Ado about Nothing. Richmond Style Weekly,* 15 June.

Brockbank, Philip, ed. 1985. *Players of Shakespeare I.* Cambridge: Cambridge University Press.

Brodie, Amanda. 1993. *King Lear* Production Pack. RSC Education.

Brook, Peter. 1987. *The Shifting Point.* New York: Perennial.

Brown, Geoff. 1993. Review of Branagh *Much Ado about Nothing. Times,* 26 August.

Brown, John Mason. 1936. Review of John Gielgud's *Hamlet. New York Post,* 14 November.

1948. "Olivier's *Hamlet.*" *Saturday Review of Literature,* 2 October, 26–27.

Brown, John Russell. 1974. "Free Shakespeare." *Shakespeare Survey* 24: 127–35.

Brown, Stewart. 1994. "Monette's *Hamlet* a Restrained Success." *Ontario Spectator,* 3 June 1994, D-1.

Brustein, Robert. 1987. "Vaudeville and Radio." *The New Republic,* 6 July 1987, 28–29.

1988. "21st Century *Hamlet.*" Review of Ingmar Bergman's Dramaten *Hamlet. New Republic* 18 & 25 July, 28–29.

Buck, Joan Juliet. 1993. "Costume Frolics." Review of the Branagh *Much Ado about Nothing. Vogue,* May 1993, 125–28.

Bulman, James. 1988. "*As You Like It* and the Perils of Pastoral." *Shakespeare on Television,* edited by James Bulman and H.R. Coursen. Hanover, N.H.: University Press of New England.

Butler, Robert W. 1993. "It's funny, and sunny, and sexy." Review of the Branagh *Much Ado about Nothing. Kansas City Star,* 18 June, G-4.

Byles, Joan Montgomery. 1991. "Political Theatre: *Hamlet* in Romania." *Shakespeare Bulletin* 9: 25–26.

Campbell, Kathleen. 1991. "Zeffirelli's *Hamlet*—Q1 in Performance," *Shakespeare on Film Newsletter* 16, no. 1: 7.

Cartwright, Kent. 1991. *Shakespearean Tragedy and its Double: The Rhythms of Audience Response*. University Park: Penn State University Press.

Canby, Vincent. 1989. "A Down-to-Earth *Henry V* Discards Spectacle and Pomp." Review of the Kenneth Branagh *Henry V*. *New York Times*, 8 November, C-19.

1993. "A House Party of Beatrice, Benedick and Friends." Review of the Branagh *Much Ado about Nothing*. *New York Times*, 7 May, C-16.

Carr, Jay. 1993a. "Boom, Boom Go the Summer Films." *Boston Globe*, 15 August, B-1, B-4.

1993b. "Branagh's 'Much Ado' has an earthy, golden glow." *Boston Globe*, 21 May.

Chapman, Geoff. 1994. "Ouimette's Mad Hamlet Becomes Vividly Accessible." Review of the Stratford, Ontario *Hamlet*. *Toronto Star*, 6 June.

Clark, David. 1994. Review of the Open Air Theatre *Hamlet*. *What's On*, 22 June.

Clark, Paul. 1993. "'Ado' sun-drenched romp." Review of the Branagh *Much Ado about Nothing*. *Cincinnati Post*, 16 June.

Cohen, Michael. 1989. *Hamlet: in My Mind's Eye*. Athens: University of Georgia Press.

Coleman, Kevin. 1994. Program note for *Hamlet*. Shakespeare & Company: Lennox, Massachusetts.

Collick, John. 1989. *Shakespeare, Cinema and Society*. Manchester: Manchester University Press.

Connors, Joanna. 1993. "Worthy of Much Ado." Review of the Branagh *Much Ado about Nothing*. *Cleveland Plain Dealer*, 18 June.

Cook, Dorothy and Wayne. "*Henry IV, Parts 1 and 2*." *Shakespeare Bulletin* 12, no. 2: 14–15.

Cooper, Jeanne. 1995. "ART Makes War by Playing with Time." Review of the American Repertory Theatre *Henry V*. *Boston Globe*, 10 March.

Corliss, Richard. 1989. "King Ken Comes to Conquer." Review of the Branagh *Henry V*. *Time*, 13 November, 65.

1993. "Smiles of a Summer Night." Review of the Branagh *Much Ado about Nothing*. *Time*, 10 May, 72.

1994. "Something to Sing About." *Time*, 21 December, 84.

Coulbourn, John. 1994. "A Courageous *Hamlet* Graces Stratford." Review of the Stratford, Ontario *Hamlet*. *Toronto Sun*, 4 June.

Coursen, H.R. 1969. "Prospero and the Drama of the Soul." *Shakespeare Studies* 4: 316–33.

1976. *Christian Ritual and the World of Shakespeare's Tragedies*. Lewisburg, Pa.: Bucknell University Press.

1984. *The Leasing Out of England*. Washington: University Press of America.

1986. *The Compensatory Psyche*. Washington: University Press of America.

1988a. "'Morphic Resonance' in Shakespeare's Plays." *Shakespeare Bulletin* 6, no. 2: 5–8.

1988b. "Theories of History in *Richard II*." *Upstart Crow* 8: 42–53.

1990. "Vernon and Coleville." *Shakespeare Bulletin* 8, no. 1: 36–37.

1991. "Sexual Politics in Production: England, Summer 1990." *Shakespeare Bulletin* 9, no. 1: 9–12.

1992. *Performance as Interpretation*. Newark: Delaware University Press.

1993a. "The Directors and the Critics: Stratford-upon-Avon: 1992." *Shakespeare Bulletin* 11, no. 2: 10–12.

1993b. *Watching Shakespeare on Television*. Madison. N.J.: Fairleigh-Dickinson University Press.

1995. *Reading Shakespeare on Stage*. Newark: Delaware University Press.

Coveney, Michael. 1994a. "HRH to the power of two." Review of RSC *Henry V*. *Observer*, 12 May.

1994b. Review of Open Air Theatre *Hamlet*. *Observer*, 19 June.

1994c. "Warm glow all round." Review of RSC *Coriolanus*. *Observer*, 29 May.

Cox, Murray. 1992. "What Ceremony Else?" In *Hamlet* Program. London: Royal Shakespeare Company, 14.

Creelman, Elizabeth. 1936. Review of MGM *Romeo and Juliet*. *New York Sun*, 21 August.

Cross, Brenda, ed. 1948. *The Film "Hamlet": A Record of Its Production*. London: Saturn Press.

Crowl, Samuel. 1992. *Shakespeare Observed*. Athens: Ohio University Press.

1993a. Review of Christine Edzard *As You Like It*. *Shakespeare Bulletin* 11, no. 3: 41.

1993b. Review of Branagh *Much Ado about Nothing*. *Shakespeare Bulletin* 11, no. 3: 39–40.

1994. "The Roman Plays on Film and Television." In *Shakespeare and the Moving Image*, edited by Anthony Davies and Stanley Wells. Cambridge: Cambridge University Press.

Crowther, Bosley. 1967. *The Great Films: Fifty Years of Motion Pictures*. New York: G.P. Putnam's Sons.

Cunningham, James P. 1936. Review of MGM *Romeo and Juliet*. *Commonweal* 42, 4 September.

Curtis, Quentin. 1993. Review of Branagh *Much Ado about Nothing*. *Independent on Sunday*, 29 August.

Davenport, Hugo. 1993. Review of Branagh *Much Ado about Nothing*. *London Daily Telegraph*, 27 August.

David, Hal, ed. 1982. *Hit Songs*. New York: American Society of Composers, Authors, and Publishers.

Davies, Anthony. 1988. *Filming Shakespeare's Plays*. Cambridge: Cambridge University Press.

1994a. "Preface," *Shakespeare and the Moving Image*, edited by Anthony Davies and Stanley Wells. Cambridge: Cambridge University Press.

1994b. "Shakespeare on Film and Television: A Retrospect." *Shakespeare and the Moving Image*, edited by Anthony Davies and Stanley Wells. Cambridge: Cambridge University Press.

Davison, Peter. 1983. *Hamlet: Text & Performance*. London: Macmillan.

Dawson, Anthony. 1988. *Watching Shakespeare*. London: Macmillan.

Deats, Sara Munson. 1992. "Rabbits and Ducks: Olivier, Branagh, and *Henry V*." *Literature/Film Quarterly* 20. no. 4: 284–93.

DeChick, Joe. 1993. "Branagh's Comedy Lacks 'Nothing'." Review of the Branagh *Much Ado about Nothing. Cincinnati Enquirer*, 18 June.

Dehn, Paul. 1954. "Filming Shakespeare." In *Talking of Shakespeare*, edited by John Garrett. London: Hodder & Stoughton.

de Jongh, Nicholas. 1993. Review of RSC *King Lear. London Evening Standard*, 21 May.

⸻. 1994a. "New Hero Is Born." Review of RSC *Henry V. London Evening Standard*, 11 May.

⸻. 1994b. "No Sex Please." Review of RSC *Twelfth Night. London Evening Standard*, 26 May.

⸻. 1994c. Review of the RSC *Tempest. London Evening Standard*, 14 July.

Dent, Alan, ed. 1948. *"Hamlet": The Film and the Play*. London: Saturn.

Derrick, Patty. 1993. "Richard Mansfield's *Henry V* in the Aftermath of 'A Splendid Little War.'" Paper presented at the annual meeting, Shakespeare Association of America, Atlanta.

Desai, R.W. 1991. Review of Gary Taylor's *Reinventing Shakespeare. Hamlet Studies* 14, no. 1: 112–14.

Dessen, Alan. 1986. "The Supernatural on Television." *Shakespeare on Film Newsletter* 11, no. 1: 1, 12.

⸻. 1992. "Resisting the Script: Shakespeare Onstage in 1991." *Shakespeare Quarterly* 43, no. 4: 472–78.

⸻. 1994. "The Image and the Script: Shakespeare on Stage in 1993." *Shakespeare Bulletin* 12, no. 1: 5–8.

Devine, Elizabeth, ed. 1984. *Annual Obituary: 1983*. Chicago: St. James Press.

DeVine, Lawrence. 1994. "A Good Night, Sweet Prince: Clarity Is Soul of this 'Hamlet'." Review of Stratford, Ontario *Hamlet. Detroit Free Press*, 6 June, 1-E, 3-E.

Donaldson, Peter S. 1990. *Shakespearean Films/ Shakespearean Directors*. Boston: Unwin Hyman.

⸻. 1991. "Taking on Shakespeare: Kenneth Branagh's *Henry V*." *Shakespeare Quarterly* 42, no. 1: 60–71.

Doran, Terry. 1994. "Streamlined 'Hamlet' Is As Good As It gets." Review of Stratford, Ontario *Hamlet. Buffalo News*, 9 June, B-11.

Doughty, Louise. 1994. "Horray, Henry." Review of RSC *Henry V. London Mail on Sunday*, 15 May.

D.R.C. 1936. "An Epilogue to 'Romeo'." *New York Times*, 19 April, Sec. 9, 4.

Dudgate, Ron. 1994. Review of RSC *Henry V. Plays and Players*, May, 31.

Duffy, Robert A. 1976. "Gade, Olivier, Richardson: Visual Strategy in *Hamlet* Adaptation," *Literature/Film Quarterly* 4, no. 2: 141–52.

Dyer, Richard. 1995. "*Henry V* at War with Words." Review of American Repertory Theatre *Henry V. Boston Globe*, 24 February.

Eckert, Charles W. 1972. *Focus on Shakespearean Films*. Englewood Cliffs, N.J.: Prentice-Hall.

Edgerton, Ellen. 1994. "'Your Answer, Sir, Is Cinematical': Kenneth Branagh's *Much Ado about Nothing.*" *Shakespeare Bulletin* 12, no. 1: 42–44.

Edmonds, Richard. 1994. "Classic Humour in a Wintry Landscape." Review of RSC *Twelfth Night. Birmingham Post,* 26 May.

Edwards, Anne. 1974. *Judy Garland.* New York: Simon & Schuster.

Elgin, Kathy. 1993. "The Man Behind Elgar's Moustache." *RSC Magazine,* Autumn, 13–15.

Eliot, T.S. 1960. "Hamlet and His Problems." In *Hamlet: Enter Critic,* edited by Claire Sachs and Edgar Whan. New York: Appleton-Century-Crofts.

Elsom, John, ed. 1989. *Is Shakespeare* Still *Our Contemporary?* London: Routledge.

Elston, Laura. 1936. Review of MGM *Romeo and Juliet. Canadian Magazine,* September.

Empson, William. 1960. *Some Versions of Pastoral.* Norfolk, Connecticut: New Directions.

Fabricius, Johannes. 1989. *Shakespeare's Hidden World.* Copenhagen: Munksgaard.

Fabricius, Susan. 1994. "The Face of Honour. On Kenneth Branagh's Screen Adaptation of *Henry V.*" In *Screen Shakespeare,* edited by Michael Skovmand. Aarhus, Denmark: Aarhus University Press.

Farley, Barbara Stuart. 1994. Review of the RSC *Tempest. Shakespeare Bulletin,* 12, no. 1: 13.

Feay, Suzi. 1994a. Review of Open Air Theatre *Hamlet. Time Out,* 22–29 June.
1994b. Review of Open Air Theatre *Hamlet. Time Out,* 10–17 August.

Fenster, Bob. 1993. "Branagh's 'Ado' Makes Much of Bard's Comedy." *Arizona Republic,* 18 June, D-1, D-11.

Ferguson, Otis. 1936. "Young Love, Etc." Review of MGM *Romeo and Juliet. New Republic,* 2 September, 104.

"Films." 1936. Review of MGM *Romeo and Juliet. The London Mercury,* November, 57.

Fitter, Chris. 1991. "A Tale of Two Branaghs" *Henry V,* Ideology, and the Mekong Agincourt." In *Shakespeare Left and Right,* edited by Ivo Kamps. London: Routledge.

Flamini, Roland. 1994. *Thalberg.* New York: Crown.

Foakes, R. A. 1993a. *Hamlet versus Lear.* Cambridge: Cambridge University Press, 1993.
1993b. "The Reception of Hamlet." *Shakespeare Survey* 45: 1–13.

Fox, Alistair. 1983. *Thomas More, History and Providence.* New Haven: Yale University Press.

Francis, Dick. 1984. *Proof.* London: Pan.

Freeman, John. 1990. "Filling in the Margins of Shakespeare's Texts: The New Historicism in the Classroom." *Nebraska English Journal,* edited by Edmund Taft IV. 35, nos. 3 & 4: 108–15.

French, Philip. 1993. Review of Branagh *Much Ado about Nothing. Observer,* 29 August.

Freud, Sigmund. 1959. *Psychoanalysis. The Complete Works,* edited by James Strachey. Vol. 20. London: Hogarth Press.

Frey, Charles. 1992. "Shakespearience! What to Teach? What to Learn." First Clemson Shakespeare Conference. 11 March.

Friedman, Michael D. 1994. "'To Be Slow in Words is Woman's Only Virtue': Silence and Satire in *The Two Gentlemen of Verona.*" In *Selected Papers: Shakespeare and Renaissance Association of West Virginia,* edited by Edmund M. Taft IV. 17: 1–9.

Frost, Robert. 1930. Lecture presented at Amherst College. In *Selected Prose,* edited by Hyde Cox and Edward C. Lathem. New York: Holt, Rinehart, and Winston. Reprinted in *The Norton Reader,* edited by Arthur M. Eastman. New York: W.W. Norton, 1025–33.

Frye, Northrop. 1957. *Anatomy of Criticism.* Princeton: Princeton University Press.

———. 1963. *Fables of Identity.* New York: Harcourt, Brace, and World.

Furse, Roger. 1948. "Designing the Film *Hamlet.*" In *"Hamlet": The Film and the Play,* edited by Alan Dent. London: Saturn.

Fussell, Paul. 1975. *The Great War and Modern Memory.* New York: Oxford University Press.

Fuzier, J. 1978. Review of RSC *Comedy of Errors. Cahiers Elisabethains* 12, 74–75.

Gardner, Helen. 1963. *The Business of Criticism.* Oxford: Oxford University Press.

Garner, Jack. 1993. "Summery and Smart." Review of Branagh *Much Ado about Nothing. Rochester Democrat & Chronicle,* 17 June, 1-C, 4-C.

Geckle, George. 1994. Review of RSC *King Lear. Shakespeare Bulletin* 12, no. 1: 10.

Gibney, Liz. 1993. "Interview with Robert Stephens." *Plays International,* May.

Gielgud, John. 1992. *Acting Shakespeare.* New York: Scribners.

Gilbert, Matthew. 1993. "Much Ado About Branagh." Review of Branagh's *Much Ado about Nothing. Boston Sunday Globe,* 16 May, B-33, B-37.

Gillespie, Ian. 1994. "Festival's *Hamlet* Minimal, Majestic." Review of Stratford, Ontario *Hamlet, London* [Ontario] *Free Press,* 4 June.

Goddard, Harold. 1951. *The Meaning of Shakespeare,* Chicago: University of Chicago Press.

Goldman, Michael. 1992. *"Hamlet:* Entering the Text." *Theater Journal* 44: 449–460.

Gomery, Douglas. 1986. *Actors and Actresses.* New York: St. James Press.

Gore-Langton, Robert. 1994. Review of RSC *Henry VI. London Daily Telegraph,* 15 August.

Gottlieb, Sidney. 1992. Review of *Still in Movement: Shakespeare on Screen,* by Lorne M. Buchman. *Shakespeare Quarterly* 43, no. 2: 244–47.

Graham, Renee. 1995. "Another view of Henry V's triumph." Review of ART *Henry V. Boston Globe,* 19 February, B-25, B-30.

Granville-Barker, Harley. 1936. "Alas Poor Will." *The Listener*, 3 March, 387–89, 425–26.

Green, Douglas E. 1992. "Staging the Evidence: Shakespeare's Theatrical Revengers" *The Upstart Crow* 12: 29–40.

Greenblatt, Stephen. 1980. *Renaissance Self-Fashioning: From More to Shakespeare*. Chicago: University of Chicago Press.
    *Learning to Curse: Essays in Modern Culture*. London: Routledge, 1990.

Gross, John. 1994a. "Leading His People Off the Roman Road." Review of RSC *Coriolanus*. *London Sunday Telegraph*, 29 May.
    1994b. Review of RSC *Henry VI*. *London Sunday Telegraph*, 14 August.

Gross, Sheryl W. 1980. "Poetic Realism in Olivier's *Hamlet*," *Hamlet Studies* 2, no. 2: 62–68.

Gukringa, Frank. 1993. "'Nothing' is really something." Review of the Branagh *Much Ado about Nothing*. *Columbus Dispatch*, 18 June.

Gussow, Mel. 1987, Review of Karamazov *Comedy of Errors*. *New York Times*, 1 June.

Hagerty, Bill. 1994. Review of Open Air Theatre *Hamlet*. *Today*, 17 June.

Hall, Peter. 1969. "Shakespeare's *Dream*." *Times*. 26 January.

*Hamlet*. 1991. Stratford Festival Program: Stratford, Ontario.

Hampton, Wilbron. 1994. "Theater Reviews." *New York Times*, 26 January, C-16.

Hanks, Robert. 1994a. Review of the RSC *Tempest*. *Independent on Sunday*, 17 July.
    1994b. "Thrust and Harry." Review of RSC *Henry V*. *Independent*, 12 May.

Hapgood, Robert. 1986. "Shakespeare on Film and Television." In *The Cambridge Companion to Shakespeare Studies*, edited by Stanley Wells. Cambridge: Cambridge University Press.

Hardison, O.B. 1969. "Three Types of Renaissance Catharsis." *Renaissance Drama*, n.s., 2: 3–22.

Hattaway, Michael. 1987. *Hamlet: The Critics Debate*. Atlantic Highlands, N.J.: Humanities Press International.

Hawkes, Terry. 1985. "*TELMAH*." In *Shakespeare and the Question of Theory*, edited by Geoffrey Hartmann and Patricia Parker. London: Metheun.
    1992. *Meaning by Shakespeare*. London: Routledge.

Hazlitt, William. 1845. *Characters of Shakspeare's Plays*. New York: Wiley and Putnam.

Hearst, Stephen. 1978. "It Ain't Necessarily So." *New Review* 5, no. 1: 3–13.

Hemingway, Ernest. 1929. *A Farewell to Arms*. New York: Scribner's.

Herold, Niels. 1995. "Performance Criticism and the New Historicism." *Shakespeare and the Classroom* 3, no. 1: 48–50.

Herzberg, Max J. 1936. *A Preliminary Study Guide to the Screen Version of Shakespeare's "Romeo and Juliet"*. Newark, N.J.: Educational and Recreational Guides, Inc.
    1949. *"Hamlet": An Introduction to the Photoplay*. New York: Theater Guild.

Hinson, Hal. 1993. "Nothing Much About 'Ado.'" Review of Branagh *Much Ado about Nothing. Washington Post,* 21 May, B-7.

Hirshhorn, Clive. 1994. Review of RSC *King Lear. London Sunday Express,* 5 June.

Hitchcock, Alfred. 1936. "Much Ado About Nothing?" *Listener,* 10 March, 448-50.

Hodgdon, Barbara. 1985. "Parallel Practices, or the *Un*-Necessary Difference." *Kenyon Review* 7, no. 3: 57-65.

1991. *The End Crowns All.* Princeton: Princeton University Press.

Holderness, Graham. 1985. *Shakespeare's History.* New York: St. Martin's Press.

1993. "Shakespeare Rewound." *Shakespeare Survey* 45: 63-77.

Holland, Peter. 1992. "Shakespeare Performances in England." *Shakespeare Survey* 44: 175-78.

1993a. "The Eyes Have It." *Times Literary Supplement,* 7 May: 3-4.

1993b. "Shakespeare Performances in England, 1990-1." *Shakespeare Survey* 45: 115-44.

Home Box Office, 1990. "The Making of *Hamlet.*" Documentary on the Franco Zeffirelli film of *Hamlet.*

Hornby, Richard. 1988. "Shakespeare in New York," *Hudson Review* 40, no. 2: 339-44.

Howard, Jean E. 1979. "Shakespearean Counterpoint: Stage Technique and the Interaction between Play and Audience." *Shakespeare Quarterly* 30, no. 3: 343-57.

1986. "The New Historicism in Renaissance Studies." *English Literary Renaissance* 16: 13-43.

Howard, Richard. 1994. "The Danger and Fun of Diving into Hamlet." *News Notes.* Ashland: Oregon Shakespeare Festival.

Howe, Desson. 1993. "'Much Ado' Is Something." Review of Branagh *Much Ado about Nothing. Washington Post Weekend,* 21 May, 53.

Humphreys, A.R., ed. 1991. *Henry IV, Part II.* London: Routledge.

Hush, Jeff. 1991. Letter to the author, 30 October.

Impastato, David. 1991. "Zeffirelli's *Hamlet:* Sunlight Makes Meaning." *Shakespeare on Film Newsletter* 16, no. 1: 1-2.

1992. "Zeffirelli's *Hamlet* and the Baroque." *Shakespeare on Film Newsletter* 16, no. 2.: 1-2.

"Inconsistencies Hamper 'Hamlet'." 1994. Review of Oregon Shakespeare Festival *Hamlet. Eugene Register-Guardian,* 4 March.

Ingram, Raymond. 1992. In "Angles of Perception," *As You Like It: Audio Visual Shakespeare,* edited by Cathy Grant. London: British Universities Film and Video Council.

"Irving Thalberg." 1936. *New York Times,* 15 September, 29.

Jackson, Russell. 1994a. Review of RSC *Twelfth Night. Times Literary Supplement,* 26 May, 7.

1994b. "Shakespeare at Stratford-upon-Avon." *Shakespeare Quarterly* 45, no. 3: 332-48.

1994c. "Shakespeare's Comedies on Film." In *Shakespeare and the Moving*

*Image,* edited by Anthony Davies and Stanley Wells. Cambridge: Cambridge University Press.

Jackson, Russell, and Robert Smallwood, eds. 1988. *Players of Shakespeare 2.* Cambridge: Cambridge University Press.

1993. *Players of Shakespeare 3.* Cambridge: Cambridge University Press.

Jacobs, Tom. 1991. "Hamlet Is No Wimp," *Brunswick-Bath (Maine) Times-Record,* 7 January.

James, Caryn. 1993. "Why Branagh's Bard Glows on the Screen." Review of the Branagh *Much Ado about Nothing. New York Times,* 16 May, H-17.

Johnson, Barry. 1993. "A Prince without Passion." Review of Oregon Shakespeare Festival *Hamlet. Oregonian,* 28 February.

Johnson, Ian. 1972. "Merely Players." In *Focus on Shakespearean Films,* edited by Charles W. Eckert. Englewood Cliffs, N.J.: Prentice Hall.

Johnstone, Iain. 1993. Review of Branagh *Much Ado about Nothing. Sunday Times,* 29 August.

Jones, Ernest. 1949. *Hamlet and Oedipus.* New York: Doubleday.

Jonson, Ben. 1925. *Works.* Vol. 1. Edited by C.H. Herford, E. Simpson, and P. Simpson. Oxford: Oxford University Press.

Jorgens, Jack. 1977. *Shakespeare on Film.* Bloomington: Indiana University Press.

1988. Review of BBC-TV *As You Like It.* In *Shakespeare on Television,* edited by James Bulman and H.R. Coursen. Hanover, N.H.: University Press of New England.

Julian, Patrick. 1994. "A Grudging Part in Real History: Shakespeare's *Henry V* and War in the Twentieth Century." *Selected Papers of the Shakespeare and Renaissance Association of West Virginia* 17: 112–19.

Juillerat, Lee. 1994. "Something Is Rotten in Ashland." Review of Oregon Shakespeare Festival *Hamlet. Klamath Falls* (Oregon) *Herald & News,* 18 March.

Kallaway, Kate. 1991. Review of RSC *Henry IV, Part II. Observer,* 2 June.

Keats, John. "The Eve of St. Agnes." *Poems of John Keats.* New York: Macmillan, 1898.

Kelly, Kevin. 1993. "ART's 'Henry IV' For All Times." *Boston Globe.* 3 December.

Kennedy, Dennis. 1993. *Looking at Shakespeare: A Visual History of Twentieth-Century Performance.* Cambridge: Cambridge U.P.

Kent, Roberta. 1994. "*Hamlet:* 'The Time Is Out of Joint.'" *Ashland Gazette,* March-April, 12.

Kernan, Alvin B. 1970. "*The Henriad:* Shakespeare's Major History Plays." In *Modern Shakspearean Criticism: Essays on Style, Dramaturgy and the Major Plays,* edited by Alvin Kernan. New York: Harcourt.

1974. "This Goodly Frame, The Stage: The Interior Theater of Imagination in English Renaissance Drama." *Shakespeare Quarterly* 25, no. 1: 1–5.

Kerr, Walter. 1969. Review of Michael Kahn *Henry V. New York Times,* June 1969.

Kettle, Arnold, ed. 1964. *Shakespeare in a Changing World*. New York: New Directions.

Kimbrough, R. Alan. 1988. Review of BBC-TV *As You Like It*. *Shakespeare on Television*, edited by James Bulman and H.R. Coursen. Hanover, N.H.: University Press of New England.

Kingston, Jeremy. 1994. "Midsummer in a Monotone." Review of RSC *A Midsummer Night's Dream*. *Times*, 16 June.

Kirchhoff, H.J. 1994. "*Hamlet* Cut to the Bone." Review of Stratford, Ontario *Hamlet*. *Ontario Globe and Mail*, 4 June.

Kliman, Bernice W. 1988. *Hamlet: Film, Television, and Audio Perfomance*. Cranbury, N.J.: Associated University Presses.

———. 1989. "Branagh's *Henry V*: Allusion and Illusion." *Shakespeare on Film Newsletter* 14, no. 1: 1, 9–10.

———. 1994. "Welles's *Macbeth*, a Textual Parable." In *Screen Shakespeare*, edited by Michael Skovmand. Aarhus, Denmark: Aarhus University Press.

Knapp, Jeanne. 1993. "A King and a Nation in Crisis." *Asides*. Washington, D.C.: Shakespeare Theatre. Fall, 1, 7.

Knight, Arthur. 1970. "Still There, Old Mole?" *Saturday Review of Literature*, 17 February, 37.

Knights, L.C. 1947. *Explorations*. New York: New York University Press.

Koenig, Rhoda. 1994. "Dreaming Colour." Review of RSC *A Midsummer Night's Dream*. *Independent*, 5 August.

Kozintsev, Grigori. 1962. "*Hamlet*." "Films and Filming." September.

———. 1966. *Shakespeare: Time and Conscience*. London: Dennis Dobson.

———. 1971. "*Hamlet* and *King Lear*." In *Shakespeare: 1971*, edited by Clifford Leech and J.M.R. Margeson. Toronto: University of Toronto Press, 1972.

Kramer, Mimi. 1992. "Theater," *New Yorker*, 22 June.

Kroll, Jack. 1989. "A Henry V for Our Time." Review of Branagh *Henry V*. *Newsweek*, 20 November, 78.

———. "Shakespeare, As You Like It." 1993. Review of Branagh *Much Ado about Nothing*. *Newsweek*, 10 May, 60.

Krutch, Joseph Wood. 1936. Review of John Gielgud and Leslie Howard *Hamlets*. *Nation*, 21 November, 40.

Kustow, Michael. 1964. Review of Kozintsev *Hamlet*. *Sight and Sound* 33, 144–45.

Lacan, Jaques. 1977. "Desire and the Interpretation of Desire in *Hamlet*." Translated by James Hulbert. French text edited by Jacques-Alain Miller. *Yale French Studies* 55–56: 11–52.

Lane, Anthony. 1993. Review of Branagh *Much Ado about Nothing*. *New Yorker*, 10 May, 97–99.

Lasch, Christopher. 1978. *The Culture of Narcissism*. New York: Norton.

Lehman, Jon L. 1995. "Superb *Henry V* Triumphantly Concludes A.R.T. Trilogy." *Quincy, Mass. Patriot Ledger*, 24 February.

Lewis, John. 1993. "Don't Mess With Bill." Review of Branagh *Much Ado about Nothing*. *Dallas Observer*, 16 June.

Lindsay, Heather. 1995. "The King Is But a Man: The Personal Epic of Henry V." In *Henry V* Program. Cambridge, Mass.: American Repertory Theatre.

Lusardi, James. 1985. Review of the Shakespeare and Company *Comedy of Errors*. *Shakespeare Bulletin* 3, no. 2: 7.

Lyons, Richard. 1994. "Allan G. Odell, 90; Burma Shave Executive Linked Beards to Bards." *New York Times*, 22 January.

Macaulay, Alastair. 1994a. "Mixed Feelings." Review of RSC *Coriolanus*. *Financial Times*, 27 May.

1994b. "*Hamlet* in the Park." Review of Open Air Theatre *Hamlet*. *Financial Times*, 11 June.

1994c. "Henry VI—the Battle for the Throne." Review of RSC *Henry VI*. *Financial Times*, 12 August.

1994d. Review of RSC *Henry V*. *Financial Times*, 12 May.

1994e. Review of RSC *Tempest*. *Financial Times*, 14 July.

MacCambridge, Michael. 1993. "Shakespeare for the '90s." Review of Branagh *Much Ado about Nothing*. *Austin American-Statesman*, 18 June.

Mahood, Molly. 1992. *Bit Parts in Shakespeare*. Cambridge: Cambridge University Press.

Malcolm, Derek. 1993. Review of Branagh *Much Ado about Nothing*. *Guardian*, 26 August.

Mangan, Michael. 1991. *A Preface to Shakespeare's Tragedies*. London: Longman.

Manheim, Michael. 1994. "The English History Plays on Screen." *Shakespeare and the Moving Image*, edited by Anthony Davies and Stanley Wells. Cambridge: Cambridge University Press.

Manvell, Roger. 1971. *Shakespeare and the Film*. New York: Praeger.

Marks, John. 1936. Review of Reinhardt-Dieterle *A Midsummer Night's Dream* and Cukor-Thalberg *Romeo and Juliet*. *Sight and Sound* 5, Autumn, 37–38.

"Masterpiece." 1946. *Time*. Review of the Olivier *Hamlet*, 8 April.

Matheson, Thomas. 1994. "Hamlet's Last Words: Remaining Silent?" Paper presented at the biennial International Shakespeare Association Conference. Stratford-on-Avon, 24 August.

Matthews, Brander. 1913. *Shakspere as a Playwright*. New York: Columbia University Press.

Maupin, Elizabeth. 1994a. "Actors Bring a Freshness that 'Hamlet' Often Lacks." Review of Orlando Festival *Hamlet*. *Orlando Sentinal*, 3 April, A-2.

1994b. "Shakespeare Projects into Electronic Age." *Orlando Sentinal*, 1 April.

Maxwell, Glyn. 1993. "Reality and recreation." Review of Branagh *Much Ado about Nothing*. *Times Literary Supplement*, 3 September, 18.

Mazer, Cary M. 1993. "Shakespeare in Heat." Review of Branagh *Much Ado about Nothing*. *Philadelphia City Paper*, 21–28 May.

McCarten, John. 1946. Review of Olivier *Henry V*. *New Yorker*, 22 June.

McCarthy, Mary. 1956. "A Prince of Shreds and Patches." In *Sights and Spectacles: 1937-1956.* New York: Farrar, Straus & Giroux.

McElroy, Bernard. 1989. "Odd Couple: *Hamlet* and *Rosencrantz and Guildenstern* at the New Jersey Shakespeare Festival." *Shakespeare Quarterly* 40, no. 1: 94-96.

McGuire, Philip. 1979. Introduction to *Shakespeare: The Theatrical Dimension,* edited by Philip C. McGuire and David A. Samuelson. New York: AMS Press, 1979.

1985. *Speechless Dialect: Shakespeare's Open Silences.* Berkeley: University of California Press.

McLuhan, Marshall. 1964. *Understanding Media.* New York: McGraw Hill.

McLuskie, Kathleen. 1985. "The Patriarchal Bard: Feminist Criticism and Shakespeare: *King Lear* and *Measure for Measure.* In *Political Shakespeares: New Essays in Cultural Materialism,* edited by Jonathan Dollimore and Alan Sinfield. Manchester: Manchester University Press.

1988. *Renaissance Dramatists.* Atlantic Highlands: Humanities Press International.

McQueen, Max. 1991. "Mel Gibson as Hamlet: Not the Definitive Dane," *Kennebec* (Maine) *Journal,* February 2-3, D-10.

Meeker, Joseph. 1980. *The Comedy of Survival.* Los Angeles: Guild of Tutors Press.

Meltz, Marty. 1991. "Now Playing." *Portland* (Maine) *Press-Herald,* 31 January.

1993a. "'Firm' grips with power, suspense." *Portland* (Maine) *Press-Herald,* 8 July.

1993b. "'Line of Fire' the place to be." *Portland* (Maine) *Press-Herald,* 15 July.

Miller, Mark C. 1980. "The Shakespeare Plays." *Nation,* 12 July, 46-61.

Mills, John. 1985. *Hamlet on Stage: The Great Tradition.* Westport, Ct.: The Greenwood Press.

Milton, Joyce. 1993. *Loss of Eden.* New York: Harper, Collins.

Mondello, Bob. "Tour de Fourth." Review of Shakespeare Theatre *Henry IV.* *Washington City Paper,* 30 September 1994.

Monette, Richard. 1994. "On Playing Hamlet." Lecture presented at Concordia College, Stratford, Ontario, January.

Montrose, Louis. 1979-80. "The Purpose of Playing: The Playwright's Reflections on a Shakespearean Anthropology." *Helios* 7, no. 2: 51-52.

1989. "The Poetics and Politics of Culture." *The New Historicism,* edited by H. Aram Veeser. London: Routledge.

Morley, Sheridan. 1994a. Review of RSC *King Lear. Spectator,* 11 June.

1994b. Review of RSC *Tempest. Spectator,* 23 July.

Morrison, Bill. 1993. "Something from 'Nothing'." Review of Branagh *Much Ado about Nothing. Raleigh Notes & Observer,* 18 June.

Morrison, Blake. 1994. "Letter from Liverpool: Children of Circumstance." *New Yorker,* 14 February, 48-60.

Moseley, C.W.R.D. 1988. *Shakespeare's History Plays.* London: Penguin.

"Much Ado about Dinosaurs." 1993. Review of Branagh *Much Ado about Nothing*. *Hartford Advocate*, 17 June.

Mullin, Michael. 1976. "Tony Richardson's *Hamlet:* Script and Screen," *Literature/Film Quarterly* 4, no. 2: 123–33.

———. 1994. "Our Shakespeare: Shakespeare Across Cultures." Paper presented at the biennial International Shakespeare. Association Conference, Stratford-on-Avon, August.

Mulvey, Laura. 1985. "Visual Pleasure and Narrative Cinema." *Film Theory and Criticism*, edited by Gerald Mast and Marshall Cohen. New York: Oxford University Press.

Murray, David. 1994. Review of RSC *King Lear*. *Financial Times*, 2 June.

Nardo, Anna. 1983. "*Hamlet:* A Man to Double Business Bound." *Shakespeare Quarterly* 34, no. 2: 181–99.

Nathan, David. 1993. Review of RSC *King Lear*. *Jewish Chronicle*, 28 May.

Neely, Carol Thomas. 1981. "Feminist Modes of Shakespearean Criticism." *Woman's Studies* 9: 9–17.

———. 1994. "Madmen and Strong Women in *Twelfth Night* and *Comedy of Errors*." Lecture presented at Clemson University, 18 March.

Neman, Daniel. 1993. " 'Much Ado" is funny, romantic, ultimately satisfying." Review of Branagh *Much Ado about Nothing*. *Richmond Times-Dispatch*, 18 June.

Newell, Alex. 1991. Review of 1991 Stratford Festival *Hamlet*. *Shakespeare Bulletin* 9, no. 4: 31–32.

Nightingale, Benedict. 1994a. "Jung Man's Guide to Fairyland." Review of RSC *A Midsummer Night's Dream*. *Times*, 5 August.

———. 1994b. "Preaching His Way to Victory." Review of RSC *Henry V*. *Times*, 12 May.

———. 1994c. Review of RSC *Henry IV, Part II*. *Times*, 1 June.

———. 1994d. Review of RSC *King Lear*. *Times*, 2 June.

———. 1994e. Review of RSC *Tempest*. *Times*, 15 July.

———. 1994f. "Rough Theatre, Rough Times." Review of RSC *Henry VI*. *Times*, 12 August.

Noble, Adrian. 1994. "The RSC Season." Biennial International Shakespeare Association Conference, 26 August.

Nugent, Frank. 1936a. "The Bard Passes His Screen Test." Review of MGM *Romeo and Juliet*. *New York Times*, 30 August, sec. 9, 3.

———. 1936b. "The Screen." *New York Times*, 21 August.

———. 1937. "Films of 1936." *New York Times*, 5 January, sec. 10, 5.

O'Connor, Donal. 1993. "Masterful Acting, Unadorned Text Team for a Superb *Hamlet*." Review of Stratford Festival *Hamlet*. *Stratford Beacon-Herald*, 3 June.

O'Connor, Joseph. 1988. Review of BBC-TV *As You Like It*. In *Shakespeare on Television*, edited by James Bulman and H.R. Coursen. Hanover, N.H.: University Press of New England.

Olivier, Laurence. 1948. "An Essay in *Hamlet*." In *The Film "Hamlet," a Record of Its Production*, edited by Brenda Cross. London: Saturn.

Orgel, Stephen. 1983. "Shakespeare Imagines a Theater." In *Shakespeare: Man of the Theater,* edited by Kenneth Muir, Jay L. Halio, and D.J. Palmer. Newark, Del.: University of Delaware Press.

Osborne, Robert. 1994a. *"Romeo and Juliet:* the 1936 MGM Film." Turner Classic Movies, 20 April.

1994b. *"Smilin' Through:* the 1932 MGM Film." Turner Classic Movies, 30 October.

Paton, Maureen. 1994. "Mad Midsummer Dream Turns into a Nightmare." Review of RSC *A Midsummer Night's Dream. London Daily Express,* 4 August.

Peachment, Chris. 1994. "Beardless into the Breach." Review of RSC *Henry V. London Sunday Telegraph,* 15 May.

Pearce, G.M. 1984. Review of BBC-TV *Comedy of Errors. Cahiers Elisabethains* 25: 113–15.

Peter, John. 1991. Review of RSC *Henry IV, Part II. Sunday Times,* 2 June.

1994a. "A King and Officers of Sorts." Review of RSC *Henry V. Sunday Times,* 15 May.

1994b. Review of RSC *Coriolanus. Sunday Times,* 29 May.

1994c. Review of RSC *Henry VI. Sunday Times,* 14 August.

1994d. Review of National Theatre *Pericles. Sunday Times,* 31 July.

1994f. Review of RSC *Twelfth Night. Times,* 27 May.

Peterson, Douglas. 1995. "Beginnings and Endings: Structure and Mimesis in Shakespeare's Comedies." In *Entering the Maze: Shakespeare's Art of Beginning,* edited by Robert F. Willson, Jr. New York: Peter Lang.

Pickford, Mary. 1956. *Sunshine and Shadow.* London: Dennis Dobson.

Pigott-Smith, Tim. 1994. *Hamlet* Program. London: Open Air Theatre.

Pilkington, Ace. 1994. "Zeffirelli's Shakespeare," *Shakespeare and the Moving Image,* edited by Anthony Davies and Stanley Wells. Cambridge: Cambridge University Press.

Polunsky, Bob. 1993. "Branagh Triumphs." Review of Branagh *Much Ado about Nothing. San Antonio Express-News,* 18 June.

Portman, Jamie. 1994. "Less-Is-More *Hamlet* Triumphs." Review of Stratford Ontario *Hamlet. Windsor Ontario Star,* 3 June.

Potter, Lois. 1975. "Realism Versus Nightmare: Problems of Staging *The Duchess of Malfi. The Triple Bond,* edited by Joseph G. Price. University Park: Penn State University Press.

Pressley, Nelson. 1994a. " 'Cut!' 'Henry' Gets Snipped to Fit Shakespeare Stage." Review of Shakespeare Theatre *Henry V. Washington Times,* 25 September, D-1, D-3.

1994b. "Smaller 'Henry' Is Still in Fine Form." *Washington Times,* 27 September.

Prior, Moody. 1973. *The Drama of Power.* Evanston: Northwestern University Press.

Proctor, Roy. 1994. "Marathon Is Worthy Idea, But 'Henry IV' Is Exhausting." Review of Shakespeare Theatre *Henry V. Richmond Times Dispatch,* 27 September.

Pursell, Michael. 1992. "Playing the Game: Branagh's *Henry V.*" *Literature/Film Quarterly* 20, no. 4: 268–75.

Quigley, Pat. 1994. "Conversation with Richard Monette." *Stratford for Students.* Spring, 3–7.

Quinn, Edward. 1991. "Zeffirelli's *Hamlet.*" *Shakespeare on Film Newsletter* 15, no. 2: 1–2.

Rabkin, Norman. 1977. "Rabbits, Ducks, and *Henry V.*" *Shakespeare Quarterly* 28, no. 3: 279–96.

———. 1981. *Shakespeare and the Problem of Meaning* Chicago: University of Chicago Press. 1981.

Rackin, Phyllis. 1990. *Stages of History.* Ithaca: Cornell U.P.

Rafferty, Terrence. 1994. "Mad Love." *New Yorker.* 3 October, 109.

Ranald, Margaret Loftis. 1993. Review of Theatre for a New Audience *Henry V. Shakespeare Bulletin* 11, no. 2: 13–14.

Rauchut, E.A. 1993. "The Siege Oration in Branagh's *Henry V.*" *Shakespeare Bulletin* 11, no. 1: 39–40.

Reid, Robert. 1994. "Vital, Working Words." Review of Stratford Ontario *Hamlet. Kitchner-Waterloo (Ontario) Record,* 3 June.

Reinhardt, Max. *Max Reinhardt and His Theatre.* ed. Oliver M. Sayler. New York: Brentano's, 1926.

Reiss, Al. 1994. "The Tragedy in OSF's 'Hamlet' Comes from Poor Direction, Not Plot." *Medford* (Oregon) *Mail-Tribune,* 3 March.

"Report from Hollywood." 1936. *New York Times,* 19 April, sec. 9, 4.

Review of MGM *Romeo and Juliet.* 1936a. *Scholastic,* 19 September.

Review of MGM *Romeo and Juliet.* 1936b. *Time,* 24 August, 30, 32.

Review of MGM *Romeo and Juliet.* 1936c. *Variety,* 23 August.

Review of RSC *Coriolanus.* 1994. *Time Out,* 10–17 August.

Rich, Frank. 1992. "Branagh's Hamlet as a Young Conservative." *New York Times,* 24 December, C-9, C-14.

Roberts, Jeanne. A. 1984. Review of BBC-TV *Comedy of Errors. Shakespeare on Film Newsletter* 9, no. 1: 4.

Rooks, John. 1990. "Shakespeare in a West African Context: Boundaries and Points of Access." In *Nebraska English Journal,* edited by Edmund M. Taft IV. 35, nos. 3 and 4: 116–22.

Rose, Lloyd. 1994. " 'Henry IV: Shortened and Sweet." Review of Shakespeare Theatre *Henry IV. Washington Post,* 27 September.

Rosenbaum, Ron. 1994. "Kim Philby and the Age of Paranoia." *New York Times Magazine,* 10 July, 28–37, 50, 53–54.

Rothwell, Kenneth S. 1973. "Hollywood and Some Versions of *Romeo and Juliet:* Toward a 'Substantial Pageant.' " *Literature/Film Quarterly* 1, no. 4: 343–51.

———. 1977. "Irving Thalberg's 'Picturization' of Shakespeare's *Romeo and Juliet.*" Unpublished.

———. 1994. Letter to author. 13 May.

Rothwell, Kenneth S. and Annabelle H. Melzer. 1990. *Shakespeare on Screen: An International Filmography and Videography.* New York: Neal-Schuman.

Saccio, Peter. 1982. Review of BBC-TV *Henry IV*, Part Two. *Shakespeare on Film Newsletter* 6, no. 1: 2.

Safire, William. 1994. "On Language." *New York Times Magazine*, 6 November, 18.

Salomon, Patricia. 1994. "*Communitas* in Branagh's 'Henry V'." Paper presented at the annual meeting, Shakespeare Association of America, Albuquerque, New Mexico.

Scanlan, Peter. 1993. "An Epic of Order and Misrule." In *Henry IV* Program. Cambridge, Mass.: American Repertory Theatre.

Schlueter, June. 1987. "*The Comedy of Errors*." *Shakespeare Bulletin* 5, no. 4: 10–11.

Schwartz, Amy E. 1990. "Henry Today." Review of Branagh *Henry V*. *Washington Post*, 6 February, A–25.

"Screening of America." 1994. *New Yorker*, 21 March, 12.

Senter, Al. 1994. "Pray God for Iain!" *RSC Magazine*, no. 9, 6–8.

Shapiro, Michael. 1994. Review of the Goodman Theatre *Merchant of Venice*. *Shakespeare Bulletin* 12, no. 4: 32–33.

Sharman, Leslie Felperin. 1993. "Branagh's 'Much Ado.'" *Sight and Sound*, September.

Shaw, Catherine. 1994. "Shakespeare and the American Twentieth Century Self-Image." Paper presented to the biennial International Shakespeare Association Conference.

Shaw, William P. 1992. "Textual Ambiguities and Cinematic Certainties in *Henry V*." Abstract in *The Shakespeare Newsletter* 42, no. 4: 66.

Shay, Jonathan. 1994. *Achilles in Vietnam: Combat Trauma and the Undoing of Character*. New York: Atheneum.

Sheldrake, Rupert. 1981. *A New Science of Life*. London: Blond and Briggs.
——— 1995. "Dogmas and Pet Theories." *Times Higher Education*, 5 May, 19.

Sherman, Betsy. 1994. "A Soggy, not Snappy *As You Like It*." Review of Edzard *As You Like It*. *Boston Globe*, 31 March.

Showalter, Elaine. 1985. "Representing Ophelia: Women, Madness, and the Responsibilities of Feminist Criticism." *Shakespeare and the Question of Theory*, edited by Geoffrey Hartman and Patricia Parker. London: Metheun.

Shurgot, Michael. Forthcoming. *Stages of the Play: Shakespeare's Theatrical Energies in Elizabethan Performance*.

Shuttleworth, Ian. 1994. Review of Open Air Theatre *Hamlet*. *London Evening Standard*, 17 June.

Simon, Jeff. 1993. "Poetry in Motion." Review of Branagh *Much Ado about Nothing*. *Buffalo News*, 18 June 1993.

Simon, John. 1987. Review of Kline *Hamlet*. *New York Magazine*, 15 June, 91.

Sinfield, Alan. 1992. *Faultlines: Cultural Materialism and the Politics of Dissident Reading*. Berkeley: University of California Press.
——— 1994. *Cultural Politics: Queer Reading*. London: Routlege.

Singer, Sandra S. 1978. "Laurence Olivier Directs Shakespeare: A Study in Film Authorship." Dissertation, Northwestern University, Evanston, Ill.

Skovmand, Michael, ed. 1994. *Screen Shakespeare*. Aarhus, Denmark: Aarhus University Press.

Smallwood, Robert. 1992. "Shakespeare at Stratford-upon-Avon, 1991." *Shakespeare Quarterly* 43, no. 3: 341–56.

Smith, R.C. 1993. "Branagh Lends Masterful Touch." Review of Branagh *Much Ado about Nothing*. *Durham Herald*, 18 June.

Smith, Russell. 1993. "Shakespeare's Lusty Couples Prove Slyly Engaging." Review of Branagh *Much Ado about Nothing*. *Dallas Morning News*, 18 June.

Snyder, Susan. 1979. *The Comic Matrix of Shakespeare's Tragedies*. Princeton: Princeton University Press.

Speaight, Robert. 1970. "Shakespeare in Britain." *Shakespeare Quarterly* 21, no. 4: 439–50.

Spencer, Charles. 1992. "A Hamlet of Hidden Mysteries." *London Daily Telegraph*. 21 December.

———. 1994a. "Dazzling Stars Outshine Their Productions." Review of RSC *Twelfth Night* and *Coriolanus*. *London Daily Telegraph*, 27 May.

———. 1994b. Review of RSC *Tempest*. *London Daily Telegraph*, 15 July.

Starger, Steve. 1993. "'Much Ado' is Shakespeare for Everyone." Review of Branagh *Much Ado about Nothing*. *Hartford Journal Inquirer*, 17 June.

Steele, Kenneth B. 1991. "The Stratford, Ontario, Festival 1991: A Canadian's Overview." *Shakespeare Bulletin* 9, no. 4: 24–28.

Sterritt, David. 1993. "Branagh Loses Focus in Film Version of *Much Ado*." *Christian Science Monitor*, 10 May, 14.

Stribrny, Zdenek. 1964. "*Henry V* and History." In *Shakespeare in a Changing World*, edited by Arnold Kettle. New York: International.

———. 1984. "Recent Prague *Hamlet*s." *Shakespeare Quarterly* 35, no. 1: 108–13.

Strunk, William, ed. 1936. *Romeo and Juliet: A Motion Picture Edition*. New York: Random House.

Stutzin, Leo. 1994. "*Hamlet* stands out at Oregon Shakespeare Festival." *Modesto* (California) *Bee*, 10 April, G–1, G–5.

Styan, John. 1978. "Psychology and the Study of the Drama." *College Literature* 5, no. 2: 77–93.

———. 1981. *Symbolism, Surrealism and the Absurd*. Vol. 2 of *Modern Drama in Theory and Practice*. Cambridge and New York: Cambridge University Press.

Suczek, Alex. 1994. "*Hamlet*: Intricate Play of Words and Ideas." Review of Stratford, Ontario *Hamlet*. *Gross Pointe* (Michigan) *News*, 3 June.

Swander, Homer. 1985. "In Our Time: Such Audiences We Wish Him." *Shakespeare Quarterly* 35, no. 5: 528–40.

Tanitch, Robert. 1985. *Olivier* New York: Abbeville.

Tannenhouse, Leonard. 1986. *Power and Display: The Politics of Shakespeare's Genres*. New York: Metheun.

Taylor, Gary. 1994. "Program Note." In *Henry V* program. Stratford-on-Avon: Royal Shakespeare Company.

Taylor, Neil. 1994. "The Films of *Hamlet.*" In *Shakespeare and the Moving Image,* edited by Anthony Davies and Stanley Wells. Cambridge: Cambridge University Press.

Taylor, Paul. 1991. Review of RSC *Henry IV, Part II. Independent,* 4 June.

——— 1994a. "The Horror, the Horror." Review of RSC *Henry VI. Independent,* 12 August.

——— 1994b. "Inglorious Twelfth." Review of RSC *Twelfth Night. Independent,* 27 May.

——— 1994c. "Prince Who's Fit for a King." Review of Open Air Theatre *Hamlet. Independent,* 16 June.

——— 1994d. Review of RSC *Coriolanus. Independent,* 26 May.

——— 1994e. Review of RSC *King Lear. Independent,* 2 June.

——— 1994f. Review of RSC *Tempest. Independent,* 15 July.

Thomas, Sidney. 1943. *The Antic Hamlet and Richard III.* London: King's Crown Press.

Thompson, Ann. 1988. *King Lear.* Atlantic Highlands: Humanities Press International.

Tinker, Jack. 1994a. "Glorious Twelfth." Review of RSC *Twelfth Night. London Daily Mail,* 26 May.

——— 1994b. "Marching Onward." Review of RSC *Henry V. London Daily Mail,* 11 May.

——— 1994c. Review of Open Air Theatre *Hamlet. London Daily Mail,* 17 June.

Toppman, Lawrence. 1993. *"Much Ado* Is Worth Making a To-Do Over." Review of Branagh *Much Ado about Nothing. Charlotte Observer,* 18 June.

T.R. 1991. "Zeffirelli's *Hamlet.*" *The New Yorker,* 11 February, 22.

Trewin, J.C. 1978a. *Going to Shakespeare.* London: Allen & Unwin.

——— 1978b. "Shakespeare in Britain." *Shakespeare Quarterly* 28, no. 2: 212–22.

——— 1987. *Five & Eighty Hamlets.* London: Hutchinson.

Tyler, Parker. 1949. "Hamlet and Documentary." *Kenyon Review.* o.s. 11: 517–32.

Vernon, Grenville. 1936. "Leslie Howard's Hamlet." *Commonweal* 42, 27 November.

Vickers, Brian. 1993. *Appropriating Shakespeare.* New Haven: Yale University Press.

von Franz, Marie-Louise. 1959. *Complex/ Archetype/ Symbol in the Psychology of C.G. Jung.* New York: Pantheon.

Wall, Stephen. 1994. Review of RSC *Henry V. Times Literary Supplement,* 20 May, 18.

Waller, Gary. 1992. Review of H.W. Fawkner, *Deconstructing* Macbeth: *The Hyperontological View. Shakespeare Quarterly* 43, no. 1: 102–3.

Walter, John H., ed. 1954. *King Henry V.* London: Methuen.

Wardle, Irving. 1994a. "Just Mad about the Boy." Review of RSC *Coriolanus, Independent on Sunday,* 29 May.

——— 1994b. Review of RSC *Henry VI. Independent on Sunday,* 14 August.

——— 1994c. Review of RSC *King Lear. Independent on Sunday,* 5 June.

1994d. "To Play the King." Review of RSC *Henry V*. *Independent on Sunday*, 15 May.

Warren, Roger. 1977. "Theory and Practice: Stratford, 1976." *Shakespeare Survey* 30: 169-77.

1984. "Shakespeare in England." *Shakespeare Quarterly* 34, no. 3: 334-40.

Watterson, William. "Prospero's Closet." Forthcoming.

Watts, Richard. 1935. "Films of a Moonstruck World." *Yale Review* 34: 311-20.

Webster, Margaret. 1961. *Shakespeare Without Tears*. New York: Premier.

Weimann Robert. 1985. "Mimesis in *Hamlet*," *Shakespeare and the Question of Theory*, edited by Geoffrey Hartman and Patricia Parker. New York: Metheun.

1991. "Bi-Fold Authority in Shakespeare's Theatre." *Shakespeare Quarterly* 39, no. 4: 462-71.

Wells, Stanley, editor. 1972. *The Comedy of Errors*. London: Penguin.

Willis, Susan. 1992. *The BBC Shakespeare Plays*. Chapel Hill: University of North Carolina Press.

Wineke, Donald. 1992. "Henry V as Solitary Hero." Abstract in *Shakespeare Newsletter* 42, no. 4: 66.

Wing, Susan. 1994. "Ophelia on Film." Paper presented to the annual meeting, Shakespeare Association of America. Albuquerque, New Mexico.

Winn, Steven. 1994. "Ashland 'Hamlet' Surprise." Review of the Oregon Shakespeare Festival *Hamlet*. *San Francisco Chronicle*, 2 March, E-1, E-3.

Woddis, Carole. 1994a. Review of RSC *Henry V*. *London Theatre News* 7, no. 3: 5, 8.

1994b. Review of RSC *Henry V*. *What's On*, 18 May.

Woodhead, M.R. 1979. "'The Murder of Gonzago.'" *Shakespeare Survey* 32: 151-61.

Worthen, W.B. 1989. "Deeper Meanings and Theatrical Technique: The Rhetoric of Performance Criticism." *Shakespeare Quarterly* 40, no.4: 441-55.

Wyatt, Euphemia V.R. 1936. "Shakespeare on the Screen." Review of MGM *Romeo and Juliet*. *Catholic World*, October, 85.

Yardley, Jonathan. 1990. "The Metamorphosis of 'Henry'." Review of Branagh *Henry V*. *Washington Post*, 26 February, C-2.

1993. "Power, Politics and the Press." *The Washington Post National Weekly Edition*, 18-24 October, 36.

Yeats, William Butler. 1937. *A Vision*. London: Macmillan.

Yungblut, Andrea. 1991. "Colm Feore: Title Role in *Hamlet* Surprisingly Fun." *Beacon Herald Festival Edition*. Stratford, Canada.

Zeigler, Henry A. 1969. "Kahn's *Henry V*." *New Leader*, 23 June.

Zenger Media Catalogue. 1994. Culver City, California: Zenger.

Zitner, Sheldon. 1981. "Wooden O's in Plastic Boxes: Shakespeare & Television." *University of Toronto Quarterly* 51: 1-12.

# Index

# A Note about the Author

H. R. Coursen is Director of Education in the Northeastern United States for the Shakespeare Globe Centre (London) and teaches at the University of Maine, Augusta. His most recent critical work is *Reading Shakespeare on Stage* (University of Delaware Press, 1995).